Lecture Notes
in Business Information Processing   165

Series Editors

Wil van der Aalst
  Eindhoven Technical University, The Netherlands
John Mylopoulos
  University of Trento, Italy
Michael Rosemann
  Queensland University of Technology, Brisbane, Qld, Australia
Michael J. Shaw
  University of Illinois, Urbana-Champaign, IL, USA
Clemens Szyperski
  Microsoft Research, Redmond, WA, USA

Janis Grabis
Marite Kirikova
Jelena Zdravkovic
Janis Stirna (Eds.)

The Practice of Enterprise Modeling

6th IFIP WG 8.1 Working Conference, PoEM 2013
Riga, Latvia, November 6-7, 2013
Proceedings

 Springer

Volume Editors

Janis Grabis
Riga Technical University
Department of Management Information Technology
Riga, Latvia
E-mail: grabis@iti.rtu.lv

Marite Kirikova
Riga Technical University
Department of System Theory and Design
Riga, Latvia
E-mail: marite.kirikova@cs.rtu.lv

Jelena Zdravkovic
Stockholm University
Department of Computer and Systems Sciences
Stockholm, Sweden
E-mail: jelenaz@dsv.su.se

Janis Stirna
Stockholm University
Department of Computer and Systems Sciences
Stockholm, Sweden
E-mail: js@dsv.su.se

ISSN 1865-1348   e-ISSN 1865-1356
ISBN 978-3-642-41640-8   e-ISBN 978-3-642-41641-5
DOI 10.1007/978-3-642-41641-5
Springer Heidelberg New York Dordrecht London

Library of Congress Control Number: 2013951012

Typesetting: Camera-ready by author, data conversion by Scientific Publishing Services, Chennai, India

Printed on acid-free paper

Springer is part of Springer Science+Business Media (www.springer.com)

Preface

The EM research discipline aims to solve business-IT alignment in a holistic manner by providing the techniques, languages, tools, and best practices for using models to represent organizational knowledge and information systems from different perspectives. Described complex business and technology conditions upraise the role of enterprise modeling (EM) in its responsibility in reaching the alignment. The quality attributes such as agility, sensitivity, responsiveness, adaptability, autonomy, and interoperability are emerging as the norms for modern enterprise models. Solving them will allow all components of an enterprise to operate together in the cooperative manner for the purpose of maximizing overall benefit to the enterprise. PoEM 2013—the 6th IFIP WG 8.1 Conference on the Practice of Enterprise Modeling—took place in November 2013 in Riga, Latvia. The conference series is a dedicated forum where the use of EM in practice is addressed by bringing together the academic community and practitioners from industry to contribute to improved EM practice, as well as to share knowledge and experience. PoEM 2013 attracted 80 submissions with authors from 31 countries (Argentina, Austria, Belgium, Canada, Chile, Colombia, Czech Republic, Estonia, France, FYR Macedonia, Germany, Greece, Italy, Kazakhstan, Latvia, Lithuania, Luxembourg, Malaysia, Morocco, The Netherlands, Norway, Pakistan, Poland, Portugal, Romania, Russia, South Africa, Sweden, Switzerland, UK, and USA), out of which the Program Committee selected 19 high-quality papers for the presentation on the conference, which are included in this proceedings volume. Furthermore, selected short papers were accepted for publication as CEUR online proceedings (CEUR-WS.org). The program of PoEM 2013 reflected different topics of EM, including modeling approaches and tools for agility and flexibility, quality, transformations and management of models, as well as technical aspects, tools, and cases. Additionally, the program featured two keynotes: *Keynote 1: "A New Contract Between Business and Business Analyst,"* by Dr. Baiba Apine, from PricewaterhouseCoopers Consulting, Latvia. This keynote summarized the conclusions from ten years of business modeling practice in Latvia, highlighted the major challenges, and discussed the latest tendencies faced by business analysts. The focus of business analysis has changed significantly over the years. Initially business analysts focused on discovery and modeling of business processes. They aimed to identify opportunities for application of information technologies in business process automation and to determine resources needed for business process execution. More recently, the attention has shifted toward business process monitoring and optimization, while current trends are concerned with business process intelligence for agile decision-making. Businesses expect that the business analysts will identify opportunities for continuous business process improvement by providing contextualized, high-quality, and secure information. In light of these new business expectations, the keynote speech identified today's challenges faced by the business analysts and described the current practice in dealing with these challenges. *Keynote 2: "Designing Intelligent Enterprises with the Viable Systems Approach,"* by Jose Perez Rios, Professor at the University of Valladolid, Spain. Managers in companies or organizations, politicians in their different areas of responsibility and, in general, any decision-maker should have at their disposal the necessary tools for tackling the problem facing them. At the start of the 1970s, Conant and Ashby had argued, in the famous theorem that bears their name, that a good regulator of a system must be a model of the system. However, both this model and the regulating system should possess a degree of variety (complexity) in accord with that of the system they are trying to regulate (manage). The aim of this keynote was to show how the Viable System Model, a systemic methodological approach created by S. Beer, can provide us with the possibility of constructing models with sufficient variety (the capacity to deal with complexity) to respond to current problems. After exploring the functions that the VSM considers necessary and sufficient for viability in an enterprise/organization, along with the model's recursive nature, we will show the role played by the communication channels that connect all the VSM functions/systems and other internal and external elements. This side of the VSM application is fundamental for designing an organization's or company's information systems. A deep understanding of the different functions (systems) of an organization and the communication channels that connect them offers a comprehensive framework for both designing information systems and diagnosing the quality and adaptation of existing ones.

The conference program also included short paper sessions presenting research in progress – new research ideas, including method and tools. Furthermore, the panel session and the exhibition offered the possibility for researchers and practitioners to explore the topics of enterprise practice through open discussions. We owe special thanks to the members of the International Program Committee for promoting the conference, their support in attracting submissions, as well as for providing valuable reviews for the submitted papers. We also thank the external reviewers. Special thanks go to Riga Technical University for an engaging organization of the conference.

September 2013

Janis Grabis
Marite Kirikova
Jelena Zdravkovic
Janis Stirna

Organization

Steering Committee

Anne Persson   Skóvde University, Sweden
Janis Stirna   Stockholm University, Sweden

Organizers

Jānis Grabis   Riga Technical University, Latvia
Gundega Lazdane   IIBA Latvia Chapter, Latvia
Lilita Sparane   Latvian IT Cluster, Latvia
Renate Strazdina   Riga Technical University (Industrial Cooperation Chair)
Jānis Kampars   Riga Technical University, Latvia

Program Committee

Daniel Amyot   University of Ottawa, Canada
Marko Bajec   University of Ljubljana, Slovenia
Janis Barzdins   University of Latvia, Latvia
Guiseppe Berio   University of South Brittany, France
Robert Buchmann   University of Vienna, Austria
Rimantas Butleris   Kaunas University of Technology, Lithuania
Albertas Caplinskas   VU IMI, Lithuania
Steinar Carlsen   Computas, Norway
Wolfgang Deiters   Fraunhofer ISST, Germany
Sergio España   Universitat Politècnica de València, Spain
Xavier Franch   Universitat Politècnica de Catalunya, Spain
Janis Grabis   Riga Technical University, Latvia
Norbert Gronau   University of Potsdam, Germany
Remigijus Gustas   Karlstad University, Sweden
Patrick Heymans   University of Namur, Belgium
Stijn Hoppenbrouwers   Radboud University Nijmegen, The Netherlands
Jennifer Horkoff   University of Trento, Italy
Paul Johannesson   Stockholm University, Sweden
Håvard Jørgensen   Commitment AS, Norway
Marite Kirikova   Riga Technical University, Latvia

John Krogstie
Norwegian University o fScience and
Technology, Norway

Marc Lankhorst
Novay, The Netherlands

Birger Lantow
University of Rostock, Germany

Ulrike Lechner
Munich University of the Armed Forces,
Germany

Michel Leonard
Université de Genève, Switzerland

Peri Loucopoulos
Harokopio University of Athens, Greece/
University of Loughborough, UK

Florian Matthes
Munich University of Technology, Germany

Raimundas Matulevicius
University of Tartu, Estonia

Graham McLeod
inspired.org, South Africa

Jan Mendling
Vienna University of Economics, Austria

Christer Nellborn
Nellborn Management Consulting AB, Sweden

Björn Nilsson
Anatés AB, Luxembourg

Andreas Opdahl
University of Bergen, Norway

Sietse Overbeek
University of Duisburg-Essen,Germany

Oscar Pastor
Valencia University of Technology, Spain

Anne Persson
University of Skovde, Sweden

Michael Petit
University of Namur, Belgium

Tomas Pitner
Masaryk University, Czech Republic

Naveen Prakash
GCET, India

Erik Proper
Radboud University Nijmegen,
The Netherlands

Jolita Ralyté
Université de Genève, Switzerland

Colette Rolland
Université Paris 1 Panthéon Sorbonne, France

Irina Rychkova
Université Paris 1 Panthéon Sorbonne, France

Kurt Sandkuhl
Jönköping Technical University, Sweden

Ulf Seigerroth
Jönköping International Business School,
Sweden

Khurram Shahzad
University of the Punjab, Pakistan

Nikolay Shilov
SPIIRAS, Russia

Pnina Soffer
University of Haifa, Israel

Maarten Steen
Novay, The Netherlands

Janis Stirna
University of Stockholm, Sweden

Darijus Strasunskas
DS Applied Science, Norway

Renate Strazdina
Ernst&Young SIA, Latvia

Olegas Vasilecas
Vilnius Gediminas Technical University,
Lithuania

Mathias Weske
University of Potsdam, Germany

Eric Yu
University of Toronto, Canada

Jelena Zdravkovic
Stockholm University, Sweden

Additional Reviewers

Gundars Alksnis	Riga Technical University, Latvia
Solviata Berzisa	Riga Technical University, Latvia
Nelly Condori-Fernandez	University of Twente, The Netherlands
Sybren De Kinderen	Vrije Universiteit Amsterdam, The Netherlands
Arturo Gonzalez	Universitat Politècnica de València, Spain
Matheus Hauder	Munich University of Technology, Germany
Martin Henkel	Stockholm University, Sweden
Amin Jalali	Stockholm Univeristy, Sweden (PhD student)
Oleh Khovalko	University of Potsdam, Germany
Ivan Monahov	Munich University of Technology, Germany
Laila Niedrite	University of Latvia, Latvia
Georgious Plataniotis	CRP Henri Tudor, Luxembourg
Inese Polaka Riga	Technical University, Latvia
Diego Prado-Gesto	Valencia University of Technology, Spain
Luise Pufahl	Munich University of Technology, Germany
Marcela Ruiz	Universitat Politècnica de València, Spain
Agris Sostaks	University of Latvia, Latvia
Inese Supulniece	Riga Technical University, Latvia
Vladimir Tarasov	Jönköping International Business School, Sweden
Justas Trinkunas	Vilnius Gediminas Technical University, Lithuania
André Ullrich	University of Potsdam, Germany
Dirk van der Linden	CRP Henri Tudor, Luxembourg
Marin Zec	Munich University of Technology, Germany

Table of Contents

Enterprise Modelling and Business Processes

Enterprise Modelling and Information Systems

Enterprise Modelling Cases

A New Contract between Business and Business Analysts

Baiba Apine

PricewaterhouseCoopers Ltd,
Kr. Valdemara str. 21, LV-1010, Riga, Latvia
baiba.apine@lv.pwc.com

Abstract. Since the advent of business processes management it has been recognized that its main objective is optimization of enterprise's performance. However, the focus of business analysis has changed significantly over the years. Initially business analysts focused on discovery and modelling of business processes. They aimed to identify opportunities for application of information technologies in business process automation and to determine resources needed for business process execution. More recently, the attention has shifted towards business process monitoring and optimization, while the current trends concern with business process intelligence for agile decision-making. Businesses expect that the business analysts will identify opportunities for continuous business process improvement by providing contextualized, high quality and secure information. In the light of these new business expectations, the keynote speech identifies today's challenges faced by the business analysts and describes the current practice in dealing with these challenges.

Keywords: Business process, business process modelling, optimisation.

1 Introduction

Business process modelling is a very interesting discipline. It does not provide business value per se, however it serves as a backbone for many complex projects and it is a critical factor for completing these projects successfully. Business process reengineering, information system implementation, reorganisation of the company etc. are samples of the projects involving business process modelling as a significant component. The demand for projects involving business process modelling has always been high and will remain so in the future as well. For instance, 64% of CEOs working for financial institutions have undergone a review and redesign of their organization in the last 12 months [1].

This article summarizes the ten years business modelling experience in Latvia, highlights the major challenges and discusses the latest tendencies faced by the business analysts.

The major challenges faced during the modelling of the business processes are: 1) keeping the model as simple as possible for it to serve as a communication tool among business analyst, technology provider and business; 2) finding balance

J. Grabis et al. (Eds.): PoEM 2013, LNBIP 165, pp. 1–8, 2013.
© IFIP International Federation for Information Processing 2013

between excellence of the model and cost effectiveness of the modelling process; and 3) dealing with issues of completeness and quality of the model.

While the challenges remain the same, the expectations from business analysts have changed significantly over the years. A decade ago business analysts mostly focused on discovery and modelling of processes aiming to identify opportunities for application of information technologies for process automation and to determine resources needed for business process execution. More recently, the attention has shifted towards business process optimization and business process intelligence for agile decision-making. Businesses expect that the business analysts will identify opportunities for continuous business process improvement by providing contextualized, high quality and secure information as well as have ready-made world class best practices of organizational structures and process templates.

2   Empirical Data

The conclusions made in this paper are based on consulting practice at the PricewatehouseCoopers Ltd, Latvia. The company has been involved in the modelling of the business processes for different purposes. The team of 3 – 4 business analysts has been constantly working in different projects involving the description of the business processes for 10 years (2004 – 2013). Totally 90 projects for more than 70 different companies/public sector institutions have been analysed to come up with the conclusions summarized in this article. The split per industries is given in Figure 1.

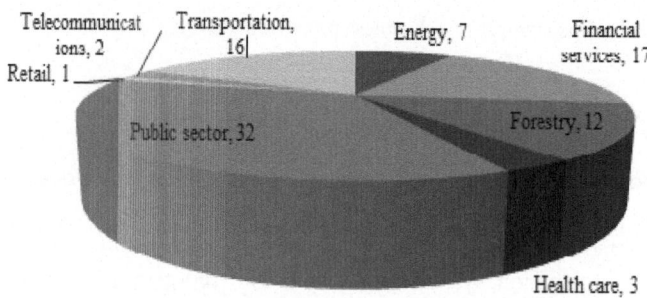

Fig. 1. Business process modelling split per industries (number of projects)

Modified BPMN notation [2] was used for the description of the processes. The average length of the projects was 4 – 7 months. All projects were done for companies/public institutions operating in Latvia. Approximately 70% of the projects involved the description of the 'as-is' processes and 'to-be' processes, while 30% involved the description of the 'to-be' processes only. For the purposes of the analysis the projects were classified in three groups by the objectives of the business process modelling (see Figure 2).

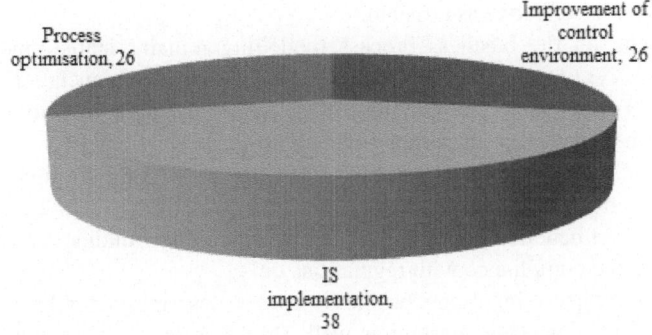

Fig. 2. Purposes of the business process modelling (number of projects)

Business process descriptions for business requirements definition for IS implementation are used (1) to define the requirements for IS implementation; (2) as a source of information about business process for system provider; and (3) to evaluate system providers' proposals for IS implementation; (4) building testing scenarios for IS testing.

Business process description for process optimisation serves (1) for communication of the existing processes among all parties involved in the optimisation and (2) as a source of information for optimisation opportunities for business analysts. Usually these process descriptions include also quantitative information about number of transactions, goods produced, etc.

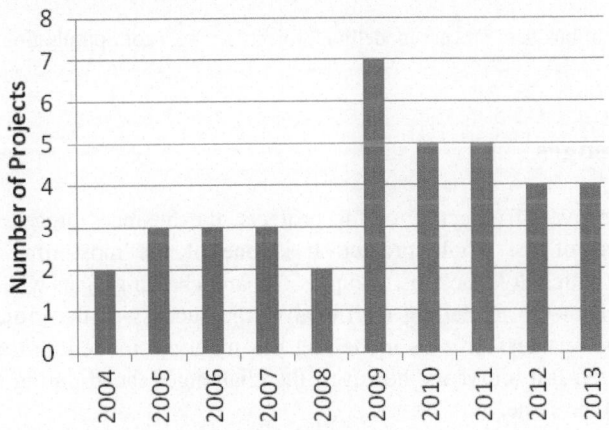

Fig. 3. Number of business process modelling projects per year for information system requirements definition

The business process description for the optimisation of control environment involves (1) identification of control weaknesses against standard/directive/framework and (2) strengthening the control environment. However, it is important to keep the business process as effective as possible.

The demand on the business process modelling remains stable since 2004 (~9 projects annually) with fall in 2008 to 4 engagements due to financial crisis in Latvia (see Figure 3). Business process modelling for information system requirements definition is the most frequent purpose of such projects.

Number of projects involving business process modelling for improvement of control environment is constantly decreasing (from 9 in 2006 to 3 in 2012). The main reason is the cost/benefit from such projects – the cost of building the model is too high to ensure the compliance with regulations only.

Number of projects involving business process description for business process optimisation purposes stays constant as well. However, the number increased during the financial crisis in Latvia (2008 – 2010), when companies were looking for inefficiencies and cost cutting opportunities (see Figure 4).

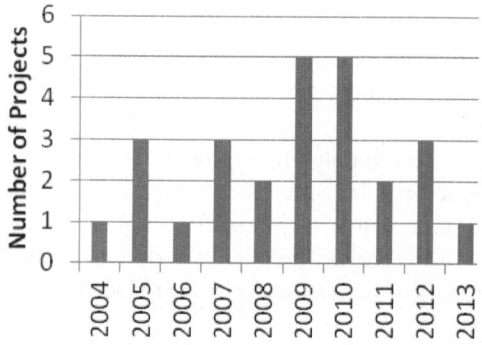

Fig. 4. Number of business process modelling projects per year for optimisation of the business processes

3   Challenges

Regardless the overall objective of the projects, the business process modelling is significant part of the whole project. It is one of the most time and resource consuming activities. It is the most complex one and challenging as well. At the same time, the result of the modelling is critical to the success of the project. The team involved in the business process modelling has matured, modelling tools used have changed over the last ten years, however, the challenges faced during the modelling have remained the same.

Regardless the purpose of the business process description, it has to serve as a communication tool among business analyst, business people and sometimes system providers. Hence, the descriptions should be understandable and kept as simple as possible. It is very easy to produce large business models attempting to describe almost all processes in the company. This is the most common mistake for inexperienced business analysts' teams paying much attention to the detail and sometimes losing the 'big picture'. Large business models, especially describing existing processes, are very comfortable for business people involved in the processes as they can argue, that processes are too complex to be changed. At the same time it is practically impossible to ensure consistency and understandability of the process descriptions. The descriptions lose their role of the communication tool and the success of the whole project can be at risk.

The following actions are found to be helpful to produce business process description serving as a communication tool:

1. Structured approach to the description of the processes is essential, limited amount of time, discussions devoted to the single process description. Limited time frame and structured approach are identified as significant influencing factors in the creation of understandable business process model in the theoretical research [3].
2. Very clear criteria should be kept in mind to select the business processes to be described to avoid the description of the 100% of cases. The most frequently practically used criteria might be different for different projects. For the purposes of process optimisation the criteria should be: (1) the most resource, time consuming processes, (2) the highest number of quality issues requiring resources for rework etc. For the IS implementation purposes the criteria should be: (1) the business processes, where the automation and new technologies will bring the most value for the business; (2) the most intensive 6 - 7 information flows out of 10 etc.

The actions mentioned above should be planned and monitored continuously by the manager of the business analysts' team or senior business analyst. The drawbacks from limiting business process modelling scope, schedule and discussions around the model are (1) the risk of building incomplete model; (2) limited use of automated tools for business process analysis, for instance, described in [4] and [5].

Business process modelling as a part of the project doesn't add any value for the business directly, i.e. the result is not implemented change, an automated information flow or any other tangible result. However, business process modelling is time and resource consuming phenomena. Business analysts often face pressure from the businesses to skip the description of the 'as-is' processes and concentrate on the 'to-be' processes only to cut costs for the analysis and produce the tangible results faster. In addition, the description of the 'as-is' processes is more time consuming and complex as the knowledge stays with the business people primary and not with the business analysts (for 'to-be' processes the situation is vice versa). In our practice, the projects skipping the 'as-is' processes description do not bring the results faster. The time and analysts' resources saved are used later by the analysts' team or business management to argue the feasibility of the changes proposed, e.g., to discuss 'it cannot be done like this' arguments from the people involved in the existing processes. Hence, the task of the manager of the business analysts' team is to insist on the description of the existing business processes at the beginning always.

The third challenge is to find the right business analysts' team for the particular project. The team is essential, because the ability to identify the right level of detail of the process description, obtaining the right information from business people involved in the process depends on the soft skills of the team and every individual analyst. The team must know the notation used, the tool and the principles of the modelling. However, the successful team should have business (industry) specific knowledge, information management techniques, pros and cons of technologies for accessing information (mobile technologies, clouds etc.). The requirements from the business towards the business analysts have changed significantly over the years.

4   Changing Paradigm

Regardless the primary objective of the project involving process modelling, companies are always looking at the optimisation opportunities to improve the overall company's performance. The most of the companies from our practice have done business process modelling more than once during the 10 years period, they are optimising business processes continuously as well. The optimisation opportunities originating from business processes have decreased, because (1) business people are more connected with other professionals, the knowledge about industry specific issues/solutions is more accessible; (2) off-shelf operational templates are available together with proven implementation approaches, [7]; (3) the best industry practices are built into ERP systems; (4) more and more tools are produced and available on the Internet providing search engines in unstructured data, hence, the businesses can skip sophisticated changes in their processes producing structured data for decision making.

The process optimisation has become one minor part of the improvement of the overall company's performance. According to my experience, the components of overall company's performance improvement are given in the Figure 5. The five components are closely interrelated and should be considered together. For example, to redefine business processes and technologies, an organization should consider which talent requirements are necessary to implement new processes or systems.

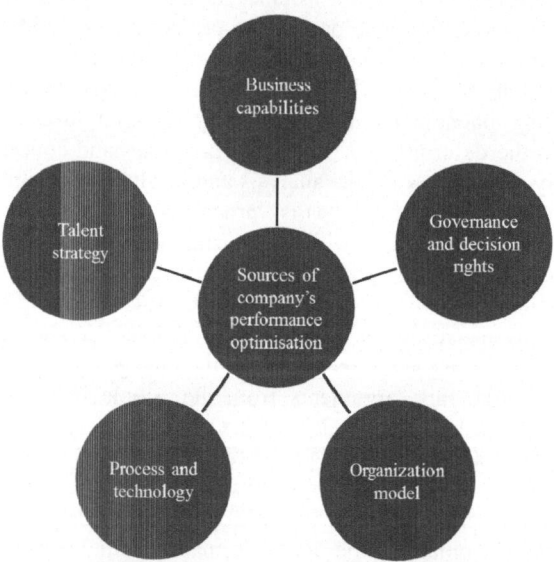

Fig. 5. Sources of company's performance optimisation

Business capabilities refer to company's core capabilities like relationship management, product design, data analytics required to execute the business. Non-core capabilities can be sourced from external service providers in line with strategic business requirements. Decision rights refer to the codification of business decisions and the accountable decision-making groups/individuals. The organization model includes two elements (1) service delivery that determines choices of location, the organization of the service delivery and (2) the functional groupings, reporting structure, target headcount, and functional responsibilities for each function. Talent strategy includes effective management of the overall talent lifecycle, such as workforce planning, recruitment, on-boarding, development, and performance management.

At the same time business process modelling serves as a backbone, where all the weak performance issues come up and the team of business analysts should be able to propose the most convenient and effective options to the business regardless the area of performance optimisation. This new role requires the wide range of new knowledge for business analysts. Now the good business analyst should be able to ensure the process, where information lands in the hands of the decision maker at the point of the decision. Hence, the methodological knowledge about business process management is not enough. He/she should understand (1) the opportunities provided by mobile technologies, cloud computing for timely information delivery; (2) best practices of the organisation structures and business processes for accounting, IT management, sales etc.; (3) best practices of keeping balance between in-house and outsource functions; (4) best practices of building effective control environment; (5) frameworks of obtaining information for decision making from social networks or other unstructured sources, for instance described in the [8], [9] etc. The new business analyst should be able to put the practices mentioned above in the context of the business and convince the business representatives about the benefits.

5   Conclusions

The demand from the business for business process modelling has been high and stable for years. It will remain so in the future as well, because the business is changing continuously due to availability of new technologies.

The key challenges in the business process modelling are (1) keeping the model understandable and complete; (2) finding the right business analysts' team suiting the best the objectives of the modelling. The solutions for the abovementioned challenges lay primarily in the management of the projects, ensuring continuous dialog with the business rather than in using advanced modelling tools and techniques.

The objectives and nature of the modelling process has changed significantly over the last ten years. Initially business analysts were expected to identify the company's performance optimisation opportunities by use of information technologies. Now the business analysts are expected to advise on the benefits of the wide range of information technologies as well as on the best practices of organisation structures, business capabilities, talent management etc. All these areas should be put in the context of the company's business to produce the process, where information lands in the hands of the decision maker at the point of the decision.

References

1. PwC analysis based on webinar survey results. How Financial Services companies can execute the right people strategy (2011)
2. Object Management Group, Business Process Model and Notation (2013), http://www.bpmn.org
3. Claes, J., et al.: Tying Process Model Quality to the Modeling Process: The Impact of Structuring, Movement, and Speed. In: Barros, A., Gal, A., Kindler, E. (eds.) BPM 2012. LNCS, vol. 7481, pp. 33–48. Springer, Heidelberg (2012)
4. Accorsi, R., Lehmann, A.: Automatic Information Flow Analysis of Business Process Models. In: Barros, A., Gal, A., Kindler, E. (eds.) BPM 2012. LNCS, vol. 7481, pp. 172–187. Springer, Heidelberg (2012)
5. Ramezani, E., Fahland, D., van der Aalst, W.M.P.: Where Did I Misbehave? Diagnostic Information in Compliance Checking. In: Barros, A., Gal, A., Kindler, E. (eds.) BPM 2012. LNCS, vol. 7481, pp. 262–278. Springer, Heidelberg (2012)
6. Handfield, R.: Best Practices in the Procure-to-Pay Cycle: Perspectives from Suppliers and Industry Experts (2013), http://www.supplychainredesign.com/publications/practix032006.pdf
7. Buchmann, A., Appel, S., Freudenreich, T., Frischbier, S., Guerrero, P.E.: From Calls to Events: Architecting Future BPM Systems. In: Barros, A., Gal, A., Kindler, E. (eds.) BPM 2012. LNCS, vol. 7481, pp. 17–32. Springer, Heidelberg (2012)
8. Scekic, O., Truong, H.-L., Dustdar, S.: Modeling Rewards and Incentive Mechanisms for Social BPM. In: Barros, A., Gal, A., Kindler, E. (eds.) BPM 2012. LNCS, vol. 7481, pp. 150–155. Springer, Heidelberg (2012)

Visualizing and Measuring Enterprise Architecture: An Exploratory BioPharma Case

Robert Lagerström[1,2], Carliss Baldwin[1], Alan MacCormack[1], and David Dreyfus[3]

[1] Harvard Business School, Soldiers Field Park, Boston, MA 02163, United States
[2] The Royal Institute of Technology, Osquldas väg 10, 10044, Stockholm, Sweden
[3] Boston University, 595 Commonwealth Avenue, Boston, MA 02215, United States
{cbaldwin,amaccormack}@hbs.edu
robertl@ics.kth.se
ddreyfus@bu.edu

Abstract. We test a method that was designed and used previously to reveal the hidden internal architectural structure of software systems. The focus of this paper is to test if it can also uncover new facts about the components and their relationships in an enterprise architecture, i.e., if the method can reveal the hidden external structure between architectural components. Our test uses data from a biopharmaceutical company. In total, we analyzed 407 components and 1,157 dependencies. Results show that the enterprise structure can be classified as a core-periphery architecture with a propagation cost of 23%, core size of 32%, and architecture flow through of 67%. We also found that business components can be classified as control elements, infrastructure components as shared, and software applications as belonging to the core. These findings suggest that the method could be effective in uncovering the hidden structure of an enterprise architecture.

Keywords: Enterprise Architecture, Design Structure Matrices, Enterprise Modeling, Architecture Visualization.

1   Introduction

Managing software applications has become a complex undertaking. Today, achieving effective and efficient management of the software application landscape requires the ability to visualize and measure the current status of the enterprise architecture. To a large extent, that huge challenge can be addressed by introducing tools such as enterprise architecture modeling as a means of abstraction.

In recent years, Enterprise Architecture (EA) has become an established discipline for business and software application management [1]. EA describes the fundamental artifacts of business and IT as well as their interrelationships [1-4]. Architecture models constitute the core of the approach and serve the purpose of making the complexities of the real world understandable and manageable [3]. Ideally, EA aids the stakeholders of the enterprise to effectively plan, design, document, and communicate IT and business related issues; i.e. they provide decision support for the stakeholders [5].

J. Grabis et al. (Eds.): PoEM 2013, LNBIP 165, pp. 9–23, 2013.
© IFIP International Federation for Information Processing 2013

In relation to supporting decisions, a key underlying assumption of EA models is that they should provide aggregated knowledge beyond what was put into the model in the first place. For instance, the discipline of software architecture does more than just keep track of the set of source files in an application; it also provides information about the dependencies between those files. More broadly, an EA covers the dependencies between the business and the software applications so that, for example, conclusions can be drawn about the consequences in the enterprise should a specific application be removed or changed.

Enabling this type of analysis is extremely important for EA to provide value to stakeholders. Unfortunately, though, EA frameworks rarely explicitly state the kinds of analyses that can be performed given a certain model, nor do they provide details on how the analysis should be performed [6].

In [7], Baldwin et al. present a method based on Design Structure Matrices (DSMs) and classic coupling measures to visualize the hidden structure of software system architectures. This method has been tested on numerous software releases for large systems (such as Linux, Mozilla, Apache, and GnuCash) but not on enterprise architectures with a potentially large number of interdependent components. This paper performs such a test using data from a biopharmaceutical company (referred to as BioPharma). The data consisted of a total of 407 architecture components and 1,157 dependencies.

We find that the BioPharma enterprise architecture can be classified as core-periphery, meaning that 1) there is one cyclic group (the "Core") of architecture components that is substantially larger than the second biggest cyclic group, and 2) the Core also makes up a large portion of the entire architecture. The analysis also shows a propagation cost of 23%, meaning that almost one-fourth of the architecture may be affected when a change is made to a randomly selected component in the architecture. In addition, we find that the Core contains 132 architecture components, which embody 32% of the architecture. And lastly, the analysis uncovers that the architecture flow through accounts for as much as 67% of the architecture, meaning that more than half of the components are either in, depend on, or are dependent on the Core.

The remainder of this paper is structured as follows: Section 2 presents related work; Section 3 describes the hidden structure method; Section 4 presents the biopharmaceutical case used for the analysis; Section 5 discusses the approach and outlines future work; and Section 6 concludes the paper.

2   Related Work

In this section, we argue that the EA frameworks available today do not provide support for architecture analysis. Then we present system architecture approaches that aim to solve these problems.

2.1   Enterprise Architecture Analysis

As stated in the introduction, EA frameworks rarely supply the exact procedure or algorithm for performing a certain analysis given an architecture model. But most do recognize the need to provide special-purpose models as well as different viewpoints intended for different stakeholders. Unfortunately, however, most viewpoints are designed from a model-entity point of view rather than from an analysis-concern point of view. Thus, they cannot perform the visualizing and measuring of the modularity or coupling of an architecture in a straightforward manner. The Department of Defense Architecture Framework (DoDAF) [8], for instance, provides products (i.e., viewpoints) such as "systems communications description," "systems data exchange matrix," and "operational activity model." These are all viewpoints based on a delimitation of elements of a complete metamodel. The Zachman framework presented in [2, 9] does connect model types describing different aspects (Data, Function, Network, People, Time, and Motivation) with abstractly described stakeholders (Strategists, Executive Leaders, Architects, Engineers, and Technicians), but it does not provide any deeper insights as to how different models should be used for analysis. The Open Group Architecture Framework (TOGAF) [4] explicitly states the concerns for each suggested viewpoint, but it does not describe the exact mechanism for analyzing the stated concerns. With respect to modularity, the most appropriate viewpoints provided would, according to TOGAF, arguably be the "software engineering view," "systems engineering view," "communications engineering view," and "enterprise manageability view." The descriptions of these views contain statements such as, "the use of standard and self-describing languages, e.g. XML, is good in order to achieve easy to maintain interface descriptions." What is not included, however, is the exact interpretation of such statements when it comes to architectural models or how they relate to the analysis of, for example, the flexibility of a system as a whole. Moreover, these kinds of "micro theories" are only exemplary and do not claim to provide a complete theory for modularity or similar concerns.

Other analysis frameworks focus on the assessment of non-functionality qualities such as availability [10], interoperability [11], modifiability [12], and security [13]. These frameworks use Bayesian analysis or probabilistic versions of the Object Constraint Language for enterprise modeling. They do not, however, provide any analysis capabilities when it comes to revealing the hidden structure of an enterprise architecture. Also, the visualization capabilities of these frameworks are limited because they all use entity-relationship modeling without any proper views dealing with large complex models.

2.2   System Architecture Visualization

If we instead turn to the discipline of system architecture, we find work that aims to solve the issue of architecture analysis and visualization. Studies that attempt to characterize the architecture of complex systems often employ network representations [14]. Specifically, they focus on identifying the linkages that exist between the different elements (nodes) in a system [15, 16]. A key concept here is modularity, which refers to the way in which a system's architecture can be decomposed into different parts. Although there are many definitions of "modularity," authors tend to agree on some fundamental features: interdependence of decisions within modules and independence between modules, and hierarchical dependence of modules on components that embody standards and design rules [17, 18].

Studies that use network methods to measure modularity have typically focused on capturing the level of coupling that exists between different parts of a system. In this respect, one of the most widely adopted techniques is the so-called Design Structure Matrix (DSM), which illustrates the network structure of a complex system in terms of a square matrix [19-21], where rows and columns represent components (nodes in the network) and off-diagonal elements represent dependencies (links) between the components. Metrics that capture the level of coupling for each component can be calculated from a DSM and used to analyze and understand system structure. For example, [22] uses DSMs and the metric "propagation cost" to compare software system architectures. DSMs have been used to visualize architectures and to measure the coupling of the internal design of single software systems.

3   Method Description

The method used for architecture network representation is based on and extends the classic notion of coupling. Specifically, after identifying the coupling (dependencies) between the elements in a complex architecture, the method analyzes the architecture in terms of hierarchical ordering and cycles, enabling elements to be classified in terms of their position in the resulting network.

In a Design Structure Matrix (DSM), each diagonal cell represents an element (node), and the off-diagonal cells record the dependencies between the elements (links): If element i depends on element j, a mark is placed in the row of i and the column of j. The content of the matrix does not depend on the ordering of the rows and columns, but if the elements in the DSM are rearranged in a way that minimizes the number of dependencies above the main diagonal, then dependencies that remain there will show the presence of cyclic interdependencies (A depends on B, and B depends on A) which cannot be reduced to a hierarchical ordering. The rearranged DSM would then reveal significant facts about the underlying structure of the architecture that cannot be inferred from standard measures of coupling or from the architect's view alone. The following subsections present a method that makes this "hidden structure" visible and describe metrics that can be used to compare architectures and track changes in architecture structures over time. (Note: A more detailed method description can be found in "Hidden Structure: Using Network Methods to Map System Architecture" by Baldwin et al. [7].)

3.1   Identify the Direct Dependencies and Compute the Visibility Matrix

The architecture of a complex system can be represented as a directed network composed of N elements (nodes) and the directed dependencies (links) between them. Fig. 1 contains an example (taken from [22]) of an architecture that is shown both as a

A Directed Graph	Design Structure Matrix	Visibility Matrix $V=\sum M^n$; n=[0,4]
	A B C D E F A 0 1 1 0 0 0 B 0 0 0 1 0 0 C 0 0 0 0 1 0 D 0 0 0 0 0 0 E 0 0 0 0 0 1 F 0 0 0 0 0 0	A B C D E F A 1 1 1 1 1 1 B 0 1 0 1 0 0 C 0 0 1 0 1 1 D 0 0 0 1 0 0 E 0 0 0 0 1 1 F 0 0 0 0 0 1

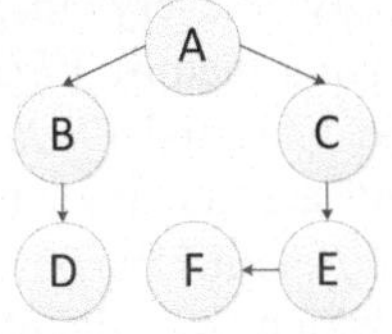

Fig. 1. A directed graph, Design Structure Matrix (DSM), and Visibility matrix example

directed graph and a DSM. This DSM is called the "first-order" matrix to distinguish it from a visibility matrix (defined below).

If the first-order matrix is raised to successive powers, the result will show the direct and indirect dependencies that exist for successive path lengths. Summing these matrices yields the visibility matrix V (Fig. 1), which denotes the dependencies that exist for all possible path lengths. The values in the visibility matrix are binary, capturing only whether a dependency exists and not the number of possible paths that the dependency can take [22]. The matrix for n=0 (i.e., a path length of zero) is included when calculating the visibility matrix, implying that a change to an element will always affect itself.

3.2 Construct Measures from the Visibility Matrix

Several measures are constructed based on the visibility matrix V. First, for each element i in the architecture, the following are defined:

- VFI_i (Visibility Fan-In) is the number of elements that directly or indirectly depend on i. This number can be found by summing the entries in the ith column of V.
- VFO_i (Visibility Fan-Out) is the number of elements that i directly or indirectly depends on. This number can be found by summing the entries in the ith row of V.

In the visibility matrix (Fig. 1), element A has VFI equal to 1, meaning that no other elements depend on it, and VFO equal to 6, meaning that it depends on all other elements in the architecture.

To measure visibility at the architecture level, the Propagation Cost (PC) is defined as the density of the visibility matrix. Intuitively, it equals the fraction of the architecture affected when a change is made to a randomly selected element. It can be computed from Visibility Fan-In (VFI) or Visibility Fan-Out (VFO) as described in Eq. 1.

$$\text{Propagation Cost} = \frac{\sum_{i=1}^{N} VFI_i}{N^2} = \frac{\sum_{i=1}^{N} VFO_i}{N^2} \qquad (1)$$

3.3   Identify and Rank Cyclic Groups

The next step is to find the cyclic groups in the architecture. By definition, each element within a cyclic group depends directly or indirectly on every other member of the group. So we sort the elements, first by *VFI* descending then by *VFO* ascending. Next we proceed through the sorted list, comparing the *VFI*s and *VFO*s of adjacent elements. If the *VFI* and *VFO* for two successive elements are the same, they might be members of the same cyclic group. Elements that have different *VFI*s or *VFO*s cannot be members of the same cyclic group, and elements for which $n_i=1$ cannot be part of a cyclic group at all. But elements with the same *VFI* and *VFO* could be members of different cyclic groups. In other words, disjoint cyclic groups may, by coincidence, have the same visibility measures. To determine whether a group of elements with the same *VFI* and *VFO* is one cyclic group (and not several), we simply inspect the subset of the visibility matrix that includes the rows and columns of the group in question and no others. If this submatrix does not contain any zeros, then the group is indeed one cyclic group.

The cyclic groups found via this algorithm are referred to as the "cores" of the system. The largest cyclic group (the "Core") plays a special role in the architectural classification scheme, described next.

3.4   Classification of Architectures

The method of classifying architectures is motivated in [7] and was discovered empirically. Specifically, Baldwin et al. found that a large percentage of the architectures they analyzed contained four distinct types of elements: 1) one large cyclic group, called the "Core," 2) "Control" elements that depend on other elements but are not themselves used by many, 3) "Shared" elements that are used by other elements but do not depend on that many others, and 4) "Periphery" elements that are not used by or depend on a large group of other elements.

From those empirical results, a core-periphery architecture was defined as one containing a single cyclic group of elements that is dominant in two senses: it is large relative to the architecture as a whole, and it is substantially larger than any other cyclic group. The empirical work also showed that not all architectures fit into the category of core-periphery. Some architectures (called "multi-core") have several similarly sized cyclic groups rather than one dominant one. Others (called "hierarchical") have only a few extremely small cyclic groups.

Based on the large dataset of software architectures analyzed in [7], the first classification boundary is set empirically to assess whether the largest cyclic group contains at least 5% of the total elements. Architectures that do not meet this test are labeled "hierarchical." Next, within the set of large-core architectures, a second classification boundary is applied to assess whether the largest cyclic group contains at least 50% more elements than the second largest cyclic group. Architectures that meet the second test are labeled "core-periphery"; those that do not (but have passed the first test) are labeled "multi-core." Fig. 2 summarizes the classification scheme.

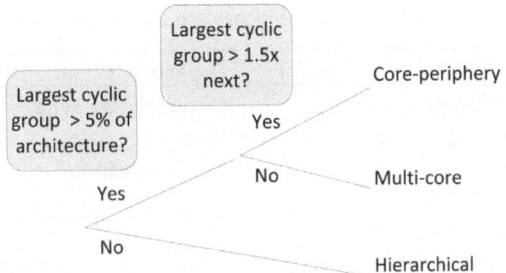

Fig. 2. Architectural classification scheme

3.5   Classification of Elements and Visualizing the Architecture

The elements of a core-periphery architecture can be divided into four basic groups:

- "Core" elements are members of the largest cyclic group and have the same VFI and VFO, denoted by VFI_C and VFO_C, respectively.
- "Control" elements have $VFI < VFI_C$ and $VFO \geq VFO_C$.
- "Shared" elements have $VFI \geq VFI_C$ and $VFO < VFO_C$.
- "Periphery" elements have $VFI < VFI_C$ and $VFO < VFO_C$.

Together the Core, Control, and Shared elements define the flow through of the architecture. (Note: For the classification of elements in hierarchical and multi-core architectures, see [7].)

Using the above classification scheme, a reorganized DSM can be constructed that reveals the "hidden structure" of the architecture by placing elements in the order of Shared, Core, Periphery, and Control down the main diagonal of the DSM, and then sorting within each group by VFI descending then VFO ascending.

4   BioPharma Case

We now apply the described method to a real-world example of a U.S. biopharmaceutical company (BioPharma). Data were collected at the research division by examining strategy documents, entering architectural information into a repository, using automated system scanning techniques, and conducting a survey. A subset of the data employed for the analysis presented in this paper was previously used in the study "Digital Cement: Software Portfolio Architecture, Complexity, and Flexibility," by Dreyfus and Wyner [23], with a more extensive exploration in [24].

4.1   Identifying the Direct Dependencies between the Architecture Components

The BioPharma dataset contains 407 architecture components and 1,157 dependencies. The architectural components are divided as follows: eight "business groups," 191 "software applications," 92 "schemas," 49 "application servers," 47 "database instances," and 20 "database hosts" (cf. Table 1).

Table 1. Component and dependency types in the BioPharma case

Component type	No. of	Dependency type	No. of
Business Group	8	Communicates With	742
Software Application	191	Runs On	165
Schema	92	Is Instantiated By	92
Application Server	49	Uses	158
Database Instance	47		
Database Host	20		

The dependencies between the architecture components belong to the following types (cf. Table 1): 742 "communicates with" (bidirectional), 165 "runs on" (unidirectional), 92 "is instantiated by" (unidirectional), and 158 "uses" (unidirectional).

We can represent this architecture as a directed network, with the architecture components as nodes and dependencies as links, and then convert that network into a DSM. Fig. 3 contains the "architect's view," with dependencies indicated by dots. (Note: We placed dots along the main diagonal, implying that each architecture component is dependent on itself.) The squares in Fig. 3 represent the architecture components, which have been ordered in terms of typical enterprise architecture layers (from top left to bottom right): business groups, software applications, schemas, applications servers, database instances, and database hosts.

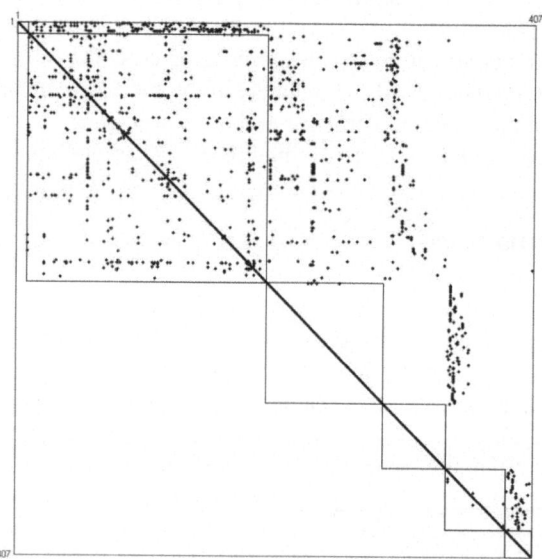

Fig. 3. The BioPharma DSM – architect's view

From the DSM, we calculate the Direct Fan-In (*DFI*) and Direct Fan-Out (*DFO*) measures by summing the rows and columns for each software application, respectively. Table 2 shows, for example, that Architecture Component 324 (AC324)

has a *DFI* of four, indicating that three other components depend on it, and a *DFO* of 2, indicating that it depends on only one component other than itself.

4.2   Computing the Visibility Matrix and Constructing the Coupling Measures

The next step is to derive the visibility matrix by raising the first-order matrix (the architect's view) to successive powers, such that both the direct and all the indirect dependencies appear. The Visibility Fan-In (*VFI*) and Visibility Fan-Out (*VFO*) measures can then be calculated by summing the rows and columns in the visibility matrix for each respective architecture component. Table 2 shows that Architecture Component 403 (AC403), for example, has a *VFI* of 173, indicating that 172 other components directly or indirectly depend on it, and a *VFO* of 2, indicating that it directly or indirectly depends on only one component other than itself.

Table 2. A sample of Biopharma Fan-In and Fan-Outs

Architecture component	DFI	DFO	VFI	VFO
AC324	4	2	140	3
AC333	2	3	139	265
AC347	2	2	140	3
AC378	8	23	139	265
AC403	29	2	173	2
AC769	1	6	1	267
AC1030	3	2	3	2

Using the *VFI* and *VFO* measures, we can calculate the propagation cost of the BioPharma architecture, as described in Eq. 2.

$$\text{Propagation Cost} = \frac{\sum_{i=1}^{407} VFI_i}{407^2} = \frac{\sum_{i=1}^{407} VFO_i}{407^2} = 23\% \tag{2}$$

A propagation cost of 23% means that almost one-fourth of the architecture may be affected when a change is made to a randomly selected architecture component.

4.3   Identifying Cyclic Groups and Classifying the Architecture

To identify cyclic groups, we first ordered the list of architecture components based on *VFI* descending and *VFO* ascending. We could then identify 15 possible cyclic groups. When inspecting the visibility submatrices of these possible clusters, we found that most groups were not cyclic. In other words, these applications had ended up with the same *VFI* and *VFO* by coincidence. But one possible cluster had 132 architecture components and proved to be the largest cyclic group, which we labeled as "Core." In Table 2, Architecture Components 333 and 378 are part of the Core. Because the Core makes up 32% of the architecture and because the second largest cluster contains only four components, the architecture is classified as core-periphery, according to the classification scheme discussed earlier (cf. Fig. 2).

4.4   Classifying the Components and Visualizing the Architecture

After identifying components that belong to the Core, the next step is to classify the remainder of the architecture components as Shared, Periphery, or Control. To do so, we compare the *VFI* and *VFO* of each component with the VFI_C and VFO_C of the Core components. A total of 133 components have a *VFI* that is equal to or larger than the VFI_C and a *VFO* that is smaller than the VFO_C, classifying them as Shared. A total of 135 architecture components have *VFI* and *VFO* numbers that are smaller than the Core, classifying them as Periphery. And seven components have a *VFI* that is smaller than the VFI_C and a *VFO* that is equal to or larger than the VFO_C, classifying them as Control. Table 3 summarizes those results.

Table 3. BioPharma architecture component classification

Classification	No. of	% of total
Shared	133	33%
Core	132	32%
Periphery	135	33%
Control	7	2%

By sorting the original DSM using the different classifications, we can uncover the hidden structure of the architecture. First, the components are sorted in the order of Shared, Core, Periphery, and Control. Then, within each group the components are ordered by *VFI* descending and *VFO* ascending.

Fig. 4. BioPharma rearranged DSM

From Fig. 4, which shows the rearranged DSM, we see a large cyclic group of architecture components that appear in the second block down the main diagonal. Each element in this group both depends on and is dependent on every other member of the group. These "Core" components account for 32% of the elements. Furthermore, the Core, the components depending on it ("Control"), and those it depends on ("Shared"), account for 67% of the architecture. The remaining components are "Periphery," in that they have few relationships with other components.

If we examine where the different types of components in the architecture end up after the classification and rearrangement, we find the following: The Shared category contains only infrastructure components (schema, application server, database instance, and database host); the Core consists of only software-application elements; the Periphery contains a mix; and the Control category consists of just business-group components (see Table 4).

Table 4. Distribution of architecture components between classification categories

	Business group	Software application	Schema	Application server	Database instance	Database host
Shared	0	0	83	27	15	8
Core	0	132	0	0	0	0
Periphery	1	59	9	22	32	12
Control	7	0	0	0	0	0

5   Discussion and Research Outlook

As presented in [7], the hidden structure method was designed based on the empirical regularity from cases investigating large complex software systems. All those cases were focused on one software system at a time, independent of its surrounding environment, analyzing the dependencies between its source files. In other words, that work considered the internal coupling of a system. In this paper, the same method is tested on the dependencies between architecture components; i.e., the current work considers the external coupling between not only software applications but also other enterprise architecture components.

For the BioPharma case, the method revealed a hidden structure (thus presenting new facts) similar to those cases on software systems investigated in previous studies. And the method also helped classify the architecture as core-periphery using the same rules and boundaries as in the previous cases. However, because this is only one set of data from one company, additional studies are needed. We present one such study using enterprise application architecture data from a Telecom company in [25].

Compared to many other complexity, coupling, and modularity measures, the hidden structure method considers not only the direct network structure of an architecture but also takes into account the indirect dependencies between components (not unlike some measures used in social networks). Both these features provide important input for management decisions. For instance, components that are classified as Periphery or Control are probably easier (and less costly) to modify because of the lower probability of a change spreading and affecting other components. In contrast, components that are classified as Shared or Core are more difficult to modify because of the higher probability of changes having an impact elsewhere. This information can be used in change management, project planning, risk analysis, and so on.

From just the architect's view (cf. Fig. 3), we see some of the benefits of using Design Structure Matrices for enterprise architecture visualization. If the matrix elements are arranged in an order that comes naturally for most companies, with the business layer at the top, infrastructure at the bottom, and software in between, we see that 1) the business groups depend on the software applications, 2) the software applications communicate with each other in what looks like a clustered network of dependencies, 3) the software applications depend on the schemas and application servers, 4) the schemas depend on the database instances, and 5) the database instances depend on the database hosts. Although these observations are neither new nor surprising, they do help validate that the components in the investigated architecture do interact as expected.

From Table 2, we see that architecture components 324, 333, 347 769, and 1030 all have rather low Direct Fan-In (*DFI*) and Direct Fan-Out (*DFO*) numbers. As such, those components might be considered as low risk when implementing changes. But if we also look at the Visibility Fan-In (*VFI*) and Visibility Fan-Out (*VFO*) numbers, which measure indirect dependencies, we see that application 333 belongs to the Core of the architecture. Thus any change to it might spread to many other components (even though it has few direct dependencies). The same goes for components 324, 347, and 403, which are classified as Shared. Therefore, we argue that the hidden structure method, which considers indirect dependencies, provides more valuable information for decision-making.

In our experience, we have found that many companies working with enterprise modeling have architecture blueprints that describe their organization, often with entity-relationship diagrams containing boxes and arrows. When the entire architecture is visualized using this type of model, however, the result is typically a "spaghetti" tangle of many components and dependencies that are difficult to interpret. But this representation can be translated directly to the architect's view DSM (cf. Fig. 3), which, along with the entity-relationship model, can be used to trace a dependency between two components, thus enabling better decision-making (compare with the discussion above on *DFI/DFO* versus *VFI/VFO* measures). Moreover, if we instead use the hidden structure method and rearrange the DSM, as in Fig. 4, we can actually see what components are considered to be Core, Shared, Control, and Periphery, which gives us much more insight about the structure of the architecture. Lastly, measures such as the propagation cost, the architecture flow through, and the size of the core can be useful when trying to improve an architecture because future scenarios can be compared in terms of these metrics.

In the explored BioPharma case, we found that the Control category contains only business groups; the Core consists of only software applications; the Shared elements are all infrastructure-related components (schemas, application servers, database instances, and database hosts); and the Periphery category contains a mix of all types. These results provide support for the method, as we would expect that the business controls the underlying components in the architecture (e.g. a business group depends on the software it uses but not the other way around). Also, infrastructure components such as databases are supposed to be shared among the applications in a sound architecture.

A first step in future research is to test the hidden structure method with additional enterprise architectures, like the one in [25]. This will provide valuable input either supporting the method as currently constructed or with suggested improvements for future versions.

Both in the previous work by Baldwin et al. [7], Lagerström et al. [25], and in this case, the architectures studied have a single large Core. A limitation of the hidden structure method is that it only shows which elements belong to the Core but does not help in describing the inner structure of that Core. Thus, future research might extend the hidden structure method with a sub-method that could help identify the elements within the Core that are most important in terms of dependencies and cluster growth. The hypothesis is that there are some elements in a Core that bind the group together or that make the group grow faster. As such, removing these elements or reducing their dependencies (either to or from them) may decrease the size of the Core and thus the complexity of the architecture. Identifying these elements might also help pinpoint where the Core is most sensitive to change.

We have also seen in previous work that enterprise application architectures often contain non-directed dependencies, thus forming symmetric matrices that have special properties and behave differently from matrices with directed dependencies. This could, for instance, be due to the nature of the link itself (as in social networks), or, as in most cases we have seen, it could be due to imprecision in the data (often because of the high costs of data collection). For companies, the primary concern is whether two applications are connected, and the direction of the dependency is secondary. In one of our cases, the company had more than a thousand software applications but did not have an architecture model or application portfolio describing them. For that firm, collecting information about what applications it had and what those applications did was of primary importance. That process was costly enough, and consequently the direction of the dependencies between the applications was not a priority.

Effective tools could help lower the high costs associated with data collection. In the prior work of Baldwin et al. [7], the analysis of internal coupling in a software system was supported by a tool that explored the source files and created a dependency graph automatically. In the enterprise architecture domain, such useful practical tools generally do not exist. Consequently, data collection requires considerable time. The most common methods are interviews and surveys of people (often managers) with already busy schedules. As such, future work needs to be directed towards data collection support in the enterprise architecture domain. Some work has already been done but is limited in either scope or application, as described in [26, 27].

For the hidden structure method to be useful in practice, it needs to be incorporated into existing or future enterprise architecture tools. Most companies today already use modeling tools like Rational System Architect [28] and BiZZdesign Architect [29] to describe their enterprise architecture. Thus, having a stand-alone tool that supports the hidden structure method would not be feasible or very cost efficient. Moreover, if the method is integrated with current tools, companies can then perform a hidden structure analysis by re-using their existing architecture descriptions. The modeling software Enterprise Architecture Analysis Tool (EAAT) [30] is currently implementing the hidden structure method, and future studies will use it.

Last, but not least, the most important future work is to test the *VFI/VFO* metrics and the element classification (Shared, Control, Periphery, and Core) with performance outcome metrics such as change cost. Doing so will help prove that the method is actually useful in architectural work. Currently, we can argue its benefits only with respect to other existing methods.

6   Conclusions

Although our method is used in only one case, the results suggests that it can reveal new facts about the architecture structure on an enterprise level, equal to past results in the initial cases of single software systems. The analysis reveals that the hidden external structure of the architecture components at BioPharma can be classified as core-periphery with a propagation cost of 23%, architecture flow through of 67%, and core size of 32%. For BioPharma, the architectural visualization and the computed coupling metrics can provide valuable input when planning architectural change projects (in terms of, for example, risk analysis and resource planning). Also the analysis shows that business components are Control elements, infrastructure components are Shared elements, and software applications are in the Core, thus providing verification that the architecture is sound.

References

1. Ross, J.W., Weill, P., Robertson, D.: Enterprise Architecture As Strategy: Creating a Foundation for Business Execution. Harvard Business School Press (2006)
2. Zachman, J.A.: A Framework for Information Systems Architecture. IBM Systems Journal 26(3), 276–292 (1987)
3. Winter, R., Fischer, R.: Essential Layers, Artifacts, and Dependencies of Enterprise Architecture. Journal of Enterprise Architecture 3(2), 7–18 (2007)
4. The Open Group: The Open Group Architecture Framework (TOGAF). Version 9, The Open Group (2009)
5. Kurpjuweit, S., Winter, R.: Viewpoint-based Meta Model Engineering. In: The 2nd International Workshop on Enterprise Modelling and Information Systems Architectures: Concepts and Applications, pp. 143–161 (2007)
6. Johnson, P., Lagerström, R., Närman, P., Simonsson, M.: Enterprise Architecture Analysis with Extended Influence Diagrams. Information Systems Frontiers 9(2-3), 163–180 (2007)
7. Baldwin, C., MacCormack, A., Rusnack, J.: Hidden Structure: Using Network Methods to Map System Architecture. Harvard Business School Working Paper, no. 13-093 (May 2013)
8. Department of Defense Architecture Framework Working Group: DoD Architecture Framework. Version 1.5, Technical report, Department of Defense, USA (2007)
9. Zachman International, http://www.zachmaninternational.com
10. Franke, U., Johnson, P., König, J., Marcks von Würtemberg, L.: Availability of Enterprise IT Systems: An Expert-based Bayesian Framework. Software Quality Journal 20(2), 369–394 (2012)
11. Ullberg, J., Johnson, P., Buschle, M.: A Language for Interoperability Modeling and Prediction. Computers in Industry 63(8), 766–774 (2012)

12. Lagerström, R., Johnson, P., Höök, D.: Architecture Analysis of Enterprise Systems Modifiability: Models, Analysis, and Validation. Journal of Systems and Software 83(8), 1387–1403 (2010)
13. Sommestad, T., Ekstedt, M., Holm, H.: The Cyber Security Modeling Language: A Tool for Assessing the Vulnerability of Enterprise System Architectures. IEEE Systems Journal (2013) (online-first)
14. Barabási, A.: Scale-Free Networks: A Decade and Beyond. Science 325(5939), 412–413 (2009)
15. Simon, H.A.: The Architecture of Complexity. The American Philosophical Society 106(6), 467–482 (1962)
16. Alexander, C.: Notes on the Synthesis of Form. Harvard University Press (1964)
17. Mead, C., Conway, L.: Introduction to VLSI Systems. Addison-Wesley Publishing Co. (1980)
18. Baldwin, C., Clark, K.: Design Rules. The Power of Modularity, vol. 1. MIT Press (2000)
19. Steward, D.: The Design Structure System: A Method for Managing the Design of Complex Systems. IEEE Transactions on Engineering Management 3, 71–74 (1981)
20. Eppinger, S.D., Whitney, D.E., Smith, R.P., Gebala, D.A.: A Model-Based Method for Organizing Tasks in Product Development. Research in Engineering Design 6(1), 1–13 (1994)
21. Sosa, M., Eppinger, S., Rowles, C.: A Network Approach to Define Modularity of Components in Complex Products. Transactions of the ASME 129, 1118–1129 (2007)
22. MacCormack, A., Baldwin, C., Rusnak, J.: Exploring the Duality Between Product and Organizational Architectures: A Test of the "Mirroring" Hypothesis. Research Policy 41(8), 1309–1324 (2006)
23. Dreyfus, D., Wyner, G.: Digital Cement: Software Portfolio Architecture, Complexity, and Flexibility. In: The Americas Conference on Information Systems (AMCIS). Association for Information Systems (2011)
24. Dreyfus, D.: Digital Cement: Information System Architecture, Complexity, and Flexibility. PhD Thesis. Boston University Boston, MA, USA (2009) ISBN: 978-1-109-15107-7
25. Lagerstrom, R., Baldwin, C.Y., MacCormack, A., Aier, S.: Visualizing and Measuring Enterprise Application Architecture: An Exploratory Telecom Case. Harvard Business School Working Paper, no. 13–103 (June 2013)
26. Holm, H., Buschle, M., Lagerström, R., Ekstedt, M.: Automatic Data Collection for Enterprise Architecture Models. Software & Systems Modeling (2012) (online first)
27. Buschle, M., Grunow, S., Matthes, F., Ekstedt, M., Hauder, M., Roth, S.: Automating Enterprise Architecture Documentation using an Enterprise Service Bus. In: The 18th Americas Conference on Information Systems, AMCIS (2012)
28. IBM Rational System Architect,
    http://www.ibm.com/software/products/us/en/ratisystarch
29. BiZZdesign Architect, http://www.bizzdesign.com/tools/bizzdesign-architect
30. The Enterprise Architecture Analysis Tool, http://www.ics.kth.se/eaat

An Empirical Evaluation of Design Decision Concepts in Enterprise Architecture

Georgios Plataniotis[1,2,3], Sybren de Kinderen[3], Dirk van der Linden[1,2,3], Danny Greefhorst[4], and Henderik A. Proper[1,2,3]

[1] Public Research Centre Henri Tudor, Luxembourg, Luxembourg
[2] Radboud University Nijmegen, Nijmegen, The Netherlands
[3] EE-Team, Luxembourg, Luxembourg*
[4] ArchiXL, The Netherlands
{georgios.plataniotis,dirk.vanderlinden,erik.proper}@tudor.lu,
sybren.dekinderen@gmail.com, dgreefhorst@archixl.nl

Abstract. Enterprise Architecture (EA) languages describe the design of an enterprise holistically, typically linking products and services to supporting business processes and, in turn, business processes to their supporting IT systems. In earlier work, we introduced EA Anamnesis, which provides an approach and corresponding meta-model for rationalizing architectural designs. EA Anamnesis captures the motivations of design decisions in enterprise architecture, alternative designs, design criteria, observed impacts of a design decision, and more. We argued that EA Anamnesis nicely complements current architectural languages by providing the capability to learn from past decision making.

In this paper, we provide a first empirical grounding for the practical usefulness of EA Anamnesis. Using a survey amongst 35 enterprise architecture practitioners, we test the perceived usefulness of EA Anamnesis concepts, and compare this to their current uptake in practice. Results indicate that while many EA Anamnesis concepts are perceived as useful, the current uptake in practice is limited to a few concepts - prominently 'rationale' and 'layer'. Our results go on and show that architects currently rationalize architectural decisions in an ad hoc manner, forgoing structured templates such as provided by EA Anamnesis. Finally, we interpret the survey results discussing for example possible reasons for the gap between perceived usefulness and uptake of architectural rationalization.

Keywords: Enterprise Architecture, Design Rationale, Design Decision concepts, Evaluation, Survey.

1 Introduction

Enterprise Architecture (EA) modeling languages, such as the Open Group standard language ArchiMate [1], connect an organization's IT infrastructure and

---

* The Enterprise Engineering Team (EE-Team) is a collaboration between Public Research Centre Henri Tudor, Radboud University and HAN University of Applied Sciences (www.ee-team.eu)

J. Grabis et al. (Eds.): PoEM 2013, LNBIP 165, pp. 24–38, 2013.

applications to the business processes they support and the products/services that are in turn realized by the business processes. Such a holistic perspective on an enterprise helps to clarify the business advantages of IT, analyze cost structures and more [2].

While EA modeling languages allow for modeling an enterprise holistically, the design decisions behind the resulting models are often left implicit.

As discussed in our earlier work [3], the resulting lack of transparency on design decisions can cause design integrity issues when architects want to maintain or change the current design [4]. This means that due to a lacking insight of the rationale, new designs are constructed in an adhoc manner, without taking into consideration constraints implied by past design decisions. Also, according to a survey for software architecture design rationale [5], a large majority of architects (85,1%) admitted the importance of design rationalization in order to justify designs.

Furthermore, anecdotal evidence from six exploratory interviews we conducted with senior enterprise architects suggests that enterprise architects are often external consultants. This situation increases the architectural knowledge gap of the Enterprise Architecture, since without rationalization architects lack insights into design decision making in an organization that is new to them.

In earlier work [3,6,7], we introduced an approach for the rationalization of enterprise architectures by capturing EA design decision details. We refer to this approach as EA Anamnesis, from the ancient Greek word ανάμνησις (/ˌænæmˈniːsɪs/), which denotes memory and repair of forgetfulness. The EA Anamnesis meta-model is grounded in similar approaches from the software engineering domain, prominently in the Decision Representation Language (DRL) [8]. At this stage, EA Anamnesis complements the ArchiMate modeling language [1] by conceptualizing decision details (alternatives, criteria, impacts) and by grouping EA decisions in three different enterprise architecture layers (Business, Application, Technology) in accordance with the ArchiMate specification.

In this paper we evaluate empirically the design decision concepts from the EA Anamnesis meta-model by means of a survey amongst enterprise architecture practitioners. On the one hand, our study shows that a majority of EA practitioners deem EA Anamnesis's concepts, such as "motivation" and "observed impact", as useful, in that these concepts help them with the maintenance and justification of enterprise architectures. On the other hand, however, our study shows a limited uptake of rationalization in practice. For one, while many architects capture a decision's motivations, there is less attention for capturing the observed impacts of decisions. Finally we find that, currently, there is little reliance on a structured rationalization approach, such as provided by EA Anamnesis. Rather, rationalization of decisions (if any) is done in an ad hoc manner, relying on unstructured tools such as MS Word or Powerpoint.

Also, we speculate that the distinction between perceived usefulness and uptake in practice is, at least partially, due to a lacking awareness of rationalization, and potential usefulness it has for architectural practice.

This paper is structured as follows. Sect. 2 presents the EA Anamnesis concepts and a short illustration of them. Sect. 3 presents the evaluation setup, while Sect. 4 presents the results of our study. Subsequently, in Sect. 5 we discuss the survey results. Sect. 6 concludes.

2   Background

To make the paper self contained, this section presents the design rationale concepts of the EA Anamnesis approach that were confronted to practitioners during our study (in Sect. 2.1), accompanied by an illustration of our approach with a case study from the insurance sector (in Sect. 2.2).

2.1   EA Anamnesis Design Decision Concepts

In this paper we focus on decision detail concepts that provide qualitative rationalization information for design decisions. According to [4], architectural rationale can be discriminated in three different types: qualitative design rationale, quantitative design rationale and alternative architecture rationale.

The meta-model of the EA Anamnesis approach is depicted in Fig. 1. To limit survey length we focus our study on a set of key concepts. Concepts of the meta-model that provide additional details, such as title (a descriptive name of a decision), are not discussed.

Below we provide a brief description of the concepts used in our survey.

Rationale. The reason(s) that leads an architect to choose a specific decision among the alternatives. According to Kruchten [9] a rationale answers the "why" question for each decision.

Alternative. This concept illustrates the EA decisions that were rejected (alternatives) in order to address a specific EA issue [10,11].

Layer. In line with the ArchiMate language [1], an enterprise is specified in three layers: *Business, Application and Technology*. Using these three layers, we express an enterprise *holistically*, showing not only applications and physical IT infrastructure (expressed through the application and technology layers), but also how an enterprise's IT impacts/is impacted by an enterprise's products and services and its business strategy and processes.

Observed Impact. The observed impact concept signifies an *unanticipated* consequence of an already made decision to an EA artifact. This is opposed to anticipated consequences, such as signified by decision impact relationships (discussed next). Observed impacts can be positive or negative consequences.

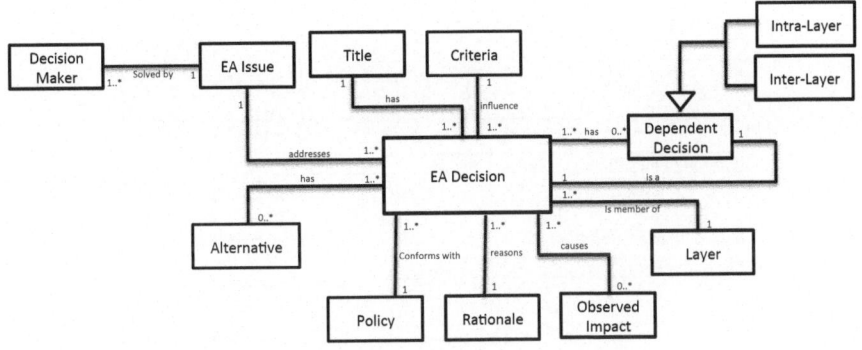

Fig. 1. The EA Anamnesis meta-model

In current everyday practice, architects model *anticipated* consequences using what-if-scenarios [2]. Unfortunately, not every possible impact of made EA decisions can be predicted. This is especially true for enterprise architecture, where one considers impacts across the enterprise rather than in one specific (e.g. technical) part. Some of the consequences of EA decisions are revealed during the implementation phase, or during the maintenance of the existing architecture design [12]. These unanticipated consequences are exactly captured by the concept of an observed impact.

For us the main usefulness of capturing observed impacts is that they can be used by architects to avoid decisions with negative consequences in future designs of the architecture.

Impact (Decision Traceability). The "Impact" concept makes explicit relationships between EA decisions. For example, how an IT decision affects a business process level decision or vice versa.

2.2 Illustrative Example

We now briefly illustrate how the concepts of our approach can be used to express architectural design rationale, using a fictitious insurance case presented in our previous work [3].

ArchiSurance is an insurance company that sells car insurance products using a direct-to-customer sales model. The architectural design of this sales model, created in the EA modeling language ArchiMate, is depicted in Fig. 2.

Two business services support the sales model of ArchiSurance: "Car insurance registration service" and "Car insurance service". ArchiMate helps us to understand the dependencies between different perspectives on an enterprise. For example, in Fig. 2 we see that the business service "Car insurance registration service" is realized by a business process "Register customer profile". In turn, we also see that this business process is supported by the application service "Customer administration service".

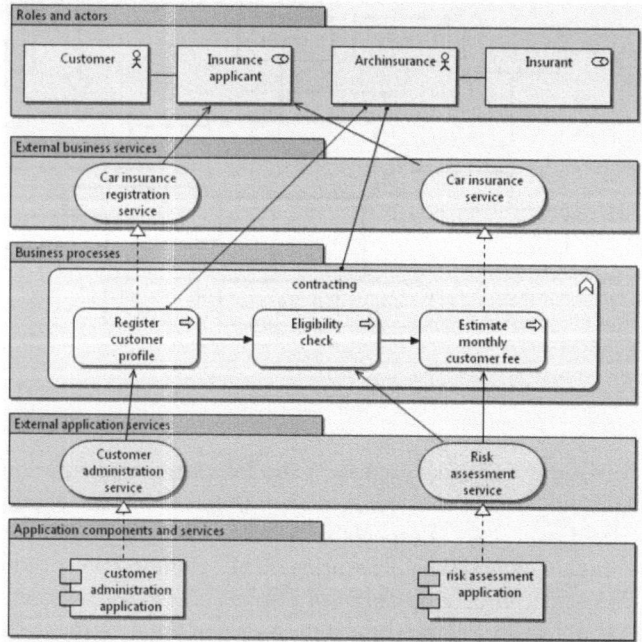

Fig. 2. ArchiSurance direct-to-customer EA model

Although disintermediation reduces operational costs, it also increases the risk of adverse risk profiles [13], incomplete or faulty risk profiles of customers. These adverse profiles lead insurance companies to calculate unsuitable premiums or, even worse, to wrongfully issue insurances to customers. As a response, ArchiSurance decides to use intermediaries to sell its insurance products. After all, compiling accurate risk profiles is part of the core business of an intermediary [13].

In our example scenario, an external architect called *John* is hired by ArchiSurance to help guide the change to an intermediary sales model. John uses ArchiMate to capture the impacts that selling insurance via an intermediary has in terms of business processes, IT infrastructure and more. For illustration purposes we will focus on the translation of the new business process "Customer profile registration" to EA artifacts in the application layer. The resulting ArchiMate model is depicted in Fig. 3.

In Fig. 3 we see for example how a (new) business process "customer profile registration", owned by the insurance broker (ownership being indicated by a line between the broker and the business process), is supported by the IT applications "customer administration service intermediary" and "customer administration service ArchiSurance".

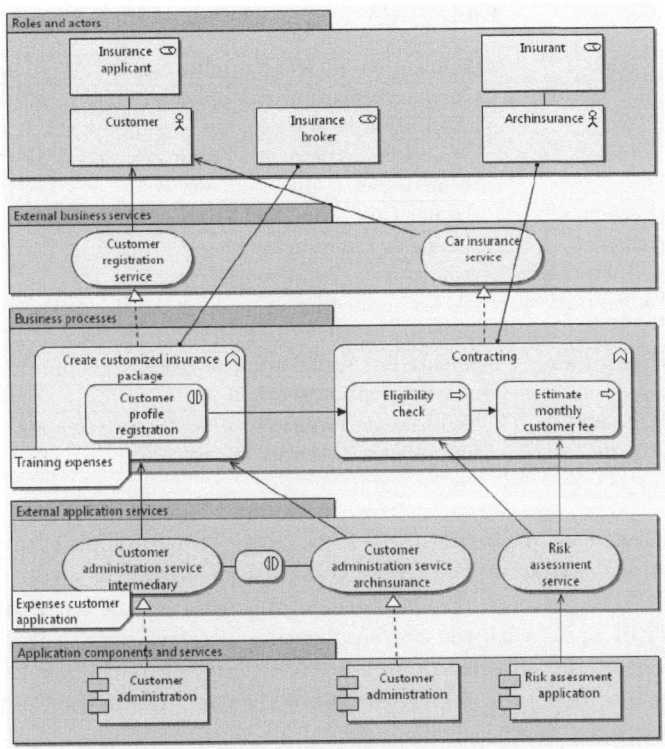

Fig. 3. ArchiSurance intermediary EA model

For this simplified scenario, 13 architectural design decisions were taken. These design decisions, in terms of our design decision concepts, were captured with EA Anamnesis by John during the transformation process.

Let us assume that a newly hired Enterprise Architect, Bob, wants to know the rationale behind the architectural design that supports the new business process of Archisurance. To this end, he relies on decision rationales captured by John. Table 1 shows one such rationalized decision: design decision 13, for the IT application "customer administration service intermediary".

As can be observed, design decision 13 regards the acquisition of the Commercial off-the-shelf (COTS) application B. Bob can determine the **alternatives**, "COTS application A" and "upgrade of the existing IT application". Furthermore, Bob determines that John's **rationale** for the selection of COTS application B was that COTS application B was more scalable.

Next, let us assume that Bob is interested in reviewing the relationship of this individual decision with other decisions. Firstly, he can identify by examining the **Layer** field that this decision is an application Layer decision. Moreover, by examining the **Impact relationship** field, he can understand that this decision is related with 2 other decisions, decision 07 (a business layer decision) and decision 10 (an application layer decision).

Table 1. EA decision 13 details

Title:	Acquisition of COTS application B
EA issue:	Current version of customer administration application is not capable to support maintenance and customers administration of intermediaries application service
Layer:	Application
Impact relationships:	Business: Decision 07 Application: Decision 10
Alternatives:	COTS application A Upgrade existing application (in-house)
Rationale:	Scalability: Application is ready to support new application services
Observed Impact:	Reduced performance of customer registration service business process

Last but not least, Bob can inspect the possible unanticipated outcomes of this decision. By examining the **Observed impact** field, he is aware of an issue that arose in the customer profile registration business process because of the unfamiliarity of clerks with the new application interface.

For a more detailed illustration of EA Anamnesis approach, how the different concepts are interrelated and how this rationalization information is visualized, see earlier work [7].

3   Evaluation

In this section we describe the objectives of our study, the evaluation method for the validation of our decision design concepts, and limitations and considerations of the evaluation.

3.1   Objectives

The main objective of this study is to identify the usefulness of design rationale approaches in the context of Enterprise Architecture. As we mentioned in the introduction, anecdotal interviews with EA practitioners gave us a first insight regarding the perceived usefulness of design rationale approaches in EA. In particular, we aim at identifying the perception of EA practitioners regarding our design rationale concepts.

For our study we address three research questions:

Question 1:
Do enterprise architecture practitioners perceive EA Anamnesis's concepts as useful for the justification and maintenance of EA Designs?

Question 2:
To what extent do EA practitioners currently capture EA Anamnesis's concepts?

Question 3:
If rationalization information is captured, to what extent are structured templates used? (such as provided by EA Anamnesis)

3.2   Study Setup

Participants: Participants were gathered during a professional event on enterprise architecture organized by the Netherlands Architecture Forum (NAF). NAF is a leading Dutch (digital) architecture organization, concerned with the professionalization of Enterprise and IT Architecture. A total of 65 people started the survey, 35 out of which actively finished the study. Given the different focus of the individuals, the number of participants for each individual part of the survey fluctuated between 33 and 35. The majority of the participants were of Dutch nationality, had at least several years of professional experience in enterprise architecture, and were fluent in the language the survey was taken in (English).

Materials: The questions and input used for this survey derived from previous research and professional workshops on the use and creation of architecture principles in Dutch knowledge management and enterprise modeling organizations. The data analyzed and used for this study derives from a subset of the total survey, which contained additional sections dealing with other, related, factors of architecture principle creation and use. All questions were presented in English because non-Dutch speakers were expected. Furthermore, the survey was planned to be extended to other European countries afterwards.

Method: The survey consisted mostly of structured and closed questions. The participants were given the context that the questions dealt with the larger area of architecture principles, specifically introducing them to the fact that principles provide a foundation for EA decisions, and what factors are important for such decisions.

To investigate to what extent the concepts of EA Anamnesis are grounded in reality, we queried for each concept (a short explanation of each concept was provided) whether participants considered them to 1) help with the maintenance of an enterprise architecture, 2) help them to justify an enterprise architecture, and 3) be currently actively documented in the participant's organization or professional experience.

For each of these dimensions participants could answer whether they disagreed, agreed, or strongly agreed with the dimension applied to the given concept. The format of the answers was adopted from a bigger survey, which was executed by an outside party. The outside party had already structured the questions' format of this survey and as such we adopted the same answering formats in order to reduce any potential confusion as much as possible.

To follow up on the current practical state of design decisions, we then enquired whether any standardized approaches or processes existed for the capturing of EA design decisions.

Participants were given the choice of either stating that, for their organization, such approaches exist, do not exist, or that they were uncertain of their existence. In the case of nonexistence of documentation approaches, participants had the possibility to expose the reasons for this through a hybrid structure with predefined answers as well as free text comments.

Data analysis: The data resulting from the main questions (whether our use case concepts help in the maintenance and justification of an EA and whether they are documented) were quantified by assuming "strongly agree" implied "agree", and that such answers could be treated as "agrees". Based on this, we calculated the total amount of "agree" and "disagree" answers for each of our concepts as they pertained to the investigated dimensions. Of course, questions that were not filled in were disregarded in our calculation. While the size of these groups did not differ much (resp. 33, 34 and 35 participants), and comparison between them should thus be a valid endeavor, care should also be taken not to assume they represent a breakdown of opinions in the exact same group. The data resulting from the question regarding the use of standardized templates for documenting EA design decisions were analyzed in a straightforward way, calculating the percentages of yes, no and uncertain answers for the group (n=35) of participants who answered this question.

3.3   Survey Limitations

The main difficulty in executing this study was that our questions had to be integrated into a larger study, of which the structure and answer formats were already determined. Unfortunately, the opportunity to conduct a dedicated survey regarding design rationale with such a number of participants was quite limited due to time unavailability of practitioners. Therefore, we had a limitation regarding the number of questions we could incorporate into this larger study.

Thus, in order to ensure that participants would not feel confused by radically different question and answering formats, we had to deal with a suboptimal set of answers for our first question. Ideally, the question of whether certain concepts apply to a given dimension, would be done on a Likert scale, with equal amounts of negative and positive answers. However, as the goal of the wider survey was to elicit as much (strong) opinions as possible from practitioners, it was chosen to use answer structures which contained no neutral grounds and thus forced people to make a polarized choice.

We will take these issues into account during the analysis of our data, and attempt to account for the possible loss of nuance.

4 Results

Tables 2, 3, 4 show the survey results on to what extent EA Anamnesis's concepts help the EA practitioner to (1) maintain the architecture, (2) justify the architecture, by which we mean that the EA Anamnesis concepts can aid in motivating design decisions, and (3) to what extent EA practitioners document EA Anamnesis concepts in current practice.

For each question, we provide a division into "positive" and "negative", and a subsequent division of "positive" into "agree" and "strongly agree". We do this for the sake of transparency: on the one hand, we want to show aggregate results on positive reactions to a concept, but on the other hand we do not want to hide that the questions were posed in a possibly biased manner (as discussed in Sect. 3.3).

Furthermore, Table 5 shows us to what extent practitioners use standardized templates to capture EA design rationales. In case practitioners forego the use of standardized templates, Table 6 shows why this is so, by means of closed answers (such as "no time/budget") and open answers, whereby the architects could provide a plaintext description (such as "Enterprise Architecture is not mature enough").

Table 2. To what extent study participants (n=35) find that EA Anamnesis's concepts help with the maintenance of the enterprise architecture

| Concept | Helps with the maintenance of EA | | | |
	Negative	Positive	Positive-Agree	Positive-Strongly agree
Rationale	9%	91%	42%	49%
Rejected Alternatives	26%	74%	43%	31%
EA Layer	9%	91%	46%	45%
Observed Impact	23%	77%	43%	34%
Decision Impact	14%	86%	40%	46%

5 Discussion

Generally, the results from Tables 2, 3 indicate that EA practitioners perceive that the EA Anamnesis concepts will help them with the maintenance and justification of Enterprise Architecture designs. This can be concluded from the fact that, for each concept, a majority of architects agrees with its usefulness for both maintenance and justification. Yet, the results from Table 4 indicate that while the design rationale concepts are considered useful, the majority of them is not documented by practitioners. While many EA practitioners capture the rationale for a decision (70%) and the EA layer (79%), a majority of them does not capture either the observed impact, decision impact or rejected alternatives.

Table 3. To what extent study participants (n=35) find that EA Anamnesis's concepts help with the justification of the enterprise architecture

Concept	Helps with the justification of EA			
	Negative	Positive	Positive-Agree	Positive-Strongly agree
Rationale	18%	82%	29%	53%
Rejected Alternatives	29%	71%	44%	27%
EA Layer	38%	62%	38%	24%
Observed Impact	18%	82%	50%	32%
Decision Impact	26%	74%	44%	29%

Table 4. To what extent study participants (n=33) currently document the EA Anamnesis concepts

Concept	Current documentation practice			
	Negative	Positive	Positive-Agree	Positive-Strongly agree
Rationale	30%	70%	55%	15%
Rejected Alternatives	73%	27%	27%	0%
EA Layer	21%	79%	40%	39%
Observed Impact	73%	27%	24%	3%
Decision Impact	58%	42%	36%	6%

Table 5. To what extent study participants (n=35) use a standardized template for documenting EA design decisions

Question	Uncertain	Yes	No
Does your organization use a standardized template for documenting EA design decisions?	23%	40%	37%

Table 6. The proportions of the reasons that practitioners (n=33) do not use standardized templates for documenting EA design decisions.

Not useful	30%
No time/budget	3%
No suitable tool	9%
Other comments:	58%

Design decisions are documented inside PSA/PEA (Word or Powerpoint)
Depends mostly on the client
EA is not mature enough
Our organization is not mature enough when it comes to EA
General immaturity of EA departments
We use several templates, but they are not exactly the same
Company standard is the TOGAF template

Moreover, in cases where practitioners document decisions, 40% of them use standardized templates for documentation, while 23% of them is not aware of the existence of such templates. The remaining 37% of practitioners, that do not use standardized templates, finds that standardized templates are not useful (30%), or that there are no available resources in terms of time/budget (3%), or that there no suitable tool for this (9%). Furthermore 58% of the EA practitioners do not use standardized templates because they feel covered by documenting design decisions inside MS Word/Powerpoint. Others insist the Enterprise Architecture is not a mature practice in the organization.

A possible reason for the currently limited rationalization of Enterprise Architecture designs is that practitioners are insufficiently *aware* of the potential usefulness of design rationale techniques. This may be caused by the relative immaturity of the Enterprise Architecture field compared to areas in which decision rationalization and their tool support is well established, such as the field of Software Architecture.

Let us now discuss our findings per concept:

Rationale. The Rationale concept, which captures why a decision is taken, is considered an important concept for the majority of practitioners. Specifically 91% believe that this concept helps with the maintenance of the EA, and 82% believe that it helps to justify existing Enterprise Architectures. Interestingly however, as opposed to capturing other concepts, the current practice of documenting rationale of decisions is quite high (70%). We argue that this happens, because architects usually have to justify their design decisions to other stakeholders and the management of the organization.

Rejected Alternatives. The majority of practitioners (74%) acknowledges that captured rejected alternatives information assists them with the maintenance of the enterprise architecture and (71%) of them that they are helped with the justification of the enterprise architecture. Practitioners seem to understand that this information provides a better insight into the rationalization process. We speculate that rejected alternatives, in combination with selection criteria, provide them with additional rationalization information by indicating the desired qualities which were not satisfied by these alternatives.

However Table 4 indicates that only (27%) of the EA practitioners capture rejected alternatives. We reason that the capturing effort of rejected alternatives in combination with the ignorance of the potential usefulness of this information do not motivate practitioners to document this concept. Even if this information is documented, the added value it provides is not so high because of the lack of structured documentation. However when rejected alternatives are combined with other rationalization concepts (such as criteria) it does allow one to better trace the decision making process, as is commonly done in structured rationalization templates for software architecture (see e.g. [11]).

Layer. 91% of the practitioners agree that the concept of layer helps them with the maintenance of an enterprise architecture. The proportion of practitioners that agree that this concept helps them to justify enterprise architectures is 62%. Although the proportion itself is quite supportive, we can observe quite a big variation compared with the question on "helps with maintenance". We argue that this is because the Layer concept is not a justification concept in itself, but when it is combined with the other design rationale concepts it can actually contribute to justification. For example, design decisions that belong to the business layer can impact decisions in the application layer.

Observed Impact. A majority of Enterprise Architects (77%) recognize that the explicit information of observed impacts helps them with the maintenance of the enterprise architecture. We speculate that practitioners, while they maintain existing architectures, are expected to use information of the unanticipated outcomes of past decisions in the enterprise to avoid past mistakes. Furthermore 82% of Enterprise Architects agree that the observed impact concept helps them with the justification of the EA.

Interestingly however, despite the fact that practitioners recognize the usefulness of capturing the observed impact, only the 23% of them has a standard practice to document this concept. We believe that when an unanticipated outcome of a design decision is observed, practitioners are focused on immediately solving this issue. From a short term perspective, the documentation of this observed impact is a minor issue for them. However, in the long term, the awareness of observed impacts raises awareness of unanticipated outcomes. Another reason could be the lack of a structured environment for architectural rationalization, which would allow architects to relate observed impacts to decisions, layers (impacts on a business process or IT level), and more.

Impact (Decision Traceability). A majority of the practitioners (86%) find that the impact concept can assist them with the maintenance of the enterprise architecture. Moreover, 74% indicate that this concept helps them with the justification of the enterprise architecture. Our approach provides impact (decision traceability) information by making explicit how design decisions are related to each other. The different types of decision relationships, described by decision relationships concept, provide different types of impact traceability. Regarding the documentation practice, some of the practitioners (42%) capture this concept but still the majority of them (58%) does not document it. In our view this indicates a tendency of practitioners to interrelate their design decisions and EA artifacts. However, on the other hand, we think that the capturing of decision impacts is still limited since architects lack structured ways to capture design decisions, as we can see in Table 6.

6   Conclusion

In this paper, we reported on a first empirical evaluation of the EA Anamnesis approach for architectural rationalization. Using data from a survey amongst enterprise architecture practitioners, we found that EA Anamnesis concepts are largely perceived as useful to architectural practice. Yet, we also found that the uptake of rationalization in practice is currently limited to only a few concepts, prominently "rationale". Furthermore, these few concepts are captured in an ad hoc manner, thereby forgoing structured rationalization approaches such as EA Anamnesis.

Finally, we speculated on (1) the distinction between perceived usefulness of rationalization concepts on the one hand, and the uptake in practice on the other, and (2) the seeming current limited use of a structured template for rationalization. A possible explanation is the relative immaturity of the field of Enterprise Architecture, compared to fields where rationalization is well accepted, such as Software Architecture. Such immaturity manifests itself in a lack of awareness of rationalization, including recognizing its potential usefulness for tracing design decisions, as well as in a lack of structured templates for documenting design decisions in enterprise architecture.

However, as we test only the *perceived* usefulness of EA Anamnesis concepts, we should use a single in depth case study to further investigate the claims made in this article. For one, the difference between perceived usefulness and uptake may also be caused by the effort that it takes to capture rationalization information, in addition to a lack of structured templates and usefulness awareness.

Acknowledgments. This work has been partially sponsored by the *Fonds National de la Recherche Luxembourg* (www.fnr.lu), via the PEARL programme.

References

1. The Open Group: ArchiMate 2.0 Specification. Van Haren Publishing (2012)
2. Lankhorst, M.: Enterprise architecture at work: Modelling, communication and analysis. Springer (2009)
3. Plataniotis, G., Kinderen, S.D., Proper, H.A.: Ea anamnesis: towards an approach for enterprise architecture rationalization. In: Proceedings of the 2012 Workshop on Domain-specific Modeling, DSM 2012, pp. 27–32. ACM, New York (2012)
4. Tang, A., Jin, Y., Han, J.: A rationale-based architecture model for design traceability and reasoning. Journal of Systems and Software 80(6), 918–934 (2007)
5. Tang, A., Babar, M.A., Gorton, I., Han, J.: A survey of architecture design rationale. Journal of Systems and Software 79(12), 1792–1804 (2006)
6. Plataniotis, G., de Kinderen, S., Proper, H.A.: Capturing decision making strategies in enterprise architecture – A viewpoint. In: Nurcan, S., Proper, H.A., Soffer, P., Krogstie, J., Schmidt, R., Halpin, T., Bider, I. (eds.) BPMDS 2013 and EMMSAD 2013. LNBIP, vol. 147, pp. 339–353. Springer, Heidelberg (2013)
7. Plataniotis, G., Kinderen, S.D., Proper, H.A.: Relating decisions in enterprise architecture using decision design graphs. In: Proceedings of the 17th IEEE International Enterprise Distributed Object Computing Conference, EDOC (2013)
8. Lee, J.: Extending the potts and bruns model for recording design rationale. In: Proceedings of the 13th International Conference on Software Engineering, pp. 114–125 (1991)

9. Kruchten, P.: An ontology of architectural design decisions in software intensive systems. In: 2nd Groningen Workshop on Software Variability, pp. 54–61 (2004)
10. Kruchten, P., Lago, P., van Vliet, H.: Building up and reasoning about architectural knowledge. In: Hofmeister, C., Crnković, I., Reussner, R. (eds.) QoSA 2006. LNCS, vol. 4214, pp. 43–58. Springer, Heidelberg (2006)
11. Tyree, J., Akerman, A.: Architecture decisions: Demystifying architecture. IEEE Software 22(2), 19–27 (2005)
12. Proper, H.A., Op 't Land, M.: Lines in the water. In: Harmsen, F., Proper, E., Schalkwijk, F., Barjis, J., Overbeek, S. (eds.) PRET 2010. LNBIP, vol. 69, pp. 193–216. Springer, Heidelberg (2010)
13. Cummins, J., Doherty, N.: The economics of insurance intermediaries. Journal of Risk and Insurance 73(3), 359–396 (2006)

Evaluating Data Quality for Integration of Data Sources

John Krogstie

Norwegian University of Science and Technology (NTNU),
Sem Sælandsvei 7-9, N-7030 Trondheim, Norway
krogstie@idi.ntnu.no

Abstract. Data can be looked upon as a type of model (on the instance level), as illustrated e.g., in the product models in CAD and PLM-systems. In this paper we use a specialization of a general framework for assessing quality of models to be able to evaluate the combined quality of data for the purpose of investigating potential challenges when doing data integration across different sources. A practical application of the framework from assessing the potential quality of different data sources to be used together in a collaborative work environment is used for illustrating the usefulness of the framework for this purpose. An assessment of specifically relevant knowledge sources (including the characteristics of the tools used for accessing the data) has been done. This has indicated opportunities, but also challenges when trying to integrate data from different data sources typically used by people in different roles in an organization.

Keywords: Product modelling, data integration, data quality.

1 Introduction

Data quality has for a long time been an established area [2]. A related area that was established in the nineties is quality of models (in particular quality of conceptual data models) [21]. Traditionally, one has here looked at model quality for models on the M1 (type) level (to use the model-levels found in e.g., MOF [4]). On the other hand, it is clear especially in product and enterprise modeling that there are models on the instance level (M0), an area described as containing data (or objects in MOF-terminology). Thus our hypothesis is that also data quality can be looked upon relative to more generic frameworks for quality of models. Integrating data sources is often incorrectly regarded as a technical problem that can be solved by the IT-professionals themselves without involvement from the business side. This widespread misconception focus only on the data syntax and ignores the semantic, pragmatic, social and other aspects of the data being integrated that can lead to costly business problems further on.

Discussions on data quality must be looked upon in concert with discussions on data model (or schema) quality. Comprehensive and generic frameworks for evaluating modelling approaches have been developed [13, 19, 23], but these can easily

J. Grabis et al. (Eds.): PoEM 2013, LNBIP 165, pp. 39–53, 2013.

become too general for practical use. Inspired by [22], suggesting the need for an inheritance hierarchy of quality frameworks, we have earlier provided a specialization of the generic SEQUAL framework [13] for the evaluation of the quality of data and their accompanying data models [16]. Whereas the framework used here is the same as in [16], the application of the framework for looking at quality aspects when integrating data sources is novel to this paper.

In section 2, we present the problem area and case study for data integration. Section 3 provides a brief overview of SEQUAL, specialized for data quality assessment. An example of action research on the case, using the framework in practice is provided in section 4. In section 5, we conclude, summarizing the experiences applying the SEQUAL specialization.

2   Description of the Problem Area of the Case-Study

LinkedDesign[1] is an ongoing international project that aims to boost the productivity of engineers by providing an integrated, holistic view on data, actors and processes across the full product lifecycle. To achieve this there is a need to evaluate the appropriateness of a selected number of existing data sources, to be used as a basis for the support of collaborative engineering in a Virtual Obeya [1]. Obeya – Japanese for "large room" – is a term used in connection with project work in industry, where one attempted to collect all relevant information from the different disciplines involved in the same physical room. Realizing a Virtual Obeya means to provide a "room" with similar properties, which is not a physical room, but exists only on the net.

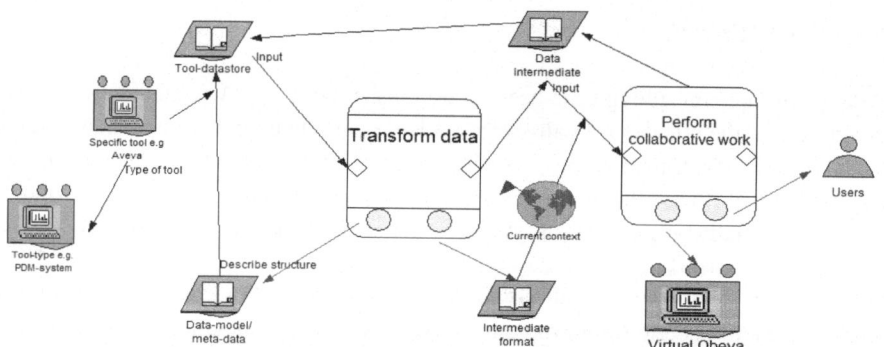

Fig. 1. Approach to knowledge access and creation in a Virtual Obeya [1]

The selected data sources are of the types found particularly relevant in the use cases of the project. When we look of *quality* of a data source (e.g., a PDM tool), we look on both the structure of the stored data in the left of Fig 1. (the data model, including meta-data) and the characteristics of the data itself, in light of our goal for

---

[1] www.linkeddesign.eu/

reuse and revisualization of data, in a way that might be annotated and/or updated through use. The users are meant to perform collaborative work using the Virtual Obeya. The Obeya presents context specific information based on the persons involved in the collaboration and other relevant information on products, projects, locations, tasks, tools, rules and guidelines etc. The data is mediated from existing work tools and is transformed depending on the context. The data presented and worked on in the Virtual Obeya can be annotated with other context-oriented information that potentially is stored for future use.

3   Introduction to Framework for Data Quality Assessment

SEQUAL [13] is a framework for assessing and understanding the quality of models and modelling languages. It has earlier been used for evaluation of modelling and modelling languages of a large number of perspectives, including data [15], object [11], process [14, 26], enterprise [17], and goal-oriented [10, 12] modelling. Quality has been defined referring to the correspondence between statements belonging to the following sets:

- G, the set of goals of the modelling task.
- L, the language extension.
- D, the domain, i.e., the set of all statements that can be stated about the situation. Domains can be divided into two parts, exemplified by looking at a software requirements specification model:
  - o   Everything the computerized information system is supposed to do. This is termed the *primary domain*.
  - o   Constraints on the model because of earlier baselined models. This is termed the *modelling context*. In relation to data quality, the underlying data model is part of the modelling context.
- M, the externalized model itself.
- K, the explicit knowledge that the audience have of the domain.
- I, the social actor interpretation of the model
- T, the technical actor interpretation of the model

The main quality types are:

- Physical quality: The basic quality goal is that the externalized model M is available to the relevant actors (and not others) for interpretation (I and T).
- Empirical quality deals with comprehensibility of the model M.
- Syntactic quality is the correspondence between the model M and the language extension L.
- Semantic quality is the correspondence between the model M and the domain D.
- Perceived semantic quality is the similar correspondence between the social actor interpretation I of a model M and his or hers current knowledge K of domain D.
- Pragmatic quality is the correspondence between the model M and the actor interpretation (I and T) of it. Thus whereas empirical quality focus on if the model is

understandable according to some objective measure that has been discovered empirically in e.g., cognitive science, we at this level look on to what extend the model has actually been understood.

- The goal defined for social quality is agreement among actor's interpretations.
- The deontic quality of the model relates to that all statements in the model **M** contribute to fulfilling the goals of modelling **G**, and that all the goals of modelling **G** are addressed through the model **M**.

When we structure different aspects according to these levels, one will find that there might be conflicts between the levels (e.g., what is good for semantic quality might be bad for pragmatic quality and vice versa). This will also be the case when structuring aspects of data quality. We here discuss means within each quality level, positioning the areas that are specified by *Batini* et al. [2], Price et al. [24, 25] and *Moody* [21]. Points from these previously described in [16] are emphasised using italic.

3.1   Physical Data Quality

Aspects of persistence, data being *accessible* (Price) for all (*accessibility* (Batini)), *currency* (Batini) and *security* (Price) cover aspects on the physical level. This area can be looked upon relative to measures of persistence, currency, security and availability that apply also to all other types of models. Tool functionality in connection with physical quality is based on traditional database-functionality.

3.2   Empirical Data Quality

This is addressed by *understandable (Price)*. Since data can be presented in many different ways, this relates to how the data is presented and visualized. How to best present different data depends on the underlying data-type. There are a number of generic guidelines within data visualization and related areas that can be applied. For computer-output specifically, many of the principles and tools used for improving human computer interfaces are relevant at the empirical level.

3.3   Syntactic Data Quality

From the generic SEQUAL framework we have that there is one main syntactic quality characteristics, **syntactical correctness**, meaning that all statements in the model are according to the syntax and vocabulary of the language.

Syntax errors are of two kinds:

- **Syntactic invalidity**, in which words not part of the language are used.
- **Syntactic incompleteness**, in which one lack constructs or information to obey the language's grammar.

Conforming to metadata (Price) including that the data conform to the expected data type of the data (as described in the data model) are part of syntactic data quality.

This will typically be related to syntactic invalidity when e.g., the data is of the wrong data-type.

3.4   Semantic Data Quality

When looking upon semantic data quality relative to the primary domain of modelling, we have the following properties:

Completeness in SEQUAL is covered by *completeness (Batini)*, *mapped completely (Price)*, and *mapped unambiguously (Price)*.

Validity in SEQUAL is covered by *accuracy (Batini)*, both syntactic and semantic accuracy as Batini has defined it, the difference between these is rather to decide on how incorrect the data is, *phenomena mapped correctly (Price)*, *properties mapped correctly (Price)* and *properties mapped meaningfully (Price)*. Since the rules of representation are formally given, *consistency (Batini)/mapped consistently (Price)* is also related to validity. The use of meta-data such as the source of the data is an important mean to support validity of the data.

Properties related to the model context are related to the adherence of the data to the data model. One would expect for instance that

- All tables of the data model should include tuples
- Data is according to the constraints defined in the data-model

The possibility of ensuring high semantic quality of the data is closely related to the semantic quality of the underlying data model. When looking upon semantic quality of the data model relative to the primary domain of modelling, we have the following properties: *Completeness (Moody and Batini)* (number of missing requirements) and *integrity (Moody)* (number of missing business rules).

Completeness (Moody) (number of superfluous requirements) and *integrity (Moody)* (number of incorrect business rules) relates to validity. The same applies to Batini's points on *correctness with respect to model* and *correctness with respect to requirements*.

3.5   Pragmatic Data Quality

Pragmatic quality relates to the comprehension of the model by the participants. Two aspects can be distinguished:

- That the interpretation by human stakeholders of the data is correct relative to what is meant to be expressed.
- That the tool interpretation is correct relative to what is meant to be expressed.

Starting with the human comprehension part, pragmatic quality on this level is the correspondence between the data and the audience's interpretation of it.

The main aspect at this level is *interpretability* (Batini), that data is *suitably presented* (Price) and data being *flexibly presented* (Price). Allowing *access to relevant metadata* (Price) is an important mean to achieve comprehension.

3.6   Social Data Quality

The goal defined for social quality is *agreement*. The area *quality of information source (Batini)* touches important mean for the social quality of the data, since a high quality source will increase the probability of agreement.

In some cases one need to combine different data sources. This consists of combing the data-models, and then transferring the data from the two sources into the new schema. Techniques for schema integration [5] are specifically relevant for this area.

3.7   Deontic Data Quality

Aspects on this level relates to the goals of having the data in the first place. Aspects to decide *volatility (Batini)* and *timeliness (Batini)/ timely (Price)* needs to relate to the goal of having and distributing the data. The same is the case for *type-sufficient (Price)*, the inclusion of all the types of information important for its use.

4   Application of the Framework

Looking at the sets of SEQUAL in the light of the case of the LinkedDesign project, we have the following:

- *G:* There are goals on two levels. The goal to be achieved when using the base tool and the goal of supporting collaborative work using data from this tool as one of several sources of knowledge to be combined in the Virtual Obeya. Our focus in the case is on this second goal.
- *L:* The language is the way data is encoded (e.g., using some standard), and the language for describing the data model/meta-model.
- *M:* Again on two levels, the data itself and the data-model.
- *A:* Actors i.e., the people in different roles using the models, with a specific focus on the collaborators in the use-cases of the project.
- *K:* The relevant explicit knowledge of the actors (A) in these roles
- *T:* Relates to the possibilities of the languages used to provide tool-support in handling the data (in the base tools, and in the Virtual Obeya)
- *I:* Relates to how easy it is for the different actors to interpret the data as it can be presented (in the base tool, and also in a Virtual Obeya)
- *D:* Domain: The domain can on a general level be looked upon relative to the concepts of an upper-level ontology. We focus on perspectives captured in the generic EKA - Enterprise Knowledge Architecture of Active Knowledge Models (AKM) since these have shown to be useful for context-based user interface development in other projects [19, chapter 5]. Thus we look on information on: Products, tasks, goals and rules (from standards to design rules), roles (including organizational structure and persons, and their capabilities) and tools.

Based on this we can describe the quality of data more precisely for this case:
- **Physical quality** relates to:
  - If the data is available in a physical format (and in different versions when relevant) so that it can be reused in the Virtual Obeya.

o   Possibility to store relevant meta-data e.g., on context
o   Availability of data for update or annotation/extension in the user interface
o   Availability of data from other tools
o   Data only available for those that should have access in case of there being security aspects

- **Empirical quality** is not directly relevant when evaluating the data-sources per se. Guidelines for this is relevant when we look upon how data can be presented in tools (and in the Virtual Obeya).
- **Syntactic quality**. Are the data represented in a way following the defined syntax including standards for the area?
- **Semantic quality**. Do the data sources potentially contain the expected type of data? Note that we here look on the possibility of representing the relevant types of data, obviously the level of completeness is dependent on what is represented in the concrete case. Tools might also have mechanisms for supporting the rapid development of complete models.
- **Pragmatic quality**. Is data of such a type that it can be easily understood (or visualized in a way that can be easily understood) by the stakeholders.
- **Social quality**. Is there agreement on the quality of the data among the stakeholders? Since different data comes from different tools, and often need to be integrated in the Virtual Obeya, agreement on interpretation of data and of the quality of the data sources among the involved stakeholders can be important.
- **Deontic quality**: Shall we with the help of data from the data source be able to achieve the goals of the project? Whereas the treatment at the other levels is meant to be generic, we have here the possibility to address the particular goals of the case explicitly. An important aspect of the case is to reduce waste in lean engineering processes [20]. In LinkedDesign, the use case-partners and other project partners have prioritized the waste areas, and we have used this input to come up with the following list of waste to be avoided as the most important:
o   Searching: time spent searching for information
o   Under-communication: Excessive or not enough time spent in communication
o   Misunderstanding:
o   Interpreting: time spent on interpreting communication or artifacts
o   Waiting: delays due to reviews, approvals etc.
o   Extra processing: excessive creation of artifacts or information

4.1 Evaluations of Relevant Tool-Types

In this project, based on the needs of the use cases, we have focused on the following concrete tools and tool types in the assessment.

- Office automation: Excel
- Computer-Aided Design (CAD): PDMS, Autocad, Catia V5
- Knowledge-based Engineering (KBE): KBEdesign
- Product Lifecycle Management (PLM/ PDM): Teamcenter, Enovia
- Enterprise Research Planning (ERP): SAP ERP (R/3), MS Dynamics

Not all the case organizations used all tool-types. We here focus on one of the organizations which had a need for integration of Excel-data, KBE and PLM-data. In the following we present the treatment of these areas.

4.2   Quality of Excel Data

Much data and information relevant for engineers and other business professionals is developed and resides in office automation tools like Excel [7].

Features Supporting Physical Quality of Excel Data. Data in tools like Excel can be saved both in the native format (.xls, .xlsx), in open standards such as .html, .xps, .dif, and .csv-files, and in open document formats (e.g., .ods), thus Excel-data can be made available in well-established forms following de jure and de facto standards, and thus can be easily made available for visualization and further use. One can also export e.g., PDF-versions of spreadsheets for making the information available without any possibility for interaction. Ensuring secure access to the data when exported is only manually enforced. Since the format is known, it is possible to save (updated) data from e.g., a Virtual Obeya, feeding this back to the original spreadsheet.

Features Supporting Empirical Quality of Excel Data. Excel has several mechanisms for data-visualizations in graphs and diagrams to ensure nice-looking visualizations and these visualizations can be made available externally for other tools. The underlying rules and macros in the spreadsheets are typically not visualized.

Features Supporting Syntactic Quality of Excel Data. Although the syntax of the storage-formats for Excel is well-defined, and standard data-types can be specified, there is no explicit information on the category of data (e.g., if the data represents product information). (Calculation) rules can be programmed, but these are undefined (in the formal meaning of the word), and the rules are in many export formats (such as .csv) not included.

Features Supporting Semantic Quality of Excel Data. You can represent knowledge of all the listed categories in a spreadsheet, but since the data-model is implicit, it is not possible to know what kind of data you have available without support from the human developer of the data, or by having this represented in some other way.

Features Supporting Pragmatic Quality of Excel Data. As indicated under empirical quality you can present data in spreadsheets visually, which can be shared (and you can potentially update the visualization directly), but as discussed under semantic quality, one do not have explicit knowledge of the category of the data represented.

Features Supporting Social Quality of Excel Data. Since Excel (and other office automation tools) typically are personal tools (and adapted to personal needs, even in cases where a company-wide template has been the starting point), there is a large risk that there are inconsistencies between data (and the underlying data model) in different spreadsheets and between data found in spreadsheets and in other tools.

Features Supporting Deontic Quality of Excel Data. Where much engineering knowledge is found in spreadsheets, it can be important to be able to include this in aggregated view in a Virtual Obeya. On the other hand, an explicit meta-model for the data matching a common ontology must typically be made in each case, thus it can be costly to ensure that all relevant data is available. As long as you keep to the same (implicit) meta-model for the data in the spreadsheet, you can update the data in the Virtual Obeya and have it transferred to the original data source. On the other hand, if you need to annotate the data with new categories it is not easy to update the spreadsheet without also updating the explicit meta-model without manual intervention.

Looking upon the waste forms we have the following

- Searching: When Excel is used, there is often data in a number of different Excel-sheets developed by a number of different people, and it is hard to know that one have the right version available.
- Under-communication: There is no explicit data-model, thus the interpretation of data might be based on labels only, which can be interpreted differently by different persons. A number of (calculation) rules are typically captured in Excel-sheets without being apparent.
- Misunderstanding: Due to potential different interpretation of terms, misunderstandings are likely.
- Interpreting: Since the meaning of data is under-communicating, the time to interpret might be quite long.
- Waiting: If data must be manually transformed to another format to be usable this might be an issue.
- Extra processing: Due to the versatility of tools like Excel, it is very easy to represent additional data and rules, even if they are not deemed useful by the organization.

4.3 Quality of Data in KBE Tools

KBE - Knowledge based engineering has its roots in applying AI techniques (especially LISP-based) on engineering problems. In [18], four approaches/programming languages are described: IDL, GDL, AML, and Intent!, all being extensions of LISP. In LinkedDesign, one particular KBE tool is used; KBEdesign™. The KBeDesign™ is an engineering automation tool developed for Oil & Gas offshore platform engineering design and construction, built on top of a commercial Knowledge Based Engineering (KBE) application (Technosofts AML), being similar to the AML sketcher. In the use case, there are two important data sources: The representation of the engineering artifacts themselves, and the way the engineering rules are represented (in AML) as part of the code.

Features Supporting Physical Quality of KBE Data. Knowledge and data is hard-coded in the AML framework. There exists classes for exporting the AML code into XML (or similar), however some information might be lost in this process. There are also classes for querying the AML code for the information you want, along with classes for automatic report creation. It is possible in KBEdesign to interact with most systems in principle. What is so far implemented is import/export routines to analysis software like GeniE, STAAD.Pro. Drawings can be exported to DWG (AutoCAD format). When the model is held within the tool, access rights can be controlled, but it is hard to enforce this when the model is exchanged to other tools. There is limited support for controlling versions both in the rule-set and in the models developed based on the rule-set. As for the rules, these are part of the overall code which can be versioned. Some rules related to model hierarchy and metadata (not geometry) for export to CAD and PLM systems are stored in a database and can be set up per project. Some capability to import data contained in the CAD-system PDMS is implemented.

Features Supporting Empirical Quality of KBE Data. Geometric data can be visualized as one instantiation of a model with certain input parameters. There are also multiple classes for different kind of finite element analysis of the model. Whereas the engineering artifact worked on is visualized in the work-tool, the AML-rules are not available for the engineer in a visual format. For those developing and maintaining the rule-base, these are represented in a code-format (i.e., structured text).

Features Supporting Syntactic Quality of KBE Data. In AML, datatypes are not defined. Programs might run even with syntax errors in formulas as there are both default values, and other mechanisms in place to ensure that systems can run with blank values. The data is stored in a proprietary XML-format, although as indicated it is also possible to make the model available using CAD-standards, but then only the information necessary for visualization is available. Options are available within AML for import and export to industry-standard file formats, including IGES, STEP, STL, and DXF. New STEP standards going beyond the current standards for CAD-tools that are interesting in connection to KBE codification are:

- The standard for construction history that is used to transfer the procedure used to construct the shape, referred to as ISO 10303-55.
- Standards for parameterization and constraints for explicit geometric product models, providing an indication of what are permissible to change refer to ISO 10303-108 for single parts and ISO 10303-109 for assemblies.
- Standard for what is known as 'design features', refer to ISO 10303-111.

Features Supporting Semantic Quality of KBE Data. The focus in KBEDesign is the representation of product data. AML is used to represent engineering rules. There are also possibilities in the core technology to represent process information related to the products. Note that an OO-framework has some well-known limitations in representing rules, e.g., for representing rules spanning many classes [8]. The AML framework also supports dependency tracking, so that if a value or rule is updated, everything that uses that value or rule is also changed. Dynamic instantiation is supported, providing potential short turnaround for changes to the rule-set.

Features Supporting Pragmatic Quality of KBE Data. The experiences from the use case indicate that it is very important to be able to provide rule visualizations, and that these can be annotated with meta-data and additional information. Standard classes in the AML framework allow you to query AML models, generating reports. Data can be visualized any way you want in AML, and if the required visualization is not part of the standard AML framework, then it can be created. It is practical to have everything working in the same environment, but it can be difficult for non-experienced users to find the right functionality.

Features Supporting Social Quality of KBE Data. KBE is a particular solution for engineering knowledge, and experiences from the use case indicate that there is not always agreement on the rules represented. The KBEDesign tool is used for developing oil-platform-designs, but for other engineering and design tasks, other tools are used. Export to tools used company-wide such as PDMS is important to establish agreement, and thus, social quality of the models.

Features Supporting Deontic Quality of KBE Data. An important aspect with object-oriented, rule-based approaches is the potential for supporting reuse across domains. Summarizing relative to factors for waste reduction in lean engineering

- Searching: Representing all rules in the KBE-system is useful in this regard, but they are to a limited degree structured e.g., relative to how rules influence each other, which rules are there to follow a certain standard etc.
- Under-communication: Since AML-rules are accessible as code only, it can be hard to understand why different design decisions are enforced.
- Misunderstanding: Can result from not having access to the rules directly;
- Interpreting: Additional time might be needed for interpretation for the above mentioned reason
- Waiting: If not getting support quickly for updating rules (if necessary), this can be an issue. The use of dynamic instantiation described under semantic quality can alleviate this, on the other hand one needs people with specific coding skills to add or change rules;
- Extra processing: Might need to represent rules differently to be useful in new situations. On the other hand if using the abstraction mechanism in a good way, this can be addressed.

4.4   Quality of Data in PDM/PLM Tools

Product lifecycle management (PLM) is the process of managing the entire lifecycle of a product from its conception, through design and manufacture, to service and disposal. Whereas CAD systems focus primarily on early phases of design, PLM attempts to take a full lifecycle view. PLM intends to integrate people, data, processes and business systems and provides a product information backbone for companies and their extended enterprise. There are a number of different PDM/PLM-tools. Some tools that were previously CAD tools like Catia have extended the functionality to become PLM-tools. The following is particularly based on literature review and interview with representatives for Teamcenter, which according to Gartner group is the market leader internationally for PLM tools. There is typically a core group of people creating information for such tools, and a vast group of people consuming this information.

Features Supporting Physical Quality of PDM/PLM Data. Core product data is held in an internal database supported by a common data model. The data can be under revision/version and security (access) control. Some data related to the product might be held in external files e.g., office documents. There can also be integration to CAD tools and ERP-tools (both ways). For Teamcenter for instance, there is CAD-integration (with Autocad, Autodesk, SolidWorks, Unigraphics, I-deas NX, Solid Edge, Catia V5, Pro Engineer) and ERP-integration (bi-directional with SAP ERP (R/3), MS Dynamics and Oracle). In addition to access on workstation, it is also possible to access the data on mobile platforms such as iPAD. Data can also be shared with e.g., suppliers supporting secure data access across an extended enterprise. This kind of functionality should also make it easier to support the access of data in the PLM-system from outside (e.g., also from a Virtual Obeya). Teamcenter have multi-site functionality, but it does not work well to work towards the same database over long distances.

Features Supporting Empirical Quality of PDM/PLM Data. PLM tools typically support 2D and 3D visualization of the products within the tool. These are typically made in CAD tools. CAD tools typically have good functionality to visualize the product data in 3D. Because of its economic importance, CAD has been a major driving force for research in computational geometry and computer graphics and thus for algorithms for visualizations that one typically focus on as means under the area of empirical quality.

Features Supporting Syntactic Quality of PDM/PLM Data. Storage of PLM-data is typically done according to existing standards. PLM XML is supported in Team-center, in addition to the formats needed for export to CAD and ERP tools mentioned under physical quality.

Features Supporting Semantic Quality of PDM/PLM Data. As the name implies, the main data kept in PLM systems is product data, including data relevant for the process the product undergoes through its lifecycle. Schedule information and work-flow modeling is supported in tools such as Teamcenter, but similar to CAD tools, the function of the parts in the product is not represented in most tools. Compliance management modules can support representation of regulations (as a sort of rules).

Features Supporting Pragmatic Quality of PDM/PLM Data. Relevant context information can be added to the product description supporting understanding. PLM systems have become very complex and as such more difficult to use and comprehend. The size of the products (number of parts) has also increased over the years. Whereas a jet engine in the 1960s had 3000 parts, in 2010 it might have 200000 parts. Reporting is traditionally in Excel, but newer tools can support running reports on the 3D-model, presenting the results as annotation to this. The Teamcenter tool has been reported to be hard to learn if you are not an engineer.

Features Supporting Social Quality of PDM/PLM Data. PLM systems are systems for integrating the enterprise. When implementing PLM-systems one needs to agree on the system set-up, data-coding etc. across the organization. Thus when these kinds of systems are successfully implemented, one can expect there to be high agreement on the data found in the tool in the organization. Note that a similar issue that is found in ERP systems, the so-called work and benefit disparity might occur (this problem was originally described in connection to so-called groupware systems [6]). Company-wide application often require additional work from individuals who do not perceive a direct benefit from the use of the application. When e.g., creating new parts, a large number of attributes need to be added, thus it takes longer time to enter product-information in the beginning.

Features Supporting Deontic Quality of PDM/PLM Data. Looking upon the waste forms we conclude the following

- Searching: Large models and a lot of extra data might make it difficult to get an overview and find all the (and only the) relevant information. On the other hand, since one have a common data-model, it should be easier to find all the data relevant for a given product.
- Under-communication: Since extra data has to be added up front for the use later in the product life cycle, it is a danger that not all necessary data is added (or is added with poor quality), which can lead to the next two issues:
- Misunderstanding: Can be a result of under-communication.
- Interpreting: When engineers and other groups need to communicate, one should also be aware of possible misunderstandings, given that it seems to be hard to learn these tools if you are not an engineer. Also given that only a few people are actually adding data a lot of people need to interpret these models without actively producing them.
- Waiting: It can be a challenge when a change is done for this to propagate also to e.g., ERP systems and supplier systems. For some type of data this propagation is automatic.
- Extra processing: Necessary to add data up front. Can be a challenge when you need to perform changes, to have the data produced in earlier phases updated.

5   Conclusion

Above, we have seen three assessments done using the specialization of SEQUAL for data quality of specifically relevant knowledge sources to be used in a Virtual Obeya. This has highlighted opportunities, but also challenges when trying to integrated data from different knowledge sources typically used by people in different roles in an organization in a common user interface, supporting collaboration. In particular it highlights how different tools have a varying degree of explicit meta-model (data model), and that this is available in a varying degree. E.g., in many export-formats one loses some of the important information on product data. Even when different tools support e.g., process data, it is often process data on different granularity. The tools alone all have challenges relative to waste in lean engineering. In a Virtual Obeya environment one would explicitly want to combine data from different sources in a context-driven manner to address these reasons for waste. Depending on the concrete data sources to combine, this indicates that it is often a partly manual job to prepare for such matching. Also the different level of agreement of data from different sources (social quality) can influence the use of schema and object matching techniques in practice.

As with the quality of a BPM [14] and data models [15], we see some benefit both for SEQUAL and for a framework for data quality by performing this kind of exercise:

- Existing work on data and information quality, as summarized in [2, 24, 25] can be positioned within the generic SEQUAL framework as described in Section 3.
- These existing overviews are weak on explicitly addressing areas such as empirical and social quality, as also described in Section 3.2 and Section 3.6. Guidelines and means for empirical quality can build upon work in data and information visualization.

- The work by Batini and Price et al. On the other hand enriches the areas of in particular semantic and pragmatic data quality, as described in section 3.4 and section 3.5.
- The framework, especially the differentiation between the different quality levels has been found useful in the case from which we have reported in Section 4, since it highlights potential challenges of matching data from different sources as discussed above. On the other hand, to be useful, an additional level of specialization of the quality framework was needed.

Future work will be to device more concrete guidelines and metrics and evaluate the adaptation and use of these empirically in other cases, especially how to perform trade-offs between the different data quality types. Some generic guidelines for this exist in SEQUAL [13], which might be specialised for data quality and quality of conceptual data models. We will also look at newer work [3, 9] in the area in addition to those we have mapped so far. Due to the rapid changes to data compared to conceptual models guidelines for achieving and keeping model quality might need to be further adapted to be useful when achieving and keeping data quality. We will also look more upon the use of the framework when integrating data from less technical areas such as CRM and ERP data.

Acknowledgements. The research leading to these results was done in the LinkedDesign project that has received funding from the European Union Seventh Framework Programme ([FP7/2007-2013]) under grant agreement n°284613

References

1. Aasland, K., Blankenburg, D.: An analysis of the uses and properties of the Obeya. In: Proceedings of the 18th International ICE-Conference, Munich (2012)
2. Batini, C., Scannapieco, M.: Data Quality: Concepts, Methodologies and Techniques. Springer (2006)
3. Batini, C., Cappiello, C., Francalanci, C., Maurino, A.: Methodologies for data quality assessment and improvement. ACM Comput. Surv. 41(3) (2009)
4. Booch, G., Rumbaugh, J., Jacobson, I.: The Unified Modeling Language: User Guide, 2nd edn. Addison-Wesley (2005)
5. Francalanci, C., Pernici, B.: View integration: A survey of current developments. Technical Report 93-053, Politecnico de Milano, Milan, Italy (1993)
6. Grudin, J.: Groupware and social dynamics: eight challenges for developers. Communications of the ACM 37(1), 92–105 (1994)
7. Hermans, F.F.J.: Analyzing and Visualizing Spreadsheets. PhD thesis, Software Engineering Research Group, Delft University of Technology, The Netherlands (2012)
8. Høydalsvik, G.M., Sindre, G.: On the purpose of object-oriented analysis. In: Proceedings of the Conference on Object-Oriented Programming Systems, Languages, and Applications (OOPSLA 1993), pp. 240–255. ACM Press (1993)
9. Jiang, L., Barone, D., Borgida, A., Mylopoulos, J.: Measuring and Comparing Effectiveness of Data Quality Techniques. In: van Eck, P., Gordijn, J., Wieringa, R. (eds.) CAiSE 2009. LNCS, vol. 5565, pp. 171–185. Springer, Heidelberg (2009)

10. Krogstie, J.: Using Quality Function Deployment in Software Requirements Specification. Paper presented at the Fifth International Workshop on Requirements Engineering: Foundations for Software Quality (REFSQ 1999), Heidelberg, Germany, June 14-15 (1999)
11. Krogstie, J.: Evaluating UML Using a Generic Quality Framework. In: Favre, L. (ed.) UML and the Unified Process, pp. 1–22. IRM Press (2003)
12. Krogstie, J.: Integrated Goal, Data and Process Modeling: From TEMPORA to Model-Generated Work-Places. In: Johannesson, P., Søderstrøm, E. (eds.) Information Systems Engineering From Data Analysis to Process Networks, pp. 43–65. IGI (2008)
13. Krogstie, J.: Model-based development and evolution of information systems: A quality approach. Springer, London (2012)
14. Krogstie, J.: Quality of Business Process Models. In: Sandkuhl, K., Seigerroth, U., Stirna, J. (eds.) PoEM 2012. LNBIP, vol. 134, pp. 76–90. Springer, Heidelberg (2012)
15. Krogstie, J.: Quality of Conceptual Data Models. In: Proceedings 14th ICISO, Stockholm Sweden (2013)
16. Krogstie, J.: A Semiotic Framework for Data Quality. In: Nurcan, S., Proper, H.A., Soffer, P., Krogstie, J., Schmidt, R., Halpin, T., Bider, I. (eds.) BPMDS 2013 and EMMSAD 2013. LNBIP, vol. 147, pp. 395–410. Springer, Heidelberg (2013)
17. Krogstie, J., Arnesen, S.: Assessing Enterprise Modeling Languages using a Generic Quality Framework. In: Krogstie, J., Siau, K., Halpin, T. (eds.) Information Modeling Methods and Methodologies. Idea Group Publishing (2004)
18. La Rocca, G.: Knowledge based engineering: Between AI and CAD. Review of a language based technology to support engineering design. Advanced Engineering Informatics 26(2), 159–179 (2012)
19. Lillehagen, F., Krogstie, J.: Active Knowledge Modeling of Enterprises. Springer (2008)
20. Manyika, J., Sprague, K., Yee, L.: Using technology to improve workforce collaboration. What Matters. McKinsey Digital (October 2009)
21. Moody, D.L.: Metrics for Evaluating the Quality of Entity Relationship Models. In: Ling, T.-W., Ram, S., Li Lee, M. (eds.) ER 1998. LNCS, vol. 1507, pp. 211–225. Springer, Heidelberg (1998)
22. Moody, D.L.: Theorethical and practical issues in evaluating the quality of concep tual models: Current state and future directions. Data and Knowledge Engineering 55, 243–276 (2005)
23. Nelson, H.J., Poels, G., Genero, M., Piattini, M.: A conceptual modeling quality framework. Software Quality Journal (2011)
24. Price, R., Shanks, G.: A Semiotic Information Quality Framework. In: IFIP WG8.3 International Conference on Decision Support Systems (DSS 2004), Prato, Italy, July 1-3, pp. 658–672 (2004)
25. Price, R., Shanks, G.: A semiotic information quality framework: Development and comparative analysis. Journal of Information Technology 20(2), 88–102 (2005)
26. Recker, J., Rosemann, M., Krogstie, J.: Ontology- versus pattern-based evaluation of process modeling language: A comparison. Communications of the Association for Information Systems 20, 774–799 (2007)

Planning Support for Enterprise Changes

Florian Lautenbacher[1], Philipp Diefenthaler[1,2], Melanie Langermeier[2],
Mariana Mykhashchuk[1], and Bernhard Bauer[2]

[1] Softplant GmbH, Munich, Germany
`firstname.lastname@softplant.de`
[2] University of Augsburg, Germany
`firstname.lastname@informatik.uni-augsburg.de`

Abstract. Enterprises have to react to changes with an increasing speed
in order to stay competitive. Many approaches support the modeling of
enterprise architectures but lack an evolution of enterprise architectures
through demonstrating a transformation path from one architecture state
to another. Enterprises know their strategic goals and are able to model
them, but are not supported towards achieving these goals in terms of developing their architecture. We want to improve the current manual creation of the transformation paths in enterprise architecture planning by
providing possible and sound sequences of actions as part of a roadmap
from the current to a desired target architecture.

Therefore, we present a solution that supports the enterprise architect with proposals for a transformation path from the current to the
target state considering dependencies to be taken into account during
the enterprise transformation.

Keywords: enterprise architecture management, transformation planning, transformation modeling, application architecture.

1 Introduction

Changing laws and regulations, a growing number of competitors, upcoming customer channels and, hence, an adapted business strategy require that enterprises
need to react flexibly. Nowadays, an IT landscape that efficiently supports the
business and can easily be adapted is a key element for the success of enterprises.

Enterprise architecture management (EAM) assists to develop the IT landscape so that it efficiently supports current and future business needs. Several
EAM frameworks were standardized (e.g. The Open Group Architecture Framework (TOGAF) [1] or the Zachman framework [2]) and are utilized and adapted
in several companies.

Enterprise architecture (EA) models describe the enterprises in an abstract
way and allow for a goal-oriented information systems development. They serve
as information basis for discussing and deciding about transformations of the
overall enterprise [3]. Models of the EA provide a holistic view on an enterprise by aggregating information about the business strategy, business processes,

J. Grabis et al. (Eds.): PoEM 2013, LNBIP 165, pp. 54–68, 2013.

the applications and interfaces, the data exchanged between the applications as well as the underlying infrastructure [4]. The relation of those elements provides enterprises with a clear picture of the current business support by IT systems.

Driven by the business strategy a desired target state can be modeled for the business, the application as well as the technological perspective. In order to close the gaps between the current and the target state, transformations from the current to the target architecture are planned by enterprise architects.

Many companies face an IT landscape which has grown over years and which comprises hundreds of systems using various technologies with complex dependencies between them. Considering all these dependencies when planning the enterprise transformations is a difficult task. Especially when focusing on the business, these dependencies are often neglected. These inherent dependencies are often revealed quite late, when implementing the transformation projects and then lead to changed project plans, higher costs and delayed deadlines.

The process of building a roadmap from a current state to a target state of an enterprise considering the EA dynamics is evaluated in the research area EA planning. Spewak [5] defines EA planning as "the process of defining architectures for the use of information in support of the business and the plan for implementing those architectures". The main goal of EA planning is to enhance and maintain the mutual alignment of business and IT [6]. The different approaches in this research area are heterogeneous and cover different topics [7]: from methodologies for EA planning [8,9] to modeling the transformation [10,11,12], describing possible actions for transformations [13] or focusing on key performance indicators to compare the current and the target architecture [14].

The contribution of this paper focuses on the creation of a transformation path from a current to a target architecture (using planning techniques from artificial intelligence, AI) and describes a solution how the enterprise architect is supported by proposed sequences of transformations, which can be performed in the enterprises' IT landscape. These sequences consider the dependencies between existing and planned IT applications (i.e. one provides an IT service that is used by others). Our solution proposes four phases to compute the proposed sequences and supports the enterprise architect during the creation of the transformation path.

The presented solution assumes that the current IT landscape as well as the target IT landscape have already been modeled and are available for the planner. Hence, the solution focuses on *how to achieve* the target rather than on *what* the target should look like. This allows the enterprise architect to stimulate alternative thinking of how the target can be reached. In this paper we describe the planning process with focus on the application architecture only, i.e. the IT applications and IT services used to exchange data. Other architecture layers (such as business or technology architecture, compare [1,15]) are outside the focus of this paper.

2   Foundations

One of the first contributors in the field of EA planning are Spewak and Hill [5] that introduce an EA planning model (wedding cake model), which describes how the blueprints for the target state are developed from the analysis of the current state, and how the changes are structured in an implementation and migration plan. More recent research on EA planning addresses the different levels which have to be considered in the planning process and how decisions in different architectures, i.e. business, application, data and technology, may affect the others [9]. Aier et al. [7] derive an EA planning process from the work of Spewak and Hill [5], Niemann [16] and Pulkkinen [9]. The derived process consists of the steps: (1) define vision, (2) model current architecture, (3) model alternative target architectures, (4) analyze and evaluate target alternatives, (5) plan transformation from current to target and, before a new planning cycle is initiated, (6) implement transformation.

The current architecture describes the status quo and the target architecture describes a desired state in the medium-dated future (approximately 3 to 5 years). A vision or ideal architecture is a blueprint of a desired architecture which will possibly never be reached, but serves as guidance for defining a target architecture.

2.1   Changes in Application Landscapes

In the context of the transformations of application landscapes the entities that are changed consist at least of the applications and the services they provide and use (c.f. [17] and [18]). Several sources in literature consider different types of changes in application landscape transformation. All of these sources distinguish between changes that *create* and *delete* entities ([19], p.95; [20], p. 172; [21]; [22], p. 11; [23], p. 59). Furthermore, an *update* of an entity is considered as a change in several sources ([21]; [22], p. 11; [23], p. 59). Sousa et al. [21] take additionally a *read* dependency for changes into account. This type of dependency is used to denote that an entity which creates and deletes certain entities needs another entity which it does not actively change by itself.

According to Aier and Gleichauf [24] the models of the current and target state can be linked through a transformation model which contains information about the successor relationships of entities. A successor relationship always links exactly one element in one state with an element in another state. It is possible that one element has zero or more than one outgoing or incoming successor relationship.

2.2   Graph Transformations for Planning Purposes

Several different approaches, techniques and representations to planning problems have been developed over the last decades in the research field of artificial intelligence planning and scheduling. These approaches range from state space model based planning to task networks, where tasks for reaching a goal are decomposed and sequenced. A state space based approach is preferable, because models of the current and target architecture are used in many EA approaches and are present in many tools used in practice.

Graph transformations for AI planning purposes solve a planning problem by applying graph transformations on a model until a solution for the planning problem is found. The result of such a planning process can be a sequence of actions changing a model into another model.

However, graph transformations have the disadvantage that they provide a huge state space regarding the states, which have to be examined when all states in the graph are computed, and as a consequence influence the computation time. With graph transformations a planning problem can be solved by searching for graph patterns in the state represented by a graph and applying graph transformations to the state [25]. Graph transformations have the benefit that they have a sound theoretical foundation.

By reusing the knowledge from existing contributions in the field of enterprise architecture planning and the existing techniques from AI planning we can create a solution which supports the enterprise architect in gaining an overview on alternative transformation paths.

3   Solution for Transformation Planning

Our solution comprises the steps analyze models and plan transformation from current to target architecture of EA planning as defined by Aier et al. [7].

The planning of the transformation takes place in four steps: (1) the connection of the architectures, (2) the segmentation analysis, (3) the creation of an action repository and (4) the creation of the transformation path. As prerequisite the current and target architecture have to be determined. The current architecture consists of the applications and their used and implemented services at present. In contrast, the target architecture contains all applications and their used and implemented services at future. As a result of the process a partial plan will be created, which describes how to reach the target. Figure 1 shows an overview of the concept which was modeled and tested.

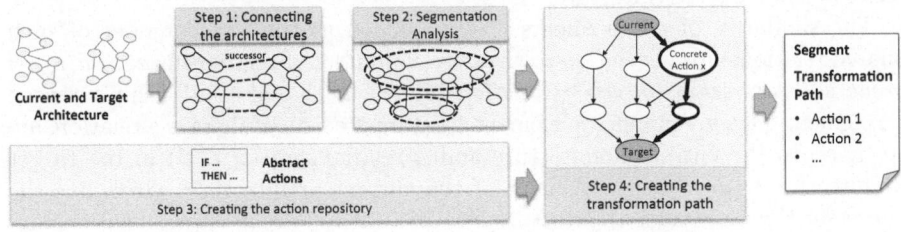

Fig. 1. The proposed solution with its four phases

The first step of our solution supports the linking of the current and target architecture and thereby the definition of the transformation model. With the segmentation analysis in the second step, we narrow the scope for the following transformation path creation. Independent of those steps is the creation of the action repository, where the abstract actions that are taken into account are modeled. Creating these abstract actions is done only once and can be applied on all variations of current and target architectures that satisfy the metamodel criteria specified in an abstract action. Metamodel entities must exist for the elements of the architecture models. Such metamodel entities represent the type of the element in order to apply the changes to a model. Furthermore, the metamodel restricts the relationships and attributes of the elements.

After finishing these three phases the creation of the transformation path can be started. Thereby, different possible plans, consisting of sequences of concrete actions, are generated. Alternatively the enterprise architect can create those paths interactively through selection of the next concrete action. Based on the preferred sequence of action a project proposal can be determined. In the following sections each of those phases will be described in more detail.

3.1   Connecting the Architecture

The first step of the proposed solution supports the enterprise architect in connecting the current architecture with the target architecture. To enable the creation of a transformation path the target architecture has to be semantically connected with the current architecture in the sense of successor relationships. Similar to Aier and Gleichauf [24] we use successor relationships to link current elements to the appropriate target elements. A special unchanged successor relationship indicates those links, where the element of the current architecture exists unchanged in the target architecture. To support the enterprise architect in finding the successor relationships, we analyze the similarity of the elements in the current and target architecture. The automatic derivation of successor relationships for applications based on business support maps and suggestions for successor services is described by Diefenthaler and Bauer [26]. However, this approach is limited to architectures, where applications are localized in the cells of a business support map.

To support the enterprise architect in finding the successor relationships independently from a localization, we analyze the similarity of the elements in current and target architecture.

The similarity of two elements c, t is defined as the total number of such shared relationships in relation to the overall number of relationships: $Sim(c)_t = \#sharedRelationships(c, t) / \#Relationships(c)$. A shared relationship between an element c in current and an element t in target exists, if there is a relationship (c, r, c') in the current architecture and a relationship (t, r, t') in the target architecture with c' as an element of the current architecture, which has the successor t' in the target architecture; r is an arbitrary architectural relationship. The similarity measure has a range from 0 to 1, whereas 0 means that there are no shared relationships and 1 means that all relationships are shared.

Before determining the shared relationships, unchanged elements have to be identified. The enterprise architect has to confirm each mapping, because name-equality does not always conclude an unchanged successor relationship. After that, there are already some successor relationships given. Based on those, the shared relationships and similarity measures can be calculated iteratively until no more suggestions can be found.

For the final decision about the successor relationships the enterprise architect should not only rely on this measure but also take the total number of relationships and the expert knowledge into account. Moreover, he has to specify, whether the relationship is an unchanged successor or not. Further measures can be determined depending on the context and enterprise specific details.

3.2   Segmentation Analysis

The segmentation analysis addresses the problem that enterprise architectures typically have a huge scope and include a lot of elements. To narrow the scope, a segmentation analysis can be done before determining the transformation path. According to Aier and Gleichauf [24] architectural elements can be grouped to segments, if they do not have relationships to other elements outside the group. As there are typically no isolated cells in enterprise architectures we do this segmentation by using different successor relationships. They enable the identification of parts in the architecture where changes occur but also where no changes occur.

A segment is defined as a set of interrelated elements in the current architecture with their successor elements in the target architecture including all implement- and use-relationships between those elements. To ensure the independence of the different segments in an enterprise architecture, each group of changed elements must be surrounded by a set of unchanged elements. Then these groups of changed elements are independent of each other in the context of planning, although the segments overlap at unchanged elements. An example for a segmentation is shown in Figure 2.

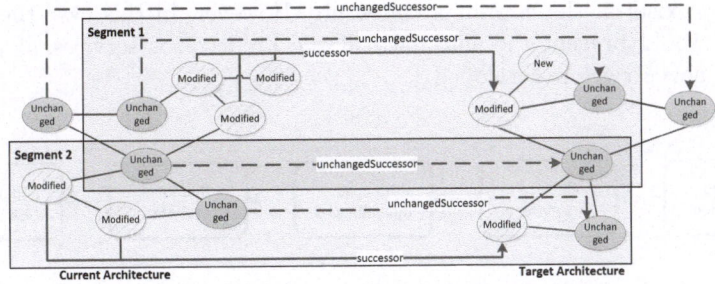

Fig. 2. Segmentation of the connected current and target architecture for narrowing the scope

The figure shows on the left side a current architecture and on the right side a target architecture. Both consist of interrelated changed and unchanged elements. Furthermore, the successor-relationships between the current and target architecture are modeled. Using the segmentation analysis two segments can be identified in this architecture. They overlap at one unchanged element. There is also one unchanged element which is neither in segment 1 nor in segment 2.

3.3   Creating an Action Repository

Before the transformation from the current to the target architecture can be planned, an action repository with abstract actions has to be modeled. An abstract action consists of two parts. One part specifies the preconditions for an action to be applicable. The other part is the effect part, which specifies the changes to an architecture if an (abstract) action is applied to it. In a technical sense the abstract action matches via a graph pattern into the concrete model of the different states. Concrete actions relate to concrete entities and relationships in an architecture and concrete changes to the state of architecture. The application of a concrete action to an architecture, may enable the application of several other concrete actions.

Logical Ordering of Abstract Actions. The abstract actions are modeled in a logical order, which means that it is only possible to apply the action if the preceding actions were already applied. For example, it is not possible to change the dependencies from a service to its successor service if it has not yet been built. Furthermore, it may be necessary to build the application first to allow the creation of a new service. After the dependencies of a service have been changed to a successor it is possible to shutdown the service. If all services of an application have been shutdown it is possible to shutdown the application. The logical ordering prevents the creation of loops in the transformation path, i.e. to shutdown and create the same application several times. It may be the case that it is not necessary to enact the *develop application* action. For example, if a segment contains a service, which has to be developed for an application that already exists, it is not necessary to develop that application again since it already exists in the current architecture. However, in this case the logical ordering would prevent the shutdown of the predecessor services, if present, until the new service is developed.

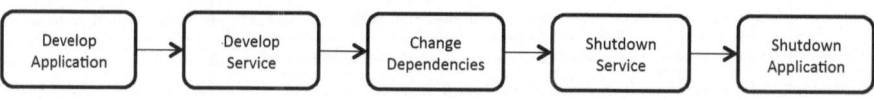

Fig. 3. The logical ordering of abstract actions

3.4   Creating the Transformation Path

With the action repository and a segment at hand it is possible to start the creation of a transformation path. It is also possible to start the creation without segments, but we advise to utilize the segmentation, because the number of possible transformation paths for an whole IT landscape is hard to grasp for a human.

We derive all applicable concrete actions for a segment by checking which preconditions of abstract actions match in a segment. This corresponds to a breadth search of applicable actions for a segment. If a concrete action is applied to a segment it changes the state of the segment. In contrast if we apply a depth search on a segment we receive a transformation path changing the segment in a sequence of concrete actions from the current to the target architecture. If no such transformation path exists the more exhaustive breadth search can be omitted and we are informed that no transformation path was found. We apply the breadth search on a segment recursively and we get the whole state space.

With the state space it is possible to determine all possible transformation paths of a segment. By selecting concrete actions we create the transformation path, change the segment and get each time a list of concrete actions which we now can apply. When the transformation path is complete, i.e. all necessary changes have been applied, no further actions are applicable and the transformation path is saved.

The selection process for choosing concrete actions can be enhanced by providing development costs for proposed applications and services, and maintenance costs for applications and services which are to be retired.

4   Use Case and Implementation Details

In the past, IT applications were often developed to address the specific business needs that a part of the organization had at that moment. However, considering the whole enterprise it is not effective to store redundant data in several IT applications as this increases the risk of outdated and inconsistent data. This is the basis for the master data management (MDM) challenge [27]. In our use case we show a typical (and simplified) example for the introduction of master data management in the research department (R & D) of an organization. Figure 4 shows a part of the current architecture of the organization's IT landscape. There has already been placed a **development master data management (DMDM)** system in the organization which provides interfaces (*MasterData_v1* and *_v2*) to other IT applications. However, not all existing systems use the master data provided by **DMDM**: the long lasting **DevManager** provides similar data that is still used by existing systems such as the product planning tool and the quality tests planning tool. Other IT applications such as the **virtual quality test result database** store the master data themselves and are not connected to **DMDM**. For the modification of products (from one test to another)

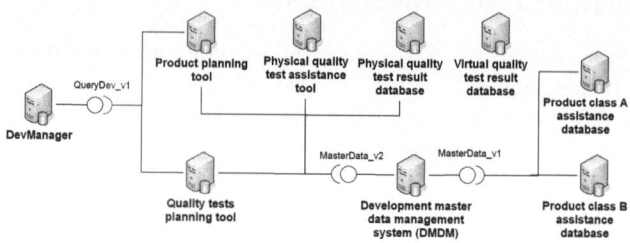

Fig. 4. Master data management: current architecture

Fig. 5. Master data management: target architecture

there exist two IT applications for the different product classes the organization provides to their customers. Additionally, IT applications to plan the product, the quality tests and store the results that have been gathered during the (physical or virtual) quality tests, exist.

In the target architecture the functionality in the different IT application shall be united and all other tools will use the data provided by **DMDM**. There will be only one planning tool that includes planning for the product as well as the quality tests. All quality tests (including the results) will be managed by one **quality test assistance and result management tool** (cf. Figure 5).

4.1 Building the Transformation Path for the Use Case

In this section we describe the transformation path created by an enterprise architect. Action prioritization is based on the principle of subject-specific importance of corresponding applications and services, the principle of redundant applications avoidance as well as the principle of using new interfaces wherever possible.

Initially, the enterprise architect has done the mapping between applications in the current and the target architecture. This mapping showed which applications and services had successor relationships. Grouping applications from current architecture by their successors in the target, the enterprise architect was able to identify three groups of applications, which had to be consolidated. One group consisted of the **Product planning tool** and **Quality tests planning tool**, both of which had the successor **Product and Quality test planning** tool. **Physical quality test assistance tool**, **Physical quality test result database** and **Virtual quality test result database** have built the second group. The third group comprised of **Product class A assistance database** and **Product class B assistance database**.

After getting an overview on forthcoming changes, the enterprise architect had to decide in which order he would perform concrete actions. Due to the high operation costs for **DevManager**, the enterprise architect had decided to start with the shutdown of this application. However, it was not possible to perform this action immediately since **DevManager** provided the service *QueryDev_v1* to **Product planning tool** and **Quality tests planning tool** and was still in use. It was also impossible to stop using the service by these systems before their successor-application was developed. Taking this into account, the enterprise architect decided to develop the **Product and quality test planning tool** together with its service *PlanningData_v1* at first. Next steps comprised the removal of connections between service *QueryDev_v1* and applications **Product planning tool** and **Quality tests planning tool**. Not until then *QueryDev_v1* and **DevManager** could be shut down. After that, once connections of **Product planning tool** and **Quality tests planning tool** to another service *MasterData_v2* have been removed, the enterprise architect could shut down these applications. In this way, the enterprise architect created the transformation path for the first group of applications.

For the remaining applications the enterprise architect decided to proceed with the second group, whilst taking into account that isolated solutions were not desirable in the organization and quality test result management had a high strategic importance for the R & D department. In the end, the transformation path for applications of the third group was created.

An excerpt of the list of actions can be seen below.

1. Develop application **Product and Quality test planning tool**
2. Develop service *PlanningData_v1* of application **Product and Quality test planning tool**
3. Remove connection between application **Product planning tool** and service *QueryDev_v1*
4. Remove connection between application **Quality tests planning tool** and service *QueryDev_v1*
5. Shut down service *QueryDev_v1*
6. Shut down application **DevManager**
7. Remove connection between application **Product planning tool** and service *MasterData_v2*
8. Remove connection between application **Quality tests planning tool** and service *MasterData_v2*
9. Shut down application **Product planning tool**
10. Shut down application **Quality tests planning tool**

4.2   Implementation Details

For the implementation of our solution we use model query languages and GROOVE[1]. Models of the segment are transformed via a model-to-model transformation into GROOVE models. The current version of GROOVE allows to import and export Ecore[2] conform models, which can for example be UML models.

The current and target architecture have to be modeled using a formally defined metamodel. The connection of the architecture as well as the segmentation analysis, are done by using a model query language. We modeled the abstract actions, depicted in Figure 3, with GROOVE. Abstract actions change the lifecycle phases of applications and services or change the usage dependencies between those. Besides theses abstract actions, also abstract actions for debugging purposes were modeled to allow the detection of states which are incorrect from an expert viewpoint. For example it should not be possible that an application consumes a service it also provides.

A segment serves as a starting state for GROOVE. It consists of the applications and services from the current and target architecture, the successor relationships between them, the implementation relationships between applications and services of the current and target architecture and, moreover, the usage dependencies of the current architecture. Upon this state concrete actions can be applied in GROOVE via graph pattern matching and graph transformation.

To be able to have a criterion when the transformation path is ready we define an action, which has no effect on the state. This action consists of the usage dependencies of the target architecture, all applications and services which have to be *shutdown* are in the corresponding lifecycle, and all applications and services which have to be built are in the lifecycle phase *live*. With this action and the initial state at hand it is possible for GROOVE to compute a transformation path. Furthermore, it is possible to create a transformation path in interaction between an enterprise architect and GROOVE, by selecting concrete actions and computing the resulting states.

5   Evaluation

The evaluation for the use case was conducted by an enterprise architect and a knowledge engineer. The knowledge engineer is the creator of the action repository, who models the actions according to certain requirements. The enterprise architect is the creator of the current and target architecture and has functional knowledge about the concrete changes.

Conducting the Evaluation. The goal of the evaluation was to determine the differences between the expectations of the enterprise architect and actual

---

[1] GRaphs for Object-Oriented VErification (GROOVE)
   http://groove.cs.utwente.nl/
[2] http://www.eclipse.org/modeling/emf/?project=emf

information provided by GROOVE. Therefore we first checked if the desired transformation path from the enterprise architect could be reproduced using the interactive alternative of our solution. Second, we verified the functional correctness of the transformation path, if it was created by GROOVE without interaction.

For the first case the knowledge engineer explained the procedure and the tool setting to the enterprise architect. Then the enterprise architect was asked to explain the concrete changes of her transformation path. The knowledge engineer performed each action in GROOVE until the transformation path was finished.

In the second case the transformation path, created by GROOVE, was extracted to a text file and relevant parts for the enterprise architect were kept in it. This means that it contained actions like Create Application: **Product and Quality test planning tool** and their ordering in the transformation path. The enterprise architect used prints of the current and target architecture with their successor relationships between the applications and services to keep track of the actions applied by the proposed transformation path.

Results of the Evaluation. It was possible to reproduce the transformation path of the enterprise architect in GROOVE. The knowledge engineer had to execute additional actions, because not every step of the path was exactly one step in the tool. For example, the change of a dependency is considered by the enterprise architect as one step, but in GROOVE this change was modeled as two steps (one delete and one create). Furthermore, the corresponding action for shutting down applications is modeled in a way that it shuts down all possible applications in one step. The enterprise architect considered the shutdown of the applications **Product planning tool** and **Quality tests planning tool** as two steps.

The enterprise architect confirmed the transformation path created from GROOVE as valid. However, other transformation paths were considered as more optimal from the viewpoint of the enterprise architect. Furthermore, it was necessary to explain to the enterprise architect that not every step in her path was exactly one step in GROOVE's path.

One insight of the evaluation was that it was possible to give a hint to the enterprise architect that one service was no longer in use and can be shutdown. Additional actions will be modeled that were considered as useful during the evaluation. Moreover, the enterprise architect asked for the possibility to specify priorities for the development and shutdown of applications. For example, it should be possible to prefer applications with a high strategic importance for development and to prefer applications to shutdown with high maintenance cost. Additionally, the possibility to take resource constraints, like available budget and staff, into account was uttered.

6   Related Work

We summarize three publications related to our solution in the following:

Postina [23] presents a method to manage service and process oriented enterprise architectures. He uses a case based reasoning approach and a case repository to provide information for the evolution of the enterprise architecture. The target state can be reached from the current state through several evolutionary steps. A case is defined by the type of an evolutionary step (create, update, delete), the element and type involved, e.g. organizational unit billing, and the viewpoints attached to it. The cases help to provide views for future evolutionary steps with the same combination of element type and evolutionary step type. However, the creation of different transformation paths is not considered, which a benefit of our approach is.

Postina and Gringel [28] present a prototypical tool for creating a target architecture by selecting gaps between an ideal and current application landscape. The target landscape is interactively designed by an enterprise architect and the tool. The term ideal landscape is tightly coupled to the Quasar Enterprise approach which considers domains, ideal interfaces, ideal components and ideal operations for interfaces. Based on the structural differences between the current and ideal landscape the tool can identify the gaps and provides an action list to close the gaps. The modeling of an ideal landscape is a prerequisite in order to create the target architecture and the resulting action list, which consists of actions to close the gaps. In contrast, our approach provides actions for sequencing changes within the transformation path and needs no ideal landscape, which makes it less approach-dependent. Furthermore, our actions are defined on an abstract level and thus allow determining the different dependencies between the necessary changes.

Sousa et al. [21] describe an approach to reconstruct enterprise architecture models from existing project information and the artifacts influenced by them. Furthermore, the Blueprint Management System (BMS) is introduced which allows to detect the temporal dependencies of projects on certain artifacts and can generate different viewpoints. Time is explicitly taken into account by providing a timeline bar in the BMS, which enables the user to browse through the different points in time. The tool is capable of providing different states as each project has a list of artifacts it creates and deletes. This implies that projects are already on the run and the information is derived afterwards. However, our solution can interactively create the transformation path including alternative paths and then allows the creation of proposals for projects, their change activities and the possible synchronization between them.

7   Conclusion and Future Work

In this paper we proposed a solution of how to close the gap between a current and a target architecture. We identify the successor relationships between those architectural states and determined transformation paths in terms of sequences of concrete actions. Thereby the dependencies between the architectural elements are considered. If necessary the architecture can be divided into smaller segments. For the analysis we use model query languages, for the definition of abstract actions and the creation of the transformation path we use graph transformation.

The solution is designed to support the enterprise architect in the task to find a way *how* to reach a defined target, starting with the current architecture. It enables the consideration of the complex dependencies between the architectural elements and thus reduces changes in project plans later on because of overlooked dependencies. The outcome of our solution, the transformation path, can be used to define the projects which will implement the changes.

The next step is to extend our solution to all architectural layers in enterprise architecture and start a broader field study. Future work will comprise a refinement analysis and actions to enable a more abstract target architecture as a starting point. Furthermore, providing support for the consideration of resource constraints and value-based weighting of the transformation steps is part of our future research. The presented solution provides a stable basis for these further extensions.

References

1. The Open Group: TOGAF Version 9.1. Van Haren Publishing (2011)
2. Zachman, J.: A framework for information systems architecture. IBM Systems Journal 26(3) (1987)
3. Rouse, W.B.: A theory of enterprise transformation. Systems Engineering 8(4), 279–295 (2005)
4. Lankhorst, M.M. (ed.): Enterprise architecture at work: Modelling, communication and analysis, 2nd edn. Springer, Berlin (2009)
5. Spewak, S.H., Hill, S.C.: Enterprise architecture planning: Developing a blueprint for data, applications, and technology. John Wiley & Sons, New York (1992)
6. Luftman, J.N., Lewis, P.O.S.: Transforming the enterprise: The alignment of business and information technology strategies. IBM Systems Journal 32(1), 198–221 (1993)
7. Aier, S., Gleichauf, B., Saat, J., Winter, R.: Complexity levels of representing dynamics in EA planning. In: Albani, A., Barjis, J., Dietz, J.L.G. (eds.) CIAO! 2009. LNBIP, vol. 34, pp. 55–69. Springer, Heidelberg (2009)
8. Aier, S., Gleichauf, B.: Towards a systematic approach for capturing dynamic transformation in enterprise models. In: Sprague, R.H. (ed.) Proceedings of the 43rd Annual Hawaii International Conference on System Sciences. IEEE Computer Society, Los Alamitos (2010)
9. Pulkkinen, M.: Systemic management of architectural decisions in enterprise architecture planning. four dimensions and three abstraction levels. In: Proceedings of the 39th Annual Hawaii International Conference on System Sciences (HICSS 2006), p. 179a. IEEE (2006)
10. Aier, S., Gleichauf, B.: Applying design research artifacts for building design research artifacts: A process model for enterprise architecture planning. In: Winter, R., Zhao, J.L., Aier, S. (eds.) DESRIST 2010. LNCS, vol. 6105, pp. 333–348. Springer, Heidelberg (2010)
11. Buckl, S., Ernst, A., Matthes, F., Schweda, C.M.: An information model for landscape management – discussing temporality aspects. In: Feuerlicht, G., Lamersdorf, W. (eds.) ICSOC 2008. LNCS, vol. 5472, pp. 363–374. Springer, Heidelberg (2009)

12. Buckl, S., Dierl, T., Matthes, F., Schweda, C.M.: Complementing the open group architecture framework with best practice solution building blocks. In: 2011 44th Hawaii International Conference on System Sciences, pp. 1–9. IEEE (2011)
13. Buckl, S., Ernst, A.M., Matthes, F., Schweda, C.M.: An information model capturing the managed evolution of application landscapes. Journal of Enterprise Architecture 5(1), 12–26 (2009)
14. Nissen, V., von Rennenkampf, A., Termer, F.: Agile it-anwendungslandschaften als strategische unternehmensressource. In: Hofmann, J., Knoll, M. (eds.) Strategisches IT-Management. HMD Praxis der Wirtschaftsinformatik, vol. 284. dpunkt.verlag, Heidelberg (2012)
15. Hasselbring, W.: Information system integration. Communications of the ACM 43(6), 32–38 (2000)
16. Niemann, K.D.: From enterprise architecture to IT governance: Elements of effective IT management. Vieweg, Wiesbaden (2006)
17. Winter, R., Fischer, R.: Essential layers, artifacts, and dependencies of enterprise architecture. Journal of Enterprise Architecture 3(2), 7–18 (2007)
18. Matthes, F.: Softwarekartographie. Informatik-Spektrum 31(6), 527–536 (2008)
19. Keller, W.: IT-Unternehmensarchitektur: Von der Geschäftsstrategie zur optimalen IT-Unterstützung, 1st edn. dpunkt.verlag, Heidelberg (2007)
20. Hanschke, I.: Strategisches Management der IT-Landschaft: Ein praktischer Leitfaden für das Enterprise Architecture Management, 1st edn. Hanser, München (2009)
21. Sousa, P., Lima, J., Sampaio, A., Pereira, C.: An approach for creating and managing enterprise blueprints: A case for IT blueprints. In: Albani, A., Barjis, J., Dietz, J.L.G. (eds.) CIAO! 2009. LNBIP, vol. 34, pp. 70–84. Springer, Heidelberg (2009)
22. Simon, D.: Application landscape transformation and the role of enterprise architecture frameworks. In: Steffens, U. (ed.) MDD, SOA and IT-Management, Gito, Berlin (2009)
23. Postina, M.: Evolutionsmanagement prozess- und serviceorientierter Unternehmensarchitekturen. PhD thesis, OlWIR Verlag für Wirtschaft, Informatik und Recht, Edewecht and Oldenburg, Germany (2011)
24. Aier, S., Gleichauf, B.: Application of enterprise models for engineering enterprise transformation. Enterprise Modelling and Information Systems Architectures 5(1), 56–72 (2010)
25. Edelkamp, S., Rensink, A.: Graph transformation and ai planning. In: Edelkamp, S., Frank, J. (eds.) Knowledge Engineering Competition (ICKEPS), Rhode Island, USA (2007)
26. Diefenthaler, P., Bauer, B.: Gap analysis in enterprise architecture using semantic web technologies. In: Proceedings of 15th International Conference on Enterprise Information Systems (ICEIS 2013), pp. 211–220 (2013)
27. Loshin, D.: Master data management. Morgan Kaufmann (2010)
28. Gringel, P., Postina, M.: I-pattern for gap analysis. In: Engels, G., Luckey, M., Pretschner, A., Reussner, R. (eds.) Software engineering 2010. Lecture Notes in Informatics, pp. 281–292. Gesellschaft für Informatik, Bonn (2010)

From Information Systems to Information Services Systems: Designing the Transformation

Jolita Ralyté, Abdelaziz Khadraoui, and Michel Léonard

University of Geneva, Institute of Services Science
CUI, Battelle bat. A, 7 Route de Drize, CH-1227 Carouge, Switzerland
{Jolita.Ralyte,Abdelazis.Khadraoui,Michel.Leonard}@unige.ch

Abstract. Service-orientation is currently considered as a promising paradigm to deal with the complexity, interoperability and evolution of enterprise Information Systems (IS), which are the foremost preoccupation in today's enterprises. However, the shift from a conventional IS architecture to a service-oriented one is not an easy task despite of the various service design approaches proposed in the literature. In this paper we promote the concepts of information service and Information Services System (ISS) and we present three different ways to design an ISS taking into account enterprise legacy IS and/or from scratch. We illustrate the three approaches with examples taken from industrial projects and case studies.

Keywords: Information service, information services system, service-oriented paradigm, IS evolution.

1   Introduction

Sustainability and evolution of legacy Information Systems (IS), including their maintenance, extension with new components, interoperability with other systems and applications, is one the foremost preoccupation in today's enterprises, not only at technical but also at information and business strategic levels. In addition, the need for inter-organizational and networked information systems, cloud platforms and services systems is growing because of the enterprise business models transformations into networked and service-oriented ones. At the same time, it is unthinkable to replace existing IS by the new ones for each enterprise business and/or organizational change. Legacy IS has to evolve together with enterprise changes, and this evolution can take different forms: integration of new components from the market or custom-made, development of services on top of the existing IS, establishment of interoperability between two or more IS, etc.

In this context, service-oriented approaches emerge as prospective ones to deal with IS fragmentation, interoperability and evolution problems [1, 5, 19] as well as to support inter-organizational IS development [14, 15, 18]. Modularity, reusability and evolution are considered as the main values that service-oriented paradigm brings to the IS domain. To reach modularity, an IS has to be composed of a collection of

J. Grabis et al. (Eds.): PoEM 2013, LNBIP 165, pp. 69–84, 2013.
© IFIP International Federation for Information Processing 2013

interrelated and autonomous components. The notion of service, and in particular information service (see section 2.1), is introduced to cope with IS modularity. Modularity is the necessary basis to ensure incremental and evolutionary IS development and therefore a prerequisite for legacy IS evolution with new components/services. It also allows to avoid chaotic IS fragmentation. Reusability, as opposed to the more expensive "from scratch" development, means the reuse of legacy data and applications to provide new business functionalities – new services. Finally, the evolution principle consists in the ability to easily replace an existing component/service by a new one.

The literature review demonstrates the advent of proposals to redesign conventional IS architectures into the service-oriented ones [5, 9, 14, 15, 19, 22]. The notion of information services system (ISS) introduced in [3] (see section 2.2) appears as a natural evolution of the IS concept. Similarly to IS, ISS emphasizes the value of information, its creation, management and sharing, while improving its modularity, agility and interoperability.

The research question considered in this paper is how enterprise information systems could evolve from conventional to the service-oriented ones. In particular, we aim to identify and explore different ways to lead the shift from traditional information systems towards information services systems. Based on the related literature survey, our previous works [3, 4, 10, 11, 12, 19] and various projects realized in collaboration with the Information Technology Center of the State of Geneva (some of them are reported in [10, 11, 12]), we present in this paper three different but complementary approaches to design information services systems based on enterprise legacy IS and/or from scratch. The three approaches have been tested in various projects and case studies that we mention in this paper.

The rest of the paper is organized as follows: in the next section we define the notions of information service and information services system. Then, in section 3 we present and illustrate three approaches supporting ISS design. We discuss the related work and how our contribution complements it in section 4. Finally, section 5 concludes the paper and highlights future perspectives.

2   Information Services and Services Systems

2.1   Information Service

In the domain of enterprise information systems, the notion of service was introduced as a potential means to improve legacy IS agility and evolution and to facilitate IS interoperability. It is built upon the concept of IS component [25], which is defined over classes, methods, integrity rules, processes, roles and events that constitute a semantic unit where several actors aim to achieve a common goal. In order to fit the IS context, a service is expected to support inter-organizational and/or intra-organizational business activities trough a collaborative creation, transformation and transmission of information. This type of service is named an *information service* [3, 4] and is defined as "a component of an information system representing a well defined business unit that offers capabilities to realize business activities and owns resources (data, rules, roles) to realize these capabilities". Therefore, an information system can be seen as built of a collection of interoperable information services. The metamodel of the information service is an extension of other computational services metamodels such as: WSPER [6] or the model proposed in [2]. The particularity of the information service definition is that it requires to make the service transparent, i.e. it explicitly distinguishes four interrelated information spaces – static, dynamic, rule and role – that are necessary to define service resources and capabilities in the organizational context. We claim that in the IS context it is not sufficient to consider services as black boxes with only interface part available for their selection and composition purposes. It is essential to make explicit the information concerning service structure, processes, rules and roles and to be able to identify those shared with other services. Fig.1 shows the simplified metamodel of the information service where only the main concepts are represented (see [3] for the detailed version).

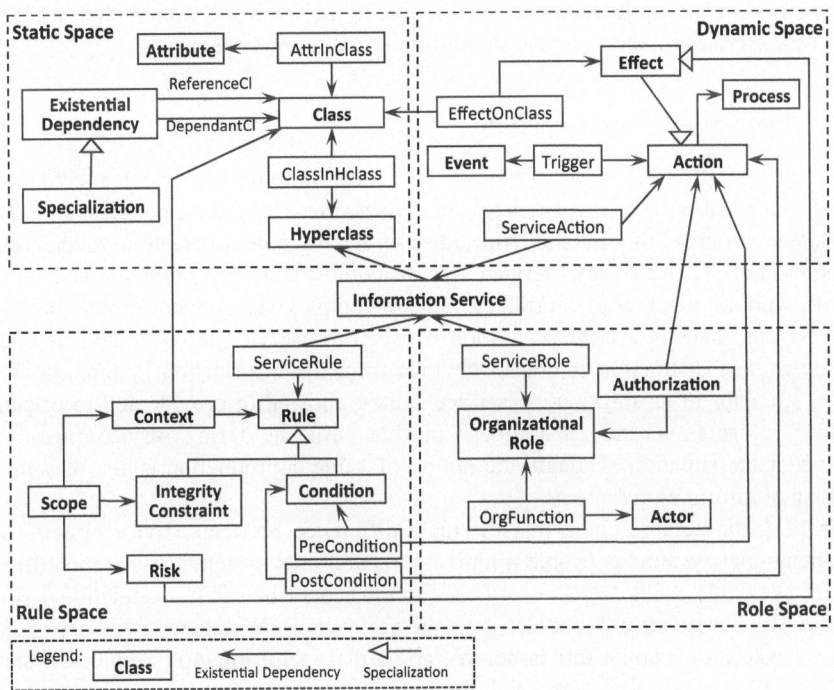

Fig. 1. Simplified metamodel of the information service.

The *static space* of the service defines its data structure in terms of classes and relationships between classes. The notion of Hyperclass (introduced in [24] to specify information system components) is used to represent complex domain concepts by putting together the corresponding set of classes. Classes are linked only via existential dependencies and specialization relationships. An existential dependency is materialized via an attribute with mandatory and permanent constraints. The *dynamic space* defines service capabilities in terms of actions that can be executed by the service and their effects on service classes. An action is triggered by an event that occurs in the service information space and is described by a process to be executed, which can be a simple function or a more complex interaction involving several actors. An action produces one or more effects on the static space (e.g. create an object of a class, modify an attribute). The notion of effect is used to characterize the result of the action and allows to evaluate the impact of the action on the rule space. The *rule space* deals with service regulation policies, which are formalized as pre-, post-conditions on service actions and integrity constraints on service data. An integrity constraint has a scope, which includes all the effects that could transgress the rule. Such an effect is called a risk of the rule. Finally, the *role space* defines service actors, the roles they play in the organization and the rights and responsibilities they have on service actions.

The metamodel presented above represents a foundation for engineering information services and services systems. In particular, it supports information services definition, composition, identification of the overlap between information services, and also new services integration into an information services system.

2.2   Information Services System

According to [21, 22], a service system is a configuration of people, technology, shared information (such as language, processes, metrics, prices, policies, and laws) and other resources that interact with other service systems to create a mutual value. Spohrer et al., [21] also say "service systems comprise service providers and service clients working together to coproduce value in complex value chains or networks". In their vision, there is a clear separation between the service provider and its client. However, this distinction is not so obvious from the information systems point of view. An actor of an information service can be allowed to provide and to consume service information and capabilities. In this case the term "service prosumer" fits better the situation. Though, the notion of value coproduction is also key in the domain of information systems.

In [21], the authors claim that the main difference between service systems and computational systems is people – unlike computational system components, the behavior of people doing work in service systems cannot be easily modeled and simulated which can create risk but also generate innovations. We agree with these authors and we take into account this issue. We argue that in Information Services Systems (ISS) people are not considered as independent system components but rather as actors enabling capabilities of information services. Their behavior is specified through the organizational roles and responsibilities involved in the information services enactment (provision and/or consumption of information resources) and governed by a set of rules implemented in the services. We also think that the unpredicted behavior of actors could be explored as a potential source of ideas for future business innovations. It could be captured in the form of initiatives. As service systems, information services systems aim to stay dynamic and open in order to enable innovation and facilitate their evolution. They have to take a risk to give people some liberty to informally and formally change rules and policies.

In our approach, an ISS is seen as a collection of interoperable information services. It aims to transform an integrated and rather rigid IS architecture into a more flexible, modular and sustainable one where services can be modified or replaced and new services can be integrated.

3   Designing Information Services Systems

There are certainly many different ways to design Information Services Systems (ISS). In this work we focus our attention on the evolution of conventional enterprise IS into the service-oriented ISS and we discuss different transformation situations and approaches. In particular, we identify and illustrate three approaches taking into consideration different organizational contexts and ISS design situations, and legacy IS reuse:

- *Services upon legacy IS*. This approach aims to bring some flexibility and modularity to the rather monolithic and fragmented legacy enterprise information systems without inflicting to them any major transformation. Indeed, in this approach services are created upon legacy IS. They utilize resources existing in various IS (their data, processes, rules, responsibilities) and provide some added value to the service users. The approach consists in identifying for each new service the existing resources that are potentially scattered in different IS and to guarantee that the execution of the service will keep these legacy IS in a consistent state, i.e. will ensure data consistency and will not violate their rules and responsibilities.
- *Fully service-oriented ISS*. This approach, in the contrary, considers an information system as a composition of information services and for that needs a more deep transformation of the existing IS into a services-oriented one. Indeed, the approach consists in "decomposing" an IS into a collection of information services and defining the overlap (common data, activities, roles, rules) between them. Information overlap management is the most important difficulty when including new services into an existing ISS.
- *Information kernel-based ISS*. This approach proposes an intermediate architecture based on a core IS and information services as its extensions. The core IS captures the kernel information – the invariant data, processes and rules, while information services offer capabilities for business activities that are subject to change. In this type of architecture the main challenges are (1) the definition of the information kernel, which is formalized as a collection of kernel services, and (2) the preservation of this kernel when adding new services to the ISS.

3.1   Information Services upon Legacy IS

Even though enterprises are constantly seeking to renew the range of their IS to be compliant with their business evolution, replacing or transforming legacy IS can be very expensive and error-prone or even impossible. Introducing a service-oriented layer upon multiple legacy systems is considered here as a potential solution to limit the transformation of legacy IS and at the same time to bring some flexibility and agility to them. In this approach we consider that several existing IS and enterprise applications are information providers to the newly defined services. The identification and selection of services to be developed has to be done prior to the application of this approach. The key step of this approach consists in the construction of a common base on top of the existing IS. This common base should help to offer each service the access to the precise and consistent information distributed in various IS and to guarantee service compliance with the existing IS and with the enterprise legal frame, which is a composition of laws and regulation policies that govern enterprise activities. Several aspects have to be considered in the construction of this common base. In particular, we need to specify the legal frame that has to be respected by the new services and to define the organizational contexts for each identified service. The approach was introduced first in [12]; its overview is shown in Fig.2a. The process model of the approach is composed of four main steps that are expressed as four engineering intentions with one or several strategies to achieve each of them (see Fig. 2c). It is represented by using Map [20] process modeling formalism, which provides a representation system based on a non-deterministic ordering of intentions and strategies in the form of a labeled directed graph. Each step is detailed below.

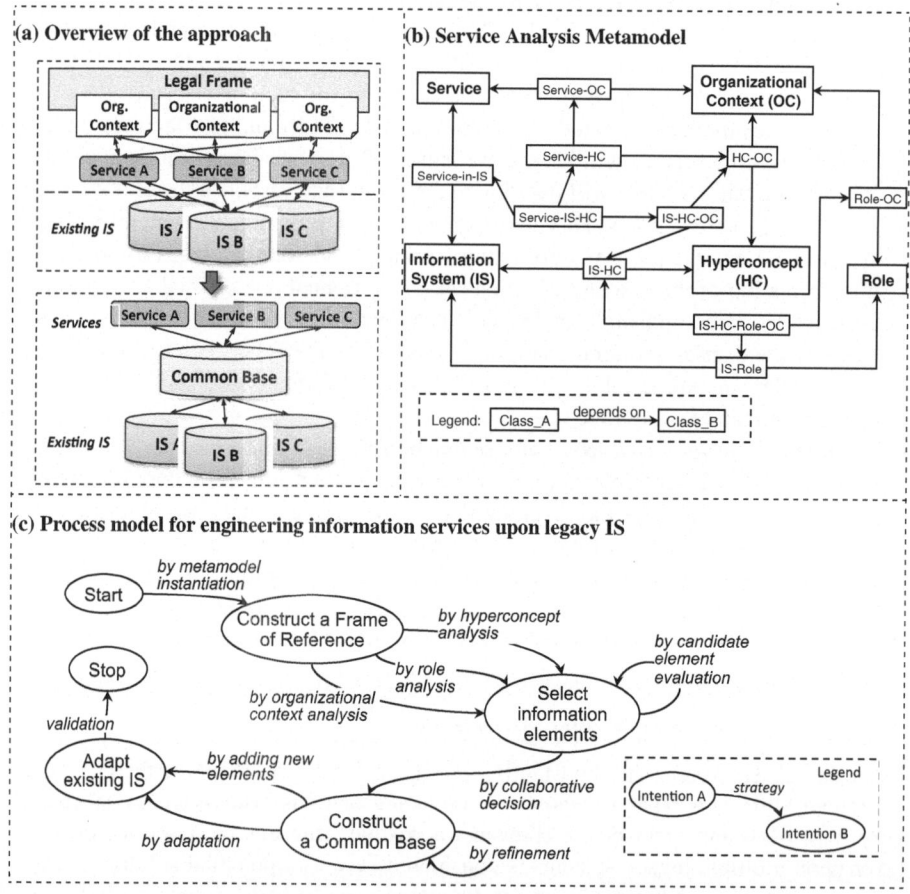

Fig. 2. The approach "Information services upon legacy IS"

Step 1: Construct a frame of reference means for each service to define: (1) its organizational contexts and the existing IS containing the information necessary for the service execution, (2) the information necessary for the service implementation in the form of a conceptual model, (3) the roles responsible for its execution. The frame of reference is constructed by instantiating the *Service Analysis Metamodel* shown in Fig. 2b. This metamodel defines the key concepts necessary to link an information service to the existing IS that provide data necessary to the service execution. A service can be defined on one or several *Organizational Contexts* that describe business rules, legal constraints and the capability of the organization to enforce laws and policies. The notion of *Hyperconcept* is used to specify how the organizational contexts are formalized in different information systems. In fact, a hyperconcept is a complex concept (composed of several sub-concepts) representing a semantic unity in the domain of analysis. Finally, the *Role* concept represents the responsibilities and authorizations to execute IS activities in a particular organizational context.

Step 2: Select the candidate informational elements for the common base by analyzing the information collected in the frame of reference. This analysis can be done in three different and complementary ways: by organizational context analysis, by organizational role and/or by hyperconcepts analysis respectively. Typically, if a hyperconcept representing a part of the service organizational context is implemented in more than one IS, the data representing it is candidate to the common base. The same applies to the roles related to the service organizational context.

Step 3: Construct a common base by collaborative decision making where all project stakeholders (business practitioners, IS architects, database architects, etc.) are invited to discuss on several formalized alternatives and to choose the elements (e.g. service related roles) to be implemented in the common base.

Step 4: Adapt the existing IS by adding new elements (e.g. adding new role) or transforming the existing ones (e.g. changing a business rule) in order to guarantee that each legacy IS is interoperable with the new common base. The number and complexity of identified transformations indicate the weight of the impact of the new service creation on the legacy IS, and this impact has to be minor.

This approach was applied in collaboration with the Information Technology Center of the State of Geneva (Switzerland) to design new services for e-administration based on five existing independent information systems (see Fig.3). Three of these IS operate at the cantonal level: (1) the Commercial Register (RC) that allows to build and identify all legal entities in the State of Geneva and to register their associated legal events, (2) the Tax IS (R-Fisc) that stores the taxation data about businesses at the cantonal level, and (3) the Geneva Business Repertory (REG) that contains administrative information on businesses and companies located in the canton of Geneva and makes this information available for administrative purposes and for the applicable dissemination in public and private sectors. These cantonal information systems have to interact with two similar IS in use at the federal level: the Federal Commercial Register (RCF) and the Federal Business Repertory (REE). Several information services were identified for this project. For example, one of them concerned the "Transmission of business statistical data" and should help companies to transmit their data to the cantonal and federal offices in order to build statistics.

The organizational context of this service is based on two laws on public statistics, one at the cantonal level (LStat)[1] and the other at the federal level (LSF)[2], and the data related to this context is available in two information systems - the REG and REE. The construction of the common base consisted in the selection of elements (data, roles, rules) common to both concerned IS and necessary for the service execution, and also the creation on new elements such as new roles for the execution of service activities. The main difficulties encountered in this project were related to the common base management, in particular to decide who will be responsible for this common base and how to manage the existing flows between the two IS (REG and REE).

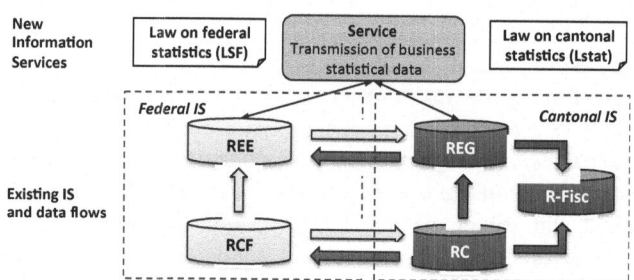

Fig. 3. Example of Service Organizational Context Analysis

3.2   Fully Service-Oriented ISS

The second approach for ISS engineering considers the enterprise IS as a composition of information services where each service provides a support for a particular business or administration activity. It differs from other service-oriented approaches in many perspectives. For example, the granularity level of information services is quite large – a service represents a full business unit not only a simple action or application. A service can represent an inter-organizational collaboration and value exchange between organizations as well as, and in particular, inter-organizational activities.

Indeed, most of the existing service-oriented approaches deal with the design of different computational services (e.g. web, mobile, cloud) and their supporting platforms in a pure "service customer vs. provider" frame. Up to now, only little attention has been paid to the intra-organizational IS context and legacy IS transformation into the service-oriented one. In [4, 19] a service-oriented and situation-driven approach for legacy IS evolution has been proposed. In this paper, we argue that this approach can be used for ISS engineering in an incremental way by progressively integrating new information services into an ISS. As said above, in this approach an IS is seen as a collection of information services, at least at the conceptual level. The main difficulty of this approach is in the fact that services composing the ISS are not totally independent components, they inevitably overlap, which is mainly because of the data sharing. In fact, the overlap between information services can exist in the four information spaces (static, dynamic, rule and role) (see Fig. 1). The construction of an ISS

---

[1] http://www.geneve.ch/legislation/rsg/f/s/rsg_B4_40.html
[2] http://www.admin.ch/ch/f/rs/431_01/index.html

consists in integrating progressively new services into the existing ISS as shown in
Fig. 4a. Of course, each new integration crates new overlap situations – some data,
activities, roles and rules can be shared between the existing and new services. Therefore, this approach is based on the analysis and resolution of the overlap between
legacy and new services by preserving the legacy ones as much as possible. The service integration approach is articulated in five main intentions with several strategies
available to reach each of them as shown in Fig. 4b.

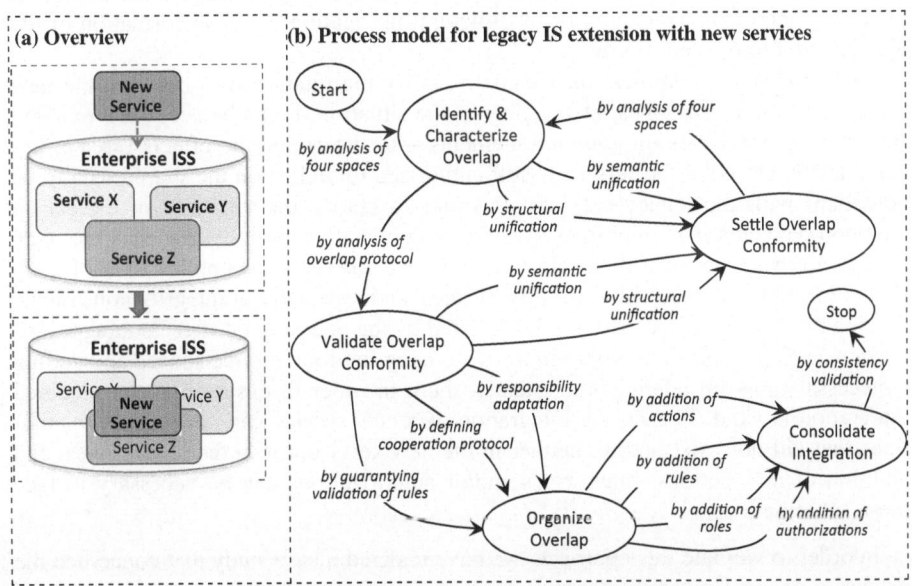

Fig. 4. The approach "Fully service-oriented ISS"

Step 1: Identify and characterize the overlap between the four information spaces
of the new service and the services already existing in the ISS. An overlap report has
to be elaborated for each space with the objective to identify similar elements and to
evaluate if they need some structural or semantic unification or not. For example, two
services can contain the same class (e.g. Student) with the same or different structure
(e.g. the attribute Birthdate is missing in one of the classes), which represents a static
space overlap. An example of the functional overlap would be when two services are
producing the same effect on a class in overlap, as for instance updating an attribute
or creating new objects of this class (e.g. create a new student). The rule overlap appears when the same class is governed by different rules in different services (e.g. the
deadline for registering new students exist in one service but not in the other). Finally,
the role space overlap means the existence of the same or similar roles in two services
(e.g. Students' administrator).

Step 2: Validate the overlap conformity for each couple of overlapping elements
(classes, actions, rules and roles respectively) identified and characterized in the overlap report. That means to check if they conform to each other, i.e. can be substituted
one by another. In the static space two classes are considered as conforming if they

have the same name, their sets of attributes and sets of methods are identical and they have the same super-classes. If two overlapping elements are not conforming, one of them (generally the element of the new service) has to be adapted in the next step.

Step 3: Settle the overlap conformity for each couple of non-conforming overlapping elements according to the type of the identified disparity. The disparities can be of semantic nature (the same name but different meaning or vice versa) or of structural nature (different set of attributes in similar classes). Therefore, it can be necessary to modify the concerned classes, actions, rules and roles by semantic unification (i.e. renaming one of the elements) or by structural unification (i.e. transformation of the element structure) accordingly.

Step 4: Organize the overlap means to clarify the relationships between the new service and the legacy ones. Depending on the situation, it can be necessary to adapt service responsibilities on common elements – to determine the effects (create, update, delete, etc.) that the service is still authorized to realize on the shared data to be compliant with the legacy services. In order to clarify the visibility of effects on common elements it is important to define a cooperation protocol for each of them. Finally, to make sure that the new service respects the regulation policy of the legacy ISS, we need to guarantee that validity of rules, and especially of integrity constraints, defined on legacy services will not be violated by the new service after its integration.

Step 5: Consolidate the integration by revising the four service spaces and adding if necessary missing elements in each of them in order to ensure that the obtained integration is valid. In fact, the integration of a new service can generate new situations that did not exist before, neither in the new service nor in the legacy ones, and addition of new actions, rules, roles and/or authorizations can be necessary to face these situations.

In order to validate this approach, we have realized a case study that concerned the extension of our University Students Management System with new information services. In particular, we have considered the Diploma Management Service (DMS) as an existing information service and the Online Registration Service (ORS) as the new service to be integrated in the existing ISS. The DMS provides several diploma management capabilities such as: to create the curriculum of each diploma by defining its courses and linking them to their lecturers, to manage students' registration to different diplomas and to the corresponding courses, to manage examination results, etc. The new service, the ORS, enables students' registration by providing a web interface for this purpose. A candidate can create a university registration request on-line by filling the registration form and by uploading different required documents. Then, the students' administrator validates the on-line created registration request and asks for additional documents if necessary. He/she is responsible for recording the candidate as a student and for registering him/her to the selected diploma.

Because, the two services have been developed independently, it is obvious that some information overlap between them is inevitable (e.g. class *Person*, class *Student*, activity *UpdatePerson*, rule *RgistrationToDiploma.RegistrationDate < Diploma.RegistrationLimitDate*, role *Student*, role *Diploma Manager*, etc.). These shared elements (identical or similar) constitute the information overlap between the existing and the new service and the integration process was to make this overlap consistent in order to enable reliable new service exploitation within the ISS and the non-violation of the already existing ISS consistency.

3.3   Information Kernel-Based ISS

The third approach for ISS engineering proposes to use a mixed architecture where a kernel IS is extended with a variety of information services. In fact, in this approach we consider that the core and invariant information (including data, processes, rules and roles) can be found in the laws and other regulation policies governing enterprise activities, and should be captured in the kernel of the IS independently of the information services that could extend this IS later. This approach is especially adapted for the ISS development in public and governmental sectors. We argue that legal documents include precise definitions of concepts, rules and constraints governing the institutional activities and represent a rich source of knowledge for the ontological information extraction and the information kernel conceptualization. Moreover, the use of laws permits to enhance the adequacy and compatibility of an institutional IS with the corresponding institution activities and to construct a stable information kernel as a basis for the sustainable ISS development. Therefore, this approach has two parts: (1) the ontological model construction based on the analysis of legal sources and (2) its mapping into the conceptual model representing the kernel IS as shown in Fig. 5a. This kernel IS then can be extended with new services following Fully Service-Oriented ISS engineering approach presented above.

Formally, the process model of the approach is defined in terms of three main intentions and several strategies to achieve each of them as depicted in Fig. 5c. The first two intentions, *Identify Hyperconcepts* and *Build Hyperconcepts*, deal with the ontological model construction in terms of a collection of interrelated hyperconcepts while the third one, *Construct Kernel Information Services*, defines the kernel IS as a collection of kernel information services.

Step1: Identify the hyperconcepts that correspond to the different ontological information spaces related to the organization activities. As depicted in Fig. 5b representing the metamodel for the kernel IS construction, we use the notion of the *hyperconcept* to capture the information related to a fragment of any legal and/or ontological source named here an *Ontological Fragment*. A hyperconcept is composed of a set of concepts extracted from ontological fragments and represents an ontological unity with precise semantics. *Ontological Business Rules* can be extracted from one or several ontological fragments and are related to one or more hyperconcepts. Besides, we use the notion of *Ontological Role*, which represents a set of responsibilities and permissions to perform business activities in the organization. Each ontological role is defined in at least one ontological fragment and is valid in the context of one or more hyperconcepts. The identification of hyperconcepts can be done in two complementary ways: (1) by selecting and analyzing different ontological fragments and (2) by analyzing the organization and identifying its ontological roles. An ontological fragment is selected if it is considered as stable and invariant for the lifespan of the organization and of the ISS under construction. It is obvious, that this type of decision requires some experience and risk management abilities.

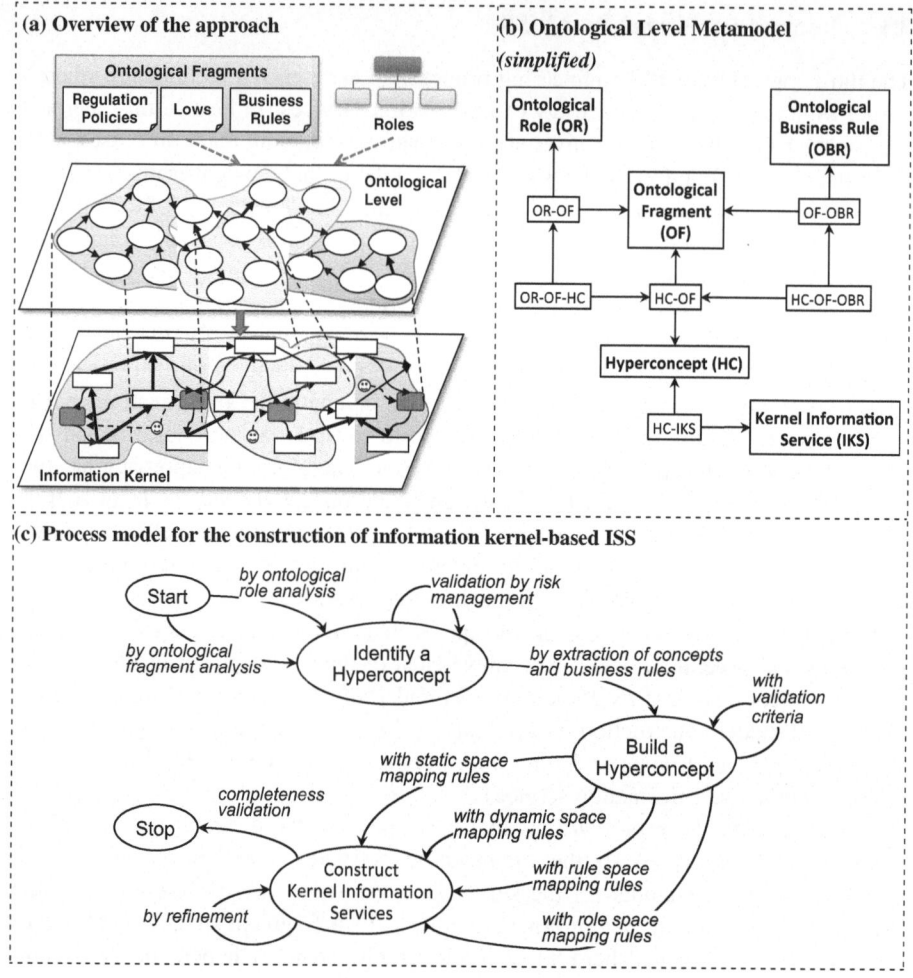

Fig. 5. The approach "Information kernel-based ISS"

Step2: Build the hyperconcepts by extracting concepts and business rules from the selected ontological fragments and refine their structure with a set of validation criteria based on the ontological level metamodel (Fig. 5b).

Step 3: Construct information services composing the kernel of the ISS. As shown in Fig. 5b, a *Kernel Information Service* is based on one or more hyperconcepts from the ontological level. The structure of the kernel information service is formalized by using information service metamodel shown in Fig. 1. We use a collection of mapping rules to extract from the ontological model the four information spaces (static, dynamic, rules and roles) of each kernel information service.

This approach was applied in several e-government projects (e.g. [11, 10]) in collaboration with the Information Technology Center of the State of Geneva (Switzerland). One of the projects concerned the development of the kernel information services system for managing the prescription and delivery of narcotics for the treatment of the addicted people. We have used the Geneva law K 4 20.06[3] as a legal source of knowledge to build and to implement the kernel ISS supporting the activities of narcotics prescription, distribution and administration. Indeed, this law describes the procedure that medical doctors have to follow in order to record a request of authorization allowing to prescribe a narcotic for the treatment of a dependent person (drug addict). For example, the law says that a doctor has to obtain an authorization from the cantonal doctor before the prescription of any narcotic to a patient. Then the pharmacist, on the basis of the authorization delivered by the cantonal doctor, provides the doctor, or directly the patient, the drug prescribed. From the law text a set of invariant concepts {*Doctor, Patient, Authorization, Cantonal Doctor, Prescription, Drug, etc.}* can be identified. The law also describes how the drug has to be distributed and administered by enumerating different cases where a patient can benefit of the administration of narcotics. Therefore, the law also defines business rules and constraints (ontological business rules) to be respected. Finally, the law allows to identify organizational roles (ontological roles) such as *Doctor, Pharmacist, Cantonal Doctor*, etc. A kernel ISS was built directly from this law.

4   Related Work and Discussion

Most of the current service-oriented approaches, like SOA [7, 13, 17] instruct how to develop service-oriented software systems from scratch and do not pay much attention to the legacy software, and in particular information systems, reuse and evolution. Moreover, the compliance of services to the laws and enterprise regulation policies is not considered. In the context of the IS engineering, these approaches can only recommend to rebuild enterprise IS in terms of autonomous services that could be composed in different ways. Such services have to be elaborated from scratch in order to avoid any overlap between them. This type of development represents a rather extreme solution and is not adapted to the legacy IS evolution. The lifecycle of an IS is a continuous incremental and evolutionary process and it is not possible to rethink the entire IS at each iteration in order to guarantee the autonomy and correctness of the existing and new services.

Up to now, we found relatively few attempts to define service-oriented architectures for information systems. We can mention the work of Chua [5] who discusses how service-oriented design should be applied in an organization in order to adopt SOA. Haesen [9] presents a research plan for developing an approach to design SOA for IS. Le Dinh and Nguyen-Hgoc [14] propose a conceptual framework for designing service-oriented inter-organizational IS. Thomas and Brocke [23] present a value-driven approach to design service-oriented IS; the approach is based on business process modeling and cost/benefit analysis to determine whether the introduction of SOA justifies the effort. Lo and Yu [16] propose a reference catalogue approach to design an SOA system. This approach uses the i* modeling technique adapted to the service-oriented business modeling for the selection of reference business models

---

[3] Today Geneva Law K 4 20.06 is abrogated and replaced by the new law K 4 20.02 http://www.geneve.ch/legislation/rsg/f/rsg_k4_20p02.html

from the catalogue and their adaptation to the particular case. Estrada et al. [8] introduce a service-oriented organizational model in order to reduce the mismatch between business models and service-oriented designs. Most of these approaches consider SOA for IS at business level rather than at information management and implementation level, and only from the customer-provider perspective – how the organization could offer services to its customers. The intra-organizational perspective of a service as a support for internal enterprise activities and information exchange is not really considered. Besides, the evolution of legacy IS into the service-oriented ones is not their major preoccupation.

Unlike the contributions mentioned above, the three approaches for ISS engineering summarized in this paper aim to support service-oriented inter- and intra-organizational ISS development taking into consideration legacy IS and their evolution. Each of the three approaches is dedicated to a particular situation but together they are considered as complementary ones.

The first approach, named information services upon legacy IS, deals with the situation where multiple legacy IS have to continue to operate and cannot be transformed drastically. It helps to preserve existing IS by creating information services upon them via a common base capturing their overlap. The main difficulties of this approach are related to the number and size of existing IS that have to be analyzed and used by the information services, the organizational changes (e.g. new roles, new responsibilities) entailed by the new services, and the data opening and sharing.

The second approach, named fully service-oriented ISS, is dedicated to support incremental ISS construction as well as legacy IS evolution by extending them with new information services. This approach is based on the analysis and resolution of the overlap between the legacy information services and the new services and helps to preserve the legacy ones as much as possible thanks to the integration impact analysis.

Finally, the third approach, named information kernel-based ISS, aims to construct a stable and invariant basis for an ISS – the kernel information services – that could then be extended with more volatile services. According to this approach, the information stability can be identified from the legal sources (laws and other regulation policies) governing enterprise activities and therefore this approach is especially suitable for the ISS engineering in public administration and governmental sectors such as e-government services. The kernel information services constitute a reference and a foundation for the ISS designers. They help to understand which information is invariant and stable during the ISS lifecycle and to design new services to be added to the ISS. Thus, various situations of services interoperability are identified, discussed and settled at early development stages.

5   Conclusion

Service-oriented paradigm seems to be well adapted to deal with the complexity, interoperability and evolution of enterprise legacy IS, and the most promising one to consider the development of the next generation information services systems.

However, the literature dealing with this topic is still modest. In this paper we aim to demonstrate how IS-specific service-oriented architectures can be elaborated, in particular to cope with the legacy IS evolution. The three approaches presented in this paper overview our work in the domain of service-oriented IS development where we introduce the notions of *information service* and *information services system (ISS)*. We aim to demonstrate that depending on the enterprise legacy IS situation and its evolution strategy the ISS development approach and the ISS architecture will be different. For example, if there is a need to open the access to the resources of multiple existing IS but the requirement to preserve these IS untouched is very strong, the approach for defining services upon legacy IS helps to deal with such situation. In the contrary, if a new services system has to be developed from scratch in order to support some new business or to computerize services that until now were provided manually or with the help of simple communication techniques like e-mail and/or fax, the information kernel-based approach seems to be the most appropriate one. Finally, the fully service-oriented approach is particularly helpful to deal with the evolution of an IS which is already designed as a composition of services. Indeed, it provides guidance for extending existing ISS with new services. The notion of information overlap is recurrent in the three approaches and it is also original in comparison with the conventional SOA, which considers software services as completely autonomous and independent modules. In the context of IS this type of autonomy is not reachable because different information services have to share data, roles and rules governing enterprise business.

The three approaches have been applied in various case studies and collaborative projects in the sector of public administration. Our future preoccupation is to apply them in different industrial settings and to extend them with additional strategies and techniques.

References

1. Abbass, A.: Accessing Enterprise Information Systems in a Service-Oriented Architecture (2006), http://www.ibm.com/developerworks/webservices/library/ws-soa-eisjca/
2. Andrikopoulos, V., Benbernou, S., Papazoglou, M.P.: Managing the Evolution of Service Specifications. In: Bellahsène, Z., Léonard, M. (eds.) CAiSE 2008. LNCS, vol. 5074, pp. 359–374. Springer, Heidelberg (2008)
3. Arni-Bloch, N., Ralyté, J.: MISS: A Metamodel of Information System Service. In: Proceedings of ISD 2008, pp. 177–186. Springer Science+Business Media (2008)
4. Arni-Bloch, N., Ralyté, J., Léonard, M.: Service-Driven Information Systems Evolution: Handling Integrity Constraints Consistency. In: Persson, A., Stirna, J. (eds.) PoEM 2009. LNBIP, vol. 39, pp. 191–206. Springer, Heidelberg (2009)
5. Chua, F.F.: Adoption of Service-Oriented Architecture by Information Systems. International J. of Autonomous and Adaptive Communications Systems 2(4), 317–330 (2009)
6. Dubray, J.-J.: Wsper an abstract SOA framework. Technical report (2007), http://www.ebpml.org/wsper/wsper/wsper_primer.pdf
7. Erl, T.: SOA Principles of Service Design. Prentice Hall PTR (2007)

8. Estrada, H., Martínez, A., Pastor, O., Mylopoulos, J., Giorgini, P.: Extending Organizational Modeling with Business Services Concepts: An Overview of the Proposed Architecture. In: Parsons, J., Saeki, M., Shoval, P., Woo, C., Wand, Y. (eds.) ER 2010. LNCS, vol. 6412, pp. 483–488. Springer, Heidelberg (2010)
9. Haesen, R.: Designing service-oriented information systems architectures. In: Proceedings of Workshops and Doctoral Consortium at CAiSE 2007, pp. 871–880 (2007)
10. Khadraoui, A., Léonard, M., Pham Thi, T.T., Helfert, M.: A Framework for Compliance of Legacy Information Systems with Legal Aspect. AIS Transactions on Enterprise Systems 1, 15–26 (2009)
11. Khadraoui, A., Opprecht, W., Aïdonidis, C., Léonard, M.: Laws-Based Ontology for e-Government Services Construction. Case Study: The Specification of Services in Relationship with the Venture Creation in Switzerland. In: Stirna, J., Persson, A. (eds.) PoEM 2008. LNBIP, vol. 15, pp. 197–209. Springer, Heidelberg (2008)
12. Khadraoui, A., Opprecht, W., Léonard, M., Aïdonidis, C.: Service Specification upon Multiple Existing Information Systems. In: Proceedings of RCIS 2011. IEEE (2011)
13. Krafzig, D., Banke, K., Slama, D.: Enterprise SOA: Service-Oriented Architecture Best Practices. Prentice Hall PTR (2004)
14. Le Dinh, T., Nguyen-Ngoc, A.V.: A Conceptual Framework for Designing Service-Oriented Inter-organizational Information Systems. In: Proceedings of SoICT 2010, pp. 147–154 (2010)
15. Le Dinh, T., Pham Thi, T.T.: A Conceptual Framework for Service Modelling in a Network of Service System. In: Morin, J.-H., Ralyté, J., Snene, M. (eds.) IESS 2010. LNBIP, vol. 53, pp. 192–206. Springer, Heidelberg (2010)
16. Lo, A., Yu, E.: From Business Models to Service-Oriented Design: A Reference Catalog Approach. In: Parent, C., Schewe, K.-D., Storey, V.C., Thalheim, B. (eds.) ER 2007. LNCS, vol. 4801, pp. 87–101. Springer, Heidelberg (2007)
17. MacKenzie, C.M., et al. (eds.): Reference Model for Service Oriented Architecture 1.0, Oasis Standard (2006), http://docs.oasis-open.org/soa-rm/v1.0/soa-rm.html
18. Ralyté, J.: Applying Transdisciplinarity Principles in the Information Services Co-creation Process. In: Proceedings of RCIS 2012. IEEE (2012)
19. Ralyté, J., Arni-Bloch, N., Léonard, M.: Information Systems Evolution: A Process Model for Integrating New Services. In: Proceedings of AMCIS 2010. Paper 431 (2010)
20. Rolland, C., Prakash, N., Benjamen, A.: A Multi-model Vew of Process Modelling. Requirements Engineering 4(4), 169–187 (1999)
21. Spohrer, J., Maglio, P.P., Bailey, J., Gruhl, D.: Steps Toward a Science of Service Systems. Computer 40(1), 71–77 (2007)
22. Spohrer, J., Vargo, S.L., Caswell, N., Maglio, P.P.: The Service System is the Basic Abstraction of Service Science. In: Proceedings of HICSS 2008, pp. 104–114 (2008)
23. Thomas, O., vom Brocke, J.: A value-driven approach to the design of service-oriented information systems—making use of conceptual models. Information Systems and E-Business Management 8(1), 67–97 (2010)
24. Turki, S., Léonard, M.: Hyperclasses: towards a new kind of independence of the methods from the schema. In: Proceedings of ICEIS 2002, vol. 2, pp. 788–794 (2002)
25. Turki, S., Léonard, M.: IS Components with Hyperclasses. In: Bruel, J.-M., Bellahsène, Z. (eds.) OOIS 2002. LNCS, vol. 2426, pp. 132–141. Springer, Heidelberg (2002)

Making Process Model Versions Comparable by Quantifying Changes

Nico Herzberg and Mathias Weske

Hasso Plattner Institute at the University of Potsdam
{nico.herzberg,mathias.weske}@hpi.uni-potsdam.de

Abstract. A central task in the business process management life cycle is the evaluation of business processes to get a solid base for process improvements. Business processes are described as process models to explicitly state the operations needed to be carried out to reach the companies' business goals. These process models evolve over time because of changing market conditions, process improvements, or legal changes, etc. and result in multiple process versions. In such circumstances, process analysis requires the comparison of several process versions, the so-called multi-version evaluation. This paper tackles this challenge and introduces a technique to identify and quantify individual influences caused by differing process versions.

Keywords: Business Process Management, Business Process Models, Process Evaluation, Process Analysis, Process Versions.

1 Introduction

Nowadays, organizations face a competitive market environment and need to be as flexible and efficient as possible. Therefore, they are managed in a process-oriented fashion to be able to react quickly on market changes. Business process management (BPM) combines concepts, methods, and techniques to support the design, administration, configuration, enactment, and analysis of these business processes in an iterative way [1]. One corner stone of the BPM life cycle is the evaluation of business process executions to identify the weak points and potential improvements. Central to BPM are process models as they explicitly describe the operations that need to be carried out to reach the companies' business goals and are used, among others, for enactment.

For instance, changing market conditions, elimination of identified weak points by implementing business process improvements, or legal changes result in business process model changes and therewith in a variety of business process models, so-called process versions. Therefore, reliable business process analysis requires all versions of a business process taken into account to get a complete picture of the business process executions so far. Most information systems that are used for business process execution collect data about the performed activities. This data can already be analyzed in the context of business processes and their

J. Grabis et al. (Eds.): PoEM 2013, LNBIP 165, pp. 85–100, 2013.

corresponding process models by using methods and techniques from the field of business process intelligence (BPI) [2,3,4]. Still, these methods and concepts are targeting on one specific process version only and are not able to handle the evolution of a process including several process versions.

In this work, we present an approach for identifying and quantifying variations of process metrics that are caused by the differences in the process versions to allow process analysis with several versions of a process. We introduce a technique to determine the actual effects of structural process model changes between process versions for a specific process metric. With the approach, we make several process versions comparable based on their common denominator. A multi-version evaluation computes a single metric, e.g., a point-to-point duration metric, using execution data from the set of all process versions or a subset of those. The studies in this work are performed using as example the point-to-point duration. This metric represents the time that elapsed between reaching a first point (A) and reaching a second point (B) during the execution of a process. In this work, we show the algorithm for determining which parts of a process model, i.e., process fragments, affect a specific point-to-point duration. These calculated process metrics can be used for process monitoring and analysis.

In the remainder, we introduce basic terms and concepts our work bases on (Section 2) followed by the description of a motivating example from health care in Section 3. In Section 4, we explain our approach in detail and present how we use newly introduced measured region models and process model structuring techniques to determine whether process model changes can be highlighted for multiple process versions analysis. In Section 5, we apply the presented approach to our motivating example and show concrete duration delta calculations. We put our work into the context concerning related work in Section 6, before we summarize and conclude the paper in Section 7.

2   Preliminaries

For this work, we rely on a simplified notion of process models defined as follows.

Definition 1 (Process Model). *A process model is a tuple $P = (N, F, \kappa)$, where N is a finite set of nodes N and $F \subseteq N \times N$ is the control flow relation. $N = A \cup G \cup E$ comprises the activity nodes A, the gateways G, and the start and end nodes $E = \{s, e\}$. $\kappa \colon G \to \{and, xor\}$ associates each gateway node with a type.* ◇

Activities have exactly one predecessor and one successor. Whereas gateways have either one predecessor and several successors (split) or several predecessors and one successor (join). We assume the process model to be structural sound, to ensure that the process model P has exactly one start node s and one end node e, and every node is part of a valid path from s to e. Refactoring techniques may be applied to normalize models that do not match these assumptions [5]. We further require process models to be block-structured and their petri-net representation to be sound [6], which ensures the absence of behavioral anomalies such as deadlocks.

The process model serves as a blueprint for the so-called process instances. A process instance is a concrete execution of the activities defined in a process model. Process monitoring and analysis is targeting on the evaluation and comparison of process instances.

As we are interested in measuring the time it takes to execute a part of a process instance, we require measurement points that denote a particular node is reached. However, positioning of such a point on process model node level only is too coarse-grained, because it is often required to track the begin and the end of an activity for instance, e.g., to distinguish between waiting times and the time it actually requires to carry out a certain activity. Therefore, we assign a *node life cycle* to each node of the process model to allow a more fine-grained positioning of the measurement points based on the state transitions of those life cycles, cf. [7].

Definition 2 (Node Life Cycle). *A* node life cycle *is a tuple* $L = (S, T)$, *where S is a finite set of* node states *and $T \subseteq S \times S$ is a finite set of* node state transitions. *Let $P = (N, F, \kappa)$ be a process model. There exists a function* $\varphi : N \to L$ *that assigns a node life cycle to every node $n \in N$ of P.* ◇

State transitions are the elementary constructs that can be leveraged to position points in the process model where measurements could be taken. A point where a measurement could be taken on a state transition of a node is called *process event monitoring point* (PEMP), cf. [7]. The set of all node state transitions of a process model $P = (N, F, \kappa)$ is comprised by $\bigcup_{n \in N} \{(n, t) | t \in T_{\varphi(n)}\}$, each of which could be potentially linked to a PEMP. $T_{\varphi(n)} \subseteq T$ represents all node state transitions $t \in T$ returned by function $\varphi(n) = (S, T)$ for node $n \in N$.

Definition 3 (Process Event Monitoring Point). *A process event monitoring point is a tuple $PEMP = (P, n, t)$, where P is the process model it is contained in, $n \in N$ is the node it is created for, and $t \in T$ is the state transition within the node life cycle of n it is assigned to.* ◇

3 Motivating Example

In our motivating example, we will look on the diagnosis of a patient's disease in a hospital, see Fig. 1a. The first activity in the initial diagnosis process version is "Withdraw Blood Samples". Afterwards the blood samples are analyzed (activity "Analyze Blood Samples") in parallel to the examination of the patient (activity "Examine Patient"). Updating the patient's records finishes the process (activity "Update Patient's Records").

For quality assurance it is essential to measure the time consumed between the point in time when the patient is introduced to the doctor (A) and the patient's data are updated according to the examination results and the blood sample analysis (B). For measuring such a point-to-point duration, we utilize PEMPs. A PEMP, cf. Definition 3, is bound to a specific state transition of a node's life cycle, cf. Definition 2 to indicate that this state transition happened by occurrence

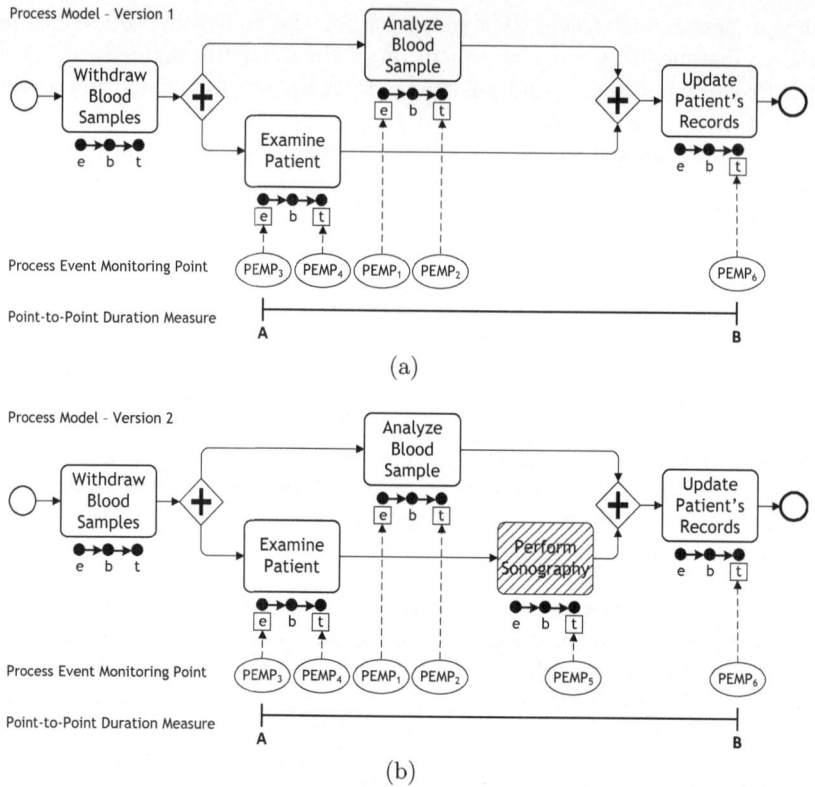

Fig. 1. Evolved process model of a diagnosis process for a patient. (a) shows process version 1 with the activities "Withdraw Blood Samples", "Analyze Blood Samples", "Examine Patient", and "Update Patient's Records". (b) shows process version 2 with the additionally inserted activity "Perform Sonography".

of the corresponding data in the information system landscape. Referring to Fig. 1a and Fig. 1b, we assigned to each activity of the process model the same node life cycle consisting of the states enabled, running and terminated with the corresponding state transitions *(e)nable*, *(b)egin* and *(t)erminate*. However, the solution allows applying individual life cycles to the nodes. In Fig. 1 the life cycles are represented by black dots and edges between them. A black dot represents a node state transition while an edge between two black dots represent the node state. In the scenario not every node state transition is observable by occurance of data from the information systems. Therefore, only PEMPs that can be observed are shown in Fig. 1. $PEMP_3$ in Fig. 1 indicates that activity "Examine Patient" is enabled for execution and $PEMP_6$ represents the end of the patient's data record update.

Due to legal changes, the hospital adjusted the diagnosis process for the patients by adding a process fragment, i.e., the activity "Perform Sonography", see Fig. 1b - shaded activity. In this second process version the termination of the sonography could be captured by $PEMP_5$. Introducing a process fragment, e.g., an activity, might affect the overall run time of the diagnosis process instances and therewith the point-to-point duration between the introduction of the patient to the doctor and the completion of patient's data update. An analysis summarizing process instances of both versions, the first version without the sonography, and the second version including the sonography, is not possible, because the results would be mixed up and falsified accordingly.

With the comparability of process instances of several different process versions several questions about the quantification of effects between the single process versions arise. For instance in our case it would be interesting to answer the following: (i) What are the diagnosis durations after adding sonography activity? (ii) Are the durations for the unchanged part of the model different before and after adding sonography?

4   Solution

Our approach targets on the determinability of effects caused by process changes. We will show the concept of our approach using the example of the point-to-point duration process metric. The point-to-point duration is a measure for the elapsed time it takes to traverse the sub-graph of a process model that is spanned by an activity indicating the start (A) and an activity indicating the end (B), see Fig. 1a and Fig. 1b. We assume that both activities can be measured by a PEMP. We use the existing process model, the defined point-to-point duration metric, the change log to the process model that captures all the changes applied to the model, and the defined PEMPs to apply our four-step approach.

First of all, a *measured region model* is derived from the source process model (version 1) based on the point-to-point duration metric. A node of the process model is part of the measured region model if its duration influences the point-to-point duration. The resulting connected sub-graph contains all such influencing nodes and builds the basis for our approach (see Section 4.1). A measured region model is a process model according to Definition 1. Secondly, the measured region model is enriched by the changes applied to the source process model contained in the change log (see Section 4.2). Afterwards the enriched measured region model is transformed to a *component tree* by utilizing the technique of the refined process structure tree (RPST) [8]. The resulting component tree is enriched with the information of defined PEMPs and an *event monitoring model* is built in a third step (see Section 4.3). In the fourth step, based on this event monitoring model it is determined whether the effects of the process model changes can be identified and quantified for more accurate process analysis (see Section 4.4).

4.1   Transformation to a Measured Region Model

The *measured region model* is the basis for determining, which structural changes might affect the point-to-point duration metric, as it contains the relevant process nodes only; see the processes shown in Fig. 2 for an example. The left side shows the original process model and the right shows the measured region model

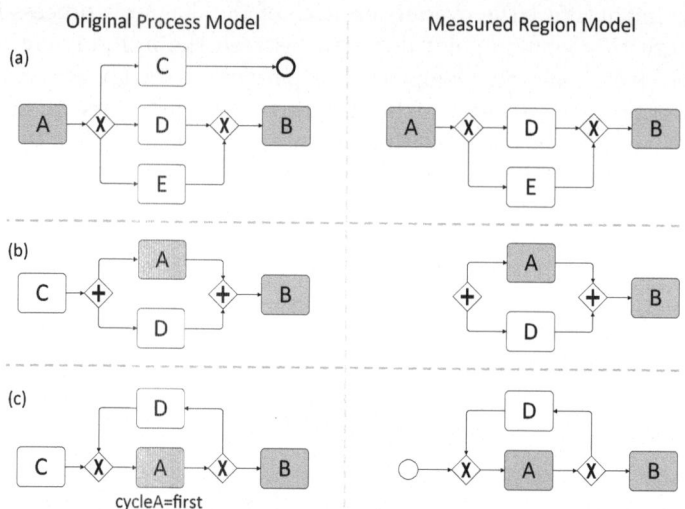

Fig. 2. A selection of measured region models for a point-to-point duration metric influenced by (a) an exclusive process fragment, (b) a parallel process fragment, and (c) a loop process fragment. In (c) a start event is added to assures that there is always a single entry and single exit point in the measured region model.

for the given point-to-point duration metric. Per definition, all elements not contained in the measured region model can be removed from the process model without affecting the given point-to-point duration metric.

Fig. 2a shows that every node on a path from node A to node B (including both nodes) is contained in the measured region model. However, this is not the case with parallel and inclusive join gateways as they represent *synchronization points* in a process, which wait for the completion of all incoming branches. If node A is contained in such a branch, then the other branches are not on a path from node A to node B, but they might still influence the point-to-point duration because of the synchronizing behavior of the joining gateway, see Fig. 2b. This does not apply to exclusive conditional join gateways, as they trigger immediately when a single branch is completed.

When considering cycles, the start point, end point, or both of the duration metric might be part of the cycle. Thus, the relating activities can be executed several times and therewith, multiple activity instances exist. Therefore, we need to consider user input to know whether the first or last activity instance is relevant for the point-to-point duration. We describe these inputs in the metric parameters $cycleA, cycleB = \{first, last\}$. It depends largely on the parameters of the metric, whether the corresponding cycle is part of the region or not, see Fig. 2c. If only node A (and not node B) is part of a cycle and $cycleA = first$, then that cycle needs to be part of the region. If $cycleA = last$, then the cycle is not part of the region, as it was not executed again after the last triggering of A. The parameter $cycleB$ has a corresponding effect on the inclusion of a cycle containing node B.

The algorithm to create a measured region model starts with the search of all relevant paths from A to B by using a traversal of the succeeding nodes starting with node A. If node B is encountered, then the current path is saved as a relevant path and that path is not traversed further. Traversal can also be stopped, if a node has no unvisited successors or node A is encountered. In the latter case, the path is also marked as relevant, if A is in a cycle and $cycleA = first$. If B is in a cycle and $cycleB = last$ we also need to find all paths from node B to itself. This case can be handled by starting a second traversal of succeeding nodes in the process model, this time starting from node B. As in the first traversal, paths to node A or node B are added depending on the mentioned parameters.

Once the set of relevant paths has been determined, each path is traversed in order and a new node is added to the measured region model for each node in the path, if the node does not exists in the model already. Further, we have to consider the case of encountering synchronizing gateways, whose start gateway is outside of all relevant paths. While traversing each path, we keep two counters, one for splitting and another for joining parallel and conditional gateways. If both counters are equal and such a joining gateway is encountered, then we know that this gateway does not have a splitting counterpart in the measured region model yet. Thus, the next step is to add all its incoming branches to the measured region model together with the splitting gateway to ensure structural soundness. The original process model is traversed backwards using the predecessors of nodes to find the first splitting gateway that is common to all branches that is then used as split in the measured region model. This backward tracing starts from the joining gateway.

To connect all the nodes, a directed edge is added from each node to it's successor in the path. Eventually, an explicit start node s or end node e is added when the measured region model includes cycles. This assures that there is always a single entry and single exit (SESE) point in the measured region model. As the final step, gateways with a single predecessor and a single successor are removed from the measured region model as they do not affect the duration and are not allowed in a process model per definition.

With this, the creation of the measured region model is complete. The measured region model contains the elements of a process model that affect a specific point-to-point duration from activity (A) to another activity (B). In the following, we will enrich this measured region model with information from the process model change log.

4.2   Enriching Measured Region Models with Change Information

In a second step, the changes to the source process model as described in the change log are applied to the measured region model created in the previous step. In this work, we assume that the change log contains only change patterns as described by Weber et. al [9]. The change patterns describe the process model change relating a particular part in the process model, the so-called process fragment. These change patterns do not contain atomic or complex activities only, but also sub-graphs that need to have a SESE. The change operations are

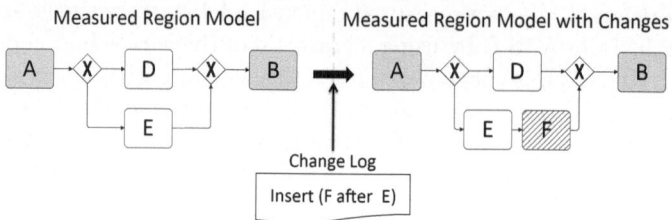

Fig. 3. Applying change operations contained in the process model change log to the measured region model

rather "simulated" in the measured region model, as the changes are marked in the model only, e.g., a removal operation applied to a measured region model's process fragment is marking that corresponding fragment only, e.g., the removal of an activity. Same holds for adding process fragments. This is necessary to keep the previous positions of the nodes for further evaluation.

For instance, the change log for our source process model shown in Fig. 2a contains an entry for the insertion of a process fragment, i.e., an additional activity F after activity E in the lower branch of the process model, e.g., stated by the change operation *Insert(F after E)*. This operation is applied to the measured region model and F is marked as inserted, see Fig. 3 - shaded activity.

A specialty in this processing step is the application of change patterns to the start and end point of the point-to-point duration metrics, i.e., to node A and B of the shown example. Changes involving node A or node B need to be handled separately, as they change the basis on which the measured region model is defined. Once the measured region model is enriched by the change information, the structure of the resulting model needs to be parsed to attach the defined PEMPs and to determine the effects of the change in the next steps.

4.3   Build the Event Monitoring Model

For parsing the structure of the measured region model, we apply the approach of the RPST introduced by Vanhatalo et. al [8]. The RPST represents the process model structured as a tree with the root symbolizing the whole graph, the nodes representing canonical elements of the parent element, and the leaves denoting the edges of the graph.

As we are interested in the nodes of the process graph, the RPST has to be transformed into a *component tree*. The component tree consists of the canonical fragments of the RPST as process components, i.e., the component tree nodes, and the measured region model nodes itself as the component tree leaves. During the transformation, canonical fragments of the RPST are transformed into process components that subsume the process elements that are contained in the corresponding canonical fragment of the RPST. From the children of the canonical fragments of the RPST, the original measured region model nodes got extracted and attached to the corresponding process component as a child. For instance, the measured region model with the applied changes from the previous

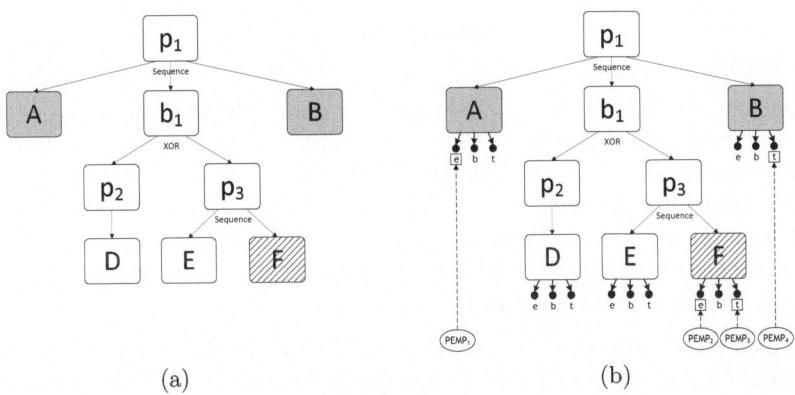

(a)   (b)

Fig. 4. (a) shows the measured region model enriched by changes structured in a component tree. To this component tree the corresponding life cycles of the process nodes are attached by $\varphi(n)$ and the defined PEMP are assigned (b).

step, see Fig. 3, is structured in a component tree as shown in Fig. 4a. Note that during the transformation of the RPST into a component tree, measured region model nodes may get duplicated in different process components of the component tree. However, this will not be an issue for our approach. The marking of the applied changes are still contained in the component tree.

To the component tree leaves, the corresponding life cycles are attached by $\varphi : N \to L$ to every node $n \in N$ of the measured region model P. With that step, every component tree leaf gets new children indicating the state transitions of the corresponding life cycle as shown in Fig. 4b. For simplicity reasons, every node gets the state transitions (e)nable, (b)egin and (t)erminate assigned.

Afterwards, the defined PEMPs are connected according their definition $PEMP = (P, n, t)$ to the component tree containing the measured region model nodes and the assigned state transitions. P is the indicator for the initial process model and the resulting measured region model, n the measured region model node the PEMP belongs to, and t the exact state transition that could be observed by the PEMP. In Fig. 4b, the enablement of node A, the termination of node B as well as the enablement and termination of the newly introduced node F can be observed by a PEMP.

With the consolidation of measured region model information and PEMP definitions the *event monitoring model* is created. Based on that, several algorithms can be run to analyze which information can be derived out of the spread PEMPs. For instance, it is possible to indicate whether the effects of a process model change can be identified and quantified to enable process analysis on multi-version processes.

4.4   Determining the Evaluation of Process Model Change Effects

Based on the event monitoring model, it is possible to determine if and how process changes influence a particular point-to-point duration metric. We categorize the determinability of effects caused by a process change to a process metric into the following four groups:

○ Unchanged—the process model changes do not effect on the process metric.
○ Indeterminable—the effects of process model changes cannot be identified nor quantified for any process instance.
○ Determinable—the effects of process model changes can be identified and quantified for all process instances.
○ Partly Determinable—the effects of changes can be identified and quantified only for some process instances.

We consider not only the process versions but the single process instances for categorization as we would like to provide a detailed indication on the determinability of the quantification of process changes. If there are changes whose effects can not be determined exactly, the algorithm determines whether this indeterminability holds for all process instances. To give an example, an indeterminable change in a sequence of process fragments will cause the effect of the whole sequence to be indeterminable. In the contrary, an indeterminable change in a branch of an XOR causes only those process instances that executed that particular branch to be indeterminable, thus, the effects are partly determinable.

Changes can be quantified, if their effects can be measured by PEMPs. This is the case when the beginning and the end of the added, removed or changed process fragment, e.g., the insertion of an activity, can be measured by a PEMP. As shown in Fig. 4b, for the added activity F the enablement and termination can be measured. Thus, additional time spend during process execution that may result from the activity F can be identified and quantified to allow a comparison between the initial process version and the changed one containing activity F.

The process model changes may not be measurable directly. One can think of only measuring the enablement or the termination of F or nothing. In this case, the predecessor resp. successor activities may provide some more insights with respect to the timestamps of the newly introduced process fragment. If we assume that two activities are in sequence and between the termination of the first activity and the enablement of the second activity no time is consumed, then we can use the rule, that the measured termination of the first activity is also the time of the unmeasured enablement of the second activity and vice versa.

With the categorization of the determinability of effects caused by a process change to a process metric, it is stated whether algorithms that quantify the changes, e.g., by calculating the duration influence, could be applied or not. Such calculations are not in scope of this paper, however, we will give an example in our case study where we validate the approach based on the motivating example.

The presented approach was illustrated along the point-to-point duration metric. However, the approach can be adapted to other metrics as well, e.g., point-to-point cost metric, the probability to reach a certain point in the process, or the number of iterations in a process. As long as the metric has a defined start and end point the approach can be applied as described with (i) transforming the process model into a measured region model based on the start and end points, (ii) enriching the measured region model with change information, (iii) build the event monitoring model, and (iv) evaluate the effects to the metric cased by process model changes if possible.

5 Case Study

In the following, we will apply the presented approach to our motivating example shown in Section 3. As shown in Fig. 1, we have a source process model (process version 1), on which the insertion of a process fragment, i.e., the insertion of the activity "Perform Sonography" is performed. This change is logged in the corresponding process model change log and described as *Insert(Perform Sonography after Examine Patient)*. This indicates that the additional activity needs to be inserted after activity "Examine Patient". As already stated in Section 3, the required point-to-point duration metrics reaches from the enablement of the activity "Examine Patient" until the completion of patient's data updates. Furthermore, in the two process versions six different PEMPs are defined. $PEMP_1$ and $PEMP_2$ representing the start and the end of the activity "Analyze Blood Samples". $PEMP_3$ and $PEMP_4$ providing time measures for the enablement resp. termination of activity "Examine Patient", $PEMP_5$ indicating the termination of the sonography, and $PEMP_6$ providing information about the termination of the activity "Update Patient's Records". Based on this information, we will evaluate if the effect of adding the sonography to the diagnosis process can be identified and quantified.

Therefore, the point-to-point duration metrics and the process model, see Fig. 1a is used to create a measured region model, as it can be seen in see Fig. 5a. The specialty with the process model in our example is that we need to consider the upper branch of the AND split as well, although the beginning of the point-to-point duration metrics is specified just in lower branch. However, the upper branch will influence the duration in cases when "Analyzing blood samples" will take more time than the patient examination (process version 1) resp. patient examination and sonography (process version 2).

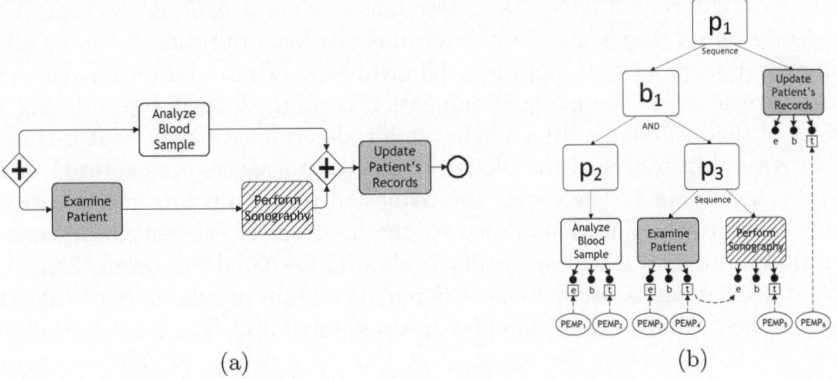

(a)   (b)

Fig. 5. (a) shows the measured region model enriched by changes from the process change log that is then transformed in an event monitoring model (b)

Afterwards, the changes contained in the change log are applied to the measured region model. In the change log only the insertion of activity "Perform Sonography" is recorded. Marking the corresponding process fragment in the measured region model simulates this change, see Fig. 5a - shaded activity.

Using the measured region model as a basis, the event monitoring model is build by constructing a component tree first, see Fig. 5b. The component tree is then enhanced by the life cycle information for each node. In the example, the same life cycle consisting of state transactions enable, begin and terminate and the corresonding states enabled, running and terminated is used for all activities. To these state transitions the corresponding PEMPs are assigned and therewith the event monitoring model is complete.

Having the event monitoring model, we can determine, that we can quantify the effects caused by the insertion of activity "Perform Sonography". The evaluation could happen due to the fact that we can measure the completion of the sonography, i.e., by $PEMP_5$. Further, we can determine the enablement of the sonography by utilizing $PEMP_4$ that is assigned to the termination of activity "Examine Patient", the predescessor of the inserted activity. Since we assume that during control flow no time is consumed this assumption holds.

In the following, we execute the approach to the motivating example for calculating the overall effect of all changes related to a particular point-to-point duration. We call these effects *duration delta*. Each structural change can be broken down to the addition or removal of process fragments. The local duration delta of such a change is thus equal to the duration of the added or removed process fragments. Once all local duration deltas are determined, we need to compute their effects on the overall duration. This can be done by applying techniques that are very similar to the aggregation of quality of service properties for process models, as described in [10] or [11]. These techniques determine the value of properties like execution time or cost for a whole process model, given the corresponding property values for each atomic process element. We can aggregate all local duration deltas to compute the duration delta for the whole process instance. We use a recursive calculation of duration deltas, which starts with the root fragment and terminates when a node is reached. When the recursion reaches a node, we determine the local duration delta for all its instances (remember that loops may be involved). The local duration deltas are then aggregated by the parent fragments according to their types during the roll-up of the recursion until a single value is determined by the root fragment.

For several instances of the diagnosis process, measures are captured by the PEMPs, see Table 1. Therewith, the requested point-to-point duration as well as the effect to the duration caused by the insertion of the sonography can be quantified. Patient 1 needs for the diagnosis after his blood was taken 82 minutes, patient 2 118 minutes, and patient 3 85 minutes. From this data, we can say that a patient needs in average 95 minutes (process version 1). The following patients where treated including the sonography. Patient 4 needs 132 minutes, patient 5 103 minutes, and patient 6 122, in average 119 minutes (process version 2). These results are not easy to compare adequately. For example, if we calculate

Table 1. Measures during patient diagnosis process correlated to PEMPs. The ID of the patient identifies process instances.

patientID	$PEMP_1$	$PEMP_2$	$PEMP_3$	$PEMP_4$	$PEMP_5$	$PEMP_6$
1	08:32	08:58	08:32	09:35		09:54
2	09:05	10:40	09:55	10:10		11:03
3	09:43	10:46	09:43	10:55		11:08
4	10:02	10:10	10:02	10:55	11:58	12:14
5	13:30	14:52	13:30	14:05	14:49	15:13
6	13:42	13:56	13:42	15:00	15:36	15:44

the average of all patient diagnoses, we will get 107 minutes. That will lower the good results of the processing time of the first versions and increase the result of the second process version. More comparable results would be achieved by hiding the results of the sonography for the multi-version process analysis. In that case, the durations of the first three patients will remain, but the results for patient 4 will change to 69 minutes, and for patient 6 to 86 minutes. For patient 5 103 minutes will remain as well, be cause in her case the blood analysis was on the critical path. With these results we will get an average of 90,5 minutes, which is more meaningful instead of comparing process versions without considering the effects of process changes.

With these numbers, the questions raised in Section 3 can be answered. (i) What are the diagnosis durations after adding sonography activity? This can be answered by comparing the average durations of process version 1 (95 minutes) and process version 2 (119 minutes). The sonography extends the diagnosis duration by 24 minutes in average. (ii) Are the durations for the unchanged part of the model different before and after adding sonography? The answer is yes, as we can see if we hide the sonography durations, the overall run time got slightly better. Process version 1 took 95 minutes in average; if we compare all process instances (process version 1 and 2) then the average is 4,5 minutes faster.

Multi-version process monitoring and analysis is enabled by these measures and the ability to quantify process model changes. It brings huge benefits to the evaluation phase of the BPM life cycle and therewith allows better improvements on business processes.

6   Related Work

The presented work builds on process versions and their process model changes. However, we abstract from actual details of version management methods and assume that the implemented version management method provide two essential functionalities: (1) retrieving a specific process version and (2) retrieving the set of change operations that transform one process version into another. The version management methods [12] and [13] meet these assumptions. [12] proposes a method for version control of process models based on change operations. The initial version of a process is stored as a whole, while all succeeding versions are only stored as the set of basic change operations. [13] decomposes process models into process fragments using SESE components, which then are used as the primary entities of a versioning system for process models.

One of the inputs for our approach is the process model change log. These changes can be described by change patterns that are investigated in multiple works. In [14] change patterns on arbitrary process fragments are used to model, store and retrieve process variants resp. versions by utilizing the concept of adjustment points. [15] defines a set of change patterns on canonical SESE components in a RPST. Based on these patterns, the authors are able to determine all changes needed to transform one process model into another. This technique could be used to determine the set of change operations between two process versions, if the version management method cannot provide them. Weber et. al [9] define an extensive and detailed classification of changes to process models into so-called *adoption patterns*. We used these adaption patterns in our approach, because they provide the right level of abstraction by being detailed enough to unambiguously define their effects on a process model, while still carrying enough semantic information to determine the intention behind the changes.

The approach presented in this paper aims to enable business process intelligence (BPI) in multi-version process execution environments. The capability to monitor, visualize, and evaluate business process execution is one core topic of BPI [2], which addresses "managing process execution quality by providing several features, such as analysis, prediction, monitoring, control, and optimization" [3]. Bringing awareness about process changes that influence process metrics can be seen as one of that features of BPI. In [2], the authors argue that process monitoring and analysis are vital to BPI and propose, based on the specific requirements of BPI, a reference architecture, composed of an integration layer, a functional layer, and a visualization layer. The approach presented in this paper targets at the functional layer, i.e., enabling the comparability of process execution measurements from several process versions.

Del-Río-Ortega et al. [16] introduced the concept of process performance indicators (PPI), the process related form of key performance indicators, to enable process evaluation. PPIs target on process measurements, e.g., time, costs, and occurrences. Our presented approach could support the measurements from several process versions and can ensure the comparability of the PPIs.

7   Conclusion

In this paper, we presented an approach to determine whether the effects of process model changes influences a particular process metric, i.e., a point-to-point duration metric. We further investigate if the influences can be quantified so that a multi-version process analysis is applicable. Therefore, we reduce the original process model to a measured region model based on the given point-to-point duration metric to identify the metric influencing process model elements. Based on the measured region model, we apply the corresponding process model changes recorded in the change log and structure the resulting model via a component tree. The component tree is enriched by the life cycle information for every node and the corresponding process event monitoring points are attached to it. This enriched component tree form the event monitoring model that could be used for determining whether the process model changes could be identified and quantified to ensure a reliable multi-version process analysis. Motivated by an example from a German hospital, we show the whole technique for a diagnosis process.

In this paper, we used the point-to-point duration process metric as example. The effects on other specific process metrics can be determined with the event monitoring model as well, which we will prove in future work. Our approach does not consider indirect dependencies between process elements nor non-structural properties of process elements. We disregard sub-process relations as such process models could be flattened. The approach does not support process models with nested loops, multi-instance nodes and loop nodes.

With the approach multi-version process analysis is possible. Effects of process model changes may can be identified and quantified and hide for several process analysis tasks. The approach applies also to process monitoring and process simulation. It is possible to simulate process model changes and evaluate the behavior of the surrounding nodes with respect to the given process metric.

Acknowledgment. Many thanks to the former student Philipp Maschke for the related initial work done during his master thesis, and the many fruitful discussions about the topic, its challenges, and the possible solutions.

References

1. Weske, M.: Business Process Management: Concepts, Languages, Architectures, 2nd edn. Springer (2012)
2. Mutschler, B., Reichert, M.: Business Process Intelligence. EMISA Forum 26(1), 17–31 (2006)
3. Grigori, D., Casati, F., Castellanos, M., Dayal, U., Sayal, M., Shan, M.C.: Business Process Intelligence. Comput. Ind. 53(3), 321–343 (2004)
4. Azvine, B., Cui, Z., Nauck, D., Majeed, D.: Real Time Business Intelligence for the Adaptive Enterprise, p. 29. IEEE (2006)
5. Vanhatalo, J., Völzer, H., Leymann, F., Moser, S.: Automatic Workflow Graph Refactoring and Completion. In: Bouguettaya, A., Krueger, I., Margaria, T. (eds.) ICSOC 2008. LNCS, vol. 5364, pp. 100–115. Springer, Heidelberg (2008)
6. van der Aalst, W.M.P.: Verification of Workflow Nets. In: Azéma, P., Balbo, G. (eds.) ICATPN 1997. LNCS, vol. 1248, pp. 407–426. Springer, Heidelberg (1997)
7. Herzberg, N., Meyer, A., Weske, M.: An Event Processing Platform for Business Process Management. In: EDOC, Vancouver (to appear, 2013)
8. Vanhatalo, J., Völzer, H., Koehler, J.: The Refined Process Structure Tree. Data & Knowledge Engineering 68(9), 793–818 (2009)
9. Weber, B., Rinderle, S., Reichert, M.: Change Patterns and Change Support Features in Process-Aware Information Systems. In: Krogstie, J., Opdahl, A.L., Sindre, G. (eds.) CAiSE 2007. LNCS, vol. 4495, pp. 574–588. Springer, Heidelberg (2007)
10. Jaeger, M.C., Rojec-Goldmann, G., Muhl, G.: QoS Aggregation for Web Service Composition using Workflow Patterns. In: EDOC, pp. 149–159. IEEE (2004)

11. Cardoso, J., Sheth, A., Miller, J., Arnold, J., Kochut, K.: Quality of Service for Workflows and Web Service Processes. Web Semantics: Science, Services and Agents on the World Wide Web 1(3), 281–308 (2004)
12. Bae, H., Cho, E., Bae, J.: A Version Management of Business Process Models in BPMS. In: Chang, K.C.-C., Wang, W., Chen, L., Ellis, C.A., Hsu, C.-H., Tsoi, A.C., Wang, H. (eds.) APWeb/WAIM 2007. LNCS, vol. 4537, pp. 534–539. Springer, Heidelberg (2007)
13. Ekanayake, C.C., La Rosa, M., ter Hofstede, A.H.M., Fauvet, M.-C.: Fragment-based Version Management for Repositories of Business Process Models. In: Meersman, R., et al. (eds.) OTM 2011, Part I. LNCS, vol. 7044, pp. 20–37. Springer, Heidelberg (2011)
14. Hallerbach, A., Bauer, T., Reichert, M.: Configuration and Management of Process Variants. In: Handbook on Business Process Management, vol. 1, pp. 237–255 (2010)
15. Küster, J.M., Gerth, C., Förster, A., Engels, G.: Detecting and Resolving Process Model Differences in the Absence of a Change Log. In: Dumas, M., Reichert, M., Shan, M.-C. (eds.) BPM 2008. LNCS, vol. 5240, pp. 244–260. Springer, Heidelberg (2008)
16. del-Río-Ortega, A., Resinas, M., Ruiz-Cortés, A.: Defining Process Performance Indicators: An Ontological Approach. In: Meersman, R., Dillon, T.S., Herrero, P. (eds.) OTM 2010. LNCS, vol. 6426, pp. 555–572. Springer, Heidelberg (2010)

Modeling the Transformation of Application Landscapes

Stefan Hofer

Software Engineering Group, Department of Informatics,
University of Hamburg, Germany
hofer@informatik.uni-hamburg.de

Abstract. Many of today's IT projects transform application landscapes. Transformation is a challenging task that has significant effect on an organization's business processes and the organization itself. Although models are necessary to accomplish this task, there are no specialized modeling approaches for transformation. We describe what such a specialized modeling approach should be capable of. This will allow the adaption of existing approaches and thus support the transformation of application landscapes.

Keywords: application landscape, enterprise architecture, transformation, migration, co-evolution.

1 Introduction

Enterprises use models of application landscapes for many purposes. One of them is to support the *transformation* of application landscapes like in the following example:

> An insurance company introduces a new customer relationship management (CRM) system which replaces a legacy application and provides new possibilities for handling documents. In addition, a back-office system replaces the previous custom-made software for commission calculation. Millions of data records need to be migrated to the new systems. Several applications (e.g. offer calculation, electronic application form, and bookkeeping) need to be adapted so they can exchange data with the new systems.
>
> Releasing all changes in a "big bang" approach seems too risky, so the company opts for an incremental transition in two steps:
>
> 1. Transition to an intermediate to-be landscape.
> 2. Transition to the final to-be landscape.
>
> The transformation affects the users because they have to adapt their work processes. For example, the "offer calculation" process has to be altered to avoid data duplication. Instead of entering the customer's data into the offer calculator, it has to be entered into the CRM system and then imported by the calculator.

J. Grabis et al. (Eds.): PoEM 2013, LNBIP 165, pp. 101–113, 2013.

Transformation may be triggered by business needs, legislation and strategic technological decisions. An organization, its business processes and its application landscape are interwoven and changes to one of them are likely to affect the others. This effect is called *co-evolution* (see [14]). Thus, transformation requires knowledge about applications and their dependencies, knowledge on how applications support business processes, and knowledge on how users work with applications. To acquire that knowledge, a vast amount of information has to be gathered and analyzed; information that changes frequently and cannot be gained by measuring and automated analysis only. Observations, interviews and assumptions add to the body of acquired knowledge. Models are a means to record this knowledge and make it accessible.

A large number of modeling tools[1] and notations support modeling of application landscapes. We claim that despite they have been in use to help transforming IT landscapes, they are not adjusted well enough for that purpose. For example, they give little guidance on how to create models from a huge amount of – possibly contradicting – information. Furthermore, it is often neglected in modeling that technical aspects and domain aspects of an application landscape need to be analyzed in conjunction with one another.

Our claim will be elaborated by presenting these contributions:

- We define what transformation of application landscapes means and how models are used in that area.
- We present six requirements that should be fulfilled by modeling approaches that are used to support application landscape transformation.
- We will show how well existing modeling approaches fulfill these requirements.

In conclusion, the reader will see that modeling approaches are currently not well suited for application landscape transformation and that adapted approaches would be useful.

The contributions presented in this paper are the result of ongoing research. Five real-world projects were analyzed to identify what characterizes "transformation" and to derive requirements for modeling approaches. The projects were conducted by companies from different domains, namely banking, logistics, and wholesale. The author was actively involved in three of those projects. Literature ([6] and [13]) served as additional input for the concept of transformation. All results presented in this paper were evaluated by seven experts that helped transform application landscapes as project manager, IT department manager, consultant, or software architect. None of the experts are affiliated with the author's employer or research group.

2 Transformation of Application Landscapes

The term *application landscape* "refers to the entirety of the business applications and their relationships to other elements, e.g. business processes in a company"

---

[1] For example, Buckl et al. list 41 of such tools in [2].

[4, p. 12]. More precisely, we will use this term only if the applications are used in the context of human work and some of the applications are directly used by people. As a counterexample, a group of applications that jointly and fully automatically carries out business processes is not considered an application landscape in the context of this paper.

Transformation is inevitable in the life cycle of application landscapes. We use the term to describe substantial, business-critical changes in an application landscape that have significant impact on an organization's business processes and on the people that work with the applications. Hence, transformation is a form of *co-evolution* which means "that the evolution of one domain is partially dependent on the evolution of the other [...], or that one domain changes in the context of the other." [14]

In this paper, we focus on the impact of transformation on business processes and on the people that execute them. This view was influenced by the concept of *application orientation* which is one of the main pillars of a software development approach called *Tools & Materials approach* (see [23]): "Application orientation focuses on software development, with respect to the future users, their tasks, and the business processes in which they are involved." [23, p. 4]. Accordingly, we aspire towards an application oriented approach to transformation of application landscapes. Yet, there are other aspects of application landscapes that are of importance for transformation, such as costs, maintainability, security, and scalability. They will, however, not be covered by this paper.

Transformation is usually carried out as a project that includes several types of activities:

- *Collect information*: Technical aspects (e.g. dependencies) and business aspects (e.g. supported business processes) of the application landscape have to be gathered. This is either done before or during modeling.
- *Evaluate and decide*: The goals of the transformation have to be defined and the current state of the application landscape has to be evaluated. For all affected applications, the necessary changes need to be identified.
- *Plan*: Planning activities for transformation are comparable with "regular" IT projects. A lot of tasks have to be aligned in order to fit into the overall roadmap.
- *Involve the organization*: Lots of communication is required to explain the goals, decisions and deadlines to all those affected by the transformation.
- *Execute*: The transformation is executed. The operations that constitute a transformation are:
  - bringing an application into service
  - changing an application
  - placing an application out of operation

More accurately, these operations are relevant to transformation projects only if they affect several applications (e.g. by adding a new dependency to the application landscape). Hence, "end-to-end" tests of business processes are required to ensure that the application landscape works as expected.

In this paper, projects that include these activities and transform an application landscape are called *transformation projects*. Although the list describes what activities are typical for transformation projects, it may not be complete. As mentioned in Sect. 1, this list of activities was derived from real-world transformation projects and evaluated by experts.

3   Modeling in Transformation Projects

The requirements we will lay down in this paper aim at increasing the value that models provide to transformation projects. To understand what value that is and who benefits from it, we will discuss the following questions:

- *How* and *what for* are models used?
- *What kinds* of models are relevant for transformation projects?
- *What* is modeled?
- *Who* uses the models?

We will answer these questions in the following subsection. Examples for use of models in transformation projects conclude this section.

3.1   Characteristics of Modeling in Transformation Projects

In transformation projects, models are often used to evaluate the current state of an application landscape and to develop possible future states. The main purpose of the latter is to explore possibilities and to anticipate the consequences of transformation. This is of particular importance for the activities summarized as "evaluate and decide" in the previous section. In general, "the purpose of a model covers a variety of different intentions and aims such as perception support for understanding the application domain, explanation and demonstration [. . .], optimization of the origin, hypothesis verification through the model, construction of an artifact or of a program" [20, p. 86].

Transformation projects require models that depict the context in which an application landscape is used – the terminology of the domain, business processes and how the application landscape supports these processes. Models that represent a domain are called *conceptual models*. They may be interpreted as a "collection of specification statements relevant to some problem" [12, p. 42].

Other types of models used in transformation projects show the internal structure of an application landscape – its software systems and their dependencies. Models depict either what software systems and dependencies exist generally in the landscape or how they work together during the execution of certain business processes. Yet other types of models focus on the dependencies between software systems and the hardware they run on.

The activities described in Sect. 2 involve various stakeholders like domain experts, IT experts, managers, and users. Since different kinds of models are commonly used to support these activities, modelers are relevant stakeholders too. A stakeholder's view on the application landscape is shaped by their goals and activities and may differ substantially from other stakeholders' views. A view can be expressed with one or several models.

3.2   Examples

The following examples illustrate how models are used in transformation projects:

- As-is models of the structure of the application landscape foster discussion about the applications that might be affected by a transformation. Also, the models serve as a baseline for the development of to-be models that show possible future states of the application landscape's structure.
- As-is and to-be models are used to analyze which dependencies have to be added, deleted, or modified and which interfaces need to be changed or introduced.
- Some transformation projects are carried out in several releases, transitioning incrementally from the as-is state to the to-be state. Models are used to determine the technical and process-related dependencies. This allows to decide which changes will be carried out in which transition.
- Models are used to develop to-be processes that fit the to-be state of the application landscape. The transformation's consequences on the way users work with their applications are communicated with the help of such models.
- To-be models allow cross-checking the planned to-be state of the application landscape and its intended use. Such cross-checks are useful to detect shortcomings in the planned to-be states.
- Models are used to develop test cases that ensure that the application landscape supports the business processes as expected – during transitions and in the final to-be state.

Creation and use of models like in these examples require a suitable modeling approach. In the next section, we will describe what constitutes such an approach.

4   Six Requirements for a Modeling Approach for Transformation Projects

A graphical modeling approach should provide a modeling language and a modeling procedure (see [10]). In addition, we consider tool support essential for use in real-world projects. Furthermore, any modeling approach should provide means to achieve high quality of models. Quality attributes that generally apply to models are for example correctness, consistency and comprehensibility (see [15]).

We claim that there are additional requirements to modeling approaches that are due to the nature of transformation projects. Also, we argue that stakeholders would benefit from using a modeling approach that meets these requirements. The following collection of requirements was compiled from an application-oriented point of view. Hence, the requirements focus primarily on how application landscape, business processes and the people who execute them are intertwined. 12 requirements – derived from the same five real-world projects described in Sect. 1 – were evaluated by the same experts who assessed what activities are typical for transformation projects. The six requirements rated as most relevant are:

Requirement 1: The modeling approach should make the available information tion manageable.

A model is an abstraction of an original (e.g. an application landscape) that contains only selected properties of that original. It is generally assumed that all the properties of the original are known and that the selection of properties that are represented in the model is driven by the goal of the model. However, this assumption does not hold in the context of application landscapes. There is extensive information available about an application landscape and its use. In large organizations this information changes constantly. Since transformation projects do not only require technical information but also information on how the landscape is used, the problem is aggravated:

> "The only complete specification of a system is the system itself, and the only complete specification of the use of a system is an infinite log of its actual use [. . .]." [5, p. 255].

For these reasons, it is not possible to create a "complete" model within limited time and effort. Information on complex application landscapes is both incomplete and beyond comprehensibility. Therefore, a modeling approach should provide some guidance on how to create and use models in such an environment.

Requirement 2: The modeling approach should be able to express contradictions.

It is tempting to assume that models of application landscapes show facts. After all, applications are technical systems and information about them can be measured or at least gathered automatically. But even if that were the case with all the technical information, some interpretation is necessary to create models from that information. In addition to technical information, transformation projects require information about how people use an application landscape (see Sect. 3). In some cases, log files can be used to analyze application usage (see [21]). But to a certain extent modelers have to rely on interviews and observations. Hence, modeling in the context of application landscapes is a *social process*. It has to account for the personal goals and needs of the people involved. For example, a stakeholder might present an assumption as a fact, withhold information, or (consciously or not) falsify information. In such an environment, contradictions will emerge.

Requirement 3: The modeling approach should be able to express *how* an application landscape supports business processes.

In transformation projects, stakeholders use models to understand which business processes depend on which applications. However, this information does not suffice to plan how work processes and organizational units are affected by the transformation. This requires knowledge of *how exactly* applications are used in business processes. In particular, this information is needed for testing.

Requirement 4: The modeling approach should be able to express an application landscape's dependencies even for business processes that use several applications and are carried out by more than one organizational unit.

Models of such processes are prone for errors as the people that are involved in them usually are familiar with fragments of the process only. The information they can provide on how application landscapes and business processes work together may be inaccurate. The division of work results in little understanding of overall processes. Modeling approaches should consider that.

Requirement 5: The modeling approach should be able to express dependencies between applications even if they cannot be mapped to technical interfaces.

There are various kinds of dependencies in an application landscape like calls (of functions, methods etc.), shared data, shared hardware (e.g. same network segment), and shared runtime environments (e.g. virtual machine). At least in theory, some information about dependencies can be gathered by analyzing interface access. This increases confidence in the information that is depicted in a model. But there is another kind of dependency that does not correspond to any technical interface and can only be recognized by analyzing business processes: Dependency by time and order. For example, a stakeholder may use the results of one task (carried out with application A) to decide, how to carry out another task with application B. If application A was to be changed or replaced in a transformation project, the way how stakeholders use application B could be affected. Such dependencies have to be considered in transformation projects and in modeling.

Requirement 6: The modeling approach should be able to express how an application landscape changes over time.

As illustrated by the example in Sect. 1, application landscapes undergo a series of changes until their desired state is reached at the end of a transformation project. Thus, it is important for stakeholders to know how and when changes will affect their work processes. This is not just a matter of project planning but of communication.

In the next section, we will evaluate how well existing modeling approaches meet the requirements.

5 Evaluation of Existing Modeling Approaches

The goal of this evaluation is to test our claim that existing approaches are not suited well enough for transformation projects. As mentioned in Sect. 1 there is a large number of modeling languages, frameworks and tools that deal with application landscapes. Our evaluation focuses on approaches that fulfill certain criteria or are open for extension so that the criteria could be fulfilled by adapting the approach. The criteria are:

- The approach consists of a modeling notation, a methodology for creation and use of models, and tool support.
- The approach can express different views on an application landscape (as described in Sect. 3). It is able to depict technical information and domain knowledge.

Since these criteria are possibly matched by many professional modeling tools we chose one tool as a representative and omitted other commercial products from the evaluation.

In the following sub-sections we will give a short introduction to the approaches that were included in the evaluation. The section is concluded with the results of the evaluation.

5.1   UML

The *Unified Modeling Language* (*UML*, see [19]) has its origins in the area of software engineering but lays claim to be much more versatile:

> "UML is a general purpose language, that is expected to be customized for a wide variety of domains" [17, p. 211].

UML is adaptable and can be modified to depict application landscapes. Such an adaption is reported by Heberling et al. in [8]. Countless modeling tools support UML. However, UML does not include a methodology for how to create or use models:

> "[UML] is methodology-independent. Regardless of the methodology that you use to perform your analysis and design, you can use UML to express the results." [16]

UML was included in the evaluation for its extensibility and widespread adoption.

5.2   ArchiMate

ArchiMate was developed to model enterprise architectures (which application landscapes are a part of). It does not include a methodology but an informal description of usage scenarios that are expressed as a collection of *viewpoints* (see [18]). Since version 2.0, ArchiMate can be used in combination with *The Open Group Architecture Framework* (*TOGAF*, see [9]) for enterprise architecture development. However, TOGAF does not provide any guidelines on how to create or use ArchiMate models.

As UML, ArchiMate is a standardized and established modeling language that is supported by many tools and was thus included in the evaluation.

5.3   EAM Pattern Catalog

The EAM patterns described in the *Enterprise Architecture Management Pattern Catalog* [2] are a collection of problems and fitting solution patterns in the area of IT enterprise architecture management. This descriptive approach presents best practices for analysis, graphical representation, and information modeling. The patterns aim at enhancing existing approaches. For example, the catalog's *methodology patterns* concretize TOGAF and the *viewpoint patterns* show applications of UML, ArchiMate, and *software maps* (see [3]). Due to the nature of this approach, the criterion of tool support can be neglected.

Methodology patterns describe the use of models. Since this approach tends to interpret graphical models as mere visualization of an underlying information model, there is no guidance on how to create models. Yet, this approach was included in the evaluation because it is grounded in practice and many of the patterns are implemented by professional modeling tools.

5.4   MEMO

Multi-perspective enterprise modeling (*MEMO*, see [7]) is a framework for the development of domain specific modeling languages for use in enterprise modeling. Examples of such languages are the business process modeling language *OrgML* and the *IT Modeling Language* (*ITML*, see [11]) for IT management.

All MEMO languages share a common meta-model that ensures interoperability of languages. MEMO is meant to be extended and provides a meta-methodology for modeling that can be used to develop a language-specific methodology. A tool prototype demonstrates that tool support is feasible.

MEMO was included in the evaluation because it provides adequate concepts to create a modeling approach for transformation projects.

5.5   ADOit 5.0

ADOit is a commercial tool for architecture management developed by the BOC Group [1]. Its meta-model can be adapted to meet the requirements of transformation projects. Yet, already the meta-model's default configuration suffices to model technical and domain aspects of application landscapes. Although ADOit is not coupled to a specific methodology for creation and use of models there are predefined views and queries that suggest certain usage scenarios.

ADOit was included in the evaluation because of its adaptable meta-model and the availability of a free-of-charge community edition. The tool is relevant to the German market and documentation is available. The vendor proved to be accessible for discussion. However, it should be noted that these criteria might also be met by other vendors (and their tools, respectively).

5.6   BEN

The *Business Engineering Navigator* (*BEN*, see [22]) developed at the University of St. Gallen is an approach for managing IT enterprise architecture. It offers support for modeling IT and its relation to business processes. BEN provides some guidance on how to analyze models of application landscapes and tool support is available. It was included in the evaluation because it covers application landscapes from a business engineering perspective.

5.7   Evaluation

In this section, we rate how well the approaches that were described briefly in the preceding sections meet the requirements laid down in Sect. 4. The results are summed up in Table 1 and explained in the remainder of this section. We use the following values for the rating:

++ Requirement is fulfilled.

+   Rudimentary but insufficient solution for requirement.

=   Requirement not fulfilled but approach offers means for enhancement.

−   Requirement not fulfilled.

Table 1. Results of the Evaluation

Requirement	UML	ArchiMate	EAM-Patterns	MEMO	ADOit	BEN
1 manageable information	=	=	+	=	=	−
2 contradictions	+	−	−	−	=	−
3 business process support	++	+	+	+	+	−
4 dependencies across boundaries	++	++	+	+	+	+
5 non-technical dependencies	=	=	−	=	=	−
6 change over time	−	+	+	=	++	+

Requirement 1 (manageable information): To make the amount of information manageable, one can simply include less of it in a model – either by constricting the modeling language or by switching to a more coarse-grained, generalized perspective that omits detail. Even if a modeling approach does not support these mechanisms explicitly they can always be applied by convention. If an approach enforces such conventions (like UML by providing *profiles*, see [19]) we rated it with "=". The EAM patterns approach was rated "+" because for every concern it addresses corresponding *information model patterns*. These patterns help a modeler to identify which information is needed to provide a model for the given concern.

Requirement 2 (contradictions): Contradictions will catch a stakeholder's eye during modeling or during use of models. The approaches presented above give little guidance on how to model and contradictions are not mentioned at all. However, some approaches offer generic means to at least annotate contradictions. UML provides *stereotypes* and *tagged values* (see [19]) for that purpose and ADOit's meta-model could be adapted to achieve a similar possibility.

Requirement 3 (business process support): Several   approaches   can express which activities an application is involved in. UML offers *activity diagrams* and *partitions* (see [19], often called "swim lanes" in other approaches). ADOit allows modelers to link activities to applications. In addition, it provides several queries to analyze the usage of an application landscape in business processes. ArchiMate's *business layer* only allows for modeling of coarse-grained process chains but they can be linked with *services* and *components* in the *application layer*. Several similar viewpoint patterns can be found in the EAM pattern catalog. MEMO's meta-model includes a relationship between business processes and applications (see [7]) which allows for the creation of a MEMO language that fulfills this requirement.

Requirement 4 (dependencies across boundaries): The dependencies described in this requirement can be expressed with UML's activity diagrams and ArchiMate (for example with the *introductory* and *layered* viewpoint described in [18]). An overview of such dependencies is provided by so-called *Process Support Maps* that show which applications support which business processes. Such visualizations are described in the EAM patterns catalog (e.g. viewpoint patterns V-29 and V-30, see [2]), in ADOit, and in BEN.

Requirement 5 (non-technical dependencies): To express dependencies between applications that cannot be mapped to technical interfaces, both modeling language and methodology have to be considered. Since no approach provides both, none was rated "+" or "++". Approaches with extensive possibilities to depict dependencies or generic relation types were rated "=".

Requirement 6 (change over time): The approaches included in the evaluation provide three different means to express how an application landscape changes over time:

The first is provided by EAM patterns, BEN, and ADOit which allow to model the *life cycle* of applications. The second possibility is a model of the application landscape that combines as-is and to-be applications. ArchiMate (viewpoint "Implementation and Migration", see [18]) and ADOit support this kind of model. Additionally, ADOit offers a time-based filter that helps tracking changes over time. Third, BEN's tool support allows for pairwise comparison of models. This functionality can be used to compare as-is and to-be models with each other.

6   Conclusions and Further Work

In this paper, we introduced a type of project that deals with extensive changes to an organization's application landscape – *transformation projects*. We look at transformation from an *application-oriented* point of view that focuses on how an application landscape is used in business processes. This point of view relies on models of the application landscape and its use.

We argued that specific requirements for modeling exist in this area and that it would be beneficial for modeling approaches to meet these requirements. This would improve their suitability for transformation projects. Six such requirements were presented. An evaluation of existing approaches showed that some approaches provide means to fulfill some of these requirements. None of the approaches met all the requirements. However, it is not necessary to invent a completely new modeling approach for transformation projects. We plan to show that existing approaches can be complemented so that they are better suited for transformation projects. Therefore, we will create an enhanced approach to show the feasibility of this idea. The enhanced approach will then be evaluated to test our initial claim: Fulfilling the presented requirements leads to a more useful modeling approach for transformation projects.

References

1. ADOit Product Website, http://www.boc-group.com/products/adoit/
2. Buckl, S., Ernst, A., Lankes, J., Matthes, F.: Enterprise Architecture Management Pattern Catalog. Technical report, Technical University Munich (2008)
3. Buckl, S., Ernst, A., Lankes, J., Schweda, C., Wittenburg, A.: Generating Visualizations of Enterprise Architectures using Model Transformations. In: Reichert, M., Strecker, S., Turowski, K. (eds.) EMISA 2007. LNI, vol. P-119, pp. 33–46. GI, Bonn (2007)
4. Buckl, S., Ernst, A., Matthes, F., Schweda, C.: An Information Model for Managed Application Landscape Evolution. Journal of Enterprise Architecture 5, 12–26 (2009)
5. Carroll, J.: Making Use. Scenario-Based Design of Human-Computer Interaction. MIT Press (2000)
6. Engels, G., Hess, A., Humm, B., Jung, O., Lohmann, P., Richter, J., Voß, M., Willkomm, J.: Quasar Enterprise. dpunkt.Verlag, Heidelberg (2008)
7. Frank, U.: Multi-perspective enterprise modeling: foundational concepts, prospects and future research challenges. Journal of Software and Systems Modeling (2012) (online first article)
8. Heberling, M., Maier, C., Tens, T.: Visual Modelling and Managing the Software Architecture Landscape in a large Enterprise by an Extension of the UML. In: Position Papers of the 2nd Workshop on Domain-Specific Visual Languages at OOPSLA (2002)
9. Jonkers H., Band, I., Quartel, D., Franken, H., Adams, M., Haviland, P., Proper, E.: Using the TOGAF 9.1 Architecture Content Framework with the ArchiMate 2.0 Modeling Language. Technical report, The Open Group (2012)
10. Karagiannis, D., Kühn, H.: Metamodelling platforms. In: Bauknecht, K., Tjoa, A.M., Quirchmayr, G. (eds.) EC-Web 2002. LNCS, vol. 2455, pp. 182–195. Springer, Heidelberg (2002)
11. Kirchner, L.: Entwurf einer Modellierungssprache zur Unterstützung der Aufgaben des IT-Managements. Technical report, University Duisburg-Essen (2007)
12. Lindland, O., Sindre, G., Solvberg, A.: Understanding quality in conceptual modeling. IEEE Software 11, 42–49 (1994)
13. Matthes, F., Wittenburg, A.: Softwarekarten zur Visualisierung von Anwendungslandschaften und ihren Aspekten. Technical report, Technical University Munich (2004)
14. Mitleton-Kelly, E., Papaefthimiou, M.: Co-Evolution Of Diverse Elements Interacting Within A Social Ecosystem. In: International Workshop on Feedback and Evolution in Software and Business Processes (2000)

15. Mohagheghi, P., Dehlen, V., Neple, T.: Towards a Tool-Supported Quality Model for Model-Driven Engineering. In: Chaudron, M. (ed.) Models in Software Engineering. LNCS, vol. 5421, pp. 74–88. Springer, Berlin (2008)
16. Object Management Group: Introduction to OMG's Unified Modeling Language, http://www.omg.org/gettingstarted/what_is_uml.htm
17. Object Management Group: OMG Unified Modeling Language (OMG UML) Infrastructure 2.4.1, http://www.omg.org/spec/UML/2.4.1/
18. The Open Group: N116 ArchiMate 2.0 Viewpoints Reference Card, https://www2.opengroup.org/ogsys/catalog/n116
19. Rumbaugh, J., Jacobson, I., Booch, G.: The Unified Modeling Language reference manual. Addison-Wesley, New York (2005)
20. Thalheim, B.: The Science and Art of Conceptual Modelling. Transactions on Large-Scale Data- and Knowledge-Centered Systems 6, 76–105 (2012)
21. van der Aalst, W.M.P.: Intra- and Inter-Organizational Process Mining: Discovering Processes within and between Organizations. In: Johannesson, P., Krogstie, J., Opdahl, A.L. (eds.) PoEM 2011. LNBIP, vol. 92, pp. 1–11. Springer, Heidelberg (2011)
22. Winter, R.: Business Engineering Navigator. Springer, Berlin (2010)
23. Züllighoven, H.: Object-Oriented Construction Handbook. dpunkt.verlag, Heidelberg (2005)

From Business Intelligence Insights to Actions: A Methodology for Closing the Sense-and-Respond Loop in the Adaptive Enterprise

Soroosh Nalchigar and Eric Yu

Department of Computer Science, University of Toronto
{soroosh,eric}@cs.toronto.edu

Abstract. Business Intelligence (BI) and analytics play a critical role in modern businesses by assisting them to gain insights about internal operations and the external environment and to make timely data-driven decisions. Actions resulting from these insights often require changes to various parts of the enterprise. A significant challenge in these contexts is to systematically connect and coordinate the BI-driven insights with consequent enterprise decisions and actions. This paper proposes a methodology for closing the gap between what an enterprise senses from BI-driven insights and its response actions and changes. This methodology adopts and synthesizes existing modeling frameworks, mainly i^* and the Business Intelligence Model (BIM), to provide a coherent step-by-step way of connecting the sensed signals of the enterprise to subsequent responses, and hence to make BI and analytics more actionable and understandable. Applicability of the proposed methodology is illustrated in a case scenario.

Keywords: Business Intelligence, Data Analytics, Adaptive Enterprise, Sense-and-Respond, Modeling framework.

1 Introduction

Business Intelligence (BI) and analytics have gained a great deal of attention from both academic and business communities over past two decades [5]. These systems serve as *sensing* mechanisms of the enterprises by providing insights about their strategic goals, operations, performance, as well as the external environment, and assist them to *respond* to critical situations and take advantage of emerging opportunities. However, a critical challenge to the adoption of these systems is the lack of understanding of how to use analytics and the insights resulting from them to improve the business [20, 31]. In other words, a leading challenge in using insights from BI is to connect them to business operations and hence shorten the latency. Latency is defined as the time taken from something happening within or around the enterprise to the moment when it reacts to it [26].

J. Grabis et al. (Eds.): PoEM 2013, LNBIP 165, pp. 114–128, 2013.

BI-driven insights can stimulate corrective actions and changes within various layers and different parts of an enterprise [31]. For example, a manufacturing company that uses BI solutions may find an increasing trend in the production costs. To reduce the costs, this company may change the manufacturing layout or may decide to modify the inventory ordering policies. A hospital which uses analytics may see a long waiting time in the reception room and decides to increase the number of physicians and/or change their work schedules. A bank whose web analytics show a decreasing trend in number of online banking users and transactions, may decide to change the interface and the web-page design to make it more user-friendly and increase its ease of use. In all of these contexts, in order to trigger new changes across the enterprise and to take action at the right time, BI-driven insights must be easy to interpret, linked to business strategy, and embedded into organizational processes [20].

To tackle this problem, we propose a model-based methodology for closing the gap between what an enterprises senses from the BI insights and their response actions and changes. The proposed methodology adopts and synthesize several requirements engineering modeling frameworks, including i^* [28, 29, 32] and Business Intelligence Model (BIM) [8, 3, 1, 14], to provide a systematic and coherent way of connecting the BI-driven insights to the consequent business action and changes. Our methodology assists business users to conceptualize strategic goals and to design the sensing mechanisms for monitoring those goals. It helps them generate and analyze the alternative response actions, to make trade-offs between them, and to find the most suitable next action. Finally, the methodology aids analysts to obtain new requirements to adapt the BI system to the new enterprise context resulting from the sense-and-respond loop.

The rest of this paper is structured as follows. Section 2 reviews related work and highlights the need for the proposed methodology. Section 3 provides an example to illustrate and motivate the research problem. Section 4 presents the proposed methodology and illustrates its applicability on the motivating example. The paper ends with concluding remarks and future work directions in Section 5.

2   Related Work

In this section we review related works and published papers and clarify the position of this paper within previous works.

Managing change and facilitating adaptiveness has been a continuous theme in enterprise architecture [31]. In 1995, Stephan Haeckel proposed a sense-and-respond model of adaptive enterprise as a new management tool for achieving competitive advantage in dynamic business environment [13]. An adaptive enterprise has the ability to sense environmental signals sufficiently and to translate them quickly into meaning and subsequent actions [11]. Haeckel described the transformation from *make-and-sell* enterprise, characterized by high-volume/low cost mass production, to *sense-and-respond* enterprise which is modular, fluid, and effectively responds to dynamic and non-linear changes. He emphasized to design adaptive enterprise based on sense, interpret, decide, and act loops [13, 11, 12]. Inspired by Haeckel's works, Buckley et al. [4] and Kapoor et al. [18] proposed a technical framework for sense and respond business and performance management. Their framework utilizes and integrates optimization and analytics models to enable proactive management and control of business resources. They implemented prototypes and showed applicability of the proposed framework for adaptive inventory management and demand/supply conditioning in two pilot projects in IBM divisions. This line of research was continued by Chowdhary et al. [6], where they applied model-driven techniques to IBM Business Performance Management (BPM) solution and illustrated their framework in a scenario of a pilot project. Also, Kapoor et al. [19] proposed a model-driven development framework for a sense-and-respond supply chain.

Nguyen et al. [23] proposed a real time service-oriented BI architecture (called SARESA) that covers sense and respond loop and thereby aims to decrease the reaction time. They implemented and illustrated their approach in a mobile phone fraud detection application which analyzes the phone calls and issues relevant alarms in fraud cases. Panian [26] discussed the notion of real-time decisioning as an analytic approach that allows enterprise to automate the "next best action" based on performance goals. He proposed six general steps which needs to be accomplished in order to make real-time decisioning work. In another work, Panian [25] discussed the characteristics and benefits of Service-oriented Architecture (SOA) and suggested to use BI solutions as Web services in an SOA environment.

Although these works contribute to the field and aim to increase enterprise adaptiveness, the proposed solutions are either in the form of technical architectures for specific settings or in terms of a set of general managerial principles and guidelines. Indeed, there is a lack of enterprise models that allow for analysis of adaptiveness as well as a systematic step-by-step way of closing the sense-and-respond loop in business contexts. Yu et al. [31] discussed various research challenges and directions about adaptive enterprise architecture. They mention the lack of a framework that includes collection of modeling constructs from various frameworks (e.g., goal modeling [7], social modeling [32], system dynamics, and BIM framework) in order to model and analyze the change and adaptiveness of the enterprise.

Recent efforts have attempted to introduce business-level modeling to provide a higher level abstraction for BI. The BIM framework [3] conceptualizes the business operations, strategies, situations and performance indicators in a way that can assist exploiting the huge amounts of data collected by enterprise. An empirical evaluation of the BIM in a Toronto hospital reported that BIM models enhance communication between technical and business stakeholders and support implementation in BI projects [2]. Horkoff et al. [14] proposed a detailed and precise definition of BIM concepts and a methodology for development of these models. It reviewed and extended BIM reasoning techniques with composite and incomplete indicators, summarized information requirements and connected them to the proposed methodology. Horkoff et al. [15] used OWL Description

Logic (DL) to provide a formal semantics for BIM language. The semantics serves as a connection to DL reasoners in order to assist various "what-if?" analyzes, to detect inconsistencies, and to automatically classify defined concepts relative to existing concepts.

While the BIM modeling framework assists enterprises to utilize their data and provides them a better understanding of business, its connection to the action side has not been elaborated. In other words, BIM framework can help business users to sense and partially interpret how well they are doing with regarding to strategic goals, but it does not address the decide-and-act side of the sense-and-respond loop. We believe that business analysts need a more complete modeling framework which can assist them to achieve enterprise adaptiveness by closing the sense-and-respond loop thus making BI and analytics more actionable. The main contribution of this paper is to fill this gap by adopting and synthesizing the BIM framework with other frameworks in order to bridge the gap between BI-driven insights and consequent enterprise actions.

3   Motivating Example

In this section we consider a hypothetical example of a North American company, *TVStars Inc.*, in the market of electronics, whose main products are TV and Home Theatre. The company has the vision of becoming a prestigious market leader recognized for its high performance products. The CEO and other senior managers of the company understand that the current business market in which they are operating is highly competitive, dynamic, and rapidly changing. To survive and thrive in this environment, they believe the company must be able to sense and adapt to changing market needs, to predict and cope with emerging threats, and still be able to monitor and satisfy stakeholder needs.

To monitor business performance and to enable managers to make data-driven and fact-based decisions, the company has recently deployed a BI solution. In this system, the performance of the business is made visible to responsible managerial positions and analysts by using monitoring dashboards and graphical display functions in the user interface. Using the BI system, the company has found a downward trend in the number of new and loyal customers. Moreover, the analytics show that the manufacturing costs of the company are above the planned targets. Having these insights, the managers and other BI users aim to improve the business performance. In this condition, they have faced a critical challenge which is lack of understanding how to use the output of BI system to improve business performance. They find it challenging to derive suitable corrective actions from the insights provided by the BI system. They want to know: What are the possible business actions (enterprise responses) to deal with the current bad performance in the indicators? Is it a good idea to target a new market in Europe and to sell our products there? Should the company change the product packaging policies from outsourcing to insourcing and hence reduce the manufacturing costs? Which of these is the most suitable business actions in this situation? After following/implementing it, how can we monitor the improvements? What are the new requirements for the current

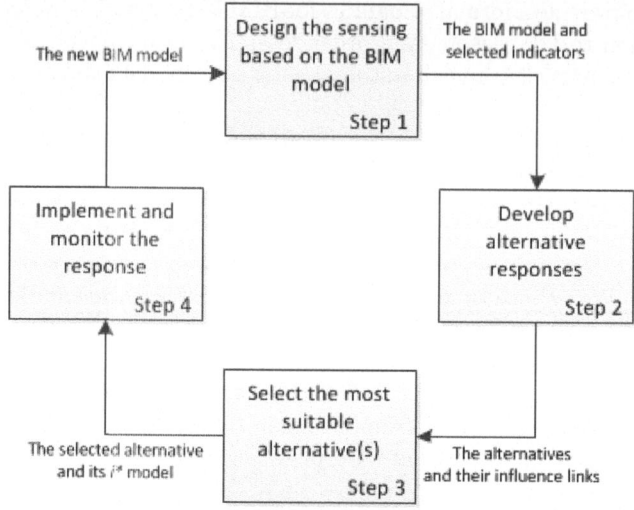

Fig. 1. Overview of the proposed methodology

BI system? How changes and enhancements to the BI system should be included as part of the response action? The main contribution of this paper is to propose a modeling framework that assist such organizations to facilitate coping with these challenges.

4   Proposed Method

In this section, we present the proposed methodology and show its application on the hypothetical example described in Section 3. Figure 1 shows an overview of the methodology and the inputs and outputs of the steps.

Step 1: Design the sensing based on the BIM model. In this phase, the first activity is to construct a business schema to support modeling and analysis of the enterprise and its performance. For this purpose, we use the BIM framework because it assists business users to utilize and make sense of huge amounts of data about the enterprise and its external environment. This framework provides business analysts with a modeling and query language to reason about business objectives, strategies, situations, tasks and performance indicators and hence to realize how well they are doing with respect to strategic goals and objectives. BIM draws upon well-known business concepts which makes it business-friendly and understandable for users. A methodology for constructing BIM models has been proposed in [14].

A BIM schema provides a picture of the goals structure of the enterprise along with the corresponding indicators and shows how well they are met. The BIM modeling concepts are adopted and synthesized from business and management literature and also requirements engineering sources, e.g. Balanced Scorecard and

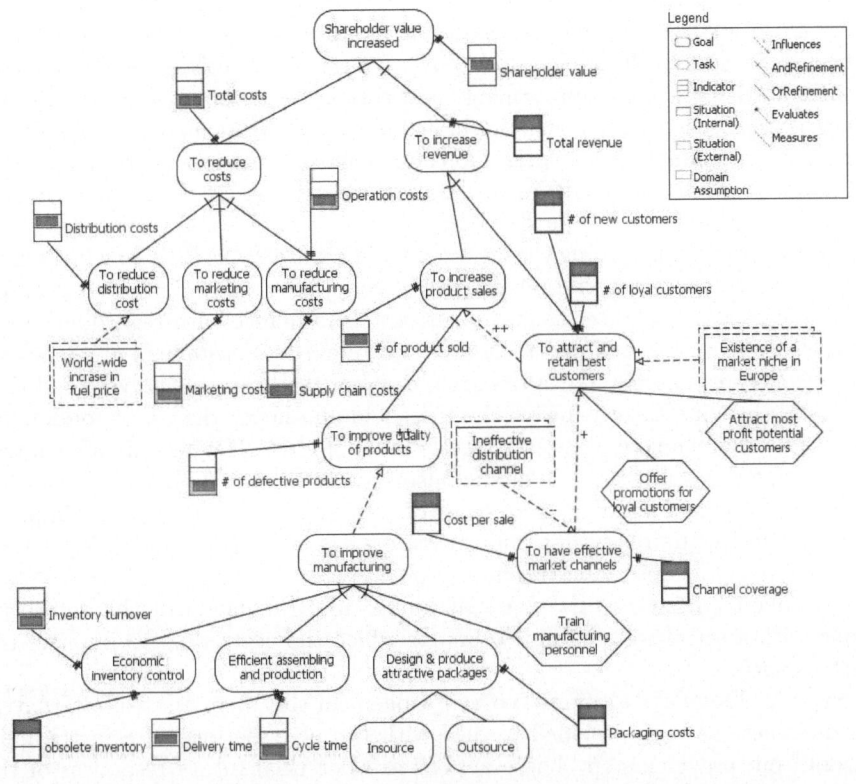

Fig. 2. Part of the *TVStars* BIM schema

Strategy Maps [17, 16], SWOT analysis (strengths, weaknesses, opportunities, and threats) [10], and goal-oriented requirements engineering [29, 9]. Reference [8] presents a full list of the concepts, definitions and examples of BIM.

Figure 2 shows part of the BIM schema of *TVStars Inc.* company, where the goal, influences and relationships, indicators (red on top, yellow on middle, green on bottom), and situations are modelled. The top level goal of the company is *shareholder value increased*. To achieve this goal, the company looks to meet the goals *to reduce costs* and *to increase revenue*. Moreover, to control the performance, the company have defined indicator(s) for each goal, e.g., *number of loyal customers* and *number of new customers* for the goal *to attract and retain best customers*. It shows how the organizational goals are refined into alternative actions that are means toward achieving those goals, e.g., a possible way *to attract and retain best customers* is to *offer promotions for loyal customers*. In addition, this model shows the external situations that are affecting the company's goals, e.g., *ineffective distribution channel* of the company, negatively affects the goal *to increase product sales*.

After constructing the BIM model, the next activity in the proposed methodology is to analyze the indicators and select those for which the current performance is not excellent (red and yellow zones). This activity results in a set of indicators for which improvements and corrective actions (i.e., enterprise response) are needed. Analyzing the indicators in the BIM model is part of the sensing step of adaptive enterprise loop and assists business people to understand how well they are doing with regarding to their strategic goals and what/where are the possible areas of improvements.

At the current time, using the BIM model in Figure 2, the *TVStars Inc.* senses that it has an average performance (yellow zone) in meeting its top goal. Moreover, the company realizes that the current performance with regarding to the goals *to increase revenue* and *to attract and retain best customers* are deficient, since the corresponding indicators are red. Also, the business analysts find that the *total costs* indicator is below the threshold and hence the corresponding indicator is in green zone, i.e., satisfactory level of costs. Having this model, and considering the competitive dynamic business market, the *TVStars Inc.* decides to undergo changes and take new course of actions in order to adapt and improve performance in the red/yellow indicators, e.g., *number of product sold, number of new customers*, and *total revenue*.

The main output of this phase, is an AS-IS BIM model of the enterprise along with a set of selected indicators for which the users want to improve the performance.

Step 2: Develop alternative responses. In this step, a set of alternative business actions are developed to deal with the poor performance in the indicators from previous step. These actions are potential future responses of the enterprise to what it has sensed. They could be in various business layers, involve different actors, and require different time, resources, and skills to be completed. The analyst adds these alternatives as new goals to the AS-IS BIM model from previous step.

After adding new alternatives, the next activity is to examine how each alternative is going to influence the other strategic goals of the enterprise. In particular, in order to model and consider the side-effects of the each alternative response, the analyst should examine how each alternative will impact the goals for which the current performance is excellent (green zone indicators). New influence links should be added to the BIM model to represents the possible effects of each alternative to other goals. These links facilitate the trade-off and decision making process among alternatives. At this step, the analysts can use the existing reasoning techniques on the BIM models to examine and answer a variety of strategic and analysis questions about effects of alternatives on the top goals of the enterprise. They can perform reasoning on the hierarchy of goals in order to evaluate different strategies for the satisfaction of top goals (forward reasoning), to evaluate the optimal input values leading to achievement of desired top goals (backward reasoning), as well as to perform analysis on goals inconsistencies and conflicts. Methods and techniques for reasoning with BIM models have been presented in [1, 14, 3, 2].

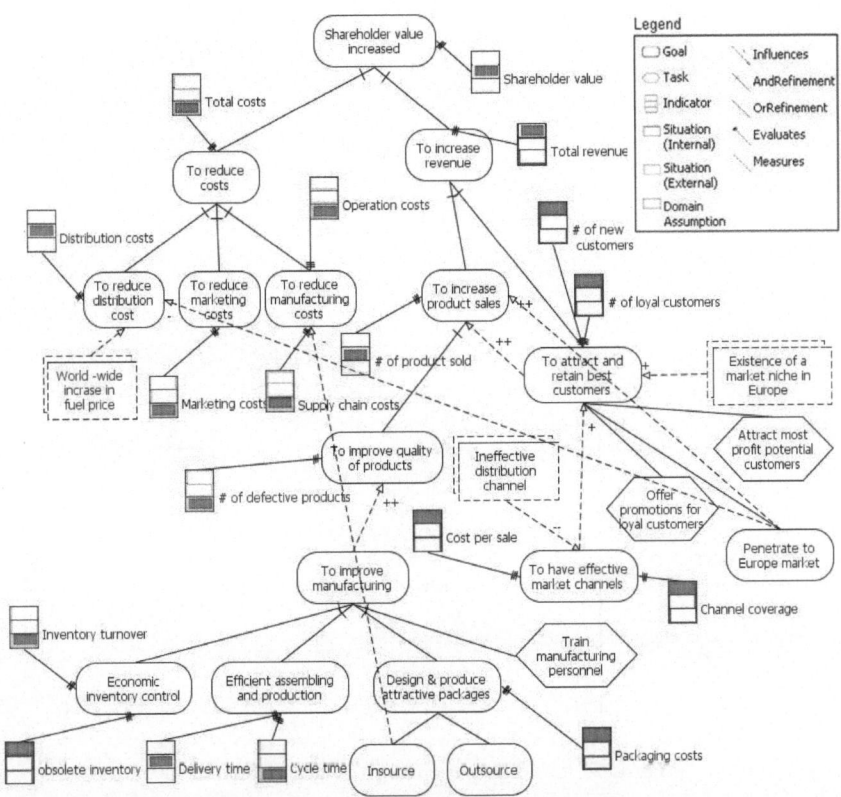

Fig. 3. BIM schema including the alternatives and their influence links

Figure 3 shows part of the new BIM schema for *TVStars Inc.* company. To generate this model, the BI analysts and the board of directors of the company examine and investigate the red and yellow zone indicators from previous step and after few meetings and discussions, they generate two alternative solutions that they believe could improve the indicators. Their first option is to *penetrate to a new market in Europe*. They believe that in this way they can increase number of new and loyal customers and hence increase the total revenue. Their second option is to change from outsourcing the package production to *insource* strategy, in which the company will design and produce the packages on its own. The analysts believe by insourcing the packaging of products, they will reduce the total costs of the company. Figure 3 also includes the new influence links of the alternative, showing that how these alternative will affect other strategic goals, e.g. penetrating to Europe market negatively affects the goal *to reduce distribution costs*.

The main output of this step is a BIM model which includes the alternatives along with their influence links to strategic goals.

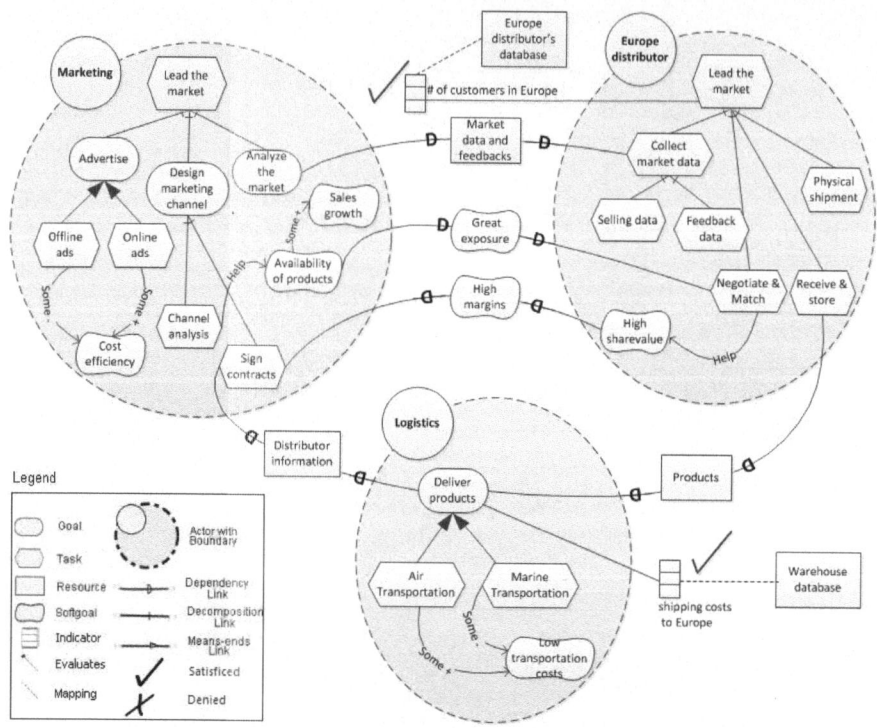

Fig. 4. i^* model representing the first alternative

Step 3: Select the most suitable alternative(s). In this step, the decision among alternative responses of the enterprise is made and the best action(s) is chosen to be implemented. To facilitate the organizational decision making process, i^* modeling framework is used to analyze each of the alternative responses. i^* models assist the analyst to provide a detailed picture of how the corresponding organizational setting would look like when the given alternative is chosen and implemented. In other words, these models are snapshots of the enterprise once the response action is adopted and help the enterprise users to know how the alternative will change the settings, e.g., new actors in the system, new dependencies and the potential TO-BE socio-technical context.

i^* models show the goal structure of social actors involved in the system and depict how the actors depend on each other to achieve their goals. Reference [30] reviews the recent applications of this modeling framework in practical industrial and business settings. Figure 4 shows the i^* model constructed for the first response alternative for *TVStars*. Using this model, the decision makers realize that if they decide to sell the products in Europe, a new actor *Europe distributor* would be part of the system. The *Marketing* department depends on this distributor to have a *great exposure* in the market which helps to achieve the softgoal *availability of products* and hence *sale growth*. The model shows them that the distributor depends on the marketing department to provide *high margins*, so he can achieve his internal softgoal *high sharevalues*. Also, the marketing department has a resource dependency to the Europe distributor to provide *market data and feedbacks* from European customers. Moreover, the analysts find that the Europe distributor will depend on the *logistics* department of the company to provide the products. In addition to external dependencies, the i^* model shows them internal goals of each actor and indicates decompositions and various ways of achieving those goals.

Figure 5 shows the i^* model constructed for the second alternative. It indicates that if the company follows the second alternative, the insource packaging task would be done as an internal task within the authority of *Manufacturing manager*. Also, it shows different productions strategies and their influences on the softgoals of manufacturing department.

After developing these models, the next activity of the proposed methodology is to decide about the new indicators that the enterprise needs to measure after implementing each alternative. This will assist enterprises to monitor, after implementation of an alternative, how well it is working and allows them to adapt again if the performance is not satisfactory. These indicators are added to the i^* models since these models are already showing the details of each alternative and can facilitate deciding about new indicators. The "measures" and "evaluates" links from the BIM meta model are used to connect the new indicators to the goals, tasks or the dependency links in the i^* model. Now, by having the new indicators in the i^* model, the analysts can examine if an indicator is accessible/computable or not. To facilitate that, the analyst connects each of the new indicators to the related existing data sources (as resources in the i^* model). The connection between indicators and data sources elements are made using mapping elements from the Conceptual Integration Modeling (CIM) framework [27]. Another way of making this connection is to use the traceability links (e.g., satisfiability) proposed in [22, 21] to connect each new indicator to the data warehouse schema of the enterprise. The accessibility/computability of indicators are used as a decision criteria while trying to find the most suitable alternative. If an analyst finds that there is not available data for measuring an indicator, this could result in removing the corresponding alternative from possible choices.

The last activity in this step is to select the most suitable alternative. As a set of criteria for this decision making, analysts and business actors consider the influence links that were developed in the second step of the methodology, the i^* models, and finally the feasibility of measuring the corresponding indicator(s) for each alternative.

Following the scenario of *TVStars Inc.* company, the analysts add two new indicators to the model in Figure 4, *number of customers in Europe* and *shipping costs to Europe* believing that these indicators are necessary for measuring the performance of this alternative. The analyst finds that the first alternative could be calculated from the *European distributor's database* and the second one could be computed from the company's *warehouse database* which is already operating in the logistics department. Hence, he marks these indicators as *satisfied* in the

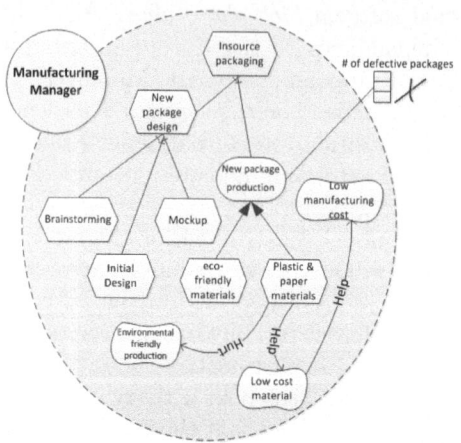

Fig. 5. i^* model representing the second alternative (See Figure 4 for legend)

model. Regarding the second alternative, the analysts realize that at the current stage, the databases of the company does not provide the required data for computing the indicator *number of defective packages*. Hence, he marks this indicator as *denied* (See Figure 5). Having this analysis and also by considering the estimated influences of the alternatives on the other strategic goals (See Figure 3), the analysts conclude that first alternative is more suitable for the current situation of *TVStars Inc.* company. Hence, they decide to follow the first alternative as the next most suitable action (i.e., the response to what they had sensed).

The main output of this step is the chosen alternative, its corresponding i^* model including new indicators, and connections to the data warehouse schema.

Step 4: Implement and monitor the response. The last step of the methodology includes the implementation of the chosen alternative, which is the enterprise's response to what it had sensed in the first step. The i^* models developed in previous step could be used to assist in the implementation. Besides, the enterprise can use the change management guidelines and principles existing in the literature. This step of the methodology also includes modifying the BI system to the new settings (i.e., chosen alternative) so the enterprise keeps track of how well it is doing with regard to its response(s). The analysts construct the TO-BE BIM model which includes the selected alternative from previous step and its associated indicators. This BIM model includes the new requirements for the BI system of the enterprise.

In the last step, the *TVStars Inc.* company penetrates to the Europe market and starts selling the products there. The company also modifies the BI system to include the new requirements, i.e., measuring the indicators related to the first alternative. After implementing the alternative and updating the BI system, the *TVStars Inc.* company has completed an iteration of the sense-and-respond loop.

To summarize, this methodology adopts and synthesizes a set of modeling frameworks to provide a systematic way of closing the sense-and-response loops of an adaptive enterprise. The methodology includes conceptualizing and modeling the strategic goals and objectives of the enterprise and thereby sensing how well the current performance is w.r.t. each of them. This is covered in the first step of the methodology (see Figure 2). The proposed methodology models various response alternatives to a given output of BIM model, as well as their associated indicators (see Figure 3). Our methodology includes modeling the social interaction and dependencies between various actors in an adaptive enterprise context. It aids business users to make trade-off between these alternatives, and finally to decide about the most suitable one (see Figures 4 and 5). Besides, it serves as a way to model the new requirements and adapt the BI system in a changing dynamic environment (see the last step of the methodology). By connecting the sensed signals of the enterprise to subsequent responses, we believe the proposed methodology can make BI and analytics more actionable and understandable for business users.

5   Summary and Future Research

BI platforms and data analytics techniques are widespread in businesses, where they assist users to sense and interpret the performance of the enterprise as well as its environment and facilitate decision making. In this context, there exist a gap between the insights resulting from these systems and the action(s) that the enterprise take to respond to the conditions. This paper proposed a methodology to fill this gap and to facilitate enterprise adaptiveness. The methodology synthesizes several existing modeling frameworks to provide a step-by-step coherent way of closing the loop between sense and response in an adaptive enterprise. Applicability of this methodology is illustrated in a hypothetical business setting.

The recent industry trend in "embedded BI" demonstrates increasing recognition of the benefits of adopting a closed-loop sense-and-respond paradigm. However, current solutions are typically limited to a single software application and aim at business process optimization and do not offer strategic enterprise modeling. The current proposal incorporates high level business modeling to support reasoning about alternative actions. The response actions include new sensing mechanisms (BI requirements) in the ongoing evolution of the sense-and-respond loops. The approach is not limited to a single application or business process, but it is intended to be enterprise-wide in scope, to be applied at all levels of business responsibility and performance management.

This research is part of a broader research agenda whose goal is to develop an adaptive enterprise architecture framework. This framework would include modeling, analysis and design tools and techniques to address adaptive enterprise requirements. Future research include implementing and evaluating the proposed methodology in a real case study. Further investigations on the understandability and communicability of the modeling concepts in proposed methodology should be made in future studies. Also, it should be examined how the proposed methodology increases the speed of reaction in the enterprise. In this paper, we showed the application of the methodology for closing closing a sense-and-respond loop at one particular level of iterative design cycles. In a complex organization, design and execution occur at many levels of time scales and scopes, as illustrated in [33]. Future works can address this. Moreover, we anticipate that there would be model libraries for various industries that could be reused as best practices for other market players. In future, the proposed methodology could be extended to include industry specific model libraries and hence to leverage the domain knowledge and existing experiences. Besides the BIM framework could be extended to include additional business level concepts, e.g., concepts from the Business Model Canvas [24], and hence to increase its expressiveness for modeling sense-and-respond loops of the enterprise. Finally, we are planning to extend the proposed methodology with a comprehensive catalog of applications of data mining and analytics techniques in business context. We aim to provide model-based support for assisting users to select the proper data mining and analytics techniques based on their business requirements. This catalog along with the modeling support will address the need of business users community for understandable ways of using data mining in an adaptive enterprise context. We leave these extensions to future work.

References

1. Barone, D., Peyton, L., Rizzolo, F., Amyot, D., Mylopoulos, J.: Towards model-based support for managing organizational transformation. In: Babin, G., Stanoevska-Slabeva, K., Kropf, P. (eds.) MCETECH 2011. LNBIP, vol. 78, pp. 17–31. Springer, Heidelberg (2011)
2. Barone, D., Topaloglou, T., Mylopoulos, J.: Business intelligence modeling in action: A hospital case study. In: Ralyté, J., Franch, X., Brinkkemper, S., Wrycza, S. (eds.) CAiSE 2012. LNCS, vol. 7328, pp. 502–517. Springer, Heidelberg (2012)
3. Barone, D., Yu, E., Won, J., Jiang, L., Mylopoulos, J.: Enterprise modeling for business intelligence. In: van Bommel, P., Hoppenbrouwers, S., Overbeek, S., Proper, E., Barjis, J. (eds.) PoEM 2010. LNBIP, vol. 68, pp. 31–45. Springer, Heidelberg (2010)
4. Buckley, S., Ettl, M., Lin, G., Wang, K.-Y.: Sense and respond business performance management. In: Supply Chain Management on Demand, pp. 287–311. Springer (2005)
5. Chen, H., Chiang, R.H., Storey, V.C.: Business intelligence and analytics: from big data to big impact. MIS Quarterly 36(4), 1165–1188 (2012)
6. Chowdhary, P., Bhaskaran, K., Caswell, N.S., Chang, H., Chao, T., Chen, S.-K., Dikun, M., Lei, H., Jeng, J.-J., Kapoor, S., et al.: Model driven development for business performance management. IBM Systems Journal 45(3), 587–605 (2006)
7. Chung, L., Nixon, B.A., Yu, E., Mylopoulos, J.: Non-functional requirements in software engineering. Kluwer Academic Publishers (2000)
8. Barone, L.J.D., Mylopoulos, J., Amyot, D.: The business intelligence model: Strategic modelling. Technical report, University of Toronto (April 2010)
9. Dardenne, A., Van Lamsweerde, A., Fickas, S.: Goal-directed requirements acquisition. Science of Computer Programming 20(1), 3–50 (1993)

10. Richard Dealtry, T.: Dynamic SWOT Analysis: Developer's Guide. Intellectual Partnerships (1992)
11. Haeckel, S.H.: Adaptive enterprise: Creating and leading sense-and-respond organizations. Harvard Business Press (1999)
12. Haeckel, S.H.: Peripheral vision: Sensing and acting on weak signals: Making meaning out of apparent noise: The need for a new managerial framework. Long Range Planning 37(2), 181–189 (2004)
13. Haeckel, S.H.: Adaptive enterprise design: the sense-and-respond model. Strategy & Leadership 23(3), 6–42 (1995)
14. Horkoff, J., Barone, D., Jiang, L., Yu, E., Amyot, D., Borgida, A., Mylopoulos, J.: Strategic business modeling: representation and reasoning. In: Software & Systems Modeling, pp. 1–27 (2012)
15. Horkoff, J., Borgida, A., Mylopoulos, J., Barone, D., Jiang, L., Yu, E., Amyot, D.: Making Data Meaningful: The Business Intelligence Model and Its Formal Semantics in Description Logics. In: Meersman, R., et al. (eds.) OTM 2012, Part II. LNCS, vol. 7566, pp. 700–717. Springer, Heidelberg (2012)
16. Kaplan, R.S., et al.: Strategy maps: Converting intangible assets into tangible outcomes. Harvard Business Press (2004)
17. Kaplan, R.S., Norton, D.P., Dorf, R.C., Raitanen, M.: The balanced scorecard: translating strategy into action, vol. 4. Harvard Business School Press, Boston (1996)
18. Kapoor, S., Bhattacharya, K., Buckley, S., Chowdhary, P., Ettl, M., Katircioglu, K., Mauch, E., Phillips, L.: A technical framework for sense-and-respond business management. IBM Systems Journal 44(1), 5–24 (2005)
19. Kapoor, S., Binney, B., Buckley, S., Chang, H., Chao, T., Ettl, M., Luddy, E.N., Ravi, R.K., Yang, J.: Sense-and-respond supply chain using model-driven techniques. IBM Systems Journal 46(4), 685–702 (2007)
20. LaValle, S., Hopkins, M., Lesser, E., Shockley, R., Kruschwitz, N.: Analytics: The new path to value. how the smartest organizations are embedding analytics to transform insights into action. MIT Sloan Management Review (2010)
21. Maté, A., Trujillo, J.: Incorporating traceability in conceptual models for data warehouses by using MDA. In: Jeusfeld, M., Delcambre, L., Ling, T.-W. (eds.) ER 2011. LNCS, vol. 6998, pp. 459–466. Springer, Heidelberg (2011)
22. Maté, A., Trujillo, J.: A trace metamodel proposal based on the model driven architecture framework for the traceability of user requirements in data warehouses. In: Information Systems, pp. 753–766 (2012)
23. Nguyen, T.M., Schiefer, J., Tjoa, M.: Sense & response service architecture (saresa): an approach towards a real-time business intelligence solution and its use for a fraud detection application. In: Proceedings of the 8th ACM International Workshop on Data Warehousing and OLAP, pp. 77–86. ACM (2005)
24. Osterwalder, A., Pigneur, Y.: Business model generation: a handbook for visionaries, game changers, and challengers. Wiley (2010)
25. Panian, Z.: Actionable business intelligence: how to make it available through service-oriented architectures. In: 2nd WSEAS International Conference on Computer Engineering and Applications, CEA 2008 (2008)
26. Panian, Z.: Just-in-time business intelligence and real-time decisioning. In: Proceedings of the 9th WSEAS International Conference on Applied Informatics and Communications, AIC 2009, pp. 106–111 (2009)
27. Rizzolo, F., Kiringa, I., Pottinger, R., Wong, K.: The conceptual integration modeling framework: Abstracting from the multidimensional model. arXiv preprint arXiv:1009.0255 (2010)

28. Yu, E.: Modelling strategic relationships for process reengineering. PhD thesis, Toronto, Ont, Canada (1995)

29. Yu, E.: Towards modelling and reasoning support for early-phase requirements engineering. In: Proceedings of the Third IEEE International Symposium on Requirements Engineering, pp. 226–235. IEEE (1997)

30. Yu, E., Amyot, D., Mussbacher, G., Franch, X., Castro, J.: Practical applications of i* in industry: The state of the art (mini-tutorial). In: 21st IEEE International Requirements Engineering Conference. IEEE CS (to appear, 2013)

31. Yu, E., Deng, S., Sasmal, D.: Enterprise architecture for the adaptive enterprise – A vision paper. In: Aier, S., Ekstedt, M., Matthes, F., Proper, E., Sanz, J.L. (eds.) PRET 2012 and TEAR 2012. LNBIP, vol. 131, pp. 146–161. Springer, Heidelberg (2012)

32. Yu, E., Giorgini, P., Maiden, N., Mylopoulos, J.: Social modeling for requirements engineering. MIT Press (2011)

33. Yu, E., Lapouchnian, A., Deng, S.: Adapting to uncertain and evolving enterprise requirements. In: Proc. 7th IEEE International Conference on Research Challenges in Information Science, pp. 155–166 (2013)

Improving Documentation by Repairing Event Logs

Andreas Rogge-Solti[1], Ronny S. Mans[2], Wil M. P. van der Aalst[2], and Mathias Weske[1]

[1] Hasso Plattner Institute, University of Potsdam
Prof.-Dr.-Helmert-Strasse 2-3, 14482 Potsdam
{andreas.rogge-solti,mathias.weske}@hpi.uni-potsdam.de
[2] Department of Information Systems, Eindhoven University of Technology, P.O. Box
513, NL-5600 MB, Eindhoven, The Netherlands
{r.s.mans,w.m.p.v.d.aalst}@tue.nl

Abstract. In enterprises, business process models are used for capturing as-is business processes. During process enactment correct documentation is important to ensure quality, to support compliance analysis, and to allow for correct accounting. Missing documentation of performed activities can be directly translated into lost income, if accounting is based on documentation. Still, many processes are manually documented in enterprises. As a result, activities might be missing from the documentation, even though they were performed.

In this paper, we make use of process knowledge captured in process models, and provide a method to repair missing entries in the logs. The repaired logs can be used for direct feedback to ensure correct documentation, i.e., participants can be asked to check, whether they forgot to document activities that should have happened according to the process models. We realize the repair by combining stochastic Petri nets, alignments, and Bayesian networks. We evaluate the results using both synthetic data and real event data from a Dutch hospital.

Keywords: documentation quality, missing data, stochastic Petri nets, Bayesian networks.

1 Introduction

Enterprises invest a lot of time and money to create business process models in order to use them for various purposes: documentation and understanding, improvement, conformance checking, performance analysis, etc. The modeling goal is often to capture the as-is processes as accurately as possible. In many cases, process activities are performed and documented manually. We call the documentation of activities in a business process *event logs*. When event logs are subject to manual logging, data quality problems are common, resulting in *incorrect* or *missing* events in the event logs [1]. We focus on the latter and more frequent issue, as in our experience it is often the case that activities are performed, but their documentation is missing.

For an enterprise, it is crucial to avoid these data quality issues in the first place. Accounting requires activities to be documented, as otherwise, if documentation is missing, potential revenues are lost. In the healthcare domain, for example, we encountered the case that sometimes the activity *preassessment* of a patient is not documented, although it is done always before treatment. In this paper, we provide a technique to automatically

J. Grabis et al. (Eds.): PoEM 2013, LNBIP 165, pp. 129–144, 2013.
© IFIP International Federation for Information Processing 2013

repair an event log that contains missing entries. The idea is to use repaired event logs to alert process participants of potential documentation errors as soon as possible after process termination. We employ probabilistic models to derive the *most likely* timestamps of missing events, i.e., when the events should have occurred based on historical observations. This novel step assists process participants in correcting missing documentation directly, or to identify the responsible persons, who performed the activities in question.

State-of-the-art conformance checking methods [2] do not consider timing aspects. In contrast, we provide *most likely* timestamps of missing events. To achieve this, we use stochastically enriched process models, which we discover from event logs [3]. As a first step, using path probabilities, it is determined which are the most likely missing events. Next, Bayesian networks [4] capturing both initial beliefs of the as-is process and real observations are used to compute the *most likely* timestamp for each inserted event. Inserted events are marked as artificial, as long as they are not corrected by the process participants. An extended version of this paper is available as a technical report [5].

The remainder of this paper is organized as follows. First, we present background on missing data methods along other related works in Section 2. Afterwards, preliminaries are given in Section 3. Our approach for repairing individual traces in an event log is described in Section 4 followed by a presentation of the algorithmic details in Section 5. An evaluation of our approach using both synthetic and real-life event data is given in Section 6. Finally, conclusions are presented in Section 7.

2   Background and Related Work

Missing data has been investigated in statistics, but not in the context of conformance checking of business processes. There are different types of missing data: missing completely at random (MCAR), missing at random (MAR), and not missing at random (NMAR), cf. the overview by Schafer and Graham in [6]. These types refer to the independence assumptions between the fact that data is missing (*missingness*) and the data values of missing and observed data. MCAR is the strongest assumption, i.e., missingness is independent of both observed and missing data. MAR allows dependencies to observed data, and NMAR assumes no independence, i.e., captures cases where the missingness is influenced by the missing values, too. Dealing with NMAR data is problematic, as it requires a dedicated model for the dependency of missingness on the missing values, and is out of scope of this paper. We assume that data is MAR, i.e., whether data is missing does not depend on the value of the missing data, but may depend on observed data values.

Over the years, multiple methods have been proposed to deal with missing data, cf. [6]. However, these techniques are focusing on missing values in surveys and are not directly applicable to event logs, as they do not consider control flow relations in process models and usually assume a fixed number of observed variables.

Related work on missing data in process logs is scarce. Nevertheless, in a recent technical report, Bertoli et al. [7] propose a technique to reconstruct missing events in process logs. The authors tackle the problem by mapping control flow constraints in BPMN models to logical formulae and use a SAT-solver to find candidates for missing events. In contrast, we use an alignment approach based on Petri nets, allowing us to deal with loops and probabilities of different paths. We also consider the time of the missing events, which allows performance analysis on a probabilistic basis.

Some techniques developed in the field of process mining provide functionality that enables analysis of noisy or missing event data. In process mining, the quality of the event logs is crucial for the usefulness of the analysis results and low quality poses a significant challenge to the algorithms [1]. Therefore, discovery algorithms which can deal with noise, e.g., the fuzzy miner [8], and the heuristics miner [9], have been developed. Their focus is on capturing the common and frequent behavior and abstract from any exceptional behavior. These discovery algorithms take the log as granted and do not try to repair missing events.

Another example is the alignment of traces in the context of conformance checking [2]. Here, the aim is to replay the event log within a given process model in order to quantify conformance by counting skipped and inserted model activities. We build upon this technique and extend it to capture path probabilities as gathered from historical observations. Note that the lion's share of work focuses on *repairing models* based on logs, rather than logs based on models. Examples are the work by Fahland and van der Aalst [10] that uses alignments to repair a process model to decrease inconsistency between model and log, and the work by Buijs et al. [11], which uses genetic mining to find similar models to a given original model.

3   Preliminary Definitions and Used Methods

In this section, we give a formal description of the used concepts, to describe the approach to the repair of missing values in process logs. We start with event logs and Petri nets.

Definition 1 (Event logs). *An event log over a set of activities A and time domain TD is defined as* $L_{A,TD} = (E, C, \alpha, \gamma, \beta, \succ)$, *where:*

- *E is a finite set of events.*
- *C is a finite set of cases (process instances).*
- $\alpha : E \to A$ *is a function relating each event to an activity.*
- $\gamma : E \to TD$ *is a function relating each event to a timestamp.*
- $\beta : E \to C$ *is a surjective function relating each event to a case.*
- $\succ \subseteq E \times E$ *is the succession relation, which imposes a total ordering on the events in E. We use* $e_2 \succ e_1$ *as shorthand notation for* $(e_2, e_1) \in \succ$. *We call the ordered set of events belonging to one case a "trace".*

Definition 2 (Petri Net). *A Petri net is a tuple* $PN = (P, T, F, M_0)$ *where:*

- *P is the set of places.*
- *T is the set of transitions.*
- $F \subseteq (P \times T) \cup (T \times P)$ *is the set of connecting arcs representing flow relations.*
- $M_0 \in P \to \mathbb{N}_0^+$ *is the initial marking.*

There have been many extensions of Petri nets to capture time, both deterministic and stochastic. In [12], Ciardo et al. give an overview of different classes. In terms of this classification, we use stochastic Petri nets with generally distributed transition durations.

Definition 3 (GDT_SPN). *A stochastic Petri net with generally distributed transition durations is a seven-tuple: GDT_SPN = $(P, T, \mathcal{P}, \mathcal{W}, F, M_0, \mathcal{D})$, where (P, T, F, M_0) is the underlying Petri net. Additionally:*

- *The set of transitions $T = T_i \cup T_t$ is partitioned into immediate transitions T_i and timed transitions T_t.*
- *$\mathcal{P} : T \to \mathbb{N}_0^+$ is an assignment of priorities to transitions, where $\forall t \in T_i : \mathcal{P}(t) \geq 1$ and $\forall t \in T_t : \mathcal{P}(t) = 0$.*
- *$\mathcal{W} : T_i \to \mathbb{R}^+$ assigns probabilistic weights to the immediate transitions.*
- *$\mathcal{D} : T_t \to D(x)$ is an assignment of arbitrary probability distribution functions $D(x)$ to timed transitions, capturing the random durations of the corresponding activities.*

Although this definition of GDT_SPN models allows us to assign arbitrary duration distributions to timed transitions, in this work, we assume normally distributed durations. Note that normal distributions are defined also in the negative domain, which we need to avoid. Therefore, we assume that most of their probability mass is in the positive domain, such that errors introduced by correction of negative durations are negligible.

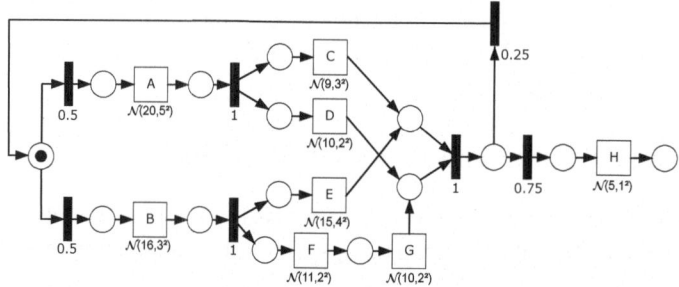

Fig. 1. Example unstructured free-choice GDT_SPN model

An example GDT_SPN model is shown in Fig. 1 and has immediate transitions (bars), as well as timed transitions (boxes). In the figure, immediate transitions are annotated with their weights, e.g., the process will loop back with a probability of 0.25, and leave the loop with 0.75 probability. We omitted priorities and define priority 1 for all immediate transitions. The timed transitions are labeled from A to H and their durations are normally distributed with the parameters annotated underneath. In this example, activity A's duration is normally distributed with a mean of 20, and a standard deviation of 5. Note that the model is sound and free-choice, and contains parallelism, choices, and a loop.

Because we allow generally distributed durations in the model, we require an execution policy [13]. We use *race semantics with enabling memory* as described in [13]. This means that concurrently enabled transitions race for the right to fire, and transitions will only be reset, if they get disabled by another transition firing.

For our purposes, we reuse the existing work in the ProM framework that extracts performance information of activities from an event log and enriches plain Petri nets to GDT_SPN models [3]. In [3], we discuss the challenges for discovering GDT_SPN models with respect to selected execution semantics of the model. The discovery algorithm uses replaying techniques, cf. [14], to gather historical performance characteristics and enriches a given Petri net to a GDT_SPN model with that performance information.

3.1 Cost-Based Fitness Alignment

Consider the example log in Fig. 2a consisting of two traces t_1, and t_2. To check, whether the trace fits to the model, we need to align them. We reuse the technique described by Adriansyah et al. in [2], which results in a sequence of movements that *replay* the trace in the model. These movements are either *synchronous moves*, *model moves*, or *log moves*. A formal description of the alignment technique is provided in [2] and remains out of scope of this paper. We only give the intuition. For an alignment, the model and the log are replayed side by side to find the best mapping of events to activities in the model. Thereby, a *synchronous move* represents an event in the log that is allowed in the

(a) example log:

t_1 :   ⟨A, C, D, B, E, F, G, H⟩
t_2 :   ⟨E, G, H⟩

(b) alignment for trace t_1:

log	A	C	D	B	E	F	G	H
model	A	C	D	B	E	F	G	H

(c) alignments for trace t_2:

(c.1)

log	≫	E	≫	G	H
model	B	E	F	G	H

(c.2)

log	≫	≫	E	G	H
model	B	F	E	G	H

Fig. 2. Example log and possible alignments for the traces

respective state in the model, such that both the model and the log progress one step together. However, if an activity in the model or an event in the log is observed with no counterpart, the model and log have to move asynchronously. Then, a *model move* represents an activity in the model, for which no event exists in the log at the current position and conversely, a *log move* is an event in the log that has no corresponding activity in the model that is enabled in the current state during replay. It is possible to assign costs to the different types of moves for each activity separately.

Fig. 2 shows some example alignments of the model in Fig. 1 and log in Fig. 2a. In Fig. 2b, a perfect alignment is depicted for trace t_1, i.e., the trace can be replayed completely by a sequence of *synchronous moves*. A closer look at trace t_2 and the model in Fig. 1 reveals that the two events B, and F are missing from the trace, which might have been caused by a documentation error. Because activity F is parallel to E, there exist two candidate alignments for t_2, as shown in Fig. 2c. The ≫ symbol denotes a step that is used to show empty moves, i.e., modeled and recorded behavior disagree. In this example, there are two model moves necessary to align the trace t_2 to the model.

Summarizing, the alignment technique described in [2,14] can be used to find the cost-optimal matches between a trace in a log and a model. However, the approach only considers the *structure* of the model and the sequence of events encountered in the log without considering timestamps or probabilities. In this paper, we enhance the alignment technique to also take path probabilities into account.

3.2 Bayesian Networks

GDT_SPN models capture probabilistic information about the durations of each activity in the process. We use Bayesian networks [4,15] to capture the dependencies between the random durations given by the GDT_SPN model structure. Fig. 3 shows an example Bayesian network that captures the relations for a part of the process model in Fig. 1.

The arcs between activities B, F, and G, and between B and E, are sequential dependencies. Note that there is no direct dependency between F and E, since they are executed in parallel, and we assume that the durations of these activities are independent. More generally, a Bayesian network is a directed acyclic graph and captures dependencies between random variables in a probabilistic model [15]. An arc from a parent node to a child node indicates that the child's probability distribution depends on the parent's values.

We use Bayesian networks to reason about our updated probabilistic beliefs, i.e., the posterior probability distributions in a model, once we assigned specific values to some of the random variables. Suppose that we observe trace t_2 in the log in Fig. 2a, with times $\gamma(E) = 30$, $\gamma(G) = 35$, and $\gamma(H) = 40$. Initially, the random variable of node B in the example has a duration distribution of $\mathcal{N}(16, 3^2)$, i.e., a normally distributed duration with mean 16, and standard

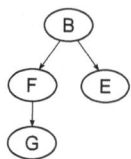

Fig. 3. Bayesian network for a fragment of Fig. 1

deviation 3. However, after inserting the observed times of events E, and event G into the network in Fig. 3, we can calculate the resulting posterior probability distributions by performing *inference* in the Bayesian network. In this case, the posterior probability distribution of B is $\mathcal{N}(14.58, 1.83^2)$. Note that by inserting evidence, i.e., constraining the variables in a Bayesian network, the posterior probability distributions get more accurate. In this example, the standard deviation is reduced from 3 to 1.83. The intuition is that we narrow the possible values of the unobserved variables to be in accordance with the observations in the log. There exist algorithms for Bayesian networks automating this process [16]. A complete explanation of Bayesian networks, however, is not the aim in this paper, and the interested reader is referred to the original work by Pearl [4] and the more recent text book by Koller and Friedman [15].

4   Repairing Events in Timed Event Logs

In this paper, we propose a method to probabilistically restore events in logs which contain missing events. In particular, we are interested in knowing when things happened *most likely*. The problem that we try to solve is to identify the parts in the model that are missing from the trace (which) and also to estimate the times of the activities in those parts (when).

In theory, we need to compare the probabilities of all possible paths in the model that are conforming to the trace. Each path may allow for different assignments of events in the trace to the activities in the model. For example, for trace t_2: $\langle E, G, H \rangle$ and the model in Fig. 1 two cost-minimal paths through the model are given by the alignments in Fig. 2.c. But, there might be further possibilities. It is possible that a whole iteration of the loop happened in reality, but was not documented. In that case, the path $\langle B, E, F, G, A, C, D, H \rangle$ would also be an option to repair trace t_2. Furthermore, the second iteration could have taken another path in the model: $\langle B, E, F, G, B, F, E, G, H \rangle$. In this case it is not clear to which iteration the events E and G belong. In general, there are infinitely many possible traces for a model that contains loops.

In order to compare the probabilities of these paths, we need to compute the probability distributions of the activities on the paths and compare which model path and which

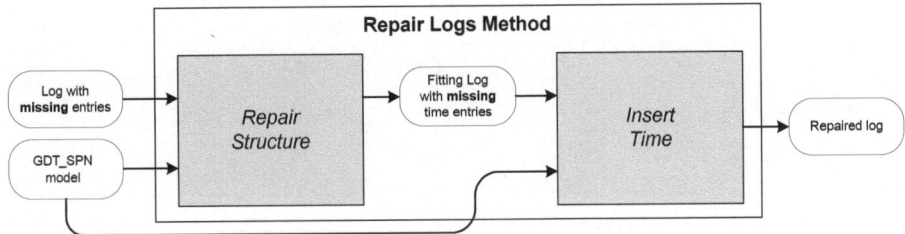

Fig. 4. We divide the problem into two subproblems: repairing the control flow, and repairing the timestamps

assignment explains the observed events' timestamps best. To reduce the complexity, we propose to decompose the problem into two separate problems, i) repair structure and ii) insert time, as sketched in Fig. 4. The method uses as input a log that should be repaired and a GDT_SPN model specifying the as-is process.

Note that by choosing this approach, we accept the limitation that missing events on a path can only be detected, if at least one event in the log indicates that the path was chosen.

5   Realization of Repairing Logs

In this section, we explain a realization of the method described above. For this realization, we make the following assumptions:

- The supported models, i.e., the GDT_SPN models, are *sound*, cf. [17], and *free-choice*, cf. [18], but do not necessarily need to be (block-)structured. This class of models captures a large class of process models and does not impose unnecessary constraints.
- The GDT_SPN model is normative, i.e., it reflects the as-is processes in structural, behavioral and time dimension.
- Activity durations are independent and have normal probability distributions, containing most of their probability mass in the positive domain.
- The recorded timestamps in the event logs are correct.
- Each trace in the log has at least one event, and all events contain a timestamp.
- The activity durations of a case do not depend on other cases, i.e., we do not consider the resource perspective and there is no queuing.
- We assume that data is MAR, i.e., that the probability that an event is missing from the log does not depend on the time values of the missing events.

The algorithm is depicted in Fig. 5, and repairs an event log as follows.

For each trace, we start by repairing the structure. This becomes trivial, once we identified a path in the model that fits our observations in the trace best. The notion of cost-based alignments [2] that we introduced in Section 3, is used for this part. It tells us exactly:

a) when the model moves *synchronously* to the trace, i.e., where the events match
b) when the *model moves* alone, i.e., an event is missing from the trace

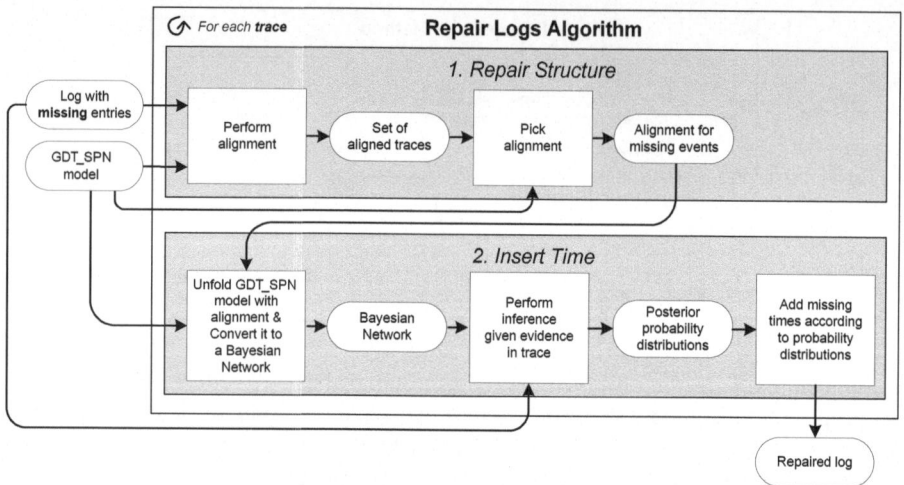

Fig. 5. The repair approach described in more detail

c) when the *log moves* alone, i.e., there is an observed event that does not fit into the model at the recorded position

We set the costs of synchronous and model moves to 0, and the cost of log moves to a high value, e.g., 1000. The alignment algorithm returns all paths through the model, where the events in the trace are mapped to a corresponding activity. This works well for acyclic models. For cyclic models, where infinite paths through a model exist, we need to assign some small costs to model moves, in order to limit the number of resulting alignments that we compare in the next step.

In the next step, cf. box *Pick alignment* in Fig. 5, we decide which of the returned cost-minimal alignments to pick for repair. The algorithm replays the path taken through the model and multiplies the probabilities of the decisions made along the path. This allows us to take probabilistic information into account when picking an alignment and enhances the alignment approach introduced in [2]. We also consider that, for one trace, paths with many forgotten activities are less likely than others. That is, we allow to specify the parameter of the missing data mechanism, i.e., the rate of missingness. We let the domain expert define the probability to forget an event. The domain expert can specify how to weigh these probabilities against each other, i.e., to give preference to paths with higher probability, i.e., determined by immediate transition weights, or to paths with less missing events that are required to be inserted into the trace. This novel post-processing step on the cost-optimal alignments allows to control the probability of paths in the model that are not reflected in a log by any event.

For example, consider a loop in a GDT_SPN model with n activities in the loop. By setting the chance of missing entries low, e.g., setting the missingness probability to 0.1 (10% chance that an event is lost), an additional iteration through the loop will become more unlikely, as its probability will be multiplied by the factor 0.1^n. This factor is the probability that all n events of an iteration are missing. We select the alignment with the highest probability. Once we decided on the structure of the repaired trace, we can continue and insert the times of the missing events in the trace, i.e., the identified *model moves*.

To insert the timing information, it is not enough to look at the GDT_SPN model alone. We need to find a way to add the information that we have for each trace, i.e., the timestamps of the recorded events. Fortunately, as mentioned in Section 3, there exists a solution for this task: *Inference* in Bayesian networks. Therefore, we convert the GDT _SPN model into a Bayesian network to insert the evidence given by the observations to be able to perform the inference.

In the previous step, we identified a probable path through the GDT_SPN model. With the path given, we eliminate choices from the model by removing branches of the process model that were not taken. We unfold the net from the initial marking along the chosen path. Consider trace $t_3 = \langle A, D, C, C, D, H \rangle$ and assume, we picked the following alignment:

log	A	D	C		C	D	H
model	A	D	C	A	C	D	H

Then, the unfolded model looks like Fig. 6, where the black part marks the path taken in the model. The grey part is removed while unfolding. Note that the unfolded model still contains parallelism, but it is acyclic. Thus, we can convert it into a Bayesian network with a similar structure, where the random variables represent timed transitions. As, due to multiple iterations of loops, activities can happen multiple times, we differentiate them by adding an index of their occurrence, e.g., $A1$ and $A2$ correspond to the first and second occurrence of the transition A. The unfolding is done by traversing the model along the path dictated by the alignment and keeping track of the occurrences of the transitions.

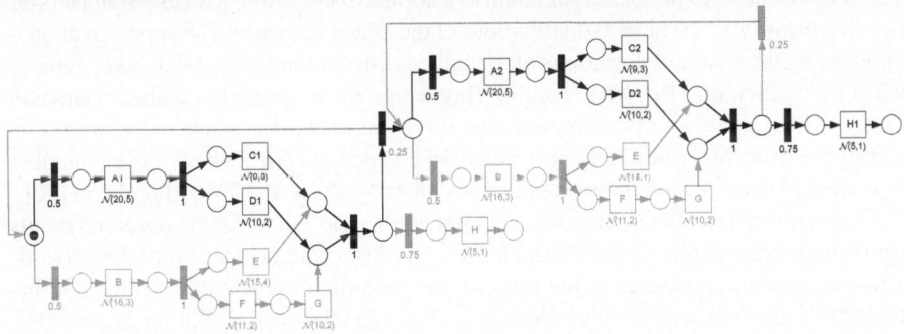

Fig. 6. Unfolded model in Fig. 1 for path $\langle A, D, C, A, C, D, H \rangle$

We transform the unfolded model into a Bayesian network with a similar structure. Most immediate transitions are not needed in the Bayesian network, as these do not take time and no choices need to be made in the unfolded process. Only immediate transitions joining parallel branches will be kept.

Fig. 7 shows transformation patterns for sequences, parallel splits, and synchronizing joins. These are the only constructs remaining in the unfolded form of the GDT_SPN model. In the resulting Bayesian network, we use the *sum* and *max* relations to define

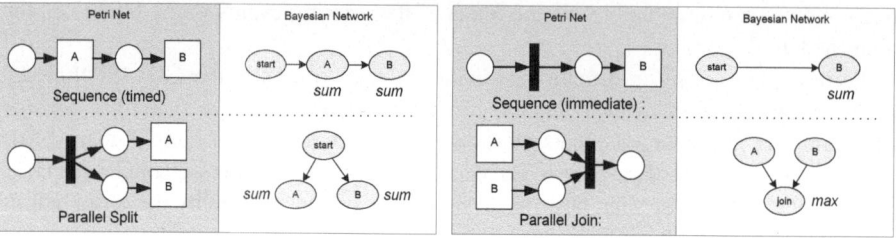

Fig. 7. Transformation of GDT_SPN models to Bayesian networks

the random variables given their parents. More concretely, if timed transition t_i is followed by timed transition t_j in a sequence, we can convert this fragment into a Bayesian network with variables X_i and X_j. From the GDT_SPN model, we use the transition duration distributions $\mathcal{D}(t_i) = D_i(x)$ and $\mathcal{D}(t_j) = D_j(x)$. Then, the parent variable X_i has the unconditional probability distribution $P(X_i \leq x) = D_i(x)$ and the child variable X_j has the probability distribution $P(X_j \leq x \mid X_i) = P(X_j + X_i \leq x)$. For each value of the parent $x_i \in X_i$, the probability distribution is defined as $P(X_j \leq x \mid X_i = x_i) = D_j(x - x_i)$, i.e., the distribution of X_j is shifted by its parent's value to the right. A parallel split, cf. lower left part in Fig. 7, is treated as two sequences sharing the same parent node.

The *max* relation that is required for joining branches at synchronization points, cf. the lower right pattern in Fig. 7, is defined as follows. Let X_i and X_j be the parents of X_k, such that X_k is the maximum of its parents. Then, $P(X_k \leq x \mid X_i, X_j) = P(\max(X_i, X_j) \leq x) = P(X_i \leq x) \cdot P(X_j \leq x) = D_i(x) \cdot D_j(x)$, i.e., the probability distribution functions are multiplied. Note that the maximum of two normally distributed random variables is not normally distributed. Therefore, we use a linear approximation, as described in [19]. This means that we express the maximum as a normal distribution, with its parameters depending linearly on the normal distributions of the joined branches. The approximation is good, when the standard deviations of the joined distributions are similar, and degrades when they differ, cf. [19]. The resulting Bayesian network model is a linear Gaussian model, which is a class of continuous type Bayesian networks, where inference is efficiently possible. More precisely, inference can be done in O (n^3) where n is the number of nodes [15]. Otherwise, inference in Bayesian networks is an NP-hard problem [20].

Once we constructed the Bayesian network, we set the values for the observed events for their corresponding random variables, i.e., we insert the evidence into the network. Then, we perform inference in the form of querying the posterior probability distributions of the unobserved variables. We use the Bayesian network toolkit for Matlab [16], where these inference methods are implemented. This corresponds to the second step in the *insert time* part of Fig. 5.

The posterior probabilities of the queried variables reflect the probabilities, when the conditions are given according to the evidence. Our aim is to get the *most likely* time values for the missing events. These most likely times are good estimators for when the events occurred in reality, and thus can be used by process participants as clues during root cause analysis. For example, in order to find the responsible person for the task in question, an estimation of when it happened *most likely* can be helpful. Note that repaired values with most likely time values need to be treated with caution, as they do not capture the uncertainty in the values. Therefore, we mark repaired entries in the log as artificial.

Once we determined probable values for the timestamps of all missing events in a trace, we can proceed with the next trace starting another iteration of the algorithm.

6   Evaluation

We have implemented our approach in ProM[1]. To evaluate the quality of the algorithm, we follow the experimental setup described in Fig. 8. The problem is that in reality we do not know whether events did not happen, or only were not recorded. Therefore, we conduct a controlled experiment. In order to have actual values to compare our repaired results with, we first acquire traces that fit the model. We do this either by selecting the fitting ones from original cases, or by simulation in artificial scenarios. In a second step, we randomly remove a percentage of the events from these fitting traces. We pass the log with missing entries to the repair algorithm, along with the model, according to which we perform the repair.

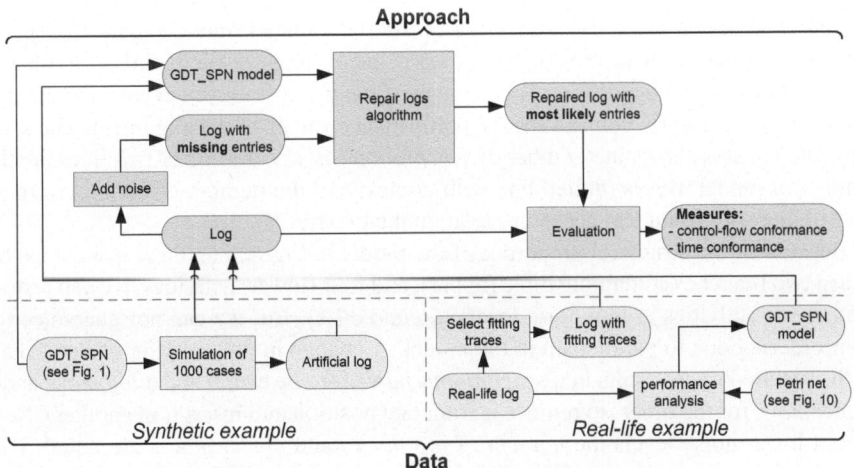

Fig. 8. Approach used to evaluate repair quality

The repair algorithm's output is then evaluated against the original traces to see, how well we could restore the missing events. We use two measures for assessing the quality of the repaired log. The cost-based *fitness* measure as defined in [2] compares how well a model fits a log. Here, we compare the traces of the original and repaired log. Therefore, we convert each original trace into a sequential Petri net model and measure its fitness with the repaired trace.

Fitness deals with the structural quality, i.e., it is a good measure to check, whether we repaired the right events in the right order. For measuring the quality of repaired timestamps, we compare the real event's time with the repaired event's time. We use the mean absolute error (MAE) of the events that have been inserted. This is the mean of the absolute differences between repaired event times and original event times.

---

[1] See package *RepairLog* in ProM http://www.promtools.org

6.1 Artificial Example

We first evaluate the repair algorithm according to the artificial model introduced in Section 3 in Fig. 1.

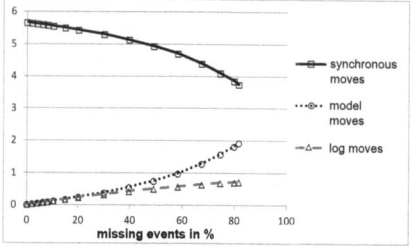 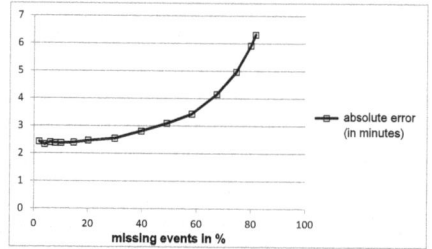

Fig. 9. Evaluation results for repairing 1000 traces of model in Fig. 1

The experiment was done with a log of 1000 simulated traces. Figure 9 displays the resulting quality measures of the repaired traces. Each dot is based on the repair results of this log with a different percentage of randomly removed events. On the left-hand side of the figure, you can see the performance values of the alignment. The solid line with squares shows the number of *synchronous moves*. The other two lines are the number of model moves (dotted line with circles) and the number of log moves (gray dashed line with triangles) necessary to align the two traces.

Because of the structural properties of the model in Fig. 1, i.e., there is a choice between two branches containing three (upper), and four (lower) activities, we can restore the *correct* activities at low noise levels (around 30%). But we can not guarantee for their ordering due to parallelism in the model. A change in the ordering of two events in the repaired trace results in a *synchronous move* for one event, and a *log move* and a *model move* for the other (to remove it from one position and insert it in another). Note that at lower noise levels the number of *log moves* and *model moves* are equal. This indicates incorrect ordering of parallel activities. At higher noise levels the number of model moves increase further. Then, it gets more likely that there remains no single event of an iteration of the loop in Fig. 1. The size of the gap between model moves and log moves shows how much the repair quality suffers from the fact that the presented algorithm, which repairs events with the most likely values, does not restore optional paths of which no event is recorded in the trace.

On the right-hand side of Fig. 9 we see the mean absolute error in relative time units specified in the model. The graph shows that the offset between original event's time and repaired event's time increases with the amount of noise non-linearly.

6.2 Repairing a Real Example Log of a Hospital

In this second part of the evaluation, we look at the results obtained from repairing a real log of a hospital. In contrast to the experimental setup, where we used the model to generate the example log, now the log is given, and we try to estimate the model parameters. To avoid using a model that was learned from the events, which we try to repair, we use 10-fold cross-validation. That is, we divide the log into ten parts and use nine parts to learn the model parameters and one to perform the repair with.

We use the log of a Dutch clinic for the ambulant surgery process, described in [21]. The process is depicted as a GDT_SPN model in Fig. 10. It is a sequential process that deals with both ambulant patients and ordered stationary patients. Each transition corresponds to a treatment step that a nurse records in a spread sheet with timestamps. In the process, the patient arrives in the lock to be prepared for the surgery. Once the operating room (OR) is ready, the patient leaves the lock and enters the OR. In the OR, the anesthesia team starts the induction of the anesthesia. Afterwards, the patient optionally gets an antibiotica prophylaxis treatment. The surgery starts with the incision, i.e., the first cut with the scalpel, and finishes with the suture, i.e., the closure of the tissue with stitches. Next, the anesthesia team performs the emergence from the anesthesia, which ends when the patient has regained consciousness. Finally, the patient leaves the OR and is transported to the recovery.

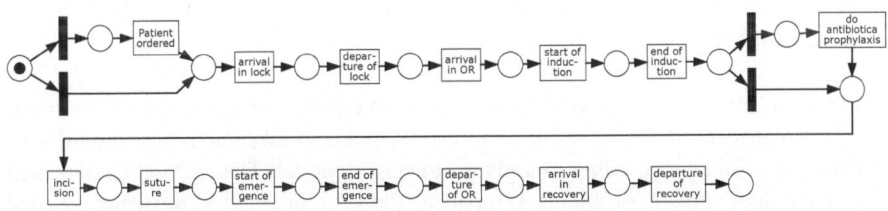

Fig. 10. Real surgery model for a surgical procedure in a Dutch hospital

Out of 1310 patient treatment cases, only 570 fit the model shown in Fig. 10 perfectly. The other cases contain one or more missing events, which motivated our research. We use the 570 fitting cases to evaluate, how well we can repair them after randomly removing events.

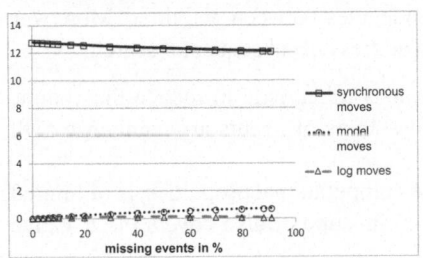
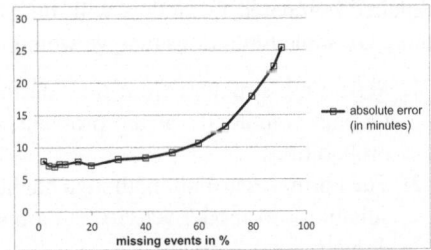

Fig. 11. Evaluation results for model in Fig. 10

Figure 11 shows the evaluation results of the hospital event log. Observe that the structure can be repaired better than in the artificial example in Fig. 9. This is due to the sequential nature of the model—it comprises twelve sequential, and two optional activities. With increasing number of missing events, the number of correctly repaired events (synchronous moves) approaches twelve. That is, only twelve activities are restored, because the algorithm is unable to repair single undetected optional events.

The mean absolute error in the restored events is higher than the artificial example. This value depends on the variance in the activity durations. In this evaluated example, the variance of certain activity durations in the model is high, due to outliers. Latter activity durations exhibit many short durations with a few outliers, which can be better captured with other distributions than the normal distribution.

Obviously, the ability to repair a log depends on the information content of observed events in the trace and the remaining variability in the model. For instance, we can repair a sequential model always with fitness 1.0 of the repaired log—if we observe only one activity. However, the chance to pick the same path through a model composed of n parallel activities with equally distributed times is only $\frac{1}{n!}$.

The presented approach is unable to restore optional branches without structural hints, i.e., at least one activity on an optional branch needs to be recorded. This affects single optional activities most, as their absence will not be repaired. Still, many real-life processes comprise only a sequence of activities, and can be repaired correctly.

7   Conclusion

We introduced a method to repair event logs to assist timely correction of documentation errors in enterprises. Thereby, we present *which*, and also *when* activities should have happened *most likely* according to a given stochastic model. The method decomposes the problem into two sub-problems: i) repairing the structure, and ii) repairing the time.

Repairing the structure is done with a novel extension of the alignment approach [2] based on path probabilities. And repairing the time is achieved by using inference in a Bayesian network representing the structure of the individual trace in the model. The algorithm can deal with a large and representative class of process models (any sound, free-choice workflow net).

Our preliminary evaluations indicate that we can repair structure and time, if noise is limited. Models exhibiting a high degree of parallelism are less likely to be correctly repaired compared to models with more dependencies between activities. Moreover, there are some limitations that we would like to address in subsequent research:

1. Separating structure from time during repair is a heuristic to reduce the computational complexity of the problem, as timestamps of events also influence path probabilities.
2. The normal distribution, though having nice computational properties, is of limited suitability to model activity durations, since its support also covers the negative domain.
3. The independence assumption between activity durations and between traces might be too strong, as resources play an important role in processes.
4. We assumed that the GDT_SPN model contains the truth, and deviations in the log are caused by documentation errors, instead of deviations from the process model. This assumption only is feasible for standardized processes with few deviations that are captured in the model. Therefore, we advise to use this approach with care and try to correct documentation errors using repaired logs as assistance.

Future work also needs to address the question of how to model causalities of activities more directly. Thus, missing events that are very likely to be documentation errors, e.g., the missing event for *enter OR*, when *exit OR* is documented, need to be separately treated from missing events of rather optional activities, e.g., missing event of *do antibiotica prophelaxe*, where it is not clear, whether the absence of the event is caused by a documentation error. An integration with the proposed technique in [7], seems promising to address this issue.

References

1. van der Aalst, W., Adriansyah, A., de Medeiros, A.K.A., Arcieri, F., et al.: Process mining manifesto. In: Daniel, F., Barkaoui, K., Dustdar, S. (eds.) BPM Workshops 2011, Part I. LNBIP, vol. 99, pp. 169–194. Springer, Heidelberg (2012)
2. Adriansyah, A., van Dongen, B.F., van der Aalst, W.M.P.: Conformance Checking using Cost-Based Fitness Analysis. In: EDOC 2011, pp. 55–64. IEEE (2011)
3. Rogge-Solti, A., van der Aalst, W.M.P., Weske, M.: Discovering Stochastic Petri Nets with Arbitrary Delay Distributions From Event Logs. In: BPM Workshops 2013. LNBIP. Springer, Heidelberg (to appear)
4. Pearl, J.: Probabilistic Reasoning in Intelligent Systems: Networks of Plausible Inference. Morgan Kaufmann (1988)
5. Rogge-Solti, A., Mans, R., van der Aalst, W.M.P., Weske, M.: Repairing Event Logs Using Stochastic Process Models. Technical Report 78, Hasso Plattner Institute (2013)
6. Schafer, J.L., Graham, J.W.: Missing Data: Our View of the State of the Art. Psychological Methods 7(2), 147–177 (2002)
7. Bertoli, P., Dragoni, M., Ghidini, C., Di Francescomarino, C.: Reasoning-based Techniques for Dealing with Incomplete Business Process Execution Traces. Technical report, Fundazione Bruno Kessler, Data & Knowledge Management (2013)
8. Günther, C.W., van der Aalst, W.M.P.: Fuzzy Mining – Adaptive Process Simplification Based on Multi-perspective Metrics. In: Alonso, G., Dadam, P., Rosemann, M. (eds.) BPM 2007. LNCS, vol. 4714, pp. 328–343. Springer, Heidelberg (2007)
9. van der Aalst, W.M.P.: Process Mining: Discovery, Conformance and Enhancement of Business Processes. Springer (2011)
10. Fahland, D., van der Aalst, W.M.P.: Repairing Process Models to Reflect Reality. In: Barros, A., Gal, A., Kindler, E. (eds.) BPM 2012. LNCS, vol. 7481, pp. 229–245. Springer, Heidelberg (2012)
11. Buijs, J.C.A.M., La Rosa, M., Reijers, H.A., van Dongen, B.F., van der Aalst, W.M.P.: Improving Business Process Models Using Observed Behavior. In: Ceravolo, P. (ed.) SIMPDA2012. LNBIP, vol. 162, pp. 44–59. Springer, Heidelberg (2013)
12. Ciardo, G., German, R., Lindemann, C.: A Characterization of the Stochastic Process Underlying a Stochastic Petri Net. IEEE Transactions on Software Engineering 20(7), 506–515 (1994)
13. Marsan, M.A., Balbo, G., Bobbio, A., Chiola, G., Conte, G., Cumani, A.: The Effect of Execution Policies on the Semantics and Analysis of Stochastic Petri Nets. IEEE Transactions on Software Engineering 15, 832–846 (1989)
14. van der Aalst, W.M.P., Adriansyah, A., van Dongen, B.: Replaying History on Process Models for Conformance Checking and Performance Analysis. In: WIREs: Data Mining and Knowledge Discovery, vol. 2, pp. 182–192. Wiley Online Library (2012)
15. Koller, D., Friedman, N.: Probabilistic Graphical Models: Principles and Techniques. MIT Press (2009)

16. Murphy, K.P.: The Bayes Net Toolbox for Matlab. In: Interface 2001. Computing Science and Statistics, vol. 33, pp. 1024–1034 (2001)
17. van der Aalst, W.M.P.: Verification of Workflow Nets. In: Azéma, P., Balbo, G. (eds.) ICATPN 1997. LNCS, vol. 1248, pp. 407–426. Springer, Heidelberg (1997)
18. Best, E.: Structure Theory of Petri Nets: The Free Choice Hiatus. In: Brauer, W., Reisig, W., Rozenberg, G. (eds.) APN 1986. LNCS, vol. 254, pp. 168–205. Springer, Heidelberg (1987)
19. Zhang, L., Chen, W., Hu, Y., Chen, C.C.: Statistical Static Timing Analysis With Conditional Linear MAX/MIN Approximation and Extended Canonical Timing Model. In: TCAD, vol. 25, pp. 1183–1191. IEEE (2006)
20. Cooper, G.F.: The Computational Complexity of Probabilistic Inference Using Bayesian Belief Networks. Artificial Intelligence 42(2), 393–405 (1990)
21. Kirchner, K., Herzberg, N., Rogge-Solti, A., Weske, M.: Embedding Conformance Checking in a Process Intelligence System in Hospital Environments. In: Lenz, R., Miksch, S., Peleg, M., Reichert, M., Riaño, D., ten Teije, A. (eds.) ProHealth 2012/KR4HC 2012. LNCS, vol. 7738, pp. 126–139. Springer, Heidelberg (2013)

An Android Tablet Tool for Enterprise Architecture Modeling in Small and Medium-Sized Enterprises

Maxime Bernaert, Joeri Maes, and Geert Poels

Department of Management Information Systems and Operations Management
Faculty of Economics and Business Administration,
Ghent University, Tweekerkenstraat 2, B-9000 Ghent, Belgium
`{Maxime.Bernaert,Joeri.Maes,Geert.Poels}@UGent.be`

Abstract. Enterprise architecture (EA) is used to improve the alignment of different facets of a company. The recognition for the need of EA in small and medium-sized enterprises (SMEs) has recently risen as a means to manage complexity and change [1]. Due to the specific problems and characteristics of SMEs, a different approach is necessary. CHOOSE was therefore developed as an EA approach focused on and adapted to the characteristics and needs of SMEs [2]. During case studies performed with CHOOSE, the need for software tool support became apparent. This paper describes a mobile software tool in support of the CHOOSE approach that should guide the CEO as enterprise architect throughout the entire EA process and facilitate the implementation, management, and maintenance of the resulting EA model. The generic development decisions make this software tool widely applicable for a multitude of models. Finally, evaluation in two Belgian SMEs is presented.

Keywords: Enterprise architecture, small and medium-sized enterprises, CHOOSE, Android tablet software tool.

1   Introduction

If you are about to build or rebuild a house, you will probably appeal to an architect to make sure the house fits your needs both structurally and functionally. The same can be said when starting, running or growing a business. An enterprise is a complex system of people, knowledge, fixed assets, projects, processes, and many more brought together to fulfill a common shared vision [3]. Enterprise architecture (EA) can help to guide this process and consists of principles, methods, and models to achieve its main objective, which is a coherent and consistent organizational design. Originally EA was focused on IT and its alignment with the business side. However, over the years the concept has grown into a much broader technique and is applied across the borders of IT and the alignment is therefore sometimes called enterprise coherence [4]. Although a lot of research is being done on EA, hardly anything is known about its use in the context of a small and medium-sized enterprise (SME) [5]. Some have pioneered in this field of study through the development of an EA approach adapted to the specific needs of this target group called CHOOSE (section

J. Grabis et al. (Eds.): PoEM 2013, LNBIP 165, pp. 145–160, 2013.
© IFIP International Federation for Information Processing 2013

2.1) [2,6]. The application and implementation of EA in general and the CHOOSE approach in particular, has proven to be a complex and challenging task. Though these techniques could offer significant benefits to SMEs, hardly any SME uses EA and adoption is far below par [1,7]. Analysis of widely accepted adoption models like the technology acceptance model (TAM) [8] and the method evaluation model (MEM) [9] has shown that software tool support could significantly contribute to solving this paradox [2]. The research question of this paper is a design science [10] question: "How could such a software tool in support of the CHOOSE metamodel and method be developed?". This software tool guides the SME's CEO in his function as enterprise architect throughout the EA process and facilitates the implementation, management, and maintenance of the resulting EA. Evaluation by means of case studies in two Belgian SMEs provides the necessary proof of both the importance and efficacy of the software tool. This evaluation process was further used to provide valuable insights and measurements for the evaluation of the efficacy of the developed software tool.

In section two, a short introduction on EA and its applicability in SMEs is discussed after which the need for tool support in this area is illustrated. The third section elaborates on the development of the tool itself and explains the design and development choices. The fourth section elaborates on the evaluation of the software tool. Finally, the paper ends with a conclusion and future research directions.

2   Enterprise Architecture Software Tool Support

EA is employed to improve the alignment in companies. If we look at the term architecture it is clear that it is not without ambiguity [3]. A definition of architecture is given by IEEE Computer Society [11] and is described as "the fundamental organization of a system embodied in its components, their relationships to each other, and to the environment, and the principle guiding its design and evolution". Multiple frameworks, models, and tools to create the structure of these components and their relationships exist. Examples of software tools currently in use include Rational System Architect [12], Aris [13], and QualiWare [14]. The drawback is that these tools are not disposing of analysis tools [15], nor are they supporting the CHOOSE metamodel, or are they adapted towards an SME target group.

2.1   CHOOSE for EA in SMEs

The current EA tools are primarily targeted at large enterprises. This focus is hard to justify since SMEs comprise up to 99.8% of all firms in the European Union while globally they account for 99% of business and 40% to 50% of the gross domestic product [16,17]. One of the major causes preventing the growth of SMEs is the lack of business skills [1]. Other than business skills, SMEs lack specialized IT knowledge and technical skills [18]. SMEs are constantly busy dealing with day-to-day business, leaving them little room for strategic issues [19]. Bernaert et al. [2] derived several requirements from these SME characteristics.

To manage the change and complexity in smaller enterprises, using EA could be a good solution [1,2]. In this light, the CHOOSE metamodel for EA (Fig. 1) is being developed based on the defined requirements for EA and SMEs [2]. CHOOSE is an acronym for "keep Control, by means of a Holistic Overview, based on Objectives and kept Simple, of your Enterprise", incorporating these requirements in its name. The CHOOSE metamodel addresses the specificities and problems SMEs face by creating an overview of the business architecture layer of EA, including elements from the information systems and technology layer. Four dimensions are distinguished to create this overview. A strategic goal dimension (why), an active actor dimension (who), an operation dimension (how) and an object dimension (what). The creation of an EA model in CHOOSE involves creating specific entities of the four dimensions and modeling the relationships between them.

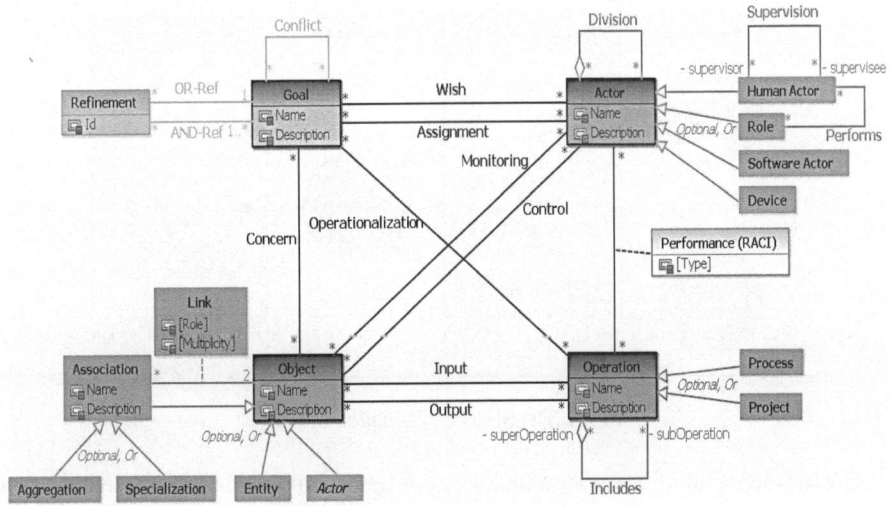

Fig. 1. CHOOSE metamodel [2]

2.2   Need for Software Tool Support

Despite the customized EA approach offered by CHOOSE with its intrinsic qualities aligned with the characteristics of SMEs, it is also very important to take the adoption of the approach into account. Techniques that are technically superior or fully customized to the needs of the user will not yield the expected benefits as long as the techniques are not effectively used in practice. To help optimize, facilitate, and speed up the adoption process, Bernaert et al. [2] investigated different adoption models and proposed the MEM [9] to evaluate the CHOOSE approach. MEM supplements the widely used TAM [8] to be better applicable for the evaluation of methods. MEM provides a model that helps discern external factors and their impact on the attitude, evaluation, and behavior of practitioners towards the adoption of IS methods, such as EA. Central determinants in this model are perceived ease of use and perceived usefulness. The conviction of the end-users that the information technology will help them better perform their job relates to the perceived usefulness. Perceived ease of use alternatively deals with the amount of effort and time needed to learn how to work with it. Both aspects influence the attitude towards the method and subsequently the behavioral intention to use. Crucial for the adoption is that the increase in performance is perceived as being of higher influence to adoption than the effort necessary to learn the developed technology and work with it [8,9]. Fig. 2 gives an overview of MEM and its main components. The biggest difference with TAM is the introduction of actual efficacy coming from Rescher [20]. This difference is subtle but nevertheless very important. It implies that when explaining human behavior, the subjective reality is often much more decisive than the objective reality and therefore perceived efficacy mediates the impact of actual efficacy on adoption in practice [2].

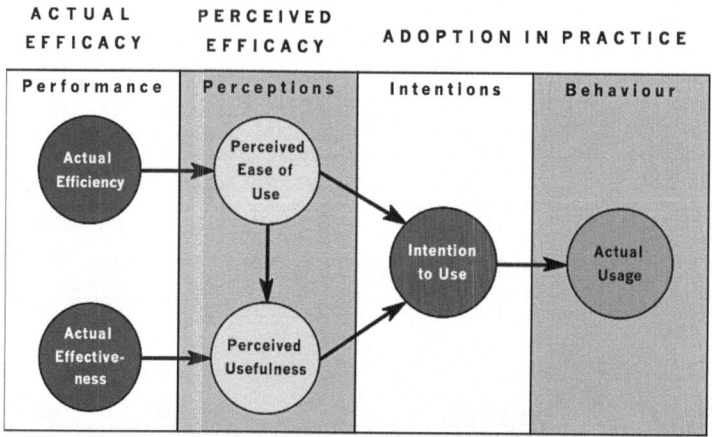

Fig. 2. The Method Evaluation Model

The development of a software tool supporting the application and implementation of CHOOSE could significantly contribute to the actual efficacy, leading to a higher adoption and added value through an increase in the subjective perception of this efficacy. Hence, measuring the perceived usefulness and perceived ease of use of the software tool during the evaluation process (section 4), will provide valuable insights with respect to the ability of this tool to increase adoption of CHOOSE, which reflects the notion of rational selection [20], which states that, generally, those methods or tools will be adopted that outperform others in achieving intended objectives.

Next to the contribution of a tool to the adoption of an approach, research concerning the implementation and use of EA in practice stresses the complexity and need for guidance by means of tool support. In general, there are three main areas where critical problems arise in the process of EA: modeling, managing, and maintaining EAs [21]. An important driver of problems in these areas is the inherent complexity of the EA process [22]. An enormous amount of information has to be transformed using the semantics and syntax of the modeling language. A tool can offer the much needed support and guidance for the development, storage, and analysis of an EA [22]. This drawback emphasizes the importance of an integrated tool for building, analyzing, and communicating the EA to all stakeholders. Other advantages of tool support include [3]:

- A tool can help to standardize the semantics and syntax used during the development of the EA within a company.
- The use of a tool contributes to the construction of correct and consistent architecture artifacts by guiding the development process and through the application of mistake proofing techniques. Tools can impose rules to make sure the desired practices and guidelines are followed.
- Tools facilitate the comparison of alternatives by providing impact of change and quantitative analysis features.
- Software tools can use computational power for the analysis of the architecture.

Although the aforementioned research confirms the importance of tool support, these findings cannot simply be extrapolated to the environment of SMEs and the importance of tool support for the implementation of the CHOOSE approach. However, case studies performed by Bernaert and Callaert (upcoming paper) confirm this need for tool support. During these case studies, the CHOOSE technique was applied in six Belgian SMEs by means of simple post-its on a whiteboard. The CEOs were convinced of the added value of having access to a software tool supporting this EA process. Fig. 3 shows a small fraction of the resulting EA model and pinpoints the importance of a tool for the development, storage, and analysis of the EA artifacts, since the use of post-its created an unmanageable EA model. The post-its should not be readable due to confidentiality issues.

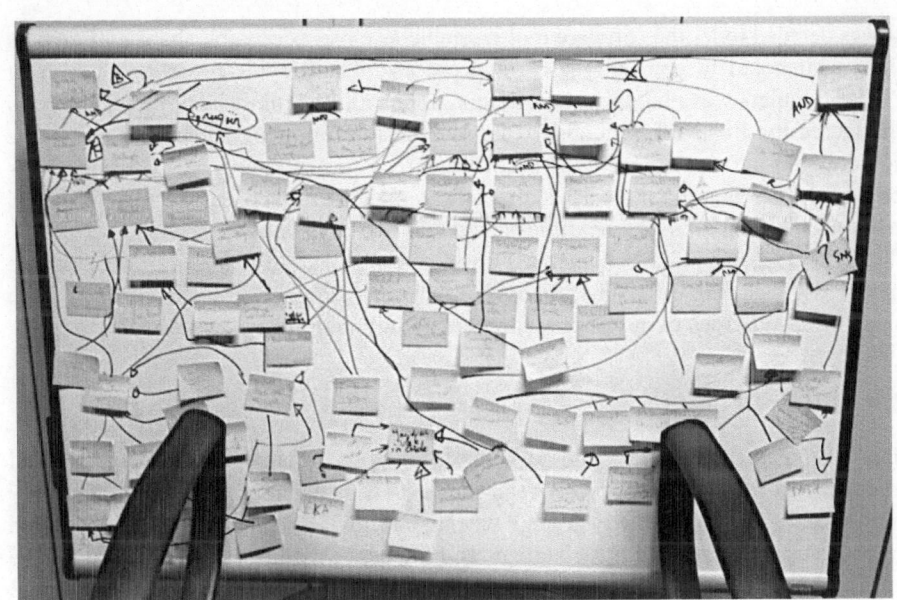

Fig. 3. Partial EA artifact of a Belgian SME

2.3   Software Tool Requirements

On the one hand, the lack of business and IT skills in SMEs causes the need for user-friendly intuitive ways to model the EA in order for the SMEs to have an overview of the company and to enable growth [1]. On the other hand, we see that in our current society, a new organizational form called the mobile enterprise is rapidly emerging [23]. Defining a mobile enterprise is difficult. In a narrow way, specific mobile solutions are used for specific problems in the organization. In a broad way, mobile solutions can be part of the strategy and are diffused throughout the entire company [23]. The combination of this particular need and the trend of increasing mobility creates a need for mobile applications to model the EA. This can help with the process of becoming a mobile enterprise and can leverage other information technology support systems. The use of the CHOOSE metamodel for such a tool is further supported by the proposition that a software tool should be based on a metamodel and be capable of representing EA information in customizable graphical and textual forms [24]. Further, a lot of companies still use Microsoft Office (29% of respondents) (e.g., Word, Excel, PowerPoint) or Visio (33% of respondents) to model their EA [25]. Export to and import from these Office tools could offer benefits.

Based on these insights, it is safe to say that the development of a software tool adjusted to the specific needs of SMEs, based on CHOOSE and incorporating these requirements could substantially improve the added value of EA for SMEs.

3   Software Tool Development

It was decided to let the software tool resemble as close as possible the use of post-its on a whiteboard to copy the case study process. The graphic processing power of Android tablets was chosen to enable this graphical drawing behavior and adhere to the increasing trend of the mobile enterprise. In the following paragraphs, a generic solution for the development of a software tool for making CHOOSE models is proposed. It is generic in the sense that any framework composed of entity types and relations between them is a possible candidate to be developed in the same way. First, the CHOOSE metamodel is mapped onto a graph data structure and the database model is developed. After this, a possible software design is proposed. During each step, the specificities of developing for the Android platform are explained.

3.1   Representation

The CHOOSE metamodel (Fig. 1) consists of four different types of entities and various possible relationships between them. This structure can be unambiguously represented by a directed graph, where entities correspond to vertices and relationships to edges. Both the vertices and the edges require a type attribute for the graph to be a correct representation of the EA. Furthermore, vertices have a name and a description. In its most basic form, the CHOOSE metamodel can be represented by the relational database model in Fig. 4 top.

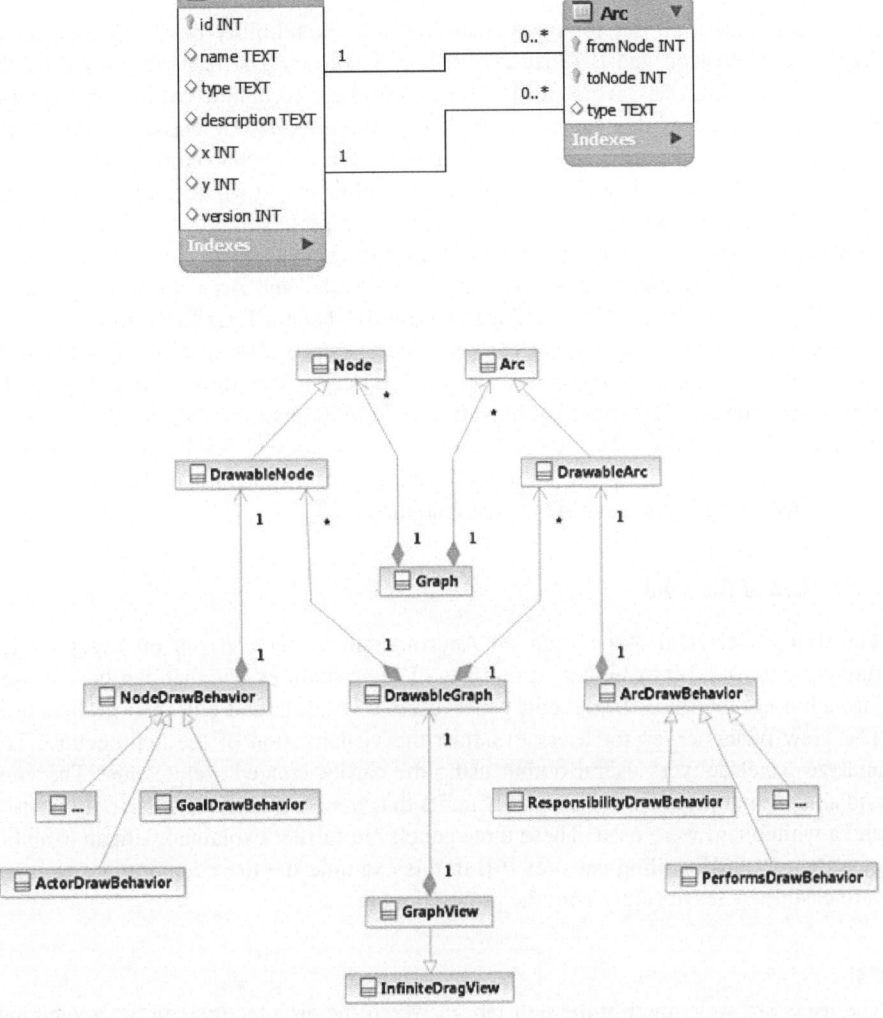

Fig. 4. Database model for a graph data structure (top) & Class diagram of the tool (bottom)

The Android framework offers an abstraction of data in the form of a content provider, which separates the user of the content provider from the backend of the storage. A content provider provides a way to add and manipulate data and is accessible from every application on the Android device. In that way, companies can create their EA in the modeling application and use this database in other applications specifically designed for the company. This could further increase the perceived usefulness of the CHOOSE approach. In this case, the SQLite database management system natively present in the Android framework is used.

3.2   Software Design

The given design allows for maintainability and extendibility of the metamodel as well as the software and is illustrated in Fig. 4 bottom. The basis is formed by the InfiniteDragView class, which allows for an infinitely scrollable field to be shown to the user. The use of this field is extended by the GraphView class, allowing for a graph structure to be shown. The graph data structure is achieved by using a Graph class, consisting of collections Node and Arc objects (Attributes are hidden) [26]. These objects are extended so they have drawing properties in order to visualize them. In that way, the GraphView class uses a DrawableGraph as input.

For the implementation of the drawing of the Nodes and Arcs, the strategy pattern is used [27]. A DrawableNode and a DrawableArc have a DrawBehavior object. All DrawBehavior classes implement the clickable interface. The specific draw behavior is added at runtime. When the GraphView calls the draw methods on the DrawableNode and DrawableArc objects, the DrawBehavior determines how a Node or Arc should be drawn. This depends on the type of Node or Arc but also on the state of this Node or Arc. It can be focused, disabled, pressed or normal. These states are chosen according to the Android design guidelines [28].

3.3   Use of the Tool

The tool is designed to be used on Android tablets but can run on every device running Android 4.0 or higher. It consists of three main panels that can be accessed through a tab interface. In the edit panel, users can create and edit their architecture. The view panel serves for users to adjust the visualization of the architecture. The analyze panel delivers useful output using the earlier created architecture. The view and analyze panels are software tool benefits that were not possible when only post-its and a whiteboard were used. These three panels are further explained with an example of a Belgian SME selling car tires [6]. In this example the tire company has to make sure customers leave safely with the proper tire pressure.

Edit

The users are welcomed in the edit tab, in which the architecture can be created and edited. In this screen, users can add, delete, and change entities and relationships of the architecture. To create a new entity, users need to press on an empty point on the plane. This plane is scrollable by swiping a finger across the screen and zooming is done by making a pinching gesture, both according to Android design guidelines [28]. Users are then subsequently asked which type of entity they want to add, which name it needs to have, and an optional description can be given. This process is done in multiple dialogs, which makes the action to complete more intuitive and clear to the user [29]. The entity is then placed where the user originally pressed. An important object in this SME is obviously a tire. The process of creating a tire object is illustrated in Fig. 5. In the last screenshot four more related objects have been created.

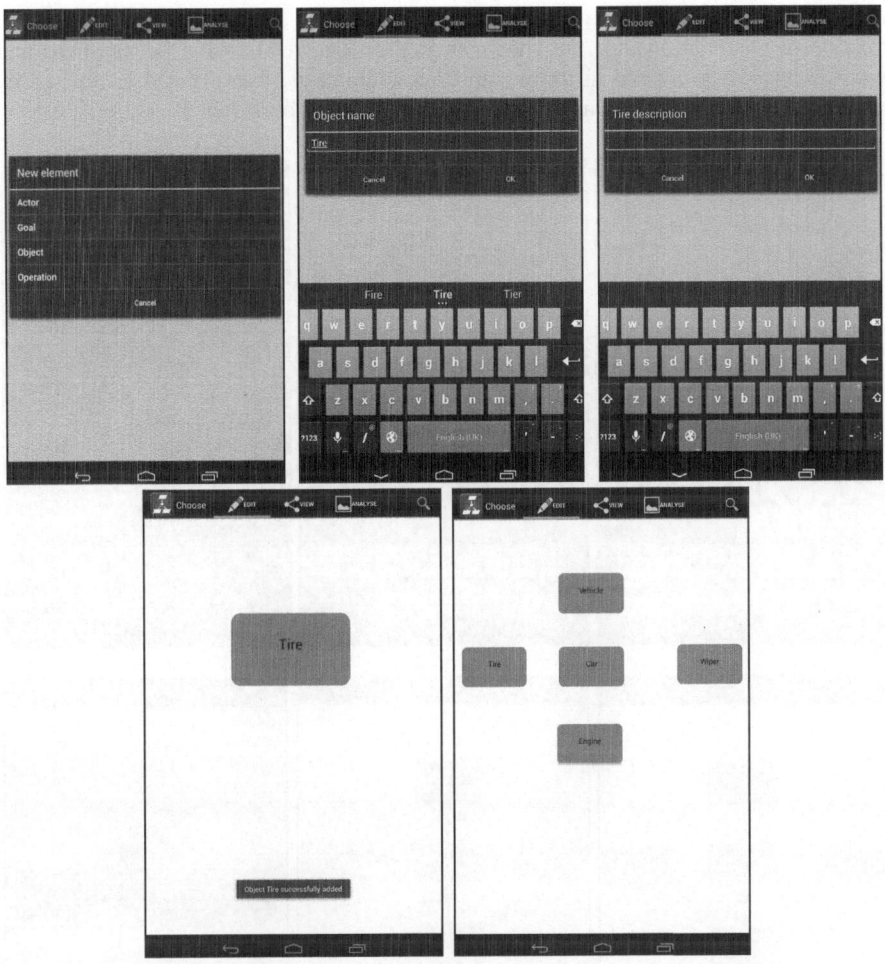

Fig. 5. Creation of entities

Changing the properties of an entity can be done by pressing on it in the edit panel, after which a dialog appears. In this dialog it is possible to change the name of the entity as well as the description. It also offers one of the two ways to create a relationship between different entities. Typing in the "Create relationship with" textbox lets the search function look for matching entities, which are then suggested. This function adds value if compared with post-its on a whiteboard. If different relationship types are possible, a dialog will ask which type it is. A second way in which a relationship can be created is by long pressing on an entity. The user hears a sound and the device will vibrate, which means it is now possible to draw a relationship between two entities. This is a fast way to model small parts of the EA.

In the car tire center example, there exists a composition relationship between the car and the engine and also between the car and the wiper. A specialization relationship exists between the car and the vehicle entity and there is also an aggregation relationship between the car and the tire. The change dialog and the creation of the relationships are shown in Fig. 6. The relationship between car and wiper is purposely created in the wrong direction and can be reversed or deleted by pressing on this relationship as shown in the last screenshot of Fig. 6.

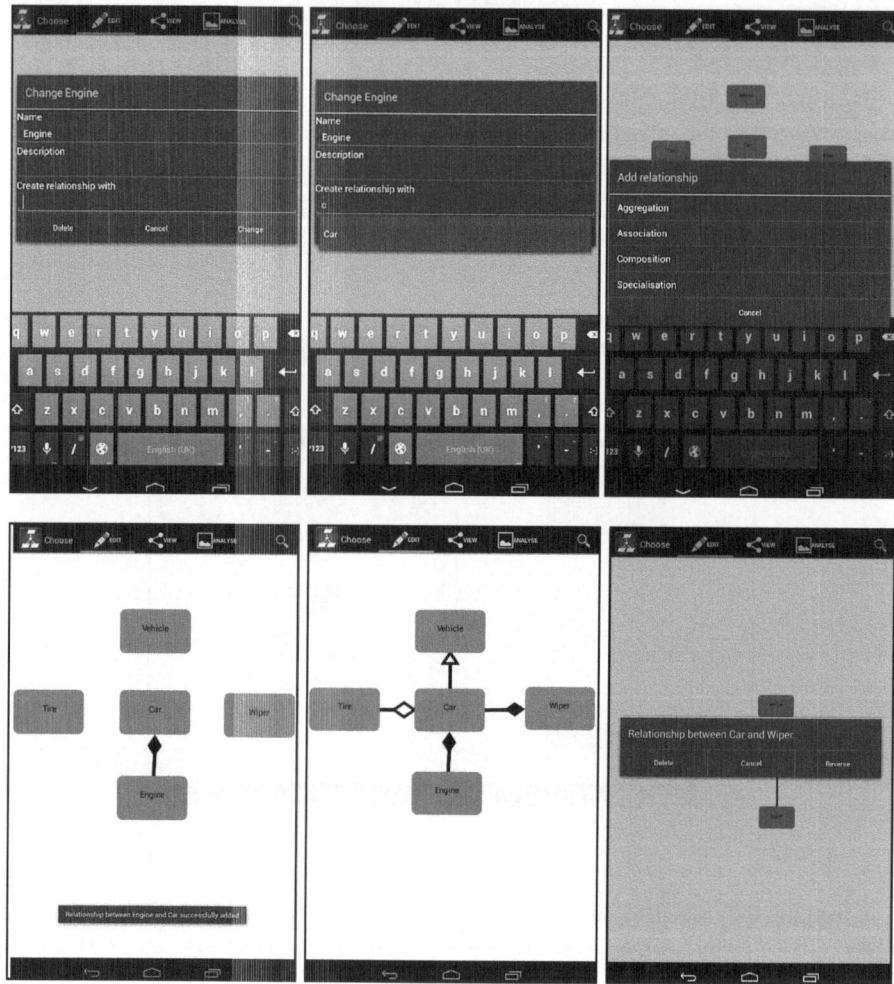

Fig. 6. Changing entities and creating relationships

During the creation, the user can let the application draw the architecture. At the moment, this happens using a force-directed algorithm around the center coordinates of the plane [30]. In its most rudimentary form, all vertex objects in the graph are modeled as point charges that are all exerting a repelling force on each other. The arcs are modeled as springs with a certain length. Letting the system react by computing the exerted forces and moving the vertices leads to a state with at least a local minimum in kinetic energy and an equilibrium in the whole system. The benefit of this algorithm is the flexibility. It allows for users to place certain vertices on fixed positions and additional positioning rules can easily be enforced. The downside is the fact that the global optimum is not guaranteed. For both small and large architectures, this creates an aesthetically pleasing structure. It must be noted that for larger architectures there is the possibility of a loss of overview on the user's side since entities will be relocated. The possibility to fixate certain vertices can help to prevent this. The process and result for a more complex graph is shown in Fig. 7.

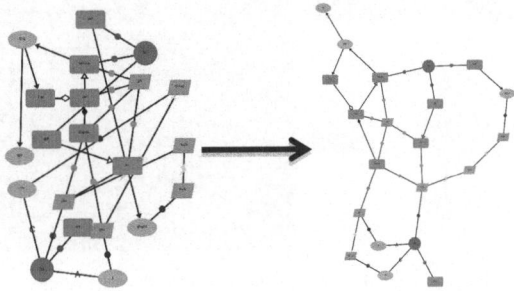

Fig. 7. Automatic drawing of the architecture

View

During the first case study it was clear that the overview is lost very quickly even with the automatic positioning due to the non-planarity of the generated graphs representing the architecture. This problem is tackled by letting users select and isolate entities on which they can work separately in the edit tab. In this way, the user will never have to deal with large unmaintainable structures. It is in this situation that the method to add relationships by typing and searching the related element is the most useful as a lot of entities will not be reachable on the screen. In the tire company example, a few more entities are added such as a safety goal, a customer actor, a process of driving a car, and others. We will isolate the objects to work on them independently (Fig. 8).

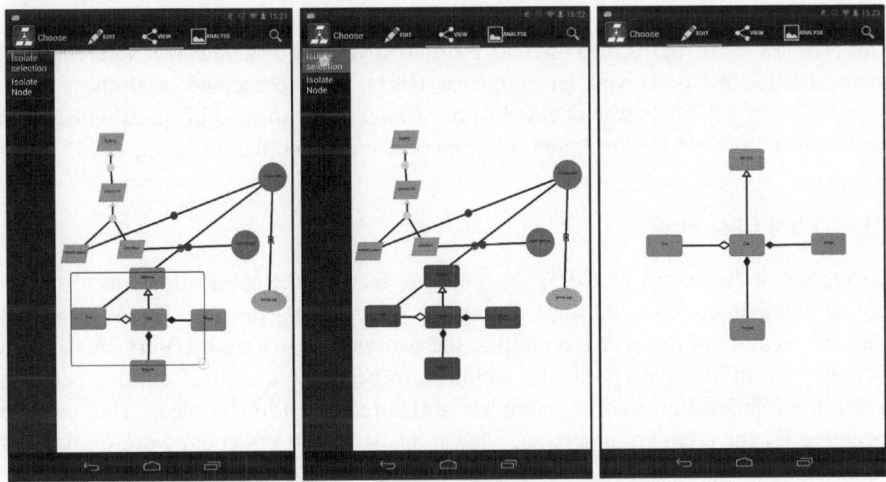

Fig. 8. Isolation of parts of the architecture and changing the visualization

The view panel also allows for multiple viewpoints to be selected, which isolate specific parts of the EA [11]. The goal viewpoint isolates all goals, allowing the generation of a goal tree. The operation viewpoint isolates all processes and projects while the operation flow viewpoint also adds the objects to show possible streams of objects throughout the operations. The other viewpoints are similar (Fig. 9).

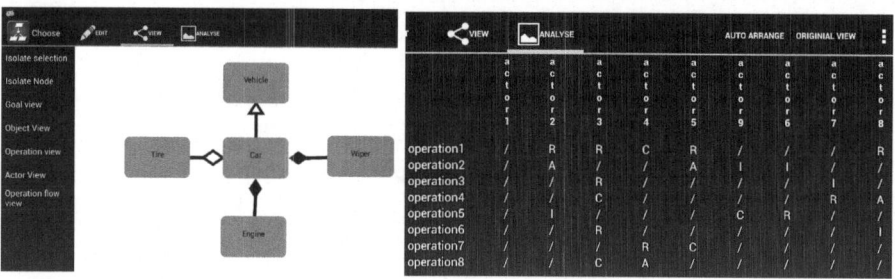

Fig. 9. The view panel (left) & RACI chart (right)

Analyze
The analyze tab is designed to create output for the user. First, it allows the user to generate a RACI chart with export functionality to Excel using the RACI relationships modeled between actors and operations. Second, reports are generated to point out suspicious loops or other problems. Third, it is also the start of an as-is/to-be analysis. Once clicked, users can edit their architecture while the tool keeps track of the changes. This feature is already implemented in the code and saves the changes in the database. The output, as well as indicating that the user is working on the as-is/to-be analysis, however still have to be implemented.

4   Case Studies

Case studies were performed in two Belgian SMEs to evaluate the software tool according to the perceived ease of use (PEU) and perceived usefulness (PU) dimensions of MEM. It was decided to have interviews instead of questionnaires to get the most possible feedback and recommendations on both dimensions of MEM.

4.1   First Case Study

During a first case study at a Belgian chocolate factory, the application was tested by adding elements and relationships during the interviewing process. It was clear that after the creation of just a dozen entities, the overview is lost easily. Very soon, when modeling at an average speed, the architecture becomes a web of entities between which the relationships and the complete structure are no longer clear. This was the incentive for the creation of separate viewpoints so that users could work on parts of the architecture (PEU). The results of the adaptations allowed for faster entry of the architecture (PEU) and let the user make an abstraction of parts of the architecture that are already modeled (PU). The CEO's recommendations were also the incentive for the as-is/to-be analysis (PU) and the RACI chart (PU), which were implemented.

4.2   Second Case Study

The second case study was performed at a Belgian vendor of window glass. The SME's CEO used the application without any further explanation and the case study led to several useful conclusions. First, although the application is made according to the Android design guidelines, it was not completely intuitive what actions the user can trigger. A tutorial when the application is started for the first time is therefore necessary (PEU). Second, for users to independently create their business architecture, it is necessary that they have an insight in how the CHOOSE model works. This is especially true for users who are not familiar with EA modeling. When the application is started for the first time, a second tutorial explaining the CHOOSE model would be very useful (PEU). A wizard based on the step-by-step guidelines of the CHOOSE method could guide the user in developing a CHOOSE model from scratch (PEU). Third, once the SME's CEO knew how the program works, the business architecture was created without much effort (PEU). The creation of entities and relationships went fast (PEU) and the CEO could fully use his mental ability to create the architecture instead of focusing on how the software works. From this perspective, the implementation of the visual approach was a success.

4.3   Case Study Conclusions

Moody's MEM [9] is proposed by Bernaert et al. [2] to assess the intention to use of CHOOSE, which is positively correlated to the actual usage. The CEOs were asked how the tool could improve their perceived ease of use and perceived usefulness, which are both positively correlated to the intention to use.

Related to the perceived ease of use, the tool was better than using only post-its on a whiteboard, but could be improved by incorporating guidance for the user, like the earlier mentioned tutorials and wizards. The search functionality and viewpoints were already implemented to increase the perceived ease of use.

The perceived usefulness was the part where most of the added value could be delivered by the software tool. This confirms the research of Moody [9] and Davis [8]. The RACI chart with export functionality, as-is/to-be analysis, and some additional viewpoints were already implemented and perceived as increasing the usefulness. Other functionalities could increase the perceived usefulness even more. As a first example, a querying functionality with export to Excel could enable different analyses and viewpoints. A CEO could for example get a list of all employees who are responsible for less than three operations. A second example of a useful functionality is automatically checking the SME's CHOOSE model based on the defined CHOOSE hard and soft constraints. This could deliver interesting insights for the CEO. For instance, an operation (process or project) which is not linked to any goal could then pinpoint a forgotten link in the CHOOSE model that could be added, or could discover operations that are not contributing to any of the company's goals.

Although some additional functionalities could be added, the feedback during the case studies revealed that during the creation of the SME's CHOOSE model, the perceived usefulness was already increased. The CHOOSE metamodel, and thus the software tool whose data model is based on this metamodel, explicitly links goals with each other in a goal tree and also links these goals to operations. This enables explicit traceability from highest-level goals all the way down to operations, which was perceived as very valuable for the SMEs' CEOs. It also triggered critically thinking about the structure of the SME.

5   Conclusion and Further Research

This research has investigated the need for a software tool in support of the implementation of EA in the environment of SMEs as pioneered by the CHOOSE approach from Bernaert et al. [2]. Both literature review and case studies have confirmed this need and the paper presents a software tool in support of this need.

An overview of the main features of the software tool was given and an initial evaluation by means of two case studies has confirmed the potential of the software tool in increasing the adoption of CHOOSE and providing the much needed guidance and support.

The software tool addresses the specific issues SMEs face (time, IT skills, and financial constraints) by being simple, intuitive, and user-friendly. By designing only parts of the EA model at once, users are capable of keeping an overview. Together with the overview users have of their company, the analysis functionalities provide them with useful information and strategic insights. Further, the generic architecture allows for other software tools using metamodels to be developed in the same way as the software tool described in this paper [31].

The case study evaluation in two SMEs revealed more insight in how the software tool helps CHOOSE in increasing its perceived ease of use and perceived usefulness. The case study evaluation was primarily used to get as much insight and as many future research directions as possible by interviewing the CEOs when they were using the software tool. Future evaluation of this software tool in accordance to other software tools or no software tool (e.g., to identify problems arising from a lack of EA modeling experience instead of arising from the tool) could be performed by means of a questionnaire based on the perceived usefulness and perceived ease of use dimensions of MEM through the adapted six-item scales of TAM [8]. This would make the evaluation more rigorous and could dig deeper into the shortcomings of the tool's prototype, like extra features enhancing the overview (e.g., drill down capabilities and extra search functionalities) or possible user-defined customizations to the metamodel (e.g., user-defined properties).

Some recommendations from the CEOs were already implemented and the software tool increased the added value of CHOOSE. Nevertheless, the software tool is still under development and the case studies have identified multiple improvement paths to be tackled. Further research with respect to additional valuable functionalities is required and continuous fine-tuning will contribute to the overall added value of the software tool in support of CHOOSE.

In this stage, only an Android version of the application exists. The architecture is made in such a way that it can be transferred easily across platforms so that it is available for most of them. A more appropriate future solution could be the development of a web application using HTML 5 in combination with the jQuery JavaScript library. These technologies have the potential to create an application accessible from every device running a browser. It also would make the transfer between different platforms [32,33] easier as users can access their architecture everywhere and it could then also support multi-user use with one common database server. Other areas of improvement include the architecture of the software and the analysis part of the business architecture. The graph structure allows for mathematical analyses generating useful information using straightforward graph algorithms.

The tool will soon be available in the Android Play store. In the meantime the tool can be installed using the following link, leading to the installation file:

https://www.dropbox.com/s/716ecd87jo3n167/BusinessModeller.apk

References

1. Jacobs, D., Kotzé, P., van der Merwe, A., Gerber, A.: Enterprise architecture for small and medium enterprise growth. In: Albani, A., Dietz, J.L.G., Verelst, J. (eds.) EEWC 2011. LNBIP, vol. 79, pp. 61–75. Springer, Heidelberg (2011)
2. Bernaert, M., Poels, G., Snoeck, M., De Backer, M.: Enterprise Architecture for Small and Medium-Sized Enterprises: A Starting Point for Bringing EA to SMEs, Based on Adoption Models. In: Information Systems and Small and Medium-sized Enterprises (SMEs): State of Art of IS Research in SMEs. Springer (2013)
3. Lankhorst, M.: Enterprise Architecture at Work: Modelling, Communication and Analysis, vol. 3. Springer (2013)
4. Wagter, R., Proper, H.A., Witte, D.: Developing the GEA Method – Design Science and Case-Study Research in Action. In: Franch, X., Soffer, P. (eds.) CAiSE Workshops 2013. LNBIP, vol. 148, pp. 43–57. Springer, Heidelberg (2013)
5. Bhagwat, R., Sharma, M.: Information system architecture: a framework for a cluster of small- and medium-sized enterprises (SMEs). Prod. Plan. Control 18(4), 283–296 (2007)
6. Bernaert, M., Poels, G.: The Quest for Know-How, Know-Why, Know-What and Know-Who: Using KAOS for Enterprise Modelling. In: Salinesi, C., Pastor, O. (eds.) CAiSE Workshops 2011. LNBIP, vol. 83, pp. 29–40. Springer, Heidelberg (2011)
7. Devos, J.: IT Governance for SMEs. University of Ghent, Ghent (2011)
8. Davis, F.D.: Perceived Usefulness, Perceived Ease of Use, and User Acceptance of Information Technology. MIS Q 13(3), 319–340 (1989)
9. Moody, D.L.: The Method Evaluation Model: A Theoretical Model for Validating Information Systems Design Methods. In: ECIS (2003)
10. Hevner, A.R., March, S.T., Park, J., Ram, S.: Design Science in Information Systems Research. MIS Q 28(1), 75–105 (2004)
11. IEEE Computer Society, IEEE Recommended Practice for Architectural Description of Software-Intensive Systems. IEEE Std 1471-2000 (2000)
12. IBM (2013), http://www-01.ibm.com/software/awdtools/systemarchitect/

13. SoftwareAG (2013), http://www.softwareag.com/corporate/products/aris_platform/default.asp

14. QualiWare (2013), http://www2.qualiware.com/RepositoryDesktop/589efbed-cd9b-463e-9164-905a9c97cdc9.htm

15. Johnson, P., Johansson, E., Sommestad, T., Ullberg, J.A.: tool for enterprise architecture analysis. In: EDOC, p. 142. IEEE (2007)

16. Small Business Administration US, What is a Small Business? Office of Advocacy (2012), http://www.sba.gov/size

17. European Commission, Are EU SMEs recovering from the crisis? Annual Report on EU Small and Medium sized Enterprises 2010/2011 (2011)

18. Haug, A., Pedersen, S.G., Arlbjørn, J.S.: Identifying the IT Readiness of Small and Medium Sized Enterprises. In: AMCIS (2010)

19. Malhotra, R., Temponi, C.: Critical decisions for ERP integration: Small business issues. Int. J. Inf. Manage 30(1), 28–37 (2010)

20. Rescher, N.: Methodological Pragmatism: Systems-Theoretic Approach to the Theory of Knowledge. Blackwell Publishers (1977)

21. Kaisler, S.H., Armour, F., Valivullah, M.: Enterprise architecting: Critical problems. In: HICSS (2005)

22. Ernst, A.M., Lankes, J., Schweda, C.M., Wittenburg, A.: Tool Support for Enterprise Architecture Management - Strengths and Weaknesses. In: EDOC, pp. 13–22 (2006)

23. Basole, R.C.: The emergence of the mobile enterprise: A value-driven perspective. In: ICMB, p. 41. IEEE (2007)

24. Braun, C., Winter, R.A.: Comprehensive Enterprise Architecture Metamodel and Its Implementation Using a Metamodeling Platform. In: EMISA, pp. 64–79 (2005)

25. Schekkerman, J.: Trends in enterprise architecture 2005: How are organizations progressing. Institute for Enterprise Architecture Developments (2005)

26. Lafore, R., Waite, M.: Data structures & algorithms in Java. Sams (2003)

27. Freeman, E., Freeman, E., Bates, B., Sierra, K.: Head First Design Patterns. O' Reilly (2004)

28. Google, Gestures (2013), http://developer.android.com/design/patterns/gestures.html

29. Krug, S.: Don't make me think! A common sense approach to Web usability. New Riders (2006)

30. Battista, G.D., Eades, P., Tamassia, R., Tollis, I.G.: Graph drawing: algorithms for the visualization of graphs. Prentice Hall (1998)

31. Buckl, S., Dierl, T., Matthes, F., Ramacher, R., Schweda, C.M.: Current and Future Tool Support for EA Management. In: MSI, pp. 9–24 (2008)

32. Dumeez, J., Bernaert, M., Poels, G.: Development of Software Tool Support for Enterprise Architecture in Small and Medium-Sized Enterprises. In: Franch, X., Soffer, P. (eds.) CAiSE Workshops 2013. LNBIP, vol. 148, pp. 87–98. Springer, Heidelberg (2013)

33. Ingelbeen, D., Bernaert, M., Poels, G.: Enterprise Architecture Software Tool Support for Small and Medium-Sized Enterprises: EASE. In: AMCIS (2013)

A Qualitative Research Approach to Obtain Insight in Business Process Modelling Methods in Practice

Céline Décosse[1], Wolfgang A. Molnar[1], and Henderik A. Proper[1,2]

[1] Public Research Center Henri Tudor, 29 Kennedy Avenue, L-1855 Luxembourg, Luxembourg
[2] Radboud University, Comeniuslaan 4, 6525 HP Nijmegen, The Netherlands
{celine.decosse,wolfgang.molnar,erik.proper}@tudor.lu

Abstract. In this paper we are concerned with the development of an observational research approach to gain insights into the performance of Business Process Modelling Methods (BPMMs) in practice. In developing this observational approach, we have adopted an interpretive research approach. More specifically, this involved the design of a questionnaire to conduct semi-structured interviews to collect qualitative research data about the performance of BPMMs. Since a BPMM is a designed artefact, we also investigated Design Science Research literature to identify criteria to appreciate the performance of BPMMs in practice. As a result, the questionnaire that was used to guide the interview is based on a subset of criteria of progress for information systems theories, while the observational research approach we adopted involves the collection of qualitative data from multiple stakeholder types. As a next step, the resulting questionnaire was used to evaluate the performance an actual BPMM in practical use; the DEMO method. Though the analysis of the collected qualitative data of the DEMO case has not been fully performed yet, we already foresee that part of the information we collected provides new insights compared to existing studies about DEMO, as is the fact that a variety of types of stakeholders have been approached to observe the use of DEMO.

Keywords: enterprise modelling in practice, information systems method evaluation criteria, qualitative research approach.

1 Introduction

In this paper we are concerned with the development of an observational research approach to obtain more insights into the actual performance of Business Process Modelling Methods (BPMM) in practice. Our initial research goal was to gain more insight into the performance of the DEMO (Design and Engineering Methodology for Organisations) method, which is a specific BPMM that is employed by enterprise architects to design concise models of organizations processes. Indeed, we knew that several projects had been performed with DEMO [1–12]. For some of these projects, the application of DEMO seems to be very promising, e.g. DEMO helped to *"construct and analyse more models in a shorter period of time"* (p.10)[2]. Therefore, we were curious about the performance of DEMO *in practice*. In addition, we had access

J. Grabis et al. (Eds.): PoEM 2013, LNBIP 165, pp. 161–175, 2013.
© IFIP International Federation for Information Processing 2013

to practitioners who have used DEMO in their projects, and who would agree to have these projects investigated by researchers.

However, rather than limiting ourselves to DEMO only, we decided to generalize our effort to BPMMs in general. In other words, rather than developing an observational approach to only observe the performance of DEMO in practice, we decided to develop an approach to observe the practical performance of BPMMs in general (still using DEMO as a specific case). Having insights about a BPMM in practice is valuable because it is easier to select, promote, improve or even better use a BPMM when knowing what can be expected when using it in practice. In doing so, we were also inspired by Winter (p.471)[13]: *"Not every artefact construction, however, is design research. 'Research' implies that problem solutions should be generic to some extent, i.e., applicable to a set of problem situations"*, where in our case the constructed artefact is the observation approach for the performance of BPMM in practice.

In developing the observation approach, we chose the interpretive research approach as a starting point, where qualitative research data pertaining to the use and performance of the specific BPMM, will be collected with semi-structured interviews. The original contribution of this paper is the way in which we defined the themes and questions of these interviews: we selected a subset of criteria of progress for information systems theories proposed by Aier and Fischer [14]. We then performed the interviews to investigate the use of DEMO in practice in several projects and contexts by several types of stakeholders acquainted with DEMO. Although the analysis of the data has not been completely performed, we nevertheless already present some first insights about DEMO in practice.

The paper is structured as follows: in the introduction we defined the problem to be addressed. Section 2 introduces definitions and positions DEMO as a specific BPMM in these definitions. In section 3, we reviewed the literature about the evaluation of DEMO in practice. Section 4 is the core of the paper: it presents the proposed research approach for getting insights about a BPMM in practice. Section 5 deals about the validity of this proposed observation approach by applying it to the use of DEMO in practice as a case study. A few first insights we gained about the use of DEMO in practice, based on the conducted interviews, are briefly presented in section 6. We then underline some limitations of our work and conclude in section 7.

2   DEMO as a Method

Method. Unlike process definitions, method definitions often refer to a modelling language and to *"underlying concepts"* [16], *"hidden assumptions"* [17] or *"way of thinking"* [18]. In the information technology domain, March and Smith define a method as *"a set of steps (...) used to perform a task."* [19]. The definition proposed by Rescher [20] and adopted by Moody [21] is more general: as methods define *"ways of doing things, methods are a type of human knowledge (the "knowledge how")*. Mettler and Rohner (p.2)[16] bring a prescriptive flavour and an ideal goal to method definition: *"methods (...) focus on the specification of activities to reach the ideal solution (how)"*. They distinguish methods *"key activities"* (that aim to reach a business goal) from their *"underlying concepts"* (that is *"the conceptual view on the world that underlies the performance of the activities"*) [16]. This distinction seems to be consistent with the view of Seligman et al. [18] on information systems methodologies, that they characterise with "*5 ways*":

— the "way of thinking", defined as "hidden assumptions" that are "used to look at organisations and information systems" [17, 18],
— the "way of working" (how to do things),
— the "way of controlling" (how to manage things),
— the "way of modelling", which they define as the "network of [the method's] models, i.e. the models, their interrelationships and, if present, a detailed description of the model components and the formal rules to check them",
— the "way of supporting", which is about the tools supporting the method.

In the current paper, we want to have an insight about methods that are used as BPMMs in practice. The method definitions above are a way for the researcher to establish a set of themes to interview stakeholders about without forgetting aspects of methods that are recurrent in the literature.

Method and modelling language. When modelling languages are mentioned in the methods definitions above, they are presented as being part of methods: March and Smith explain that "*although they may not be explicitly articulated, representations of tasks and results are intrinsic to methods.*" (p.257)[19]. For Seligman et al. [18], the way of modelling is one of the features of a method, as is the "*way of working*".

DEMO, language or method? Primarily, an artefact!
Whereas authors argue that DEMO is a modelling language [22], almost all other recent publications about DEMO usually consider it as a method [23, 24]. Winter et al. argue that a method and recommendations concerning the representation of a model can be seen as aspects of an artefact, and then propose the following artefact definition: "*A generic artefact consists of language aspects (construct), aspects referring to result recommendations (model), and aspects referring to activity recommendations (method) as well as instantiations thereof (instantiation).*" (p.12)[25].

3   Literature Review on the Evaluation of DEMO in Practice

This literature review aims at investigating whether DEMO has been evaluated in practice and how. Many papers [1–12] deal with case studies in which DEMO has been used to design situational DEMO based methods or to propose ontologies. Besides, qualities of DEMO models have been studied in several evaluations [22, 26]. We found two papers dealing with a partial evaluation of DEMO *in practice* across several cases. The first one [27] studies the adoption of DEMO by DEMO professionals in practice, in order to improve this adoption (**Table 1**). This study is restricted to the adoption of DEMO in practice so the use of DEMO in practice is not the core of the study [27]. The second one [11] investigates DEMO as a means of reflecting upon the Language/Action perspective (LAP) (**Table 2**). The DEMO related part of this paper aims at finding out how the actual application of DEMO differs from its intended application. Besides, only DEMO professionals were asked to answer the survey so the study only reflects why DEMO certified practitioners adopted (or not)

DEMO, it provides less insights about people aware of the existence of DEMO who are not DEMO professionals. Dumay et al. focused on how the professional application of DEMO differs from its intended application so only practitioners have been involved in their study [11].

Table 1. Khavas, 2010 [24] - Master thesis: the adoption of DEMO in practice

Source	Khavas, 2010 [24] - Master thesis
Subject	The adoption of DEMO in practice
Motivation	Ensure the adoption of DEMO in practical fields. This problem has been introduced in [24].
Research questions	1 What is the adoption rate of DEMO among DEMO Professionals in practice? 2 What are the factors that can influence the decision of a DEMO Professional to adopt or ignore DEMO? (p.2)
Sample	DEMO professionals [24]
Approach	— White-box approach: to define questions, DEMO is first thoroughly studied through a literature review. Then two surveys have been performed. — A researcher who understands DEMO asks people who master DEMO about adoption matters.
Methods	Based on literature review about what DEMO is and how it works on the one hand and about method adoption on the other hand, Khavas elaborated first a quantitative survey and later a qualitative analysis based on semi-structured interviews.
Results	— Identification of several levels of adoption in an organization: individual, project, unit or organization — Identification of factors that influence adoption — Recommendations to DEMO professionals to ease the adoption or DEMO

Table 2. Dumay et al., 2005, [11] – Professional versus intended application of DEMO

Source	Dumay et al., 2005, [11] - Conference Proceedings
Subject	Subject of the DEMO evaluation included in the paper: find out how the professional application of DEMO differs from its intended application.
Motivation	"Devise several recommendations on how the Language/Action Perspective (LAP) can improve its footprint in the community of Information Systems Development practice." (p.78) LAP is an approach for the design of Information Systems.
Research questions	1. What is the relationship between DEMO theory and its intended application? 2. How does the professional application of DEMO differ from its intended application? 3. Can LAP unify the apparent incompatible social and technical perspectives present in Information Systems Development practice? (p.78)
Sample	DEMO practitioners

Table 2. (*Continued.*)

Approach	DEMO evaluation by practitioners is a means of evaluating in practice the LAP. The idea is to study DEMO theory, then identify the proposed applications of DEMO; study DEMO applications by practitioners; establish the relationship between DEMO theory and practice; compare LAP theory and DEMO theory to draw conclusions about LAP thanks to DEMO analysis.
Methods	— To study DEMO theory: the framework proposed by Mingers and Brockles [28] to analyse methodologies has been used. — To study DEMO in practice: a survey has been sent by email to practitioners about DEMO application contexts (domain, duration, projects). Then a 4-hour workshop has been organised with the 19 practitioners amongst the survey respondents willing and able to attend. The subject of the workshop was DEMO areas of application.
Results	The DEMO in practice evaluation part of this study "answers the question how the professional application of DEMO differs from its intended application." (p.80)

To the best of our knowledge, no study has been performed with the aim of giving a holistic view on the use of DEMO in practice both by approaching a variety of themes and a diversity of stakeholder's profiles. The subject or the current paper is to define an observational approach to do so.

4   Observational Approach for BPMMs Performance in Practice

4.1   Observational Approach Overview: An Interpretive Approach

This section discusses the set up of the observational research approach that is to be used to gain insights about the performance of a BPMM in practice. These insights are provided by exploring stakeholders' views about the use of a BPMM in practice. For this exploratory purpose, we adopted a qualitative research approach, because it is aimed at understanding phenomena and provides modes and methods for analysing text [29]. Qualitative research can be positivist, interpretive, or critical [29]. We adopted an interpretive approach because it allows to produce "*an understanding of the context of the information system, and the process whereby the information system influences and is influenced by the context*" [30](p.4-5). "*Interpretive methods of research adopt the position that our knowledge of reality is a social construction by human actors*" [31]. We found it suitable for exploring the use of a method, because a method is an artefact that is designed, performed and evaluated by human people.

To collect these qualitative data, we selected the semi-structured interview technique. Qualitative interviews are one of "*the most important data gathering tools in qualitative research*" (p.2)[32]. The reason is that it is "*permitting us to see that which is not ordinarily on view and examine that which is looked at but seldom seen*" (p.vii)[33]. We created a questionnaire to be used as a guideline by the interviewer during the interviews to discover what can be expected from DEMO in practice.

Whether being a method or a language, DEMO is a designed artefact; so are BPMMs. We considered that to gain insights about what can be expected from a designed artefact, we could use artefacts evaluation criteria. We selected those criteria by reasoning on criteria of progress for information systems theories proposed by Aier and Fischer [14]. We based the questions of the questionnaire on the artefacts evaluation criteria we selected, and then gathered these questions in themes to ease the interviewing process. We then obtained an interview questionnaire about IS (Information Systems) DS (Design Science) artefact evaluation, to which we added a few complementary questions that are specific to DEMO.

The scope of the current paper does not involve the mode of analysis of the collected data; it is concerned with the identification of the observational approach for gaining insights about a BPMM in practice and with the first insights about DEMO provided by the interviews that have been performed.

4.2   Interview Guideline Setup

Identification of the Interview Themes

The themes of the questionnaire used as an interview guideline have been identified according to the goal of the questionnaire: gain insights about DEMO in practice. Themes have been identified from the design science literature regarding artefact and method evaluation, so that the core of the questionnaire might be used as a guideline for any IS method evaluation; from literature about DEMO, regarding stakeholders feed-back about DEMO; during a brainstorming with fellow researchers to complete the above points.

In 2010, Aier and Fischer proposed a set of Criteria of Progress for Information Systems Design Theories [14]. We call this set of criteria CriProISDT[1]. Aier and Fischer based their reflection, amongst other elements, on "evaluation criteria for IS DSR artefacts" ("IS DSR" stands for "Information Systems Design Science Research") and reviewed the literature about that. In particular, they used March and Smith [19] set of criteria for IS DSR artefacts evaluation[2]. Then, Aier and Fischer focused on IS DSR artefacts evaluation criteria that they considered as being independent of any particular artefact type (method, model, construct, instantiation), which is interesting for our purpose. They established a table of comparison of the evaluation criteria for IS DSR artefacts by March and Smith with CriProISDT. Adopting Aier and Fischer's position that "evaluation criteria for IS DSR artefacts should be strongly related to those for IS design theories"[14], we choose to use this comparison the other way round: we selected amongst CriProISDT the criteria that we thought may be applicable to artefacts (called "CriProISDT subset"), and we then used the "comparison table" to retrieve the "matching" IS DSR artefacts evaluation criteria. By doing that we obtained a set of artefact evaluation criteria (called AEC) that are:

---

[1] Aier and Fischer CriProISDT: Utility, Internal Consistency, External consistency, Broad purpose and scope, Simplicity, Fruitfulness of further research [14].

[2] March and Smith set of criteria for IS DSR *artefacts* evaluation: Completeness, Ease of use, Effectiveness, Efficiency, Elegance, Fidelity with real world phenomena, Generality, Impact on the environment and on the artefacts' users, Internal consistency, Level of detail, Operationality, Robustness, Simplicity, Understandability [19].

generic to all types of artefact evaluation; based on a recent literature review; in line with one of the most well-known set of criteria for IS DSR artefacts evaluation (March and Smith's) although refining it. Criteria we selected to be included in Cri-ProISDT subset are: Utility, External consistency, Broad purpose and scope.

Utility (usefulness).
The reason for selecting utility is that DSR literature emphasizes that DSR products *"are assessed against criteria of value or utility"* (p.253)[19]. Aier and Fischer define "utility" in (p.158)[14] and "usefulness" in [34] as *"the artefact's ability to fulfil its purpose if the purpose itself is useful. The purpose of an artefact is only useful if it is relevant for business."* Following the comparison table, "matching" IS DSR artefacts evaluation criteria are: ease of use, effectiveness, efficiency, impact on the environment and on the artefacts' users and operationality. We call this list the "utility list".

External consistency, Broad purpose and scope.
Many authors underline the interdependence between a DSR artefact and its performance environment; that evaluation criteria and results are environment dependent. [14, 19, 35, 36]. So we selected the criteria of "external consistency" (*"fidelity with real world phenomena"* [19]) and "broad purpose and scope" because they are related to the performance environment of an artefact. Following the comparison table, "matching" IS DSR artefacts evaluation criteria are: fidelity with real world phenomena, generality. We call this list the "context list". We remove from this list the "robustness" criteria, which is mainly aimed at algorithmic artefact evaluation.

IS DSR artefact evaluation criteria we used.
By aggregating the "utility list" and the "context list", we obtain a list of IS DSR artefact evaluation criteria, with the definitions adopted or proposed by Aier and Fischer in [14] when they can be applied to artefacts: ease of use, effectiveness, efficiency, impact on the environment and on the artefacts' users, operationality, fidelity with real world phenomena (external consistency), generality.

This list actually extends the list of criteria for methods evaluation proposed by March and Smith: ease of use, efficiency, operationality, generality [19]. We can see that because of the systematic way of collecting IS DSR criteria we adopted, the following criteria are not included: completeness, elegance, internal consistency, level of detail, robustness, simplicity, understandability [19].

— ease of use: the artefact shall be easily usable [14];
— effectiveness: the degree to which the artefact meets its goal and achieve its desired benefit in practice [37]. So questions about the method under evaluation added value were included in the questionnaire
— efficiency: the degree to which the modelling process utilises resources such as time and people [19]; a quotient of output and input [14]. The notion of "Return on Modelling effort" conveys the same idea. *"If an artefact resulting from a design theory is used very often, its efficiency might be the best criterion for measuring its utility."* (p.149)[14]
— impact on the environment and on the artefacts' users: a side effect. *"Side effects can increase or decrease utility"* (p.164)[14]. *"A critical challenge in building an*

artefact is anticipating the potential side effects of its use, and insuring that un-wanted side effects are avoided" (p.254)[19]

— operationality : *"the ability to perform the intended task or the ability of humans to effectively use the method if it is not algorithmic"* [14, 19]
— fidelity with real world phenomena (external consistency): Questions about to what extent the constructs of the method under evaluation reflect business concepts that stakeholders have an interest to model with BPMMs.
— generality: the same as *"broad purpose and scope"* (p.164)[14]. Questions about the possibility to tailor a BPMM to specific business context are included in the questionnaire. Besides, as DSR artefacts address classes of problems [35, 38], questions about the "kind" of problems for which it is interesting to use the method under evaluation are included in the questionnaire.

Themes of the interview guideline.
For the fluidity of the interview, the questions have been gathered in themes C to G). Themes A and B complement these themes.

— A- Interview situation - Location, date, duration, language of the interview
— B- Interview context - Actual context of use of DEMO in a particular project, also allows to determine how much the person remembers about the project
— C- Typical context of use of the Method: recommendations, factors of influence
— D- Use of the Method in practice
— E- Organisation fit: Necessary skills to apply the Method and satisfaction about the Method
— F- Method chunks identification
— G- Method construction (only for the designer stakeholder type)

Stakeholder types.
Stakeholders are part of the "impact on the environment and on the artefacts' users" criteria. Because different stakeholders have different purposes and because utility definition is related to a purpose, we defined several stakeholders types [38]. "The utility of an artefact is multi-dimensional: one dimension for each stakeholder type" (p.10)[39]. Stakeholder types we *a priori* thought of were related to their role regarding the method under evaluation (here, DEMO):

— Designers: they took part in the creation or evolution of DEMO,
— Sponsor: owner of the engineering effort, this stakeholder pays or is financially responsible for the project in which DEMO has been applied,
— Manager of the engineering effort: project manager for example,
— Modeller: this stakeholder created DEMO models,
— Final beneficiaries: they benefit from the use of the method.

Themes are common to all stakeholder types except the designers: a theme (G) dedicated only to the latter ones has been included in the questionnaire.

In themes A and B, many questions are about the stakeholders, so that new stake-holder types may emerge from the analysis of the interviews. Indeed, the semi-structured interview technique provides a guidance to help collect data on themes the researcher is interested in, but the kind and scope of answers are not predefined. Actually, surprising answers are an asset provided they relate to the goal of the study: they may enable the researcher to reconsider themes, sampling, questions and research approach.

With regard to the question if DEMO is considered as a language or a method.
As our goal is to have an insight about DEMO *in practice*, we asked the interviewees what *they* would call DEMO and whether they would consider it as being prescriptive or descriptive. Besides, we ensured that interviews were not exclusively "method oriented" by selecting evaluation criteria that are common to all types of designed artefacts. Winter et al. argue that a method and a model can be seen as aspects of an artefact (p.12) [25]. This is especially convenient in the case of asking questions about DEMO. For this reason and because of the double definition of DEMO, we added questions that are specifically related to methods as defined in Section 2, and to languages as being part of methods.

Overview of the Questionnaire Structure
Each set of questions is related to a stakeholder type, a theme, and is aimed at collecting data exclusively either about stakeholders' intentions or stakeholders' experience. The purpose of this is to collect stakeholders' a priori views when intending to do something (*"What were your original intentions/expectations when you...?"*) and a posteriori views when they had experienced this something (*"What is your experience about ...?"*)[3]. The resulting questionnaire structure is depicted in **Table 3**.

Questions are actually often similar between stakeholder types: such a structure to design a questionnaire is only a tool for the researcher to think of many types of questions related to the goal of the study. Themes A and B are about the knowledge of the context and about the stakeholders.

Table 3. Structure of the questionnaire used as a semi-structured interview guideline

Themes	Designer	Sponsor	...
A	Questions	Questions	Questions
B	Questions	Questions	Questions
C	Intention and experience questions	Intention and experience questions	Intention and experience questions
D	Intention and experience questions	Intention and experience questions	Intention and experience questions
...	Intention and experience questions	Intention and experience questions	Intention and experience questions

---

[3] " Theories seek to predict or explain phenomena that occur with respect to the artefact's use (intention to use), perceived usefulness, and impact on individuals and organizations (net benefits) depending on system, service, and information quality (DeLone and McLean 1992; Seddon 1997; DeLone and McLean 2003)", cited by Hervner et al. (p.77)[35]

5   Reflections about the Proposed Research Approach Validity

The themes of the questionnaire used as a guideline in the semi-structured interview technique influence the answers that are given by the respondents. So, we found it necessary to justify our position for referring to design science literature to define a set of criteria to evaluate a method. These criteria will be used to gain insights on a method in the current study, not to evaluate it.

Information Systems literature.
As BPMMs may not be information technology related, the question arises as to whether information systems literature is relevant to study them [13]. In this paper we assume that as BPMMs are often implemented in the context of IS projects, IS literature is relevant to reflect upon BPMMs.

Information Systems Design Sciences literature.
BPMMs evaluation can be considered as a wicked problem, because it has a critical dependence upon human cognitive and social abilities to produce effective solutions (evaluation depends both on the performance of the method under evaluation and of the evaluation process itself on the other hand) and because it is strongly context dependent [35]. Such wicked problems can be addressed by the iterative nature of design science research [35].

Besides, the design science pa explores the art of building and evaluating artefacts and especially information systems related artefacts with a strong importance given to the behavioural aspects [35]. Is DS, evaluation of an artefact is performed against the criteria of utility, which is a practical perspective. So we can then investigate the design science literature with benefits for approaching the question of how to gain insights about BPMMs *in practice*. In short, evaluating BPMMs in practice is a practical problem, as such it can be approached with DS literature [40].

Design Science literature, Design Science Research literature or both?
Winter makes the following difference between IS design research and IS design science: "While design research is aimed at creating solutions to specific classes of relevant problems by using a rigorous construction and evaluation process, design science reflects the design research process and aims at creating standards for its rigour" (p.471)[13]. With this definition, we may rather investigate more DS research literature than DS literature. But on the one hand DSR literature and DS literature are not always "self-labelled" this way and on the other hand reflections and criteria of progress that are applicable to DS can sometimes be related to those of DSR [14], we will investigated both DS literature and DSR literature.

6   Early Experience Report about the DEMO Case Study

This section exposes how we started to implement the proposed research approach, and some of the preliminary insights we gained about DEMO in practice. The data analysis is still to be performed.

6.1   Data Collection

Based on the questionnaire used as a guideline [32], for our semi-structured interviews we collected 13 interviews. Multiple stakeholder types were represented. Interviews took place in interviewee's offices except one, which was performed with Skype. Each interviewee was interviewed individually by two researchers: one interviewer to ask the questions and one "shadow" interviewer to complete questions and take notes. Interviewees agreed to be interviewed and that the interviews were recorded. Only one interviewee asked us not to disclose his name. Immediately after each interview, the interviewer and the "shadow" wrote down notes about the interview that involved what had been said or interviewee's reaction to some specific subject for example. In order to capture the actual experience of the individuals in practice with DEMO, interviewers tried to avoid "leading the witness" by: following the interview guideline, asking questions in which the answer is not included, not giving their own opinions. They attempted to reduce their role to information collectors, influencing as less as possible the content of the collected data and encouraging interviewees to keep talking. One of the interviewers was a DEMO expert, the other one was a business analyst whose knowledge about DEMO could be summarised in a few short lines. The questionnaire used as a guideline contained about 100 questions, but as not every question was meant at every stakeholder types, around 60 questions were asked to each interviewee – or not, in case interviewee spontaneously provided the information while answering another question. Average time of interviews is one hour an thirty minutes. A total amount of twenty hours of recording have been collected.

6.2   Interview Data Analysis and Initial Insights about DEMO in Practice

Interviews have been transcribed by interviewers. Scripts have been coded [41]. The full analysis still has to be performed, so only first insights can be presented here.

DEMO is seen as a way of thinking that comes with a way of modelling. Interviewees mentioned a set of concepts helping enterprise engineer analysts to analyse organizations and reveals what is actually going on when it is about responsibility, authority, role, transaction. According to the interviewees, DEMO seems to be suited for complex problems. Interviewees often mention that DEMO models were implementation independent and that to apply DEMO to produce DEMO models, abstract thinking is required, but reading DEMO models seem to require only a few hours of training. When interviewees were asked about DEMO return on modelling effort, they all were very positive about it, sometimes adding "provided it is used by trained people". Several interviewees deplore a lack of interfaces with other methods. Still, all interviewees would use DEMO again if they would have to work in their project again.

7   Conclusion and Further Work

The current paper is about setting up an observational research approach for an exploratory goal: having insights about BPMMs in practice. We adopted a qualitative research approach with semi-structured interviews for collecting research data.

To define the interview guideline, we relied on criteria of progress for information systems design theories.

The main criteria against which we could assess the proposed observational research approach may be the appropriateness of the insights we obtained during the interviews against the purpose of the research effort. Still, interview guideline themes are only a parameter to ensure this appropriateness: among other things, interviewees sampling, interviewees background compared to interviewers background, way of asking question, interviewers' attitude and degree of remembrance of interviewees regarding the case studies also influence the nature and quality of the collected data.

This paper provides an interview guideline structure that may be adapted from the DEMO interview experience and then potentially used to get insights about other BPMMs. Although interviews analysis has not been performed yet, we may already say that during the interviews performance, no understanding problems between interviewers and interviewees occurred, collected information was actually related to the themes and questions, new information appeared compared to the literature review about DEMO. Besides, the diversity of interviewed stakeholder types allowed the collection of various points of views, sometimes conflicting ones. All interviewees encouraged us both to carry on in DEMO investigation effort and to contact them again in case we would need further information.

The proposed observational research approach has some limitations, amongst which are the following ones:

— As we defined the list of evaluation criteria with a systematic process (gathering two lists), we should investigate for each criterion we included or not what the implications are, then we may (certainly) integrate again some criteria.
— Aier and Fischer explain that the set of criteria of progress they propose for information systems design theories [14] might not be complete. So, for this reason again we should reflect upon the completeness of the criteria we proposed.
— Criteria we proposed are generic to all types of artefacts, further reflection is required whether add aspects specific criteria (model, constructs, method, instantiation).
— We have not reflected upon the limitations that are inherent to the interview technique to evaluate a method.
— Whatever the research approach to get insights about an artefact, the influence of some parameters should be discussed, namely the amount of knowledge of the interviewers and researchers have about the artefact they want to have insights on.
— Various frameworks have been proposed to evaluate methods in IS literature, e.g. [42]. Though, they have not been taken into account in the current paper because our scope is about having insights about a method, so only method evaluation criteria were used for this purpose.

Some of these limitations may be addressed in future work: we plan to analyse the interviews, this will generate insights about the application of DEMO in practice and allow us to reflect upon the practical use of the themes and evaluation criteria that are proposed in the current paper. According to the findings, we may adapt these criteria and investigate in case studies BPMMs other than DEMO to have a variety of experiences with the proposed observational research approach.

References

1. Dias, D.G., Lapão, L.V., Mira da Silva, M.: Using enterprise ontology for improving emergency management in hospitals. Studies in Health Technology and Informatics 180, 58–62 (2012)
2. Dias, D.G., Mendes, C., Mira da Silva, M.: Using Enterprise Ontology for Improving the National Health System-Demonstrated in the Case of a Pharmacy and an Emergency Department. In: Filipe, J., Dietz, J.L.G. (eds.) Proceedings of the International Conference on Knowledge Engineering and Ontology Development (KEOD 2012), pp. 441–451. SciTe-Press, Barcelona (2012)
3. Dias, D.G., Mira da Silva, M., Helfert, M., Shuyan, X.: Using Enterprise Ontology Methodology to Assess the Quality of Information Exchange Demonstrated in the case of Emergency Medical Service. In: Proceedings of the 18th Americas Conference on Information Systems (AMCIS 2012), pp. 1–11. Association for Information Systems, Seattle (2012)
4. Guerreiro, S., Vasconcelos, A., Tribolet, J.: Enterprise dynamic systems control enforcement of run-time business transactions - Lecture notes. In: Albani, A., Aveiro, D., Barjis, J. (eds.) EEWC 2012. LNBIP, vol. 110, pp. 46–60. Springer, Heidelberg (2012)
5. Maij, E., Toussaint, P.J., Kalshoven, M., Poerschke, M., Zwetsloot-Schonk, J.H.M.: Use cases and DEMO: aligning functional features of ICT-infrastructure to business processes. International Journal of Medical Informatics 65, 179–191 (2002)
6. Henriques, M., Tribolet, J., Hoogervorst, J.: Enterprise Governance and DEMO - Guiding enterprise design and operation by addressing DEMO's competence, authority and responsibility notions, 473–476 (2010)
7. Pombinho, J., Aveiro, D., Tribolet, J.: Towards Objective Business Modeling in Enterprise Engineering–Defining Function, Value and Purpose. In: Albani, A., Aveiro, D., Barjis, J. (eds.) EEWC 2012. LNBIP, vol. 110, pp. 93–107. Springer, Heidelberg (2012)
8. Op 't Land, M., Zwitzer, H., Ensink, P., Lebel, Q.: Towards a fast enterprise ontology based method for post merger integration. In: Shin, S.Y., Ossowski, S. (eds.) Proceedings of the 24th Annual ACM Symposium on Applied Computing (SAC 2009), Honolulu, Hawaii, USA, pp. 245–252 (2009)
9. Nagayoshi, S., Liu, Y., Iijima, J.: A study of the patterns for reducing exceptions and improving business process flexibility. In: Albani, A., Aveiro, D., Barjis, J. (eds.) EEWC 2012. LNBIP, vol. 110, pp. 61–76. Springer, Heidelberg (2012)
10. Barjis, J.: A business process modeling and simulation method using DEMO. In: Filipe, J., Cordeiro, J., Cardoso, J. (eds.) ICEIS 2007. LNBIP, vol. 12, pp. 254–265. Springer, Heidelberg (2009)
11. Dumay, M., Dietz, J.L.G., Mulder, J.B.F.: Evaluation of DEMO and the Language / Action Perspective after 10 years of experience. In: The Language Action Perspective on Communication Modelling, Kiruna, Sweden, pp. 77–105 (2005)
12. Enterprise Engineering Institute website, http://www.demo.nl/publications
13. Winter, R.: Design science research in Europe. European Journal of Information Systems 17, 470–475 (2008)
14. Aier, S., Fischer, C.: Criteria of progress for information systems design theories. Information Systems and e-Business Management 9, 133–172 (2010)
15. Henderson-Sellers, B.: Method Engineering: Theory and Practice. In: Karagiannis, D., Mayr, H.C. (eds.) Proceedings of the 5th International Conference on Information Systems Technology and Its Applications (ISTA 2006), Klagenfurt, Austria. Lecture Notes in Informatics (LNI), p. 84 (2006)

16. Mettler, T., Rohner, P.: Situational maturity models as instrumental artifacts for organizational design. In: Proceedings of the 4th International Conference on Design Science Research in Information Systems and Technology (DESRIST 2009), p. 1. ACM Press, New York (2009)

17. Kensing, F.: Towards Evaluation of Methods for Property Determination: A Framework and a Critique of the Yourdon-DeMarco Approach. In: Beyond Productivity: Information Systems Development for Organizational Effectiveness, pp. 325–338 (1984)

18. Seligmann, P.S., Wijers, G.M., Sol, H.G.: Analyzing the structure of IS methodologies, an alternative approach. In: Maes, R. (ed.) Proceedings of the First Dutch Conference on Information Systems, Amersfoort, The Netherlands, pp. 1–28 (1989)

19. March, S.T., Smith, G.F.G.: Design and natural science research on information technology. Decision Support Systems 15, 251–266 (1995)

20. Rescher, N.: Methodological pragmatism: A systems-theoretic approach to the theory of knowledge. Blackwell, Oxford (1977)

21. Moody, D.L.: The method evaluation model: a theoretical model for validating information systems design methods. In: Ivan (ed.) Proceedings of the 11th European Conference on Information Systems (ECIS 2003), Naples, Italy (2003)

22. Hommes, B.-J., van Reijswoud, V.E.: Assessing the quality of business process modelling techniques. In: Proceedings of the 33rd Hawaii International Conference on System Sciences (HICSS 2000), pp. 1–10 (2000)

23. Weigand, H.: LAP: 10 years in retrospect. In: The Language Action Perspective on Communication Modelling, Kiruna, Sweden, June 19-20, pp. 1–8 (2005)

24. Khavas, S.S.: The Adoption of DEMO in Practice - Dissertation for a Master of Science in Computer Science (2010)

25. Winter, R., Gericke, A., Bucher, T.: Method versus model – two sides of the same coin? In: Albani, A., Barjis, J., Dietz, J.L.G. (eds.) CIAO! 2009. LNBIP, vol. 34, pp. 1–15. Springer, Heidelberg (2009)

26. Huysmans, P., Ven, K., Verelst, J.: Using the DEMO methodology for modeling open source software development processes. Information and Software Technology 52, 656–671 (2010)

27. Ven, K., Verelst, J.: The adoption of DEMO: A research agenda. In: Albani, A., Barjis, J., Dietz, J.L.G. (eds.) CIAO! 2009. LNBIP, vol. 34, pp. 157–171. Springer, Heidelberg (2009)

28. Mingers, J., Brocklesby, J.: Multimethodology: Towards a framework for mixing methodologies. Omega 25, 489–509 (1997)

29. Myers, M.D.: Qualitative research in information systems 21(2), 241–242 (June 1997), MISQ Discovery, archival version: http://www.misq.org/supplements/; Association for Information Systems (AISWorld) Section on Qualitative Research in Information Systems, updated version: http://www.qual.auckland.ac.nz (last modified March 21, 2013)

30. Walsham, G.: Interpreting information systems in organizations. John Wiley & Sons, Inc. (1993)

31. Walsham, G.: The Emergence of Interpretivism in IS Research. Information Systems Research 6, 376–394 (1995)

32. Myers, M.D., Newman, M.: The qualitative interview in IS research: Examining the craft. Information and Organization 17, 2–26 (2007)

33. Rubin, H.J., Rubin, I.S.: Qualitative interviewing: The art of hearing data. Sage (2011)

34. Aier, S., Fischer, C.: Scientific Progress of Design Research Artefacts. In: Proceedings of the 17th European Conference on Information Systems (ECIS 2009) (2009)

35. Hevner, A.R., March, S.T., Park, J., Ram, S.: Design Science in Information Systems Research. Information Systems Research 28, 75–104 (2004)
36. Gregor, S., Jones, D.: The anatomy of a design theory. Journal of the Association for Information Systems 8, 312–335 (2007)
37. Venable, J., Pries-Heje, J., Baskerville, R.: A comprehensive framework for evaluation in design science research. In: Peffers, K., Rothenberger, M., Kuechler, B. (eds.) DESRIST 2012. LNCS, vol. 7286, pp. 423–438. Springer, Heidelberg (2012)
38. Venable, J.R.: Identifying and Addressing Stakeholder Interests in Design Science Research: An Analysis Using Critical Systems Heuristics. Information Systems–Creativity and Innovation in Small and Medium Enterprises, 93–112 (2009)
39. Aier, S., Fischer, C., Winter, R.: Theoretical Stability of Information Systems Design Theory Evaluations Based upon Habermas's Discourse Theory. A Journal on the Theory of Ordered Sets and Its Applications (2011)
40. Wieringa, R.J.: Design science as nested problem solving. In: Proceedings of the 4th International Conference on Design Science Research in Information Systems and Technology (DESRIST), p. 8 (2009)
41. Miles, M.B., Huberman, A.M.: Qualitative Data Analysis: An Expanded Sourcebook. SAGE (1994)
42. Vavpotic, D., Bajec, M.: An approach for concurrent evaluation of technical and social aspects of software development methodologies. Information and Software Technology 51, 528–545 (2009)

A Dynamic Approach to Process Design: A Pattern for Extending the Flexibility of Process Models

Jiri Kolar, Lubomir Dockal, and Tomas Pitner

Masaryk University, Faculty of Informatics,
Botanicka 68a, 602 00 Brno, Czech Republic
kolar@fi.muni.cz
http://fi.muni.cz/~xkolar2/

Abstract. This paper presents a specific approach to Business Process design by combining selected principles of Adaptive Case Management, traditional modeling of processes executable in Business Process Management Systems, and a constraint-based approach to process design. This combined approach is intended for business situations, where traditional process models with rigid structures can lead to limitations of business flexibility. We propose a process design pattern that is suitable for the modeling of ad-hoc processes within common BPMS-based systems. The pattern can be used to define a process structure in a declarative constraint-based manner. Further, we present an application of the approach in an actual project, which is an end-to-end BPM project from an insurance business. The project uncovered needs for an extended flexibility of process structures. This along with requirements based on ad-hoc processes led to advancement in the presented approach. This paper presents a versatile, generally applicable solution, which was later tailored for the purpose of the aforementioned project and led to the successful satisfaction of the requirements. The approach is part of a more comprehensive research effort – complex BPM adoption methodology BPM4SME designed primarily for Small and Medium Enterprises, which put emphasis on the agility of the BPM adoption process and consequent flexible implementations of BPMS-based systems.

Keywords: BPM, process design pattern, Agile process design, process flexibility, ad-hoc processes, ad-hoc process pattern process discovery.

1 Introduction

In the scope of traditional business process models, we usually define a set of work tasks, their performers, and an explicit order in which those tasks should be performed [1]. Nowadays, an increasing amount of process models are defined in modeling languages such as Business Process Modeling Notation (BPMN), based on Petri-nets formalism [2], [3]. BPMN 2.0 was recently recognized as an industry standard for process modeling and is widely accepted in practice [4]. By modeling a process in such a language, we define the allowed sequences

J. Grabis et al. (Eds.): PoEM 2013, LNBIP 165, pp. 176–190, 2013.

in which process tasks can be performed by defining possible paths through the process graph. Such rigidly defined process models are well applicable to situations where the explicit definition of task order is known in design-time. This has several positive outcomes, such as the establishment of a uniformed work-process, efficient Business Activity Monitoring [5] and other general outcomes of Business Process Management (BPM) [6], [7]. Such BPMN process models can also be consequently executed on a process execution engine - a core component of every Business Process Management System (BPMS) [1].

In business, situations other than the ones outlined above may also arise. For certain type of work, it is optimal to decide about task ordering in run time, according to decisions carried out by task performers. For this kind of work, we will use the well-established term, knowledge work [8],[9].

For knowledge work, the desired order of tasks can differ from case to case. In these situations, process models would have to cover all possible scenarios. This can result in very chaotic process models and model clarity - the important benefit of process modeling [7] is lost. Therefore, there are different needs in the context of supportive Information Systems for knowledge intensive work. Systems built on approaches such as Adaptive Case Management (ACM) provide *palettes* of tasks [9] which can be performed in any order. Such systems do not put hard restrictions on ordering. Instead, they help knowledge workers find similarities among cases and provide soft recommendations based on the orders of tasks previously performed in similar or related cases. In this way, another very important outcome of the BPM-based approach, the codification of business know-how, is preserved and the flexibility of knowledge work is not limited [10], [11], [9].

However, in business practice, it is very common to mix these two kinds of work [12]. Management processes are often performed on the top level [13] where traditional rigid process definitions lead to better monitoring and process unification. Such management processes consequently instantiate sub-processes dealing with certain business activities and only these sub-processes are often knowledge-intensive. The schism of selection among these approaches during consequent Information System development often leads to a paralysis in decision-making, as it is not clear which paradigm to follow. This was recognized in practice as a strong showstopper of many BPMS-based system implementations.

One could clearly argue that BPMS systems should not be used in the business context where such ad-hoc processes appear. However, in practice, we often find situations where traditional BPM seems to be a perfect solution for major amounts of work and some minor cases involving ad-hoc processes are identified much later when BPM adoption is already in progress. In such cases, it often does not make sense to combine BPM with different paradigms such as ACM. This is because it would significantly raise costs, increase complexity, and confuse business users, which already have problems understanding the process-based BPM paradigm. This is also the case of the BPM project presented later in this paper.

Before we clearly define this problem and propose a solution, we should clarify the terminology of Dynamic characteristics of Process Models. We will follow the terminology of [12] and define three terms related to business process dynamics:

- **Dynamism** is a characteristic related to the evolution of process model initiated either by changes in business environment or process re-engineering efforts. These changes are made in design-time and they involve a non-trivial problem - the migration of previously executed instances [12]. Although this characteristic is not directly in scope with this paper, the proposed solution should decrease the number of situations where a change in the process model is needed.
- **Adaptability** is the process ability to cope with exceptional circumstances and non-standard behavior. This can be partially solved in design-time by adjusting the process model structure. However, there are still many situations when we have to rely on BPMS-specific technological solutions and run-time work-arounds. We will partially touch on this problem later in the paper.
- **Flexibility** is a characteristic of the process model related to loose or partially defined model structures specified in design-time. The full specification of the process is completed at run-time and it may differ for each process instance. Flexibility is the main focus of this paper, and its improvement is the main objective of our pattern-based approach.

2   Problem Description

Let us sum up three important facts for a clearer definition of the problem.

1. Traditional process models with an explicit ordering of tasks can limit work-process flexibility in certain cases of knowledge-intensive work in which we are not able to determine the exact ordering of tasks before executing a particular process instance [14]. On the other hand, traditional process models significantly help to codify the know-how in their structure [15], [16].
2. To codify know-how of knowledge work, the previous individual decisions of knowledge workers have to be recorded and related to new cases with similar characteristics [9].
3. In practice, major parts of the process models often correspond to traditional rigid structure and only relatively small parts demand a high level of flexibility [12].

Our focus is restricted to situations where we generally want to have a traditional BPMS-based solution. This is due to the fact that nowadays, BPMSes are generally available technologies and we can find relatively mature BPM products [17]. In opposition, ACM-based solutions are usually developed as a custom solution [9]. Therefore, our desire is to achieve the extended flexibility of process models to make them suitable for knowledge work and avoid mixing of ACM and BPM technologies. Obviously, limited flexibility is a common obstacle of

BPM adoptions [18], [19]. This was also confirmed during the practice project in which we participated.

According to the previously described circumstances, we are trying to find a process design pattern, which is applicable either during the initial process design, or even to redesign the existing process. The pattern should meet the following requirements, which were defined during the aforementioned project and later refined according to the related research [12], [13]:

1. The pattern will be applicable to traditional rigid BPMN process models.
2. The pattern will isolate the ad-hoc process parts into sub-process without interfering with the rigid structure of the parent process.
3. The pattern will provide a mechanism to influence such isolated sub-processes from their parent process and provide a mechanism for defining declarative constraints on an ad-hoc sequence.
4. The pattern will record sequences of tasks claimed in run-time for each instance of an ad-hoc sub-process and provide valuable historical data for the discovery of soft structures. This gives certain guidance to the worker, recommending but not directing him on how to proceed in the work process. At the same time, it preserves the know-how codification feature of BPM.
5. The pattern should be usable within conventional modeling methods and implementable in various BPMSes. Therefore, to keep the approach as versatile as possible, it should only use standardized BPMN constructs that are available in most BPMSes.

3 Related Work

Our approach is a specific application of several autonomous principles, which were the subject of several research efforts in the past.

Research related to process design patterns has been well known since the very beginning of BPM era [20], [21]. Most of these efforts focus primarily on describing the best practices for modeling certain logical structures in processes. Other efforts [20] describe patterns for exception handling aimed towards the extension of process adaptability [22]. We can also find later updates of pattern approaches [23], [24] covering more recent advancements in BPM. Such patterns are generally applicable in any process and business context. In opposition, we propose a more specific pattern for handling ad-hocness which is suitable for situations described later in this paper.

We can find several sources related to the characteristics of process flexibility in [12] and [13]. A very relevant topic is research related to the flexibility of processes, particularly a construct called *pockets of flexibility* [12], and the later effort to solve this problem with constraints [25], [26]. The constraint approach is partially used in our work as well. We build our pattern on top of these approaches and use the terminology established mainly in [12]. However, these approaches are rather general and discuss the ad-hoc principles in a general workflow-modeling perspective. Since this research was published, BPM has made big steps forward and we are therefore able to be more specific and propose solutions, which are directly applicable in the context of currently available BPM technologies. Another interesting approach, which could solve our problem, is based on *Worklets* [27], [28]. However, this is something purely implementation-specific and therefore does not meet our requirement in versatility.

Furthermore, we can also find attempts to achieve flexibility by the adaptation of process definitions, such as [29]. Certain principles used here are also highly relevant in our context. Surveys assessing the current advancements in research on process flexibility such as [18] can be found as well.

Probably the most complete work about declarative approach to process definitions can be found in [13] and consequently in more recent publications [30], [31] related to complementary Declare tooling. Some case studies from practical applications of this approach exist such as [32].

Relevant recommendation-based approach is described in [11]. Research focused on process discovery and mining which is discussed at the end of this paper can be found in [33] and [34].

3.1   Our Research Context: BPM4SME Methodology for Agile BPM Adoption

The presented approach is a part of a more comprehensive research effort, BPM4SME methodology for small-scale BPM adoptions. As confirmed by related research sources [35], [7], the adoption of the BPM paradigm in the Small and Medium Enterprise (SME) sector has several specific obstacles. We try to overcome these obstacles and develop a methodology, which provides helpful guidelines for successful and flexible BPM end-to-end adoptions in organizations of SME sizing. Our methodology is built on the following key principles. This paper is mainly contribution to the second one.

1. The application of agile collaboration while defining the business motivation model, process architecture, and process design
2. The creation of patterns for designing non-restrictive processes, which do not interfere with the turbulent character of SME business
3. A design for lightweight BPMS-based systems resulting in easy customizable solutions with low initial and consequent maintenance costs
4. A simplified documentation structure where documented processes can be easily transformed into their executable form and vice versa

An agile practice research approach is applied; thusly we verify each component of the methodology in a practical project in an actual business environment at the end of each milestone. Results of those projects are regularly published and discussed with practitioners from different business environments. Thus far, the methodology has been applied in practice in the following projects:

1. A BPM adoption in a web-app oriented SME - the software company IT Logica s.r.o. [36].

2. Process design and optimization in the context of human resources in the ICT department of Masaryk University in Brno [37].
3. Analysis at the headquarters of Masaryk University, several results discussed in the paper related to collaboration in process design [38] and [39].
4. An end-to-end implementation of a BPMS-based solution in a global insurance company, presented at the end of this paper.

4 Proposed Solution

It is now appropriate to clarify certain terminology: *task* vs. *activity*. According to the BPMN standard, *activity* is a process element, which can contain either one task or the nested sub-process consisting of several tasks and other modeling elements. Our pattern is intended to handle not just ad-hoc sequences of tasks but also sequences of activities. Therefore, starting for now, to stay consistent with BPMN, we will use the term of *activity* without differentiating between task and nested sub-process.

We now present our pattern with a step-by-step application in process design. To model and execute ad-hoc sub-process according to our approach, the following steps must be performed:

4.1 The Separation of Ad-Hoc Process Parts

The first step is to identify parts of existing processes where an ad-hoc order of activities is desired. We should include all process activities which can be ordered ad-hoc and separate them into one or more sub-process. All activities in one ad-hoc sub-process should be logically related and ideally belonging to one unit of work. Such a separation assures that the rest of the process will be isolated from the on-demand order of activity execution. The separated sub-process will be managed from the parent process. This means that it can be multi-instantiated, repeated several times, or terminated on-demand by events triggered from the parent process.

4.2 The Application of an Ad-Hoc Pattern

As depicted in (Fig. 1), the pattern consists of three basic sections. The two on the left serve for assigning tasks. This can be done either by performers, which can freely choose any allowed activity they want, or the assignment can be directed from the *Managing process* with the use of inter-process communication. These sections are synchronized and re-executed in loops. In these sections we also record the sequence of performed activities, evaluate Constraint Business Rules on the recorded sequence and determine which activities are allowed to be assigned in each process state. We will explain the details of the constraint concept in following paragraph. In the *activity section*, assigned activities are being performed and they are either completed or re-assigned. This mechanism is used for delegation, which is common in the context of ad-hoc processes. The process can be terminated either by the intervention of the Managing process or it can terminate itself after conditions defined by the business rules are met.

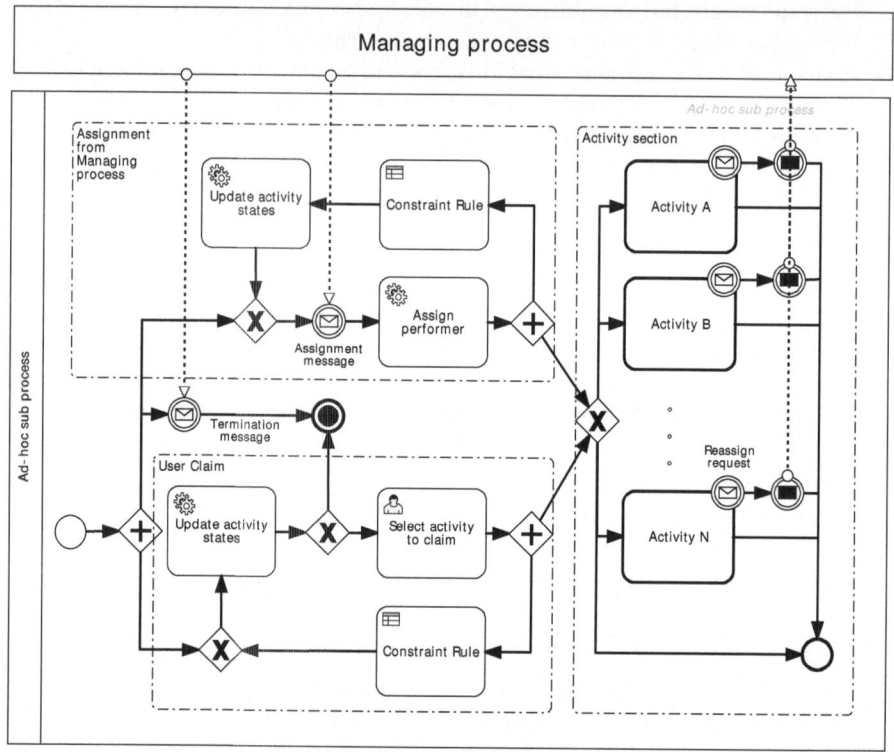

Fig. 1. Process pattern

4.3   The Definition of Constraints

The pattern contains business rule tasks, which are responsible for deciding which activities can be assigned to a performer in a certain moment. As an input, this business rule takes a list of assigned activities ordered by time, evaluates constraints that can prohibit the assigning of certain activities in the next assignment step, and produces a list of activities, which can be assigned as an output. Those lists are saved into dedicated objects in process data in the case of data-model-based BPMS, or into an external business object in the case of pure service-based BPMS.

For particular constraint scenarios, we can use the declarative structural patterns defined in a constraint-based approach [13]. In this way we can use the rule language to define complex Linear Time Logic (LTL) based constraints. In practice this concept can be eventually replaced by simple if-then-else rules. Nevertheless, the sophisticated usage of the rule language for defining adequate LTL [40] provides mechanisms for an implementation of the declarative constraint-based approach [13] within a conventional BPMN 2.0 based BPMS.

4.4   The Identification of Common Patterns in Activity Order

Suppose we have an ad-hoc process modeled according to our pattern with constraint rules. To achieve the last goal and satisfy the requirement for detecting the relationship between activity order and case characteristics, we record each path through ad-hoc process and group similar sequences into a set of common patterns. Consequently we compare these patterns to the active process instance and we are able to provide soft recommendations based on similarities. For that, we have to use two mechanisms not described by the pattern. First, we have to use some mechanism to find similarities. This has to be performed by a service outside of the process. Secondly, we use such a similarity detection mechanism to provide just-in-time intentions to the user in a user interface. For example, we can highlight certain activities, which are usually successors of the last claimed activity. The implementation of this construct can be different for each BPMS and therefore we do not propose any general solution.

4.5   Approach Limitations

Let us discuss the limitations of our approach. Despite the fact that we try to propose a generally applicable solution, we presume that the used BPMS will provide several core functionalities. First, it must implement BPMN 2.0 specifications to the extent in which used modeling elements are covered. Second, for a full-blown constraint driven solution, an adequate Business Rule Management System (BRMS) must be used. Third, there must be a mechanism for in-process reassigning of activity executors. All of these features are generally available in many BPMS products, however, not necessarily in all of them. Last, we expect a certain business setting in which we are able to identify Managing processes in the process architecture; moreover, the *ad-hocness* is mostly present in nested processes, not processes on the top level. Our pattern is also generally applicable for cases where the last condition is not met. However, some modifications of terminology and eventually of the pattern itself may be needed.

5   Application of the Approach in Insurance Business

We are going to present a real BPM project from an insurance business. The problem we present in this paper was introduced in this project. We searched for an optimal solution, which led to the creation of the presented approach. The light-weighted version of the approach was later applied in this project and led to the process redesign, which satisfied given requirements on extended process flexibility. Certain customizations of the approach were made in accordance to specifics of used Bizagi BPMS.

The project was elaborated in a global insurance company. The company recently acquired several smaller insurance companies across Eastern Europe. These acquired companies had similar business processes customized to local regulations and business environments in particular countries. Acquisitions were transformed into Business Units (BU) of the new owner. The transformation typically brought about the need for process unification and the development of a centralized process-driven Information System, which could be used across these newly created BUs. For the implementation of such a system, Bizagi BPMS was chosen as a main BPM platform.

5.1   Project Goals

Three main goals were set in the project:

1. The unification of processes across all business units with small customizations per country respecting differences in country-specific legal restrictions and locally used systems
2. The consequent unification of process monitoring and reporting processes, which could enable the mother company to compare business results achieved across BUs
3. The integration of locally used systems to collect critical business data in one system.

5.2   A Change in Requirements and Process Redesign

According to the initial settings and consequent prototype developed by the BPMS supplier Bizagi, all of the processes were modeled as hard-ordered and the groups of related ad-hoc activities were typically concentrated into one form-based *blob task* executed in loops. Therefore, performers of *blob tasks* had to wait for other performers to complete their all activites before they could claim the *blob task*. From the outer process, there was no control over activities performed inside these *blob tasks*.

The problem was identified after initial testing in one BU, where related ad-hoc parts of the process were performed by various performers. Local project coordinators in the BU complained about inefficient collaboration and they expressed several change requests to solve this issue. Such change requests were analyzed on the side of the BPM team and led to the advancement of the presented approach and consequent application of the pattern to the process redesign. An important influence on the redesign had also the RIVA method [41] used in the initial process design.

About 15 core processes were implemented in the first iteration. However, some of those were nested in each other. A need for *ad-hocness* was identified in three cases. We mention two of the most important top-level processes to understand the context and then we take a closer look at the *Quote evaluation* sub-process, one of three processes, where our pattern was applied.

1. The Opportunity management process
   This is the most important top-level process used for managing potential business opportunities, the state of each opportunity, and communication

with the potential customer. The process is started by the first contact with a potential customer and ends ideally with the acceptance of a proposed offer from the customer's side, which leads to consequent signatures of the policy document. This process usually instantiates the important underwriting process described below. The underwriting process is executed in parallel with Opportunity management and the results of underwriting are sent back to the Opportunity Management process.

2. The Underwriting process
   This top-level process is selecting risks for insurance in respect of a plan and classifying members according to their degrees of insatiability so that the appropriate premium may be charged and the terms offered may be reviewed. This is the process responsible for handling particular offers consisting of the assessment of the customer's requests regarding insurance products. Underwriting itself, and carrying out the quoting process and agreements on particular business contracts is the ideal case.

3. The Quote evaluation sub-process
   In this process parameters for each product included in the resulting quotes are considered. There are one or more Underwriters assigned to the preparation of each particular product and one Chief Underwriter responsible for the whole quote. He must confirm every completed product preparation. He also has the rights to re-initiate any of the Prepare product activities, assign particular Underwriter to a particular *product preparation* activity, and terminate the whole process by quote completion. This sub-process was the subject of redesign in accordance with our pattern and the result is depicted in (Fig. 2).

We applied several specific customizations of the general pattern presented in this paper due to the specifics of Bizagi BPMS:

1. Business rules were hard-coded into a complex event gateway
2. Re-assignment messaging was not applied as Bizagi BPMS has built-in features for delegation
3. The activity of *Manage Quote* allows the Quote supervisor to perform all management tasks, such as activity re-assignment, delegation, termination of activities, parametric changes in constraint conditions, etc. and has the same role as the Managing process in our pattern

5.3   Results

Redesigned processes were deployed for testing in one BU and offered to others. Within two months, other local project coordinators of three other countries also requested the redesign of their version of the process according to this approach. Finally, four out of five BUs are now working according to the new processes. In two BUs the process change was deployed into production environment, in the other two the change was made during the pilot system testing period. For evaluation of results, three employees from each BU were asked to provide feedback. In each BU, each of the following roles was represented by one individual

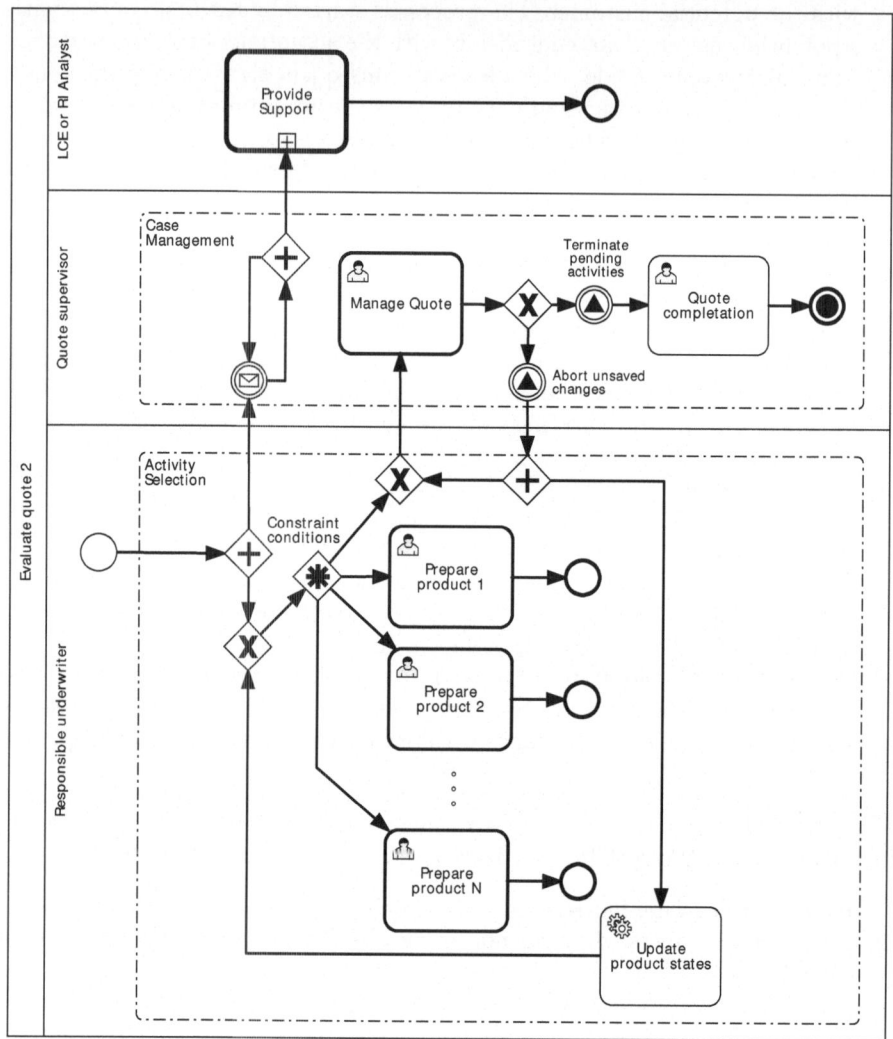

Fig. 2. Figure 2. (Evaluate quote process)

- Project Coordinator (PC) - the person responsible for the definition of requirements on the system, customization of the processes in respective BU
  and moderation of the communication between the users and the system
  developers.
- Chief Underwriter (CU) - the person responsible for managing the underlying
  sub-processes, thus the performer of the Managing Process
- Underwriter (U) - the employee performing particular ad-hoc ordered product preparation tasks.

Each of them was asked to compare the former and the redesigned process and rate the impact of the process redesign against the aspects listed in (Table 5.3). For each aspect, there were the following possible ratings: "-1" for worse than before the change, "0" for no improvement, "1" for improvement and "-" for no answer.

	BU1 (production)			BU2 (production)			BU3 (pilot)			BU4 (pilot)			Sum per aspect <-12,12>
Role	PC	CU	U	PC	CU	U	PC	CU	U	PC	CU	U	
Process model clarity	-1	0	0	0	-1	0	0	-1	0	0	0	0	-3
Work-flow flexibility	1	1	1	0	1	1	-	1	1	-	1	1	9
Time efficiency	-	0	1	-	0	1	-	1	1	1	0	1	6
Process manageability	-	1	1	1	1	1	1	0	1	-	1	-1	7
Sum per role <-4,4>	0	2	3	1	1	3	1	1	3	1	2	1	
Sum per BU <-12,12>	5			5			5			4			

According to acquired figures in (Table 5.3), there is a slight decrease of process model clarity observed by the Project Coordinators and some of the Chief Underwriters, the main users of the process model. On the other hand, there was a significant improvement of work-flow flexibility observed by all the Underwriters and more than half of the Chief Underwriters, as they could operate more flexibly without dependence on each other's tasks. As we can see in (Table 5.3), the overall perception of the process redesign was rather positive, especially in BUs where the system was deployed into the production environment with more intensive system usage. The best rating was generally given by Underwriters, thus we claim that the highest improvement was perceived by ad-hoc task performers.

6   Discussion and Conclusions

The presented approach evolved from the request for process redesign during the elaboration of the presented project. We developed the approach as a general solution of the change request, as generally applicable pattern for the modeling of ad-hoc processes with standard BPMN. We consider the approach versatile enough to be used within most modern BPMS platforms. We further customized this approach for purposes of the presented project and applied it during the process redesign. The redesign impact was evaluated by several process performers and well accepted across four out of five BUs of the company, as we describe in Results section. Our future aim is to verify this approach in different business environments and to perform further extensions to establish a versatile best practice, which can be used in the context of our BPM4SME methodology.

During the advancement of the approach, we noticed interesting fact that will be the subject of further research. The recorded sequences of activities in ad-hoc parts of the process produce data, which can be used for several purposes. First, we are able to use it to find common ordering patterns related to process data. Second, we can use them to improve our constraints on fly to make them more restrictive to achieve higher determinism. Third, these data can be used for a semi-automatic process discovery. Therefore, in the future, we plan to perform a process discovery experiment in an organization interested in BPM adoption.

Concerning limitations, we have to admit that it can be used to extend process Flexibility and partially process Adaptability. However, it does not provide any improvement to process Dynamism as it was defined at the beginning of this paper. Therefore, once we want to add completely new activities into an ad-hoc process, we still have to solve the same problems related to process model changes in a traditional approach to process modeling. This problem remains unsolved and we are not able find any satisfactory solution applicable on a BPMN level. There were some discussions about generic activities, but they are not defined in BPMN standards and such a solution could be done by hacking particular BPMS. All other proposed solutions ended up with this result as well. Something similar is described by [27], but this is also a proprietary solution and far from being generalized the way our pattern is. Therefore, this problem, which could significantly extend our approach, remains as another challenge for further research.

References

1. Jeston, J., Nelis, J.: Business Process Management: Practical Guidelines to Successful Implementations. Taylor & Francis Group (2006)
2. van der Aalst, W.M.P.: The application of Petri nets to workflow management. The Journal of Circuits, Systems and Computers 8(1), 21–66 (1998)
3. Ramadan, M., Elmongui, H.G., Hassan, R.: Bpmn formalisation using coloured petri nets. In: Proceedings of the 2nd GSTF Annual International Conference on Software Engineering & Applications (SEA 2011) (2011)
4. Ko, R.K.L., Lee, S.S.G., Lee, E.W.: Business process management (BPM) standards: a survey. Business Process Management Journal 15(5), 744–791 (2009)
5. Kolar, J.: Business activity monitoring. Master's thesis, Masaryk University (2012)
6. Rudden, J.: Making the case for bpm–a benefits checklist. BPTrends (2007)
7. Mertens, W., Van den Bergh, J., Viaene, S., Schroder-Pander, F.: How bpm impacts jobs: An exploratory field study. In: 2011 44th Hawaii International Conference on System Sciences (HICSS), pp. 1–10 (2011)
8. Magal, S.R., Word, J.: Essentials of Business Processes and Information Systems, 1st edn. Wiley Publishing (2009)
9. Swenson, K.D.: Mastering the Unpredictable: How Adaptive Case Management Will Revolutionize the Way That Knowledge Workers Get Things Done, 1st edn. Meghan-Kiffer Press, Tampa (2010)

10. van der Aalst, W.M., Weske, M., Grünbauer, D.: Case handling: A new paradigm for business process support. Data and Knowledge Engineering 53 (2005)
11. Schonenberg, H., Weber, B., van Dongen, B.F., van der Aalst, W.M.P.: Supporting flexible processes through recommendations based on history. In: Dumas, M., Reichert, M., Shan, M.-C. (eds.) BPM 2008. LNCS, vol. 5240, pp. 51–66. Springer, Heidelberg (2008)
12. Sadiq, S., Sadiq, W., Orlowska, M.: Pockets of flexibility in workflow specification. In: Kunii, H.S., Jajodia, S., Sølvberg, A. (eds.) ER 2001. LNCS, vol. 2224, pp. 513–526. Springer, Heidelberg (2001)
13. Pesic, M.: Constraint-Based Workflow Management Systems: Shifting Control to Users. PhD thesis, Eindhoven University of Technology (2008)
14. Deng, S., Yu, Z., Wu, Z., Huang, L.: Enhancement of workflow flexibility by composing activities at run-time. In: Proceedings of the 2004 ACM Symposium on Applied Computing, SAC 2004, pp. 667–673. ACM, New York (2004)
15. Wyssusek, B., Schwartz, M., Kremberg, B., Baier, F., Krallmann, H.: Business process modelling as an element of knowledge management - a model theory approach (2001)
16. Kalpic, B., Bernus, P.: Business process modeling through the knowledge management perspective. Journal of Knowledge Management 10(3), 40–56 (2006)
17. Jim Sinur, J.B.H.: Magic quadrant for business process management. Gartner RAS Core Research Note G00205212, Gartner (October 2010)
18. Schonenberg, H., Mans, R., Russell, N., Mulyar, N., van der Aalst, W.: Process flexibility: A survey of contemporary approaches. In: Dietz, J.L.G., Albani, A., Barjis, J. (eds.) CIAO! 2008 and EOMAS 2008. LNBIP, vol. 10, pp. 16–30. Springer, Heidelberg (2008)
19. Imanipour, N., Talebi, K., Rezazadeh, S.: Obstacles in business process management (bpm) implementation and adoption in smes. working papers series (2012)
20. van der Aalst, W., ter Hofstede, A., Kiepuszewski, B., Barros, A.: Workflow patterns. Distributed and Parallel Databases 14(1), 5–51 (2003)
21. Aalst, W.M.P.v.d., Barros, A.P., Hofstede, A.H.M.t., Kiepuszewski, B.: Advanced workflow patterns. In: Proceedings of the 7th International Conference on Cooperative Information Systems. CoopIS 2002, pp.18–29. Springer, London (2000)
22. Russell, N., van der Aalst, W.M.P.: Arthur: Exception Handling Patterns in Process-Aware Information Systems. Technical report, BPMcenter.org (2006)
23. Russell, N., ter Hofstede, A.H.M., van der Aalst, W.M.P., Mulyar, N.: Workflow Control-Flow Patterns: A Revised View. Technical report, BPMcenter.org (2006)
24. Russell, N., ter Hofstede, A.H.M., Edmond, D., van der Aalst, W.M.P.: Workflow data patterns: Identification, representation and tool support. In: Delcambre, L.M.L., Kop, C., Mayr, H.C., Mylopoulos, J., Pastor, Ó. (eds.) ER 2005. LNCS, vol. 3716, pp. 353–368. Springer, Heidelberg (2005)
25. Sadiq, S.W., Orlowska, M.E., Sadiq, W.: Specification and validation of process constraints for flexible workflows. Inf. Syst. 30(5), 349–378 (2005)
26. Mangan, P., Sadiq, S.: On building workflow models for flexible processes. Aust. Comput. Sci. Commun. 24(2), 103–109 (2002)
27. Adams, M., Hofstede, A.H.M.T., Edmond, D.: Worklets: A service-oriented implementation of dynamic flexibility. In: Workfows (2005)
28. van der Aalst, W.M.P., Adams, M., ter Hofstede, A.H.M., Pesic, M., Schonenberg, H.: Flexibility as a service. In: Chen, L., Liu, C., Liu, Q., Deng, K. (eds.) DASFAA 2009. LNCS, vol. 5667, pp. 319–333. Springer, Heidelberg (2009)

29. Weber, B., Rinderle, S., Reichert, M.: Change patterns and change support features in process-aware information systems. In: Krogstie, J., Opdahl, A.L., Sindre, G. (eds.) CAiSE 2007 and WES 2007. LNCS, vol. 4495, pp. 574–588. Springer, Heidelberg (2007)

30. van der Aalst, W., Pesic, M., Schonenberg, H.: Declarative workflows: Balancing between flexibility and support. Computer Science - Research and Development 23(2), 99–113 (2009)

31. Pesic, M., Schonenberg, H., Aalst, W.: Declarative workflow. In: Hofstede, A.H.M., Aalst, W.M.P., Adams, M., Russell, N. (eds.) Modern Business Process Automation, pp. 175–201. Springer, Heidelberg (2010)

32. Mulyar, N., Pesic, M., van der Aalst, W.M.P., Peleg, M.: Declarative and procedural approaches for modelling clinical guidelines: Addressing flexibility issues. In: ter Hofstede, A.H.M., Benatallah, B., Paik, H.-Y. (eds.) BPM Workshops 2007. LNCS, vol. 4928, pp. 335–346. Springer, Heidelberg (2008)

33. Van der Aalst, W.M.P., Giinther, C.: Finding structure in unstructured processes: The case for process mining. In: Seventh International Conference on Application of Concurrency to System Design, ACSD 2007, pp. 3–12 (2007)

34. Maggi, F., Mooij, A., Van der Aalst, W.M.P.: User-guided discovery of declarative process models. In: 2011 IEEE Symposium on Computational Intelligence and Data Mining (CIDM), pp. 192–199 (2011)

35. Singer, R., Zinser, E.: Business process management — S-BPM a new paradigm for competitive advantage? In: Buchwald, H., Fleischmann, A., Seese, D., Stary, C. (eds.) S-BPM ONE 2009. CCIS, vol. 85, pp. 48–70. Springer, Heidelberg (2010)

36. Kolar, J.: Process analysis at it logica s.r.o. Business analytical document, Jiri Kolar, BPM analyst (2011)

37. Kolar, J.: Process analysis at ict department faculty of arts masaryk unversity. Business analytical document, Jiri Kolar, BPM analyst (2011)

38. Kolář, J., Pitner, T.: Collaborative process design in cloud environment. In: Haller, A., Huang, G., Huang, Z., Paik, H.-y., Sheng, Q.Z. (eds.) WISE 2011 and 2012. LNCS, vol. 7652, pp. 55–69. Springer, Heidelberg (2013)

39. Kolar, J.: Agile BPM in the age of cloud technologies. Scalable Computing: Practice and Experience 13(4) (2012)

40. Rozier, K.Y.: Survey: Linear temporal logic symbolic model checking. Comput. Sci. Rev. 5(2), 163–203 (2011)

41. Ould, M., Ltd, V.C., Society, B.C.: Business Process Management: A Rigorous Approach. Meghan-Kiffer Press (2005)

Creating and Updating Personalized and Verbalized Business Process Descriptions

Jens Kolb[1], Henrik Leopold[2], Jan Mendling[3], and Manfred Reichert[1]

[1] Ulm University, Germany
{jens.kolb,manfred.reichert}@uni-ulm.de
www.uni-ulm.de/dbis
[2] Humboldt-Universität zu Berlin, Unter den Linden 6, 10099 Berlin, Germany
henrik.leopold@wiwi.hu-berlin.de
[3] Wirtschaftsuniversität Wien, Augasse 2-6, A-1090 Vienna, Austria
jan.mendling@wu.ac.at

Abstract. The increasing adoption of process-aware information systems (PAISs) has resulted in large process model collections. To support users having different perspectives on complex processes and related data, a PAIS should enable personalized process views, i.e., user-specific abstractions of process models. Despite the abstraction achieved through views of the graphical process models, many end users still struggle with understanding these graphical models and their details. For selected user groups, therefore, a PAIS should provide verbalized process descriptions describing their role in the process. Existing PAISs neither provide mechanisms for managing process views nor verbalized process descriptions. While process views have been used as visual abstractions for large process models, so far no work exists on how to provide both personalized and verbalized process descriptions based on respective views. This paper presents an approach for creating such personalized and verbalized process descriptions based on process views. Furthermore, textual changes of a personalized and verbalized process description are correctly mapped to corresponding updates of the underlying process model. In this context, all other views and process descriptions related to this process model are migrated to the new version of the process model as well. Overall, our approach enables end users to understand and evolve large process models based on personalized and verbalized process descriptions.

Keywords: process model abstraction, updatable process view, process change, natural language, process visualization, human-centered processes.

1 Introduction

Process-aware information systems (PAISs) provide support for business processes at the operational level. Usually, a PAIS separates process logic from application code, relying on graphical *process models*. In turn, this enables a separation of concerns, which is a well established principle in computer science to increase maintainability and reduce costs of change [1].

J. Grabis et al. (Eds.): PoEM 2013, LNBIP 165, pp. 191–205, 2013.

The increasing adoption of PAISs has resulted in large process model collections often including hundreds or thousands of process models [2]. Each of these process models may refer to different organizational units or user groups, and comprise dozens or hundreds of activities [3]. Usually, the different user groups require customized views on process models, enabling a personalized process abstraction and visualization for them [4,5,6]. For example, managers rather prefer an abstract process overview, whereas process participants need a detailed view of those process parts they are involved in. Several approaches for creating such process model views, which are based on well-defined abstraction techniques, have been proposed [7,8,9]. However, in many cases providing a customized process view is not sufficient for making the relevant part of a process model understandable for the end user. To be more precise, many domain experts are unfamiliar with process modeling languages and the confidence to understand process models in detail. In such a situation, a verbalization (i.e., textual representation) of process model and its corresponding process views would enable domain experts to properly understand process details relevant for them [10].

Generally, real-world processes are frequently subject to change and evolution [1,11]. In contemporary PAIS, it is not possible to modify a process model through editing and updating one of its view-based process descriptions (i.e., model abstractions). Hence, any process change must be always applied directly to the core process model, which constitutes a complex and error-prone task for domain experts, particularly in the context of large process models. To overcome this limitation, users should be enabled to change large process models through updating their personalized and verbalized process descriptions.

This paper proposes an approach which enables users to create and modify personalized *process descriptions*. Note that a process description is a textual documentation of the real-world process. Therefore, our approach combines existing research on process views [5,12] and text generation [10]. Furthermore, it is enriched with the possibility to apply changes directly to a personalized process description. In turn, respective changes are then propagated to the underlying core process model. Figure 1 illustrates this approach.

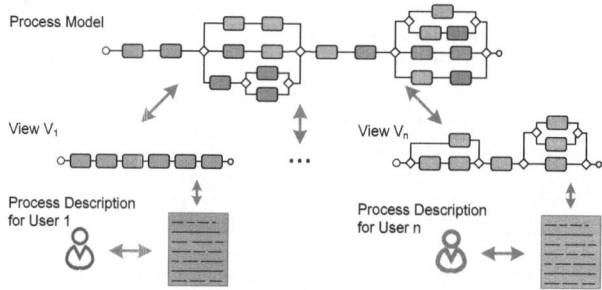

Fig. 1. Providing Personalized and Verbalized Process Descriptions

The remainder of the paper is structured as follows: Section 2 introduces basic notions. Section 3 discusses how process views as well as verbalized and personalized process descriptions may be created from an underlying process model. Section 4 shows how personalized and verbalized process descriptions and the corresponding process model may be modified through text changes. Subsequently, Section 5 presents our proof-of-concept implementation. Section 6 discusses related work and Section 7 concludes the paper.

2   Basic Notions

A process model is described in terms of a directed graph whose node set comprises *activities*, *gateways*, and *data elements*. Gateways can be categorized into *AND*, *XOR* and *Loop*, and may be used for modeling parallel and conditional branchings as well as repetition structures. Edges between activities and/or gateways represent precedence relations, i.e., the *control flow* of the process model (cf. Figure 2). Furthermore, *data elements* describe the data perspective of a process model. Based on this, the data flow is defined by a set of directed edges connecting data elements and activities. *Writing* a data element is expressed through an edge pointing from an activity to the data element. In turn, *reading* a data element is expressed through an edge pointing from this data element to the activity.

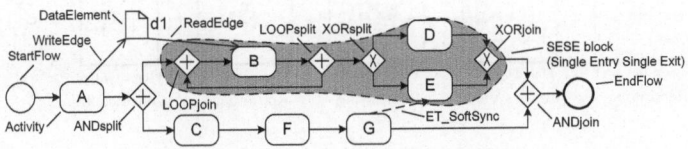

Fig. 2. Example of a Process Model

We presume that process models are *well-structured* [13,14], i.e., sequences, branchings (of different semantics), and loops are specified as blocks with well-defined start and end nodes having the same gateway type. These blocks, also known as *SESE (single-entry-single-exit)* blocks, may be nested, but are not allowed to overlap (cf. Figure 2).

3   Creating Personalized Process Descriptions

The creation of a personalized process description is a two-step approach. Section 3.1 introduces how process views are derived and Section 3.2 describes how personalized process descriptions are generated.

3.1   Process View Creation

For creating process views, we utilize the *proView*[1] framework. In particular, *proView* is to include alternative process representations (like the textual process description).

The *proView* framework aims at supporting users in intuitively interacting with large business process models as well as evolving them over time. For this purpose, personalized and updatable process views (cf. Figure 3, Part 2) are created for each user (role) abstracting from the overall process model maintained in the central process repository (cf. Figure 3, Part 1). We denote this overall process model as *Central Process Model (CPM)*.

More precisely, a process view abstracts from the CPM by hiding non-relevant process elements (i.e., applying reduction operations) or by combing and abstracting them (i.e., applying aggregation operations). Detailed information about view creation operations and their semantics can be found in [5,15,16].

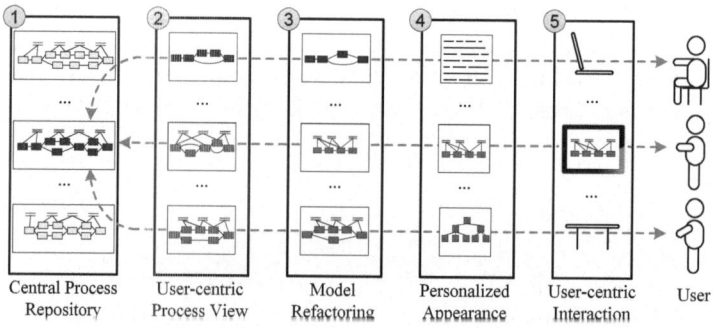

Fig. 3. Overview of proView Framework

When applying view creation operations, non-relevant gateways or empty AND branches might occur. Therefore, the model resulting from the application of such view creation operations is further simplified using behavior-preserving refactorings (cf. Figure 3, Part 3), e.g., AND gateways of a parallel branching with only one remaining branch may be removed.

Part 4 of the *proView* framework (cf. Figure 3) then transforms the process view into a personalized appearance, e.g., a form-, graph-, or tree-based representation [17,18,19]. In the context of this paper, Part 4 verbalizes the process view to obtain a textual process description as appearance. This step is described in more detail in Section 3.2. Finally, the result is presented to the user (cf. Figure 3, Part 5). Moreover, for human-centric process management end users should be able to intuitively interact with their processes (e.g., on multi-touch devices) [20].

---

[1] www.dbis.info/proView

3.2   Creating Verbalized Process Descriptions

In the following, we describe how a process model and a process view respectively can be transformed to a verbalized process description. An overview of the text generation technique applied in this context is depicted in Figure 4. Details of this transformation technique are described in [10]. Note that this transformation is applied in Part 4 of the *proView* framework, which allows creating personalized appearances (cf. Figure 3).

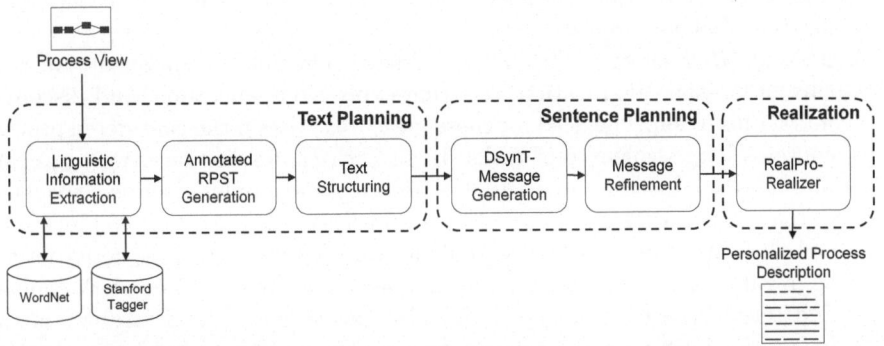

Fig. 4. Architecture for Deriving Verbalized Process Descriptions

Altogether, the transformation consists of five components:

1. *Linguistic Information Extraction*: In this component, we use the linguistic label analysis technique from [21] to recognize the different label patterns that exist for activity labels in the process view. In this way, for instance, we are able to decompose an activity label such as *Choose Contact Type* into the action *Choose* and the business object *Contact Type*.
2. *Annotated RPST Generation*: The *Refined Process Structure Tree (RPST)* generation module derives a tree representation from the given process model in order to provide a basis for a step-by-step process description. In particular, we compute an RPST, which is a parse tree containing a hierarchy of sub-graphs derived from the process view [22]. The resulting hierarchy can be visualized as a tree whose root captures the entire tree and whose leaves contain the connections between two elements of the process. After deriving the RPST, we annotate each element with the linguistic information obtained in the previous phase. Thus, for instance, the leave node pointing to activity *Choose Contact Type* is annotated with the action *Choose* and the business object *Contact Type*.

3. *DSynT-Message Generation*: The message generation component maps the annotated RPST elements to a list of intermediate messages. More specifically, each sentence is stored as a deep-syntactic tree (DSynT), which is a dependency representation introduced by the Meaning Text Theory [23]. Such a deep-syntactic tree facilitates the manageable yet comprehensive storage of the constituents of a sentence. In addition, it can be automatically mapped to a syntactically correct sentence with existing tools [24]. Taking the example of the activity *Choose Contact Type*, the corresponding DSynT consists of a root node pointing to the verb *choose* and two subordinate nodes. The first node specifies *contact type* as object and the second specifies the *clerk* as subject of *choose*.

4. *Message Refinement*: Within the message refinement component, we take care of message aggregation, referring expression generation, and discourse marker insertion. The need for these measures arises if the considered process contains long sequences of tasks. In such cases, for instance, we aggregate messages sharing the same business object. As example, imagine a sequence of the activities *Choose Contact Type* and *Select Contact Type* conducted by a clerk. Instead of generating a sentence for each activity, these activities are aggregated and communicated with a sentence such as "The clerk chooses and selects the contact type." An alternative aggregation strategy is the insertion of referring expressions such as *he* or *it* to ensure lexical variety. For the discourse marker insertion we use an extensible set of connectors to insert markers such as *then* and *afterwards*. In this way, we obtain a well readable text with sufficient variety.

5. *Surface Realization*: The complexity of the surface realization task has led to the development of publically available realizers. Existing tools significantly vary in aspects such as license costs, generation speed, and Java compatibility. Taking these aspects into account, we decided to use the DSynT-based realizer RealPro from CoGenTex [24]. RealPro requires an XML-based DSynT message as input and transforms it to a grammatically correct sentence. As a result, the DSynT for activity *Choose Contact Type* is automatically transformed into the sentence "The clerk chooses the contact type."

After applying these tasks to a process view, the resulting personalized process description may be displayed to the respective user.

Overall, Figure 5 gives an example of how we create such a personalized and verbalized process description based on a CPM. Figure 5a shows the CPM, which describes a simplified *Bank Account Creation* process. The resulting process view in Figure 5b shows the activities of role *Clerk*, i.e., the activities of the manager are reduced. Furthermore, to abstract the process the XOR branching containing activities *Select Customer* and *Create Customer* is aggregated.

Finally, the process view of the clerk is transformed into a verbalized process description. Figure 5c shows the resulting text after this transformation. Note that the AND branching is explicitly documented using bullet points.

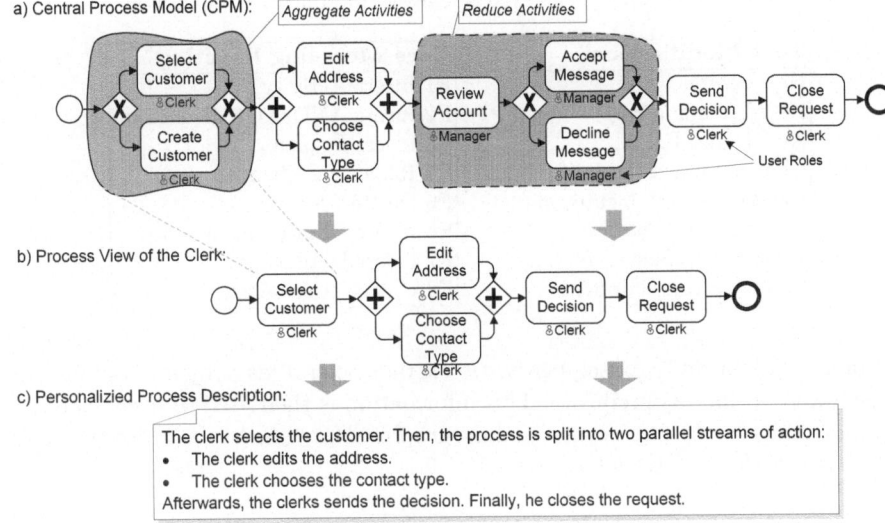

Fig. 5. Creating a Personalized and Verbalized Process Description

4   Process Model Changes through Text Modifications

For a PAIS, it is crucial to support the change and evolution of process models [11]. Consequently, authorized end users should be also enabled to modify the text of their personalized and verbalized process descriptions.

This section describes how such changes of a personalized and verbalized process description (i.e., text modifications) can be mapped to changes of the associated process view and the underlying CPM. More precisely, all modifications of a textual process description must be interpreted and mapped to changes of the corresponding process view. In this context, we build on [20], which provides a core modeling function set comprising functions $F1 - F8$. The latter cover the most common change patterns for process models [25]. Table 1 gives an overview of possible text modifications and their respective mapping to core functions. In the following, we discuss this mapping in detail.

Inserting a Sentence. When adding a new sentence to a verbalized process description, the user wants to express that an action shall be added to the process. In the context of process models, it implies to insert an activity. For this, core modeling function $F1$ *(Insert Activity)* is triggered to insert, at a certain position in the process view, an activity. Figure 6 shows an example of such an insertion. Sentence "The clerk prints the details." is added by the user to the verbalized process description and analyzed using the Stanford Parser [26]. From the parsing result, we can automatically derive the grammatical relation of the words in the sentence. Relations *nsubj(prints, clerk)* and *dobj(prints, details)* reveal that "clerk" represents the subject and "details" represents the object

Table 1. Mapping of Text Changes to Modification Functions

Text Modification	Core Modeling Function
New Sentence	F1 Insert Activity
New Enumeration	F2 Insert AND/XOR Branching
New Bullet Point	F3 Insert Branch
Change Object/Verb of Sentence	F4 Renaming Element
Delete (Part of) Sentence	F5 Delete Element
Add Part of Sentence	F6 Insert Data Element
Add Part of Sentence	F7 Insert Data Edge
Change Subject of Sentence	F8 Change User Assignments

for predicate "print." Consequently, we extract "clerk" as subject, "details" as object, and "print" as predicate. This information is then used to insert activity "Print Details," into the corresponding graphical process view. Moreover, this activity is performed by role *Clerk*.

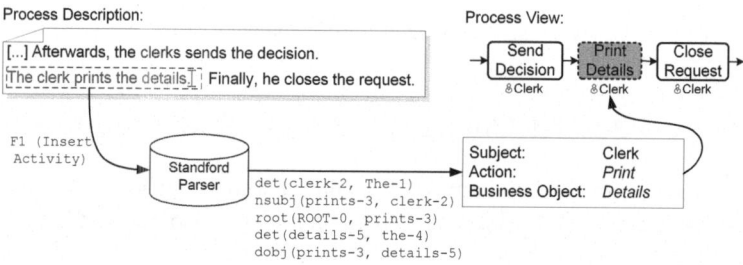

Fig. 6. Inserting a Sentence and Adapting the Corresponding Process View

Inserting an Enumeration. Inserting an enumeration block into the verbalized process description implies that the user wants to insert multiple actions that shall be performed simultaneously or alternatively. Regarding the corresponding process model, the user intends to add an AND/XOR branching, i.e., core modeling function *F2 (Insert AND/XOR Branching)* is applied to the process view. However, the user must manually add the information whether the bullet points of the enumeration should be performed simultaneously (i.e., AND branching is added) or alternatively (i.e., XOR branching is added). Inserting individual sentences to the bullet points triggers again modeling function *F1 (Insert Activity)*. Figure 7 gives an example of inserting a new enumeration block, which performs the bullet points in parallel.

Inserting a Bullet Point. The user inserts a new bullet point to an existing enumeration in the process description to add a stream of actions, which shall be performed simultaneously or alternatively, to the existing bullet points. This text

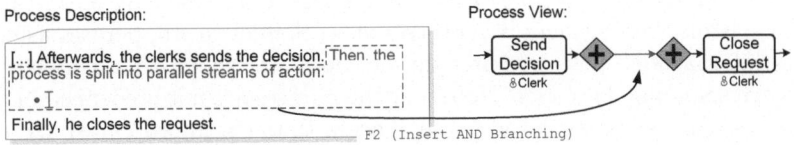

Fig. 7. Inserting an Enumeration Block and Corresponding View Adaption

modification corresponds to core modeling function *F3 (Insert Branch)*, which inserts a new branch to an existing AND/XOR branching in the corresponding process view. Initially, this branch is empty and activities may be added using core modeling function *F1 (Insert Activity)*.

Change the Object or Verb of a Sentence. When the user changes the verb or object of an existing sentence, he wants to adapt the activity described in the sentence. Mapping this to the process view, core modeling function *F4 (Renaming Element)* renames the label of an activity. The changed sentence is again analyzed using the Stanford Parser and the new verb or object is extracted (cf. *F1 (Insert Activity)*). For example, sentence "The clerk prints the order" is changed to "The clerk sends the order." This results in renaming activity "Print Order" in the corresponding process view to *Send Order* using function *F*4.

Deleting a Sentence. Deleting an existing sentence, removes the dedicated action from the personalized and verbalized process description. Thus, the corresponding activity will be deleted in the process view, as well. For this purpose, core modeling function *F5 (Delete Element)* is triggered.

Adding a Part to a Sentence. Adding a new part, like "[...] provides information customer record" to an existing sentence, details the action described through this sentence. In terms of a process model, such information is captured in the data flow. Therefore, core modeling function *F6 (Insert Data Element)* inserts a data element in the process view. Figure 8 shows an example in which the part "[...] requires the information customer record" is added to a sentence. This results in adding data element *Customer Record* to the process view. Furthermore, the verbs "require" or "provide" triggers related modeling function *F7 (Insert Data Edge)* to insert a reading or writing data edge.

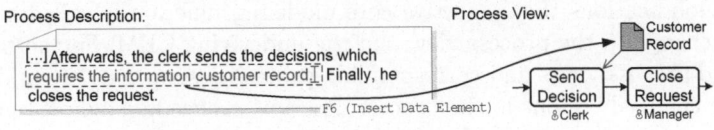

Fig. 8. Example of F6 (Insert Data Element)

Core modeling function *F7 (Insert Data Edge)* adds a reading or writing edge to an existing data element in a process view. Similar to *F6*, phrases using "provides information" and "requires information" are added to a sentence to set the corresponding data edge. Note that the phrases are not predefined in a strict sense. Instead, we parse the added sentence with the Stanford Parser and employ a set of signal verbs and nouns to detect the intention of the user.

Changing the Subject of a Sentence. If the subject of a sentence is changed by the user, he wants to dedicate the action described by the sentence to another person. For this purpose, core modeling function *F8 (Change User Assignments)* is triggered, which changes the user assignment in the corresponding process view. To detect this text modification, the Stanford Parser is used to analyze whether or not the subject is changed.

We have shown how the various text modification are analyzed and mapped to respective core modeling functions. In turn, in [27] we demonstrate how the changes of a process view can be automatically propagated to the CPM. Moreover, all associated process views are updated in this context as well. This is required in order to guarantee that all users work on the current version of the process description.

5   Proof-of-Concept Implementation

The presented *proView* framework was implemented in a proof-of-concept prototype as a client-server application. It enables users to simultaneously edit process models based on updatable process views [28,12]. Overall, the *proView* prototype demonstrates the applicability of our framework. Figure 9 shows a screen with the models depicted in Figure 5a and 5b. Note that the subprocess activity of the screenshot indicates that an aggregation operation was applied to create the respective node.

We extended *proView* with the ability to create and evolve verbalized process descriptions as described in this paper. Thus, we are able to create personalized and verbalized process descriptions for any well-structured process model and process view respectively.

Figure 10 shows the generated personalized and verbalized process description that corresponds to the process view of role *Clerk*. Pressing the *edit* button on the top right of the paper sheet will enable the user to modify the text. When finishing this editing, in turn, *proView* derives all modifications made in the verbalized process description and highlights them. Once this is accomplished, for all text modifications the respective core modeling function is called to propagate the change to the process view and the underlying CPM. Furthermore, all associated process views and corresponding process descriptions are updated as well. The changed regions in the process descriptions are highlighted again.

In future work, our proof-of-concept implementation will be used to involve practitioners in the validation of the presented abstraction approach.

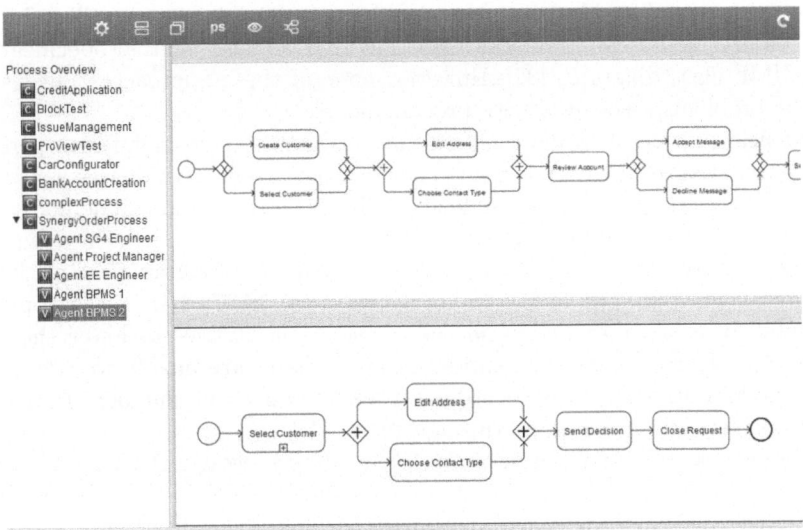

Fig. 9. Proof-of-Concept Prototype

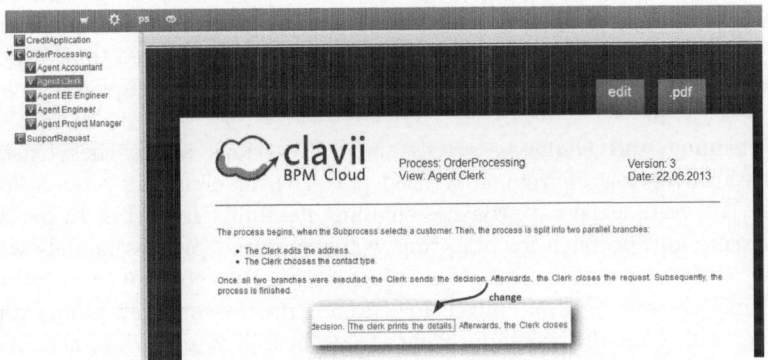

Fig. 10. Personalized and Verbalized Process Description

6 Related Work

The work presented in this paper can be related to four major streams of research: natural language generation systems, process model comprehension, process view creation, and process change.

The *generation of natural language texts* has a long tradition and has been applied in various scenarios. Examples include the generation of weather forecasts [29] or the documentation of the activities of planning engineers [30]. The application of text generation techniques on conceptual models is limited to a few examples. The ModelExplainer generates natural language descriptions from object models [31] and the GeNLangUML creates textual specifications from UML class diagrams [32]. However, none of these approaches tackles the specific problems associated with process models.

The field of *process model comprehension* is discussed from different perspectives. For instance, the results from [33] show that the number of arcs has an important effect on overall model understandability. The work in [34] demonstrates the impact the natural language in activity labels has on model comprehension. In general, most authors agree on the fact that text plus diagram provides better comprehension than any of the two in isolation [35,36,37]. Hence, the approach presented in this paper builds on these insights as it tries to lower the overall burden of process model comprehension. If users are unable to interpret a given model due to confusing wording or an overwhelming number of arcs, the generated text can guide them through the model.

In prior research, many approaches for *creating process views* have been suggested. Usually, such approaches build on different information to create an abstracted version of the model. Examples include the utilization of a tree decomposition of the process model [38], the semantic similarity of activities [39], or run time data obtained from monitoring [40,41]. However, these approaches neither enable different user perspectives on a process model nor do they provide concepts for manually creating process views. In [7], the authors introduce an approach providing predefined process view types (i.e., human tasks, collaboration views). As opposed to *proView*, however, this approach is limited to pre-specified process view types. In particular, the latter cannot be used to implement changes in the process model.

For defining and *changing process models*, various approaches exist. [25] presents an overview of frequently used patterns for changing process models. Further, [11] summarizes approaches enabling flexibility in PAISs. In particular, [42] presents an approach for adapting well-structured process models without affecting their correctness. Based on this, [43] presents concepts for optimizing process models over time and migrating running processes to new model versions properly. Still, none of these approaches takes usability issues into account, i.e., no support for user-centered changes of business processes is provided.

7   Summary and Outlook

In this paper, we introduced an approach for creating personalized and verbalized process descriptions based on process views. Such process descriptions support end-users to easily understand their tasks within a business process, which increases their process knowledge. Furthermore, modifying the text of personalized process descriptions triggers changes of the underlying process model. This enables users to perform changes and optimizations of the process without requiring process modeling knowledge. Our approach will increase process-awareness in companies especially for users without in-depth knowledge on process modeling. Furthermore, it includes such users in optimizing and evolving business processes.

We have implemented the described view mechanism in a prototype based on the *proView* framework. In future work, we plan user studies to evaluate whether personalized and verbalized process descriptions are easier to understand and maintain compared to "regular" process models and process views.

References

1. Weber, B., Sadiq, S., Reichert, M.: Beyond Rigidity - Dynamic Process Lifecycle Support: A Survey on Dynamic Changes in Process-Aware Information Systems. Computer Science - Research and Development 23(2), 47–65 (2009)
2. Rosemann, M.: Potential Pitfalls of Process Modeling: Part A. Business Process Management Journal 12(2), 249–254 (2006)
3. Weber, B., Reichert, M., Mendling, J., Reijers, H.A.: Refactoring Large Process Model Repositories. Computers in Industry 62(5), 467–486 (2011)
4. Streit, A., Pham, B., Brown, R.: Visualization Support for Managing Large Business Process Specifications. In: van der Aalst, W.M.P., Benatallah, B., Casati, F., Curbera, F. (eds.) BPM 2005. LNCS, vol. 3649, pp. 205–219. Springer, Heidelberg (2005)
5. Kolb, J., Reichert, M.: Data Flow Abstractions and Adaptations through Updatable Process Views. In: Proc 27th Symposium on Applied Computing (SAC 2013), Coimbra, Portugal, pp. 1447–1453 (2013)
6. Kabicher-Fuchs, S., Rinderle-Ma, S., Recker, J., Indulska, M., Charoy, F., Christiaanse, R., Dunkl, R., Grambow, G., Kolb, J., Leopold, H., Mendling, J.: Human-Centric Process-Aware Information Systems (HC-PAIS). CoRR abs/1211.4 (2012)
7. Tran, H.: View-Based and Model-Driven Approach for Process-Driven, Service-Oriented Architectures. TU Wien, Dissertation (2009)
8. Bobrik, R., Bauer, T., Reichert, M.: Proviado – Personalized and Configurable Visualizations of Business Processes. In: Bauknecht, K., Pröll, B., Werthner, H. (eds.) EC-Web 2006. LNCS, vol. 4082, pp. 61–71. Springer, Heidelberg (2006)
9. Chiu, D.K., Cheung, S., Till, S., Karlapalem, K., Li, Q., Kafeza, E.: Workflow View Driven Cross-Organizational Interoperability in a Web Service Environment. Inf. Techn. and Mgmt. 5(3&4), 221–250 (2004)
10. Leopold, H., Mendling, J., Polyvyanyy, A.: Generating Natural Language Texts from Business Process Models. In: Ralyté, J., Franch, X., Brinkkemper, S., Wrycza, S. (eds.) CAiSE 2012. LNCS, vol. 7328, pp. 64–79. Springer, Heidelberg (2012)
11. Reichert, M., Weber, B.: Enabling Flexibility in Process-Aware Information Systems - Challenges, Methods, Technologies. Springer (2012)
12. Kolb, J., Reichert, M.: Supporting Business and IT through Updatable Process Views: The proView Demonstrator. In: Ghose, A., Zhu, H., Yu, Q., Delis, A., Sheng, Q.Z., Perrin, O., Wang, J., Wang, Y. (eds.) ICSOC 2012. LNCS, vol. 7759, pp. 460–464. Springer, Heidelberg (2013)
13. La Rosa, M., Wohed, P., Mendling, J., ter Hofstede, A.H.M., Reijers, H.A., van der Aalst, W.M.P.: Managing Process Model Complexity Via Abstract Syntax Modifications. IEEE Transactions on Industrial Informatics 7(4), 614–629 (2011)
14. Mendling, J., Strembeck, M.: Influence Factors of Understanding Business Process Models. In: Proc. BIS 2008, pp. 142–153 (2008)
15. Kolb, J., Reichert, M.: A Flexible Approach for Abstracting and Personalizing Large Business Process. ACM Applied Computing Review 13(1) (2013)

16. Reichert, M., Kolb, J., Bobrik, R., Bauer, T.: Enabling Personalized Visualization of Large Business Processes through Parameterizable Views. In: Proc. 26th Symposium on Applied Computing (SAC 2012), Riva del Garda, Trento, Italy, pp. 1653–1660 (2012)

17. Kolb, J., Reichert, M., Weber, B.: Using Concurrent Task Trees for Stakeholder-centered Modeling and Visualization of Business Processes. In: Oppl, S., Fleischmann, A. (eds.) S-BPM ONE 2012. CCIS, vol. 284, pp. 237–251. Springer, Heidelberg (2012)

18. Lanz, A., Kolb, J., Reichert, M.: Enabling Personalized Process Schedules with Time-Aware Process Views. In: Franch, X., Soffer, P. (eds.) CAiSE Workshops 2013. LNBIP, vol. 148, pp. 205–216. Springer, Heidelberg (2013)

19. Kolb, J., Hübner, P., Reichert, M.: Automatically Generating and Updating User Interface Components in Process-Aware Information Systems. In: Proc. 10th Int'l Conf. on Cooperative Information Systems (CoopIS 2012), pp. 444–454 (2012)

20. Kolb, J., Rudner, B., Reichert, M.: Towards Gesture-based Process Modeling on Multi-Touch Devices. In: Proc. 1st Int'l Workshop on Human-Centric Process-Aware Information Systems (HC-PAIS 2012), Gdansk, Poland, pp. 280–293 (2012)

21. Leopold, H., Smirnov, S., Mendling, J.: On the Refactoring of Activity Labels in Business Process Models. Information Systems 37(5), 443–459 (2012)

22. Polyvyanyy, A., Vanhatalo, J., Völzer, H.: Simplified Computation and Generalization of the Refined Process Structure Tree. In: Bravetti, M. (ed.) WS-FM 2010. LNCS, vol. 6551, pp. 25–41. Springer, Heidelberg (2011)

23. Mel'cuk, I., Polguère, A.: A Formal Lexicon in the Meaning-Text Theory (or How to Do Lexica with Words). Computational Linguistics 13(3-4), 261–275 (1987)

24. Lavoie, B., Rambow, O.: A Fast and Portable Realizer for Text Generation Systems. In: Applied Natural Language Processing, ACL, pp. 265–268 (1997)

25. Weber, B., Reichert, M., Rinderle, S.: Change Patterns and Change Support Features - Enhancing Flexibility in Process-Aware Information Systems. Data & Knowledge Engineering 66(3), 438–466 (2008)

26. Klein, D., Manning, C.D.: Accurate Unlexicalized Parsing. In: 41st Meeting of the Association for Computational Linguistics, pp. 423–430 (2003)

27. Kolb, J., Kammerer, K., Reichert, M.: Updatable Process Views for User-Centered Adaption of Large Process Models. In: Liu, C., Ludwig, H., Toumani, F., Yu, Q. (eds.) ICSOC 2012. LNCS, vol. 7636, pp. 484–498. Springer, Heidelberg (2012)

28. Kolb, J., Kammerer, K., Reichert, M.: Updatable Process Views for Adapting Large Process Models: The proView Demonstrator. In: Proc. of the Business Process Management 2012 Demonstration Track, Tallinn, Estonia (2012)

29. Goldberg, E., Driedger, N., Kittredge, R.: Using Natural-Language Processing to Produce Weather Forecasts. IEEE Expert 9(2), 45–53 (1994)

30. McKeown, K., Kukich, K., Shaw, J.: Practical Issues in Automatic Documentation Generation. In: Applied Natural Language Processing, ACL, pp. 7–14 (1994)

31. Lavoie, B., Rambow, O., Reiter, E.: The ModelExplainer. In: Proceedings 8th Int'l Workshop on Natural Language Generation, pp. 9–12 (1996)

32. Meziane, F., Athanasakis, N., Ananiadou, S.: Generating Natural Language Specifications from UML Class Diagrams. Requirements Engineering 13, 1–18 (2008)

33. Mendling, J., Reijers, H.A., Cardoso, J.: What Makes Process Models Understandable? In: Alonso, G., Dadam, P., Rosemann, M. (eds.) BPM 2007. LNCS, vol. 4714, pp. 48–63. Springer, Heidelberg (2007)

34. Mendling, J., Reijers, H.A., Recker, J.: Activity Labeling in Process Modeling: Empirical Insights and Recommendations. Information Systems 35(4), 467–482 (2010)

35. Ottensooser, A., Fekete, A., Reijers, H.A., Mendling, J., Menictas, C.: Making Sense of Business Process Descriptions: An Experimental Comparison of Graphical and Textual Notations. Journal of Systems and Software (2012) (to appear)
36. Mayer, R.E.: Multimedia Learning. 2nd edn. Cambridge University Press (2009)
37. Hipp, M., Michelberger, B., Mutschler, B., Reichert, M.: A Framework for the Intelligent Delivery and User-Adequate Visualization of Process Information. In: Proc. 28th Symposium on Applied Computing (SAC 2013), Coimbra, Portugal (2013)
38. Polyvyanyy, A., Smirnov, S., Weske, M.: The Triconnected Abstraction of Process Models. In: Dayal, U., Eder, J., Koehler, J., Reijers, H.A. (eds.) BPM 2009. LNCS, vol. 5701, pp. 229–244. Springer, Heidelberg (2009)
39. Smirnov, S., Reijers, H.A., Weske, M.: A Semantic Approach for Business Process Model Abstraction. In: Mouratidis, H., Rolland, C. (eds.) CAiSE 2011. LNCS, vol. 6741, pp. 497–511. Springer, Heidelberg (2011)
40. Shan, Z., Yang, Y., Li, Q., Luo, Y., Peng, Z.: A Light-Weighted Approach to Workflow View Implementation. In: Zhou, X., Li, J., Shen, H.T., Kitsuregawa, M., Zhang, Y. (eds.) APWeb 2006. LNCS, vol. 3841, pp. 1059–1070. Springer, Heidelberg (2006)
41. Schumm, D., Latuske, G., Leymann, F., Mietzner, R., Scheibler, T.: State Propagation for Business Process Monitoring on Different Levels of Abstraction. In: Proc. 19th ECIS, Helsinki, Finland (2011)
42. Reichert, M., Dadam, P.: ADEPTflex - Supporting Dynamic Changes of Workflows Without Losing Control. Journal of Intelligent Inf. Sys. 10(2), 93–129 (1998)
43. Rinderle, S., Reichert, M., Dadam, P.: Flexible Support of Team Processes by Adaptive Workflow Systems. Distributed and Par. Databases 16(1), 91–116 (2004)

Modeling the Organizational Regulatory Space: A Joint Design Approach

João Barata[1,2] and Paulo Rupino da Cunha[2]

[1] CTCV, Rua Coronel Veiga Simão, 3025-307 Coimbra, Portugal
[2] CISUC, Department of Informatics Engineering, University of Coimbra, Pólo II, 3030-290 Coimbra, Portugal
{barata,rupino}@dei.uc.pt

Abstract. We present an approach for the joint design of organizational regulatory spaces (ORS). The approach was validated through action research, integrating the components of *context*, *people*, *process*, *information*, and *IT*. The design of the ORS is usually performed by distinct teams, with unconnected viewpoints, using different vocabularies and tools. Similarly to information systems, there are business experts that define the regulatory goals and rules. The ORS modeling is problematic, and is fragmented. We have adopted the O_2 framework to provide a common level of abstraction for the design. The result is a comprehensive and layered map of the ORS. This approach has proved to offer an effective representation of the ORS for external auditors and business associations. Internally, we provide organizations with new ways to model, communicate, and improve the regulatory space.

Keywords: Information system design, regulation, compliance, organizational regulatory space, O2 framework.

1 Introduction

The organizational regulatory space (ORS) is a key element of contemporary societies, shaped by laws and standards, but also by internal policies, norms, contract agreements, and corporate procedures [1, 2]. Organizational regulations may be enforced (e.g., in the case of legal requirements), or they may be voluntary, for instance when a standard is used to guide the management system or the product specification. Either way, in the majority of the cases, regulations are seen as a burden in organizations. A number of internal and external entities may influence the ORS, such as governments, private regulators, business associations, customers, or even organizational managers. The design of the ORS is then executed by distinct experts with financial, legal, technological, and managerial knowledge. However, more than a complex set of business rules, the ORS is a holistic conceptual space where people develop specific processes, interacting with each other and with the environment, exchanging information [2]. The regulatory space becomes unique for each organization.

J. Grabis et al. (Eds.): PoEM 2013, LNBIP 165, pp. 206–220, 2013.

To separate the information system (IS) from the ORS is unfeasible. On one hand, the ORS is designed with regulatory information. On the other hand, the IS design must attend to the stakeholders viewpoints, the technology, and the nature of the strategic and operational activities involved [3, 4]. Business process management presents solutions that can guide the design of IS and organizational rules [5]. Nevertheless, we must take into consideration that not all the regulations are "process-friendly" (e.g. several financial regulations), and, even when they are, problems can still exist by adopting a process approach in regulatory contexts [6]. The list of problems increases if we consider the distinct vocabulary among the ORS experts [7]; the diversity of the external legislation and standards, such as the Sarbanes-Oxley act, ISO management standards, codes of practice or business partners contracts; the need to translate the external requirements into internal procedures and practices; and the difficulty in integrating and evidencing regulatory compliance [8, 9] in audits, and voluntary or statutory reporting. The design of the ORS is critical for organizations operating in distinct regulatory spaces around the globe, each one with a specific set of rules, norms, and cultural characteristics.

Although a number of studies address the problem of compliance modeling and checking [10], we could not find a framework for cooperation in the initial phase of designing the goals, rules, and boundaries for the compliant behavior. Moreover, there is a gap concerning the compliance extraction and elicitation, and the holistic representation of regulatory space. To increase the chances of developing a joint design of the ORS, all the stakeholders must work together from the beginning. This paper address several IS and regulatory management problems identified by [8, 9], namely, the lack of compliance culture; top level management support; perception of compliance as a value-add; communication among staff; compliance knowledge base; holistic practices; and IT support/tools.

We now invite the reader to imagine the chief executive officer (CEO), the integrated systems manager (IMS – integrating quality, environmental, health and safety), the chief financial officer (CFO), the legal adviser (LA), the marketing manager (MM), and the chief information officer (CIO) in the same room and at the same time designing the ORS. The remainder of this paper is organized as follows. The next section provides the background of the research, followed by the method selection. Section 4 presents the results in three cases of action research to model the ORS. We conclude by summarizing findings, the study limitations, and future work.

2   Background

This section reviews key concepts of ORS, IS design and compliance.

2.1   The Modern Organizational Regulatory Space (ORS)

The term "regulatory space" was introduced by [1]. The authors define regulation as a combination of public and private characteristics that involve dynamic relations between and within people and organizations, sharing a common space of specific regulatory issues. In [1], the "space" metaphor is in the scope of national regulation. According to [11], the regulatory space is a social space "in which different regulatory schemes operate simultaneously [... and] the state must compete for control of regulation with other regulatory entities". In this sense, private regulators, interest groups, and distinct business experts also influence the regulatory space. For this research, we have mobilized and restricted the concept of [1] to an organizational level, representing the entire set of regulations, either imposed or voluntary, that an organization decides to implement.

The ORS includes standards, that are voluntary regulations, increasingly adopted worldwide to implement management systems. The standards address quality (e.g. ISO 9001), environmental management (e.g. ISO 14001), health and safety regulations (e.g. OHSAS 18001), and corporate responsibility (e.g. SA 8000). They also cover specificities of sectors such as food (e.g. ISO 22000), laboratorial (ISO/IEC 17025), or aeronautical (e.g. AS 9100). When a company decides to follow or be certified by a specific standard, a set of internal procedures and practices must be developed. The compliance with legislation is also required by standards, such as the environmental, health and safety. When multiple standards exist, [12] outline three possible levels of integration: (1) "compatibility with cross-references between parallel systems"; (2) "coordination of business processes"; and (3) "an organizational culture of learning, continuous improvements of performance and stakeholder involvement related to internal and external challenges".

The regulatory space is a socio-technical space combining people, processes, and information [11]. An "outside-in" perspective is needed to define the organizational regulatory context of the business. Standards and laws, combined with contract agreements, policies and norms, are then translated in procedures that regulate the "within" behavior of people, processes and information. Finally, the regulatory space also demands an "inside-out" perspective, concerning customer relationship, legal and financial information, or statutory reporting.

2.2   IS Design and Compliance

The IS design has to tackle distinct interrelated components such as the information, IT, processes, and human aspects in organizational context [13]. Compliance is a well-known research subject in IS. The literature addresses topics such as the compliance of business processes and services [14–16], requirements engineering and conceptual modeling [17, 18], auditing IS compliance [19, 20], and the alignment between law and IT compliance [21]. However, the majority of studies focus on the perspective of modeling and checking compliance [10], lacking the human behavior in that regulatory space and the guidance to allow cooperation between different experts, not specific to a technology or IT architecture.

The IS must consider not only the "formal" IT solutions that support the processes, such as an ERP or a business process management system (BPMS), but also the "informal" IT tools, such as spreadsheets and desktop databases that proliferate in the organizations [22]. To design an IT artifact, we must be concerned with the context, the designers, users and beneficiaries of the IT, processes, and the information [13,

23]. These IS components may be represented as layers, that interact and influence each other and their environment [24, 25]. The identification of the layers can integrate multiple viewpoints, according to each system stakeholder and particular field of knowledge [26]. There are similarities between the development methods of the IS and of specific systems that define the ORS, for instance, the ISO 9001 management system [27]. As stated by [2, 20, 21], both the IS and regulatory compliance should be achieved by an holistic design.

3   Method

We used action research to guide our investigation, simultaneously aiming to improve scientific knowledge and assist a practical problem [28]. As our purpose was not only to develop an ORS model and a design approach, but also to study the organizational changes, action research seemed the best approach. We have followed its canonical format, characterized by the five phases of *Diagnosing, Action planning, Action taking, Evaluating, and Specifying learning* [29]. To evaluate our research, we have relied on the principles proposed by [30]. Table 1 lists the action research cases and the main standards that influence their regulatory space.

Table 1. Action research cases

Case/Sector	Standards
1: Ceramics	ISO9001, ISO14001, OHSAS18001, EMAS, SA8000
2: Agro-food	ISO22001, ISO/IEC17025, BRC, and IFS Food Safety
3: Technological Institute	ISO9001, ISO/IEC17025, OHSAS18001

An initial *diagnosis* was conducted simultaneously in all these organizations, to understand the communication and artifacts used [31], and to prepare the mindset for the following action research phases. The *diagnosis* also included a fourth company, in the aeronautical sector, certified by ISO9001, EN9100, and AS9100. This case is a work in progress that we identify by 4w, and exclusively report in section 4.1.

The initial data gathering techniques were the document collection, and semi structured interviews with the managers [32]. The developed regulations comprise a number of policies, plans, and work instructions, be them internally decided or required by some standard, law, or customer contract. The cases 2 and 4w presented a higher complexity regarding laws and contractual agreements, when compared with cases 1 and 3.

4   ORS Modeling in Action

Section 4.1 describes the setting that we found in the four organizations. We specify which organizational management functions were most involved with regulations, their perspective of the ORS, and cooperation between functions. Then, we present our *action planning*, with the O_2 framework [27]. The subsequent sections summarize the *action taking, evaluation,* and *lessons learned.* The intervention in cases 1 to 3 occurred consecutively, each case benefiting from the previous findings.

4.1   Insights from Simultaneous Diagnosing

The four companies acknowledged the relevance of the regulatory space although they could not represent it clearly, as an holistic model. Citing the top manager of the company involved in case 2: "we need a map or we will get lost in a jungle of regulations […]".

Each interviewee had its own partial perspective of the regulatory space. Although the four companies had different managers for different standards, they all had an integrated system manager (IMS) to coordinate the company certifications. According to the interviews, the IMS primary concerns were the standards requirements, and regulatory audits. The CFO was also head of human resources management in the four cases. All the LAs were external and concerned with the legal context. The LAs recognized they made preventive work, such as to notify the organization of the most relevant legislation, although the majority of their interventions were originated at the CEO request. The contractual agreements were central issues for the MM and the CEO. While the CFO was mostly concerned with financial regulations, the CIO was specially focused on IT to support compliance, and the regulations that affected IT.

The four companies use IT to support regulatory management, including the subscription of web portals for legal information, multiple disconnected spreadsheets of legal obligations, and content management systems for regulatory documents, such as laws, standards, contracts, and procedures. The IT support was insufficient for an effective regulatory management, because it consisted of mere lists of obligations. Worse, regulatory management was burdensome, with no added value for practice.

To identify key management players of the ORS, we asked the top and intermediate managers of the four organizations to classify from 1 (none) to 5 (very high) the regulatory cooperation. We have defined regulatory cooperation as the need to work with other management functions, their communication frequency, and/or dependence on the other functions to achieve regulatory compliance. The median values of those classifications are presented in table 2.

Table 2. Regulatory space cooperation: the manager's perspectives

With / Manager	CEO	IMS	CIO	MM	LA	CFO
CEO		3	3	3	5	5
IMS	5		4	4	2	3
CIO	5	2		2	2	4
MM	4	3	2		2	2
LA	5	2	2	2		4
CFO	5	2	3	2	3	

These answers are only relevant to understand the setting of the selected cases. They suggest that all the interviewees need to communicate in the regulatory space. The CEO and CFO are core players of the space (both reported 5 in the need to cooperate with each other). Although some functions report lower levels of regulatory cooperation (e.g. the CIO and MM, with the value of 2), the purpose of our approach is that all may be involved in the ORS design. The LA does not appear to have a central role in the ORS. The reasons differ. For instance, in case 1 and 3, the legal regulations are less significant when compared with other regulation types. In all cases the LA communicates sporadically with the managers. The four CEOs reported that managing of the regulations, people, IT, and processes were independent and difficult to connect. For instance, a number of employees did not know all the essential legislation applicable to their work; internal procedures did not properly reference legislation; there was a lack of awareness on how each regulation was supported by IT; and it was difficult to link IT and organizational processes.

Subsequently we asked the managers to classify the most relevant types of regulations for their daily activities. The results are presented in table 3.

Table 3. Regulatory influence in each function, by type of regulation

Type \ Manager	Law	Standard	Contract	Internal Procedure
CEO	4,5	4	4	4,5
IMS	3	5	3	5
CIO	2,5	3	3	4
MM	2	2	5	4
LA	5	3	4,5	3,5
CFO	4,5	3	4	3,5

The median of all the table values is 4 (high). The answers show that each manager has a distinct perspective of the regulatory space (e.g. contract agreements by MM; standards goals and rules by IMS). Concerning the CEOs and IMSs, they justify the high classification of the internal procedures (median of 4,5 and 5 respectively) with the "need to set the example" to others. This effect was not found in law, standards, and contract regulations. Is possible that when defining internal policies or converting a law to internal rules or goals (internalization), the compliance may be improved by "setting the example". Nevertheless, we must be conscious of the risk to "face temptation to be content with creating appearances that will promote confidence and to be less concerned with ensuring that this confidence is actually warranted" [11].

We found that the ORS is not designed by one person; it is a result of a social constructed negotiation [1]. The experts have called for an approach to combine efforts in IS and regulatory management. The next section presents the approach for the joint design of the ORS.

4.2   Action Planning: The O_2 Framework

The O_2 framework was initially proposed by [27], for the joint design of IS and ISO 9001 management systems. The *action planning* phase of our research uses and extends the O_2 framework, presented in figure 1, and briefly described in this section.

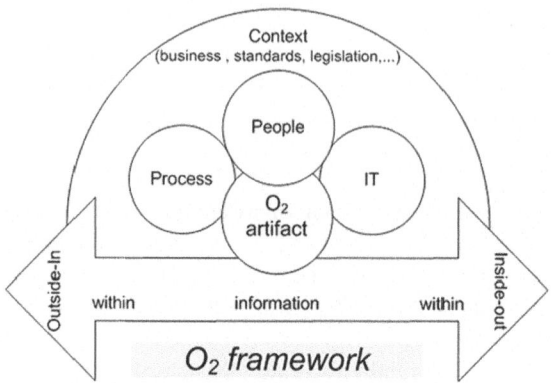

Fig. 1. The O_2 framework [27]

The O_2 framework provides a common level of abstraction to the design team. Distinct experts focus their analysis in the essential components of an IS, represented in figure 1. The regulatory goals and rules must be identified from the organizational context ("outside-in"), incorporated in daily practice by the IS ("within"), and then provide external evidence of compliance ("inside-out").

The framework was first created to complement the process approach in the joint design of the IS and an ISO 9001 management system. This need is consistent with previous studies, pointing to the insufficiency of a process approach in the ISO 9001 context [6]. The diagnosing phase presented in our research also points to a similar problem, when addressing the ORS design by a strict process perspective. As we recognize that the process approach is fundamental for the IS and for regulatory spaces, we suggest that should be complemented to achieve a holistic joint design.

In this mind set, a regulatory space is not a burden, is a space in which organizations must cooperate and learn to design with simplicity, according with multiple viewpoints and concerns [26]. The use of the O_2 framework bridges distinct paradigms of interrelations, such as the organization and the environment ("outside-in" and "inside-out" information flows), the processes and the structure (under the context layer), and the inner and outer worlds [33]. However, the O_2 framework is only a graphical representation of the main IS components that must be considered in the ORS. There are three artifacts that we use for practice: the O_2 matrix; the O_2 artifact; and the O_2 map. The artifacts and an example of their implementation are offered in figure 2.

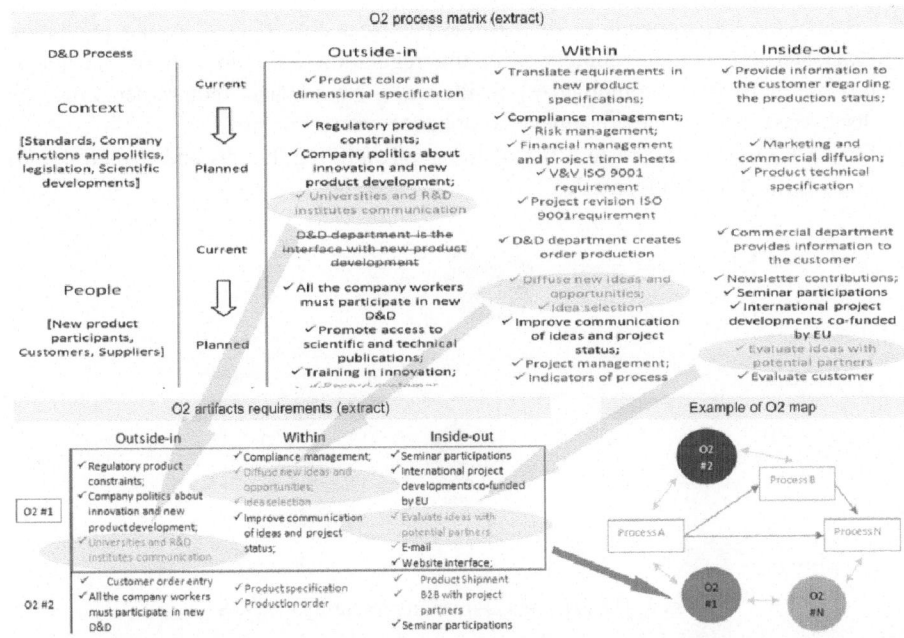

Fig. 2. The O_2 matrix (top), the O_2 artifacts (bottom-left), and an O_2 map (bottom-right) [27]

An O_2 matrix is designed for each organizational process. The example of figure 2 is for D&D – design and development process. The designers fill the matrix cells with the IS requirements for that process. Then, we extract the O_2 artifacts, that are IT artifacts [23], as illustrated in figure 2. The steps to identify the O_2 artifacts and create an O_2 map are [27]:

1. For each process, identify the requirements according with the components of process tasks, people, IT, and context needs (matrix lines). Consider the current and the planned. Take into account the dynamic of information flows, the "outside-in", "within", and "inside-out" perspective (matrix columns);

2. Group the requirements by colors (black represents a shared requirement), each color representing an O_2 artifact, which in turn are the development projects. It may be a new IT platform, a paper document, a part of an already existing system, such as an ERP, or any other means to allow the information (*oxygen*) flow, providing to end users (*system cell*) the vital process information (*breathe*);

3. Repeat 2 for every processes until an ecosystem of O_2 artifacts are designed;

4. Connect all the O_2 artifacts with the processes (*breathing system*): the O_2 map.

The O_2 framework was not initially developed for designing an ORS, so we have extended the steps of the design. After creating all the O_2 matrixes for the organizational processes, we must:

5. Identify the regulations and specify the goals and rules that must be accomplished by the organization;

6. Identify the requirements in the O_2 matrixes that are affected by the regulation ("outside-in"), help to comply with the regulation ("within") or are meant to provide evidence of compliance ("inside-out"). New matrix requirements may be discovered at this stage, to achieve compliance with regulations;
7. For each O_2 artifact, create a list of the applicable regulations and update the O_2 map, as illustrated in figure 3.

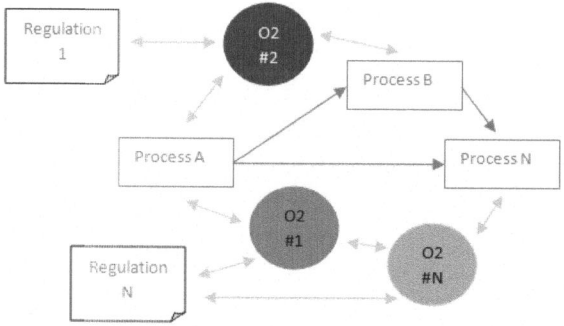

Fig. 3. The extended O_2 map, representing the ORS

The regulations are not directly connected with processes, as expressed in figure 3, but with the elements that the organization uses to manage regulations: the O_2 artifacts (IT artifacts in any form or medium). This is easier for designers that may not be so familiar with processes; for regulations that are not "process-friendly"; in organizations with deficient process approaches; and, hopefully, more effective for the IS development of the obtained IT artifacts. The O_2 artifacts can also be connected with each other, for instance, two artifacts that need to be integrated or share information.

Our decision to employ the O_2 framework as the action plan has occurred during the first action research cycle. Step 5 was simplified in our action research cases, because they already had a list of regulations, due to the multiple ISO certifications. Step 6 is the most demanding if many regulations exist. The difficulty is that for each regulatory goal or rule, we must seek the requirements in all the matrix cells that are somehow related with the regulation (influenced by the regulation, processing the regulation or providing evidence of compliance). The first case started with a fuzzy idea of joint design, as we detail in the next section.

4.3   The First Action Research Cycle

Case 1 has occurred in a large ceramics company. It exports 73% of the production to all continents, and has frequent customer audits. Due to the ISO 14001 and OHSAS 18001 certification, the company has to comply with over 500 national and international laws, each with several requirements. For each one, the company needs to establish a monitor plan and compliance actions, if applicable. The regulatory space was difficult to manage. The organization maintained a spreadsheet to describe the obligations of each regulation. This was a cumbersome mission performed almost exclusively by the IMS manager. Additionally, the IMS reported that "It is a disappointment when we realize that there is an enormous effort of regulations management, but I am the only one that uses this spreadsheet. It is difficult to make it an effective tool for other departments. Regulations are not a shared issue."

We have started to explore possibilities for our action plan. Due to the ISO certifications, we have tried to follow a process approach to design the ORS, finding regulations for each process. Although a process was a familiar concept to the CIO, CEO, and IMS; the legal, marketing, and financial managers were not comfortable with the concept. The CFO, the MM, and the legal expert stated that contractual agreements and law - their main sources of regulation, were addressed to organizations and people, not internal processes or activities. We also found problems when the IMS and CIO recognized that the process map and procedures were not detailed enough to design the ORS. A BPMS system could help, but the processes were precisely a part of the communication problem, and the CEO did not plan new investments at that moment. We also couldn't consider to immediately migrate all the IT to a new paradigm or forgetting the shadow applications [22], such as spreadsheets and desktop databases that seem to have an important role in the regulatory space. We were stuck with different viewpoints, and decided to adapt the O_2 framework.

First, the design team created the O_2 matrixes for all the organizational processes. They have selected the same processes defined for ISO 9001 certification. Then we have opted to continue steps 5 to 7 with a set of the most relevant regulations. As iterations evolve, there is a deeper understanding of the impact of a specific regulation in our context, processes, people, and IT. How that regulation affects us ("outside-in"), how we apply and monitor its compliance ("within"), and how we provide evidence of compliance in our "inside-out" activities.

This ORS design with near 100 regulations was completed and peer reviewed for 3 weeks, coinciding with an external audit from a major customer. The customer was interested in evaluating quality and social practices, such as people's work and compliance with laws. The IMS has decided to show the O_2 map to the customer. Interestingly, the O_2 map became the audit program. The customer decided to ask for each O_2 artifact, which, in some cases, was an IT application (e.g. survey platform for customers and personnel satisfaction), in other cases a documented procedure describing practices. The auditor made inquiries regarding each function expressed in the O_2 map to understand the correspondence with practice. The main conclusions were:

— The O_2 map is a possible representation of the ORS;
— The O_2 matrixes, artifacts, and map were easy to understand by internal workers, and external auditors/customers;
— The ORS designed by the O_2 framework may be used for audit programs.

Creating matrixes for regulations, even if not very detailed in a first round, was a slow task. A part of the problem is that we did not have a software tool to support the ORS design. However, by creating the matrixes we improve regulatory awareness, progressively involved more people in regulations, and discovered their real impact in the organization. When compared with the previous spreadsheets, this type of modeling is far more complete and accurate, according with the team.

4.4   The Second Action Research Cycle

In this case we dealt with an agro-food company with five lines of sauces and olive production. They export to pizza restaurant chains and supermarkets around the globe. The customer and certification audits are regular, at four times on average each month. Product traceability, law, market regulations, standards checklists, and contractual agreements are critical for the agro-food sector. We found that the company did not have a process map, because the adopted food safety standards did not require or suggest a process approach. Due to this problem, they have decided to consider their five product lines as the processes concerns. The organization told us that each line was so important that represented their core processes. However, some regulations were not specific to product lines but to other processes, such as provisioning, sales or people training. For this reason, as regulations were evaluated, new processes were identified. In one of the meetings, the IMS presented a process map to the team. Although considering that process map a first draft, they found that the O_2 matrixes have facilitated the identification of their processes. This occurred because the regulations have pointed to other critical activities they performed, not yet systematically managed as processes, or even evaluated in terms of regulations.

The O_2 map was presented to the top manager, which had to prepare a meeting in the national association of their sector. The agenda included the discussion of a specific law that required changes. The O_2 map and a fragment of the matrixes were used at the association meeting to represent the impact of the law in their organization.

Until that moment, we did not have explored the possible use of the ORS to external communication, except with auditors. The conclusions of this cycle were:

— The framework may be used for first steps of process identification and design;
— According to the managers, the CEO was now more interested in the regulatory design, seeing more benefits from an holistic ORS;
— The framework may be useful for external cooperation.

4.5   The Third Action Research Cycle

This cycle addressing ORS modeling is a sequent cycle of the research we present in [27]. The institute is a private, non-profit organization, with the mission to provide technical support to industry and to promote innovation. They have hundreds of interconnected internal procedures, required by their four certified laboratories.

Since we already had developed the O_2 matrixes for each process, we decided to concentrate this case in the development of a software tool and in a prototype of a more advanced ORS map. The experience from cases 1 and 2 was also valuable for the development of the support tool, whose main screen is presented in figure 4.

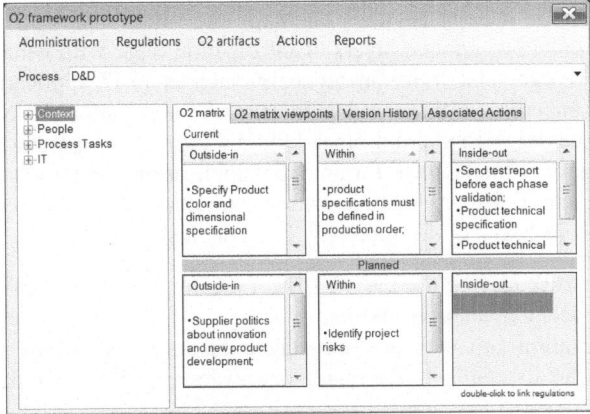

Fig. 4. The O_2 matrix software tool

The interface allows saving the distinct viewpoints from designers, and also combining the viewpoints in a single joint matrix. There is a version control, and the functionality to manage action plans to accomplish requirements. Because each requirement is now in a separate cell, it is easier to link requirements with regulations (double-click).

Another aspect that we were interested was to provide different views of the O_2 map to different stakeholders. Although a representation such as the one in figure 3 can be used, a 3D model would be more appealing and intuitive. This is possible because all the O_2 framework components of context, people, processes, and IT, are connected directly (e.g. processes and IT) or indirectly (e.g. people and IT trough processes). The ORS map evolved to a layered presentation, illustrated in the figure 5.

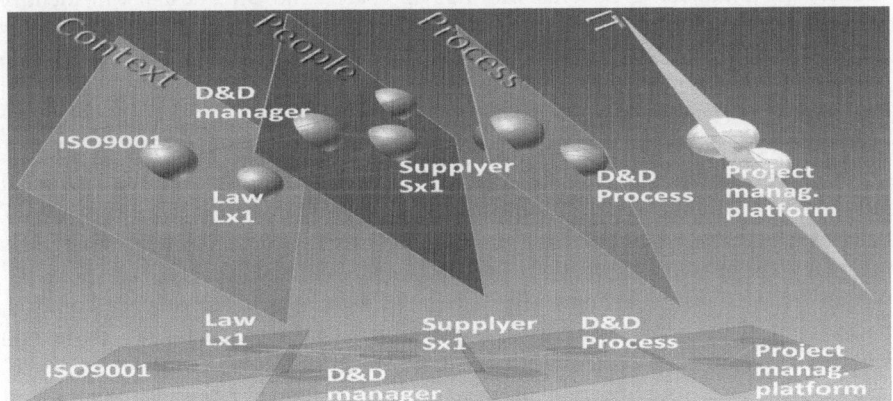

Fig. 5. The O_2 map evolution: conceptually linking different concerns at distinct layers

At this stage of the research, the tool does not create a 3D map as represented in the figure 5. We only illustrate how the representation can be achieved. The map provides a high level view when compared to BPMN models [34], but this can be an advantage in early stages of the ORS design, and for communication of the ORS with external entities. An analogy between O_2 maps and satnav maps can be made, both having options to add or remove layers of information (e.g., with/without road names or buildings). We can select only one concern, such as an IT application, and see all other related concerns of distinct layers (the IT application links with context regulations, processes, people, and other IT). We may also separately obtain one or more layers (e.g. only the IT layer for potential application integrations). We intend to continue the research with this organization, simultaneously refining the tool and improving the steps 5 to 7 of the approach. The conclusions of this cycle were:

— The framework may be used as a basis for creating 3D *models* of the ORS;
— Those models can support and *improve* the *communication* of the ORS, within the organization and with external stakeholders. The existence of a structured approach can also *improve* the regulatory awareness among the designers.

5   Conclusions

From our research findings and over 15 years of consulting experience in IS, we found that organizations have difficulties in formal mapping between regulations, processes, people, and IT. Existing approaches for managing regulations do not holistically represent the regulatory space, simultaneously addressing the cooperation with internal and external entities. Even when a business rule engine exists, its use is mostly focused in the technological aspects, and it is difficult to be used as a working tool for all the business experts and external consultants. Our work combines regulatory and IS literature. The O_2 framework provides guidance for the regulatory analysis and elicitation. During the design, distinct experts negotiate and validate the goals and rules of the ORS. The framework creates a common level of abstraction for both business and IT to align their models and improve consistency [35].

There are a number of benefits with this approach. The ORS design will identify the regulatory requirements, and there is an opportunity to reduce the "burden" of this task while improving communication in practice. With the O_2 map, the organization can provide evidence for auditors, and other external entities, such as associations and customers. The O_2 framework focuses the participants in all the dimensions of an IS, namely the (1) context, (2) people, (3) process, (4) information, and (5) IT [3, 13, 27]. A partnership is proposed from the beginning of design, as opposed to the traditional customer–supplier relation that sometimes happens [35], for instance, between IT departments (supply solutions) and other management systems experts (define goals and rules). The approach is simple to use, and technology independent.

This research has limitations. The cases represent specific regulatory contexts, mostly influenced by ISO standards. The organizational managers (ORS designers) were indicated by each organization, but other functions could be also considered. The O_2 map is a simplification of the complex system it represents, and as all regulatory models, it faces inherent uncertainties [36]. Finally, in spite of the positive results for organizational communication, joint modeling, and audit, we do not yet have evidences of compliance improvement, such as reducing non-conformances.

Future research can address distinct regulatory settings, for example, in the financial or healthcare sectors, with different company sizes and structures. There is a need to examine the runtime of the ORS and compliance management after the modeling steps. The ORS model could also be tailored for inter-organizational studies in the same or between distinct regulatory spaces. The developers of modeling tools may be inspired by our approach to provide an increased support at early stages of the joint design, and the improvement presentation and navigation of regulatory models. We intend to create new graphical functionalities to the support application, namely (1) the drill-down of the map objects, for instance, detailing a specific process in sub-processes or an IT solution in its modules; and (2) a presentation of the map layers as X3D models, providing interactivity. There is a need to research how the O_2 artifacts, designed in natural language, may be converted or even incorporated in technological solutions. Lastly, the integration with enterprise architecture approaches and other frameworks that are suitable for the sequent steps of detailed modeling, coding, and implementation [10, 17].

References

1. Hancher, L., Moran, M.: Organizing regulatory space. In: Hancher, L., Moran, M. (eds.) Capitalism, Culture and Regulation, p. 299. Clarendon Press (1989)
2. Parker, C.: Reinventing Regulation within the Corporation: Compliance-Oriented Regulatory Innovation. Administration & Society 32, 529–565 (2000)
3. Curtis, B., Krasner, H., Iscoe, N.: A field study of the software design process for large systems. Communications of the ACM 31, 1268–1287 (1988)
4. Baxter, G., Sommerville, I.: Socio-technical systems: From design methods to systems engineering. Interacting with Computers 23, 4–17 (2011)
5. Zairi, M.: Business process management: a boundaryless approach to modern competitiveness. Business Process Management Journal 3, 64–80 (1997)
6. Iden, J.: Investigating process management in firms with quality systems: a multi-case study. Business Process Management Journal 18, 104–121 (2012)
7. Syed Abdullah, N., Sadiq, S., Indulska, M.: A Compliance Management Ontology: Developing Shared Understanding through Models. In: Ralyté, J., Franch, X., Brinkkemper, S., Wrycza, S. (eds.) CAiSE 2012. LNCS, vol. 7328, pp. 429–444. Springer, Heidelberg (2012)
8. Abdullah, N.S., Sadiq, S., Indulska, M.: Information systems research: Aligning to industry challenges in management of regulatory compliance. In: Proc. PACIS (2010)
9. Syed Abdullah, N., Sadiq, S., Indulska, M.: Emerging Challenges in Information Systems Research for Regulatory Compliance Management. In: Pernici, B. (ed.) CAiSE 2010. LNCS, vol. 6051, pp. 251–265. Springer, Heidelberg (2010)
10. Kharbili, M.: Business process regulatory compliance management solution frameworks: A comparative evaluation. In: Proc. APCCM (2012)
11. Shearing, C.: A Constitutive Conception of Regulation. In: Grabosky, P., Braithwaite, J. (eds.) Business Regulation and Australia's Future, pp. 67–79. A. Inst. Criminology (1993)
12. Jørgensen, T.H., Remmen, A., Mellado, M.D.: Integrated management systems – three different levels of integration. Journal of Cleaner Production 14, 713–722 (2006)
13. Laudon, J., Laudon, K.: Management Information Systems: Managing the Digital Firm, 10th edn. Prentice Hall (2007)
14. Araujo, B., Schmitz, E., Correa, A., Alencar, A.: A method for validating the compliance of business processes to business rules. In: Proc. ACM Symposium on Applied Computing (2010)

15. Sadiq, S., Governatori, G.: Managing Regulatory Compliance in Business Processes. In: Vom Brocke, J., Rosemann, M. (eds.) Handbook of Business Process Management 2, pp. 157–173. Springer (2010)
16. Tran, H., Zdun, U., Holmes, T., Oberortner, E., Mulo, E., Dustdar, S.: Compliance in service-oriented architectures: A model-driven and view-based approach. Information and Software Technology 54, 531–552 (2012)
17. Ingolfo, S., Siena, A., Mylopoulos, J.: Establishing regulatory compliance for software requirements. In: Jeusfeld, M., Delcambre, L., Ling, T.-W. (eds.) ER 2011. LNCS, vol. 6998, pp. 47–61. Springer, Heidelberg (2011)
18. Ghanavati, S., Amyot, D., Peyton, L., Siena, A., Perini, A., Susi, A.: Integrating business strategies with requirement models of legal compliance. International Journal of Electronic Business 8, 260–280 (2010)
19. Sangkyun, K.: Auditing methodology on legal compliance of enterprise information systems. International Journal of Technology Management 54, 270–287 (2011)
20. Julisch, K., Suter, C., Woitalla, T., Zimmermann, O.: Compliance by design – Bridging the chasm between auditors and IT architects. Computers & Security 30, 410–426 (2011)
21. Bonazzi, R., Hussami, L., Pigneur, Y.: Compliance management is becoming a major issue in IS design. In: D'Atri, A., Saccà, D. (eds.) Information Systems: People, Organizations, Institutions, and Technologies, pp. 391–398. Springer (2010)
22. Handel, M.J., Poltrock, S.: Working around official applications. In: Proc. CSCW (2011)
23. Zhang, P., Scialdone, M., Ku, M.-C.: IT Artifacts and The State of IS Research. In: Proc. ICIS (2011)
24. Avison, D., Wood-Harper, A.T., Vidgen, R.T., Wood, J.R.G.: A further exploration into information systems development: the evolution of Multiview2. Information Technology People 11, 124–139 (1998)
25. Kautz, K., Madsen, S., Nørbjerg, J.: Persistent problems and practices in information systems development. Information Systems Journal 17, 217–239 (2007)
26. Sommerville, I., Sawyer, P.: Viewpoints: principles, problems and a practical approach to requirements engineering. Annals of Software Engineering 3, 101–130 (1997)
27. Barata, J., Cunha, P.R.: ISO2: A New Breath for the Joint Development of IS and ISO 9001 Management Systems. In: Proc. ISD (2013)
28. Hult, M., Lennung, S.-Å.: Towards a definition of action research: a note and bibliography. Journal of Management Studies 17, 241–250 (1980)
29. Susman, G.I., Evered, R.D.: An Assessment of the Scientific Merits of Action Research. Administrative Science Quarterly 23, 582–603 (1978)
30. Davison, R., Martinsons, M.G., Kock, N.: Principles of canonical action research. Information Systems Journal 14, 65–86 (2004)
31. Perry, M., Sanderson, D.: Coordinating joint design work: the role of communication and artefacts. Design Studies 19, 273–288 (1998)
32. Myers, M.D., Newman, M.: The qualitative interview in IS research: Examining the craft. Information and Organization 17, 2–26 (2007)
33. Van Fenema, P., Pentland, B., Kumar, K.: Paradigm Shifts in Coordination Theory Introduction. Academy of Management Annual Meeting (2004)
34. Businska, L., Kirikova, M., Penicina, L., Buksa, I., Rudzajs, P.: Enterprise Modeling for Respecting Regulations. In: Proc. PoEM (2012)
35. Branco, M.C., Xiong, Y., Czarnecki, K., Küster, J., Völzer, H.: A case study on consistency management of business and IT process models in banking. Software & Systems Modeling (in press, 2013)
36. Holmes, K.J., Graham, J.A., McKone, T., Whipple, C.: Regulatory models and the environment: practice, pitfalls, and prospects. Risk Analysis 29, 159–170 (2009)

Integrating Process Modeling Methodology, Language and Tool – A Design Science Approach

Jörg Becker, Nico Clever, Justus Holler, Johannes Püster, and Maria Shitkova

University of Muenster – ERCIS
Leonardo-Campus 3, 48149 Münster, Germany
{firstname.lastname}@ercis.uni-muenster.de

Abstract. Providing high quality process models in a timely manner can be of major impact on almost all process management projects. Modeling methodologies in the form of normative procedure models and process modeling guidelines are available to facilitate this cause. Modeling languages and according tools, however, do neglect the available methodologies. Our work searches to close this research gap by proposing a modeling environment that integrates insights from modeling methodologies with a modeling language and a tool. Main features are a simple modeling language that generalizes most existing languages, four layers of abstraction and semantic standardization through a glossary and use of attributes. Our approach allows for rapid preparation of modeling activities and ensures high model quality during all modeling phases, thus minimizing rework of the models. The prototype was evaluated and improved during two practical projects.

Keywords: Business Process Modeling, Business Process Modeling Tool, Process Modeling Methodology, Business Process Modeling Language.

1 Introduction

Business process modeling has received considerable attention in practice and theory during the last decades. Following Becker and Kahn [1], "a process is a completely closed, time-logical sequence of activities that are required for working on a process-oriented relevant business object". Process modeling as a form of conceptual modeling is guided by modeling methodologies, uses modeling languages and is supported by modeling tools [2]. Following software development terminology, the combination of methodology, language and tool will further be addressed as the modeling environment. Modeling methodologies are guidelines for the modeling process and available for different purposes, for example business process reengineering [2] or process-oriented reorganization [3]. Modeling languages are available in abundance, ranging from early languages such as EPC [4] and the more formal Petri nets [5], up to BPMN [6] and UML Activity Diagrams [7]. Tool support for all modeling languages has become a necessity, and the tools have evolved up to integrated environments, so called business process management suites [8].To ensure high model quality and, thus, to reduce costs, numerous methodologies and guidelines

J. Grabis et al. (Eds.): PoEM 2013, LNBIP 165, pp. 221–235, 2013.
© IFIP International Federation for Information Processing 2013

are available [3, 9–11]. We, however, argue that methodology insights are neglected in modeling languages and tools because they contradict the high degrees of freedom in existing modeling languages. Therefore, the research question is, how can methodological guidelines and restrictions to process modeling be integrated in the modeling language and modeling tool. The purpose of this paper is to close this research gap by proposing a modeling environment that incorporates features of modeling methodologies into the modeling language and tool for efficient and effective model creation. We have to stress that we propose a complete modeling environment and not "yet another modeling language" [12]. Furthermore, the modeling language used integrates with existing languages, such as EPC and BPMN, as it generalizes the languages by using a common subset of elements.

The development process follows the design science research methodology proposed by Peffers et al. [13], as both language and tool are design science artifacts. The remainder of the paper is structured as follows: The design science approach is described in the second section. An overview on related work is carried out in the third section to derive the research gap. Section four presents the proposed modeling environment and the results of its practical evaluation are described in section five. The paper is concluded with a discussion of the results and an outlook in section six.

2   Research Methodology

The modeling environment proposed in this paper was developed according to the design science research methodology (DSRM) introduced by Peffers et al. [13]. The DSRM consists of six consecutive phases of which the last phase, communicating the research results, is achieved with this article. The remaining five phases, along with the respective research method, are depicted in Fig. 1. To identify the problem and motivate our research, we conducted a keyword based database search [14, 15]. Based on the literature review we provide a line of argumentation to define the objectives of the proposed solution. In order to enable the subsequent implementation of our solution, a conceptual model of the modeling environment is developed in the design phase. Afterwards, the artifact was implemented as a web-based tool to demonstrate its practicability. To demonstrate the applicability of the modeling environment, we present the findings of two case studies projects with archetypical small and medium sized enterprise in which our prototype was used.

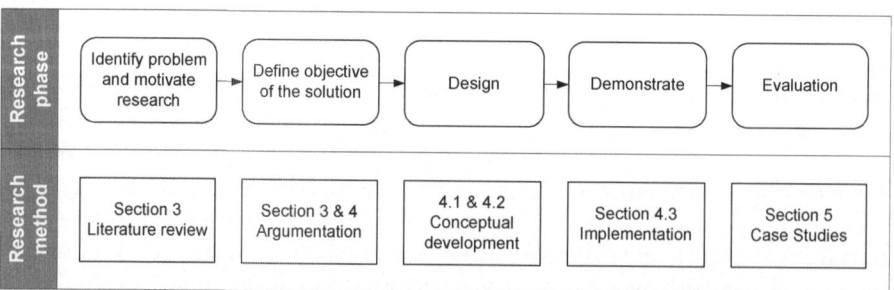

Fig. 1. Research methods applied in this paper mapped to research phases

3   Related Work

The literature review revealed several noticeable procedure models for process modeling differentiating themselves in number and naming of the phases, the purpose and intention of the procedures are nevertheless comparable. Kettinger et al. [2], performed an analysis of 25 business process reengineering (BPR) methodologies used in practice by different organizations and constructed a generalized procedure model with six phases. Due to its consolidating nature, modeling related steps are mostly concealed within the general steps of initiation, diagnosis and redesign. Allweyer [16] describes a BPR procedure model of five phases that could also be a special case of the framework by Kettinger et al. [2]. A more abstract model is proposed by Schmelzer and Sesselmann [17] that hides modeling related activities within the phases of process identification, implementation, control and optimization. In the work of Becker et al. [3], a procedure for process-oriented reorganization projects is described that consists of seven phases, including phases for the preparation of modeling, process framework design, as-is modeling and to-be modeling.

As depicted in Fig. 2, the procedures can be grouped into four steps and differentiated in the proportion of modeling related activities. All procedures start with a preparation step that is not directly related to model construction. It is followed by a step of process modeling, analysis and optimization that includes a high proportion of modeling related activities. The subsequent implementation and evaluation of the processes is less focused on the models. As modeling activities are the initial steps before the actual implementation of changes in the organization, it is important to assure their quality at earlier phases, because error correction at later stages is expensive [18, 19]. We will, therefore, focus on the phases of preparation and modeling, analysis and optimization, because they determine the quality of generated models and, thus, influence the success and costs of the whole project.

Normative approaches to ensure high model quality during preparation of modeling and the actual modeling activities are available in the form of guidelines. Six guidelines of modeling (GoM) are proposed by Becker et al. [20]. They are divided into mandatory and optional guidelines that give general advice on how modeling should be conducted. Because of their general nature, the GoM have been criticized of being too theoretical and abstract, meaning they cannot directly be operationalized [9]. Mendling et al. [9], therefore, present seven process modeling guidelines (7PMG) that provide concrete actions for modelers. Complementing the guidelines on what to do, pitfalls to avoid are listed by Rosemann [10, 11]. A detailed overview of the available guidelines and pitfalls is given in Fig. 3. Because the GoM are more abstract, all guidelines and pitfalls presented in Mendling et al. [9–11] are related to at least one or more GoM.

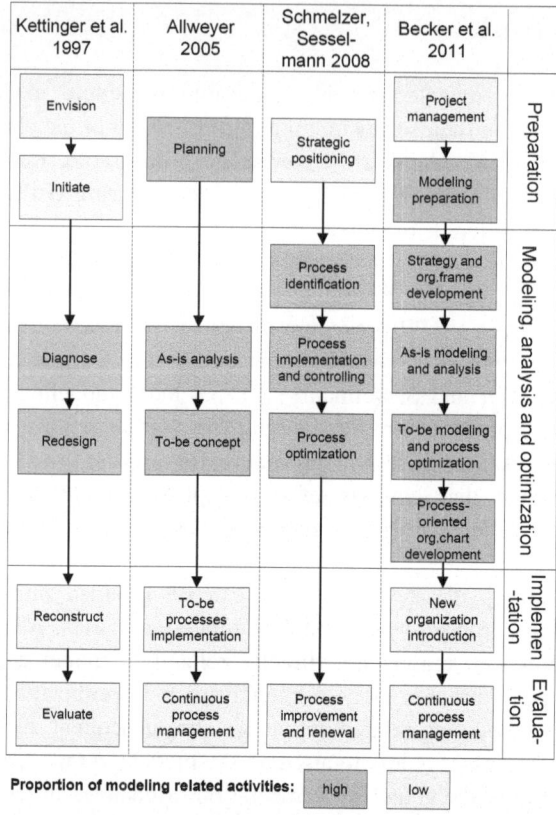

Fig. 2. Business process management procedures (Source: [2, 3, 16, 17])

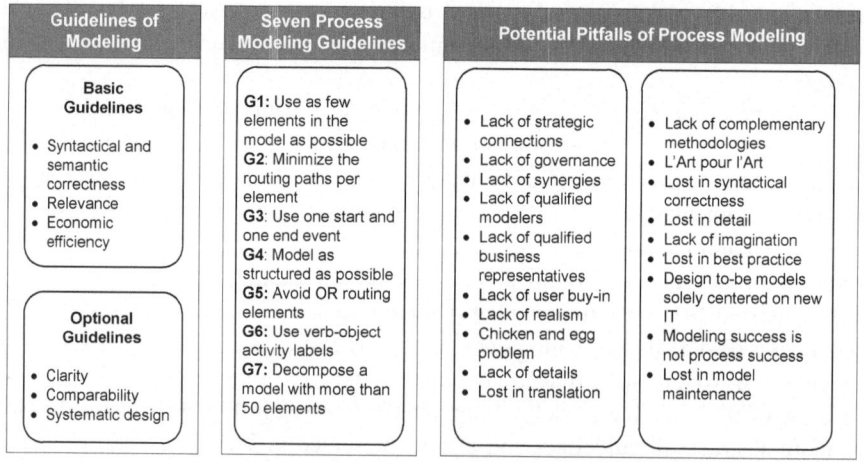

Fig. 3. Guidelines and pitfalls for process modeling

While adherence to the described guidelines can increase model quality and reduce costs, empirical results also indicate that it can cause an increase in perceived usefulness, perceived ease of use and satisfaction with the modeling language [21]. Existing process modeling languages, such as Petri nets, EPC, BPMN and UML Activity Diagrams, however, offer a high degree of freedom by the design of their meta-models. Restrictions, e. g. on how language elements like activities, connectors and flow should be used, should therefore be enforced by the modeling tool.

The process modeling tool market is vast and ranges from simple tools like Microsoft Visio up to business process management suites with many functionalities that surplus modeling functionality (see [8] and [21] for an overview on existing tools). Most tools support user in creating, standardizing, storing and sharing process models, i. e. they offer a replacement for pen and paper. Additional functionality for the analysis of process models has received academic attention lately and is already available in some tools [22]. As outlined by Mendling et al. [9], the modelers are, however, hardly supported in creating high quality and analyzable models because the available guidelines are not enforced or too abstract. We argue that this is caused by the degree of freedom in the modeling languages, which the tool vendors do not restrict [21]. An exception is an approach for the standardization of model element labels by means of naming conventions for both allowed words and phrase structures that are enforced during the modeling process [23].

We conclude that most of the available guidelines are not enforced in available tools, because tool vendors do not to limit the degree of freedom which existing modeling languages allow for. We aim to close this research gap by proposing an integrated modeling environment that tries to enforce the guidelines summarized in Fig. 3.

4   The Modeling Environment

The proposed approach consists of a modeling language and a tool and was built with the goal to integrate principles from existing methodologies and guidelines. The first design principle of the environment was simplicity to keep business process modeling projects as simple as possible and as complex as necessary. Simplicity of the modeling language reduces the degrees of freedom and therefore fosters model quality by taking the available modeling methodologies and guidelines into account. Simplicity of the modeling tool enables a wider group of users to utilize the tool and, thus, facilitates distributed modeling, which reduces modeling costs [21]. The second design principle is transparency, because the guidelines should be enforced already during modeling without the knowledge and additional interaction of the modeler.

The targeted audience of the modeling environment encompasses all the enterprises that choose or were chosen to model, discuss and analyze their processes. Our environment, however, was not built to model workflow processes that can directly be transformed into executable application code, because workflow modeling and organization-oriented process modeling differ substantially in the required level of detail [3]. Opening the environment for modeling in such detail contradicts the goal to reduce the degree of freedom and to take the modeling guidelines into account. The environment thus does not support process modeling as a preparation for the implementation of a workflow engine. It aims to support process modelling in projects focussed on the organizational issues, for example BPR, organizational documentation, knowledge management or software selection.

To address the 7PMG and the GoM as summarized in Table 1, the following rationales of the environment are presented in the upcoming sections:

- Simple syntax of the modeling language
- Layer structure to control the leveling of modeling detail
- Variants and process element references to reduce model complexity
- Glossary and semantic standardization to eliminate naming conflicts
- Attributes to adapt the environment to a concrete modeling project

While certain guidelines are enforced by the modeling tool, or imply impossible by language design, other aspects, such a the amount of elements used per model, can only be facilitated but not completely restricted.

Table 1. Guidelines and pitfalls for process modeling

7PMG		Guidelines of Modeling	Enforced (✓) or Facilitated (o) by:	
1	Use as few elements in the model as possible	Clarity, Comparability, Economic efficiency	o	Syntax, Structure
2	Minimize the routing paths per element	Clarity, Correctness	✓	Syntax
3	Use one start and one end event	Clarity, Comparability Systematic design	o	Syntax
4	Model as structured as possible	Clarity, Comparability, Economic efficiency	✓	Structure, Variants
5	Avoid OR routing elements	Clarity	✓	Syntax
6	Use verb-object activity labels	Clarity, Systematic design	✓	Glossary
7	Decompose a model with more than 50 elements	Clarity, Systematic design	o	Syntax, Structure

4.1   Syntax and Structure of the Modeling Language

While Petri-nets use 3 model elements (places, transitions, flow), EPC features over 20 elements and BPMN offers more than 90 elements, our modeling language only allows for two constructs: activities and flow. This decision was supported by empirical evidence which suggests that modelers use fractions of the available elements in other languages [24, 25]. Activities and flow are constructs that are available in virtually all process modeling languages. Therefore, we do not propose a new language, but use a subset of existing modeling languages. The meta-model of the proposed language is depicted in Fig. 4.

Our concept of flow does not include routing logic in form of connectors in order to increase model quality [25]. Activities are nonetheless allowed to have more than one predecessing or successing process element but cyclic edges are prohibited. The flow direction is top to bottom by convention within a model and only one start and end activity is allowed. Due to the secondary role of flow, all modeling detail is included in the activities and their attributes. Events are not available, because they are always connected to activities and their additional value can be included in a detailed description of the process elements, which we also call process bricks.

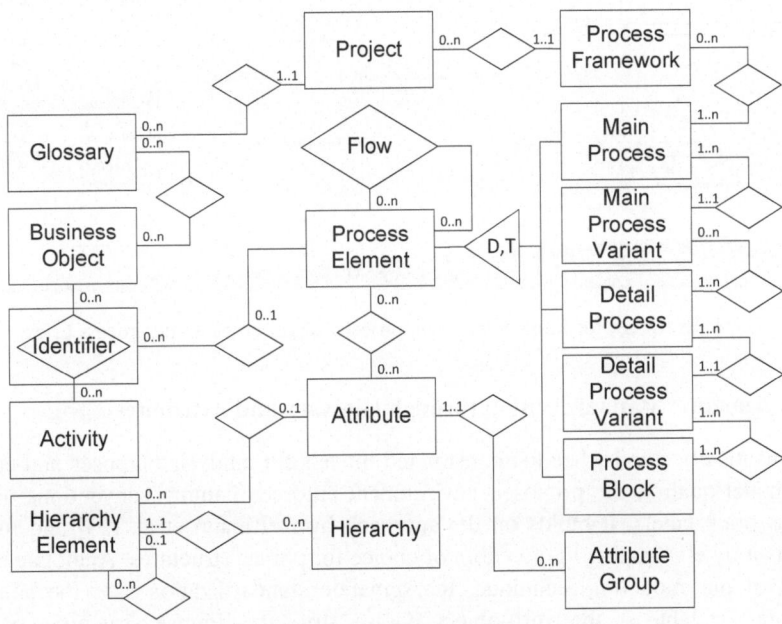

Fig. 4. Meta-model of the modeling language

Modeling within the environment is structured into four distinct layers, which enforce a comparable degree of modeling detail [9, 20]. An example of an instantiation of the meta-model is depicted in Fig. 5. The first layer is the process framework that depicts the process landscape and consists of process elements, which can be freely arranged and shaped to represent arbitrary process frameworks and thus do not require to be connected by control flow. Each process brick in the framework represents a main process. Main processes again contain process bricks, and explicitly require control flow. Each process brick in a main process in turn is a detail process. The difference between main and detail process therefore is only on a level of detail. Each detail processes consist of several process bricks.

To further reduce branching and the number of elements per process model, our modeling environment allows referencing existing elements of the same level and variants. The process brick "Print invoice", for example, can be defined in in the detail process "Handle customer order" and reused by reference in the detail process "Revise complaint". Variants can exist on the main process and detail process level and allow the modeler to depict substantially different variations of the same process. The main process "Send invoice" could for example be constituted by the two variants "Send electronic invoice" and "Send manual invoice", which do not share any process bricks. For a more detailed description, please see [26].

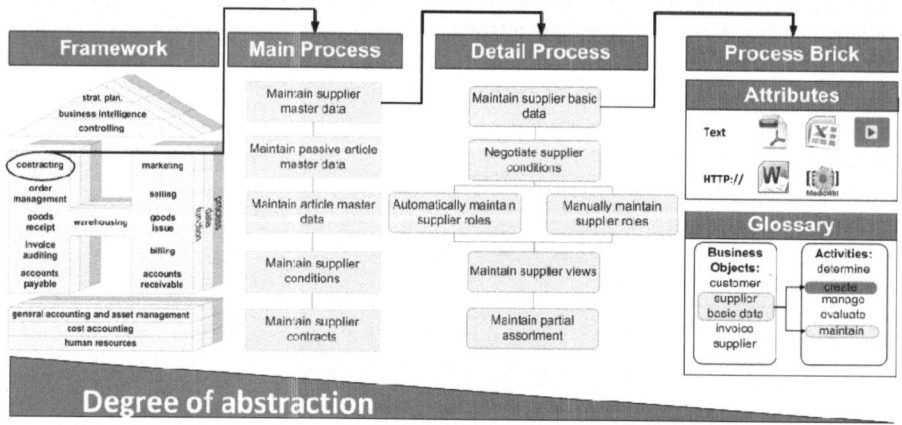

Fig. 5. Examples for framework, main process, detail process and process brick

4.2   Semantic Standardization through Glossary and Attributes

To semantically standardize the constructed models for analysis purposes and ensure high model quality, the proposed environment enforces naming conventions on the process brick labels. It builds on the approach by Delfmann et al. [23] and further extends it by eliminating the freedom of choice for phrase structures. Analogue to the syntax of our modeling technique, the semantic standardization uses the simplest structure available – the verb-object phrase structure. Phrase structures of this composition have been proven to be better understandable than other phrase structures [9]. In the context of process modeling, verb and object can furthermore be interpreted as activity and business object.

The modeling environment contains a glossary that consists of business objects, activities, and relations between both. The business object "supplier basic data", for example, allows the activities "create" and "maintain", but does not allow "determine", which in turn could be used for "customer". The naming conventions are enforced whenever a process brick is created or edited by the fact that the modeler has to use a combination of existing business object and activity to name the process brick, as shown in Fig. 5.. Similar to Delfmann et al. [23] or standardization approaches based on ontologies, the glossary requires a high initial effort of creation and subsequent maintenance. However, it allows to reuse existing content, such as domain specific business objects or generally applicable activities.

Besides their label, process bricks can own an arbitrary amount of attributes. There are a number of predefined attribute types available, which include text, number, selection, file, URL, reference and hierarchy. In order to constrain the amount of attributes the attribute groups with the corresponding attributes are defined by an administrator and the normal user is only able to select from the offered set. Attributes of type hierarchy refer to hierarchies, which can also be modeled in the environment to document, for example, the organizational structures or hierarchies of the IT-architecture and use this structured attribute to annotate process elements. Similar to the glossary, attributes can be used for process bricks on all layers, from framework to process building block. Attribution is used to increase the expressiveness of our modeling environment, because it allows for the simple annotation of detailed information without requiring new language elements.

4.3 Implementation

The prototypical implementation of our modeling environment is a web-based business process modeling tool, as presented in [27]. It is implemented as a Ruby on Rails application and integrates a role and rights management concept to support distributed modeling in large scale modeling projects with many stakeholders. See Fig. 6 for a screenshot. Process bricks of all layers are labeled using the business objects and activities that can be maintained within the glossary. Analogously, attributes can be defined within the prototype and used on all layers they are assigned to. Hierarchies for organizational structure and IT-architecture can be created and maintained directly in the prototype.

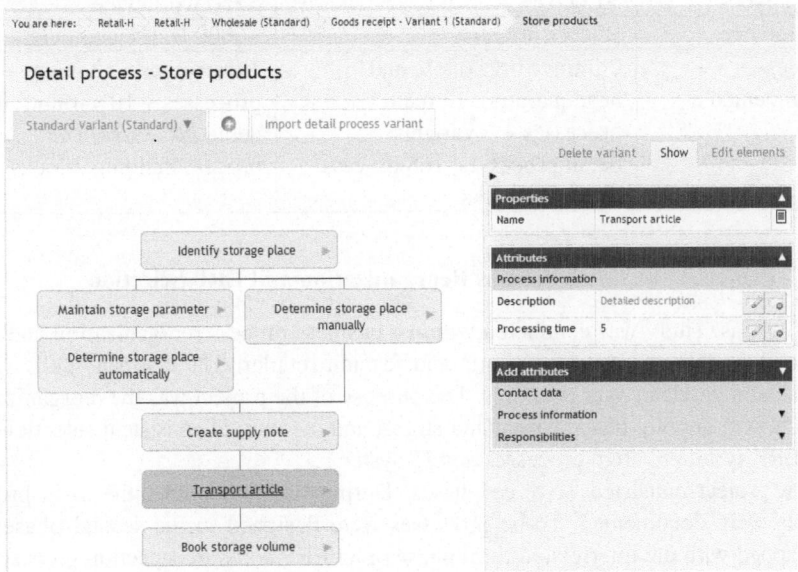

Fig. 6. Screenshot of detail process editing in the prototype

5   Case Studies

In order to evaluate the modeling environment we applied a prototypical implementation in two consulting projects that required business process modeling. Characteristics of the case study projects are summarized in Table 2. We conducted semi-structured interviews and used focus groups with the respective project leaders and key users to analyze the prototype. In both case studies, we focused on answering the question if the prototype fulfilled its purpose as efficient and effective modeling environment. Findings from the first case study were used to improve the prototype before the start of the second case study [28]. In accordance with our research methodology, we applied the enhanced prototype to the second case study and intend to keep up the iterative improvement procedure through further application.

Table 2. Case study project characteristics

	Case study 1	Case study 2
Modeling purpose	Business process reorganization, ERP selection	Organizational documentation, knowledge management
Project duration	Winter 2010 – Summer 2011	Winter 2011 – Summer 2012
Domain	Retail	Warehousing
Articles	~20.000, sports and fashion	~2.500, promotion material
Employees	>1.600	>250 worldwide
Customers	B2C customers	~6000 B2B customers
Processes documented	2 frameworks (store and headquarters), 13 main processes + 6 variants, 55 detail processes, 168 process building blocks	1 framework, 12 main processes + 10 variants, 49 detail processes, 133 process building blocks

5.1   Project 1: Business Process Reorganization and ERP Selection

The first case study was conducted within a business process reorganization and ERP selection project at a German sports and fashion retailer. The company sells sports and fashion goods in over 60 stores. The purpose of the project was the reorganization of processes in both, headquarters and stores, and the mutual consistent selection of a new ERP system to align processes and IT systems.

The project consisted of three phases. During the first phase, the as-is process models were documented. To-be processes were designed in the second phase that overlapped with the interrelated third phase of an ERP software selection process. All the phases were conducted by the company with the help of external consultants. Concerning the modeling methodologies presented in section three, the project encompassed modeling preparation and modeling conduction steps.

The modeling team consisted of external consultants and employees of the company headquarter, which were trained in the modeling environment during an initial workshop. The as-is models were created on the basis of interviews in all company departments. As the company had not undertaken any modeling activities before the project, the processes were designed on the basis of a reference model for retail processes, already available in the prototype [29]. Due to the restrictive nature of the prototype, the team did not have to discuss modeling guidelines on syntax, object types to be used, naming conventions, degree of detail or layout conventions. All adaption of the prototype to the project goals was achieved through the definition of attributes. During the first as-is modeling project phase, these company-specific attributes were defined and later on enhanced during the second to-be modeling phase. To support the final ERP choice, attributes to measure the IT-related requirements and their fulfillment were added to the modeling environment and filled out during workshop meetings with all stakeholders and process-based vendor presentations.

The case study revealed that the reduction in preparation activities was perceived very positive by the whole modeling team and allowed for a fast start into the project. Company employees stated the simplicity of the modeling language as a driver to facilitate the initial acceptance of the project in all departments. The external consultants especially complimented the four-layer architecture, because it helped to standardize the degree of detail within the models and improved inter-model comparability. The effort to prepare the models for the semi-automated creation of an ERP requirements definition could, therefore, be kept low. The main argument to use the proposed modeling environment over other modeling languages or tools in new projects, stated by almost all team members interviewed, turned out to be the ability to adapt the environment to the modeling purpose through attributes, because all models could be re-used throughout the project phases by small additions to the attributes in use. Negative comments were received during the initial preparation of the glossary. The reservations were, however, partly dissolved for the most part during later stages of the project, when renaming tasks could be executed centrally. Major criticism was furthermore voiced towards the general usability of the prototype, in particular to glossary management and the element naming. All members of the modeling team stated export (Word, Excel export and XML import/export) and analysis features, such as statistics on the used attributes, as most important missing functionalities.

We concluded that our proposed modeling environment facilitated cost-efficient modeling by accelerating modeling preparation activities and achieved high acceptance in all departments because of the simple modeling language. Re-work by the external consultants could be minimized, because model quality was ensured during all phases of the project. Adaption of the prototype to the project could be achieved through extensive use of attributes that facilitated model re-use. Nonetheless, the case study revealed improvement points, in particular usability aspects and the need for model export and analysis features.

5.2   Project 2: Organizational Documentation and Knowledge Management

After the prototype had been improved, we conducted a second case study with a leading German wholesaler of promotional material. The company has been founded two decades ago and grown ever since. In order to keep pace with the changing processes and the growing employee base, they decided to document their processes and use the documentation for knowledge management purposes. Till now, the project only included an as-is modeling phase, but as the ERP system of the company will undergo a major update by the time of this work, the models will be used to derive software test cases.

Similar to the first project, the company had not documented any processes before the project. The project team was therefore supported by external consultants. The processes were created on the basis of retail reference processes with our prototype during interviews with employees from all departments.

The second case yielded results similar to the first project. the modeling language and the enforced modeling structure were perceived very positive by all project stakeholders. All further information could be expressed using the attributes, which again allowed for extensive reuse of the models for both organizational documentation and knowledge management. Problems for the preparation of the model-based software tests are not expected.

As the prototype was improved according to the findings from the first case study, discussions of the usability of the prototype gave much more positive responses but revealed additional issues that will be addressed in the next version of the prototype. The added export functionality could be fully tested during the project and was perceived very helpful by the modeling team. In opposite, functionality for analysis could not be properly evaluated, as the project did not encompass as-is analysis or to-be modelling steps, which could have required an tool support in model analysis.

We conclude that all requirements of both projects could be met and the discussions led to a substantial improvement of the prototype. The positive comments about productivity and model quality furthermore indicate that the design goals of the modeling environment could be met. As both companies represent typical small- or medium-sized enterprises, the application results are expected to be reproducible in other companies.

6   Summary, Limitations and Outlook

This paper presented a modeling environment, consisting of a language and a tool that integrate ideas from existing methodologies. It combines a simple modeling syntax that generalizes many existing languages with a four-layer structure to control the degree of modeling detail. The use of a glossary and attributes allows for the creation of standardized process models in a cost-efficient manner. The development process of the environment is based on the design science research methodology by [13] and the resulting prototype advances the current state of the art, because it transparently operationalizes process modeling guidelines that have been proposed in literature. The prototype was successfully evaluated in two modeling projects as an easy and fast to use modeling environment for beginners but also for advanced modelers who furthermore especially appreciated the standardization regarding naming and level of detail.

The environment is limited to business modeling and analysis purposes, such as business process reengineering or knowledge documentation, and not applicable for workflow modeling. It can, however, serve as a starting point for more detailed modeling by integrating workflow models as attributes of the process bricks. The case studies on the prototype moreover only cover German companies and, thus, did not consider social factors, such as values and beliefs. Moroever, both cases were conducted within companies that had no modeling experience beforehand. An application within a company with an existing modeling landscape would be needed to reveal potential issues in model transformation. Similarly, we did not compare our approach to existing modeling languages and tools. Such a comparison could be useful to further improve the proposed environment.

During the application, we also identified potential for further research. One aspect that requires further investigation is the four-layer architecture and we intend to evaluate how it performs against structures with a different number of layers. The cases also revealed challenging usability issues, which we already address in research [30] and subsequently intend to implement in the prototype. The proposed glossary also raised need for improvements, because it was the main source of reservations in our case studies. We intend to identify methods to improve the glossary management, for example by including existing verb-hierarchies. The prototype furthermore serves as a starting point for current research on model version control [31] and modeling support features such as auto-suggestion. As it is the underlying idea behind our work, future research will also focus on the use of attributes in process modeling and the relation of attribute-based complexity with modeling language-based complexity.

References

1. Becker, J., Kahn, D.: The Process in Focus. In: Becker, J., Kugeler, M., Rosemann, M. (eds.) Process Management: A Guide for the Design of Business Processes, pp. 3–13. Springer, Berlin (2011)
2. Kettinger, W.J., Teng, J.T.C., Guha, S.: Business Process Change: A Study of Methodologies, Techniques, and Tools. MIS Quarterly 21, 55–80 (1997)
3. Becker, J., Kugeler, M., Rosemann, M.: Process Management: A Guide for the Design of Business Processes. Springer, Berlin (2011)
4. Scheer, A.-W.: Aris - Business Process Modeling. Springer, Berlin (2000)
5. Murata, T.: Petri nets: Properties, analysis and applications. Proceedings of the IEEE 77, 541–580 (1989)
6. OMG: Business Process Model and Notation (BPMN),
   http://www.omg.org/spec/BPMN/2.0/
7. OMG: Unified Modeling Language (UML),
   http://www.omg.org/spec/UML/2.4.1/
8. Gartner: Magic Quadrant for Business Process Management Suites (2010)

9. Mendling, J., Reijers, H., van der Aalst, W.M.P.: Seven Process Modeling Guidelines (7PMG). Information and Software Technology 52, 127–136 (2008)
10. Rosemann, M.: Potential pitfalls of process modeling: part A. Business Process Management Journal 12, 249–254 (2006)
11. Rosemann, M.: Potential pitfalls of process modeling: part B. Business Process Management Journal 12, 377–384 (2006)
12. Wand, Y., Weber, R.: Research Commentary: Information Systems and Conceptual Modeling - A Research Agenda. Information Systems Research 13, 363–376 (2002)
13. Peffers, K., Tuunanen, T., Rothenberger, M.A., Chatterjee, S.: A Design Science Research Methodology for Information Systems Research. Journal of Management Information Systems 24, 45–77 (2007)
14. Webster, J., Watson, R.T.: Analyzing the Past to Prepare for the Future: Writing a Literature Review. MIS Quarterly. 26, xiii–xxiii (2002)
15. Vom Brocke, J., Simons, A., Niehaves, B., Riemer, K., Plattfaut, R., Cleven, A.: Reconstructing the Giant: On the Importance of Rigour in Documenting the Literature Search Process. In: Proceedings of the ECIS 2009, Verona, pp. 2206–2217 (2009)
16. Allweyer, T.: Geschäftsprozessmanagement. W3L-Verlag, Herdecke (2005)
17. Schmelzer, H.J., Sesselmann, W.: Geschäftsprozessmanagement in der Praxis. Carl Hanser Verlag, München (2008)
18. Moody, D.: Theoretical and practical issues in evaluating the quality of conceptual models: current state and future directions. Data & Knowledge Engineering 55, 243–276 (2005)
19. Vergidis, K., Tiwari, A., Majeed, B.: Business process analysis and optimization: beyond reengineering. IEEE Transactions on Systems, Man, and Cybernetics 38, 69–82 (2008)
20. Becker, J., Rosemann, M., von Uthmann, C.: Guidelines of Business Process Modeling. In: van der Aalst, W., Desel, J., Overweis, A. (eds.) Business Process Management: Models, Techniques and Empirical Studies, pp. 30–49. Springer, Berlin (2000)
21. Recker, J.: "Modeling with tools is easier, believe me"—The effects of tool functionality on modeling grammar usage beliefs. Information Systems 37, 213–226 (2012)
22. Delfmann, P., Herwig, S., Lis, Ł., Stein, A., Tent, K., Becker, J.: Pattern Specification and Matching in Conceptual Models. A Generic Approach Based on Set Operations. Enterprise Modelling and Information Systems Architectures 5, 24–43 (2010)
23. Delfmann, P., Herwig, S., Lis, L.: Unified Enterprise Knowledge Representation with Conceptual Models - Capturing Corporate Language in Naming Conventions. In: 30th International Conference on Information Systems (ICIS 2009), Phoenix, Arizona, USA (2009)
24. Siau, K., Erickson, J., Lee, L.: Theoretical vs. Practical Complexity. Journal of Database Management 16, 40–57 (2005)
25. Muehlen, M.Z., Recker, J.: How Much Language Is Enough? Theoretical and Practical Use of the Business Process Modeling Notation. In: Bellahsène, Z., Léonard, M. (eds.) CAiSE 2008. LNCS, vol. 5074, pp. 465–479. Springer, Heidelberg (2008)
26. Becker, J., Clever, N., Holler, J., Püster, J., Shitkova, M.: Semantically Standardized and Transparent Process Model Collections via Process Building Blocks. In: Proceedings of the Fifth International Conference on Information, Process, and Knowledge Management - eKNOW 2013, Nice, pp. 172–177 (2013)
27. Becker, J., Clever, N., Holler, J., Shitkova, M.: Icebricks - Business Process Modeling on the Basis of Semantic Standardization. In: vom Brocke, J., Hekkala, R., Ram, S., Rossi, M. (eds.) DESRIST 2013. LNCS, vol. 7939, pp. 394–399. Springer, Heidelberg (2013)

28. Tremblay, M., Hevner, A., Berndt, D.: The Use of Focus Groups in Design Science Research. Design Research in Information Systems, pp. 121–143. Springer US (2010)
29. Becker, J., Schütte, R.: A Reference Model for Retail Enterprises. In: Fettke, P. and Loos, P. (eds.) Reference Modeling for Business Systems Analysis. pp. 182–205. Idea Group Publishing (2006)
30. Becker, J., Clever, N., Holler, J., Shitkova, M.: Towards A Usability Measurement Framework for Process Modelling Tools. In: Proceedings of the Pacific Asia Conference on Information Systems (PACIS), Jeju Island, Korea (2013)
31. Clever, N., Holler, J., Püster, J., Shitkova, M.: Growing Trees – A Versioning Approach for Business Process Models based on Graph Theory. In: Proceedings of the European Conference on Information Systems, ECIS, Utrecht (2013)

An Experimental Study on the Design and Modeling of Security Concepts in Business Processes

Maria Leitner[1], Sigrid Schefer-Wenzl[2,3],
Stefanie Rinderle-Ma[1], and Mark Strembeck[3]

[1] University of Vienna, Austria
Faculty of Computer Science
{maria.leitner,stefanie.rinderle-ma}@univie.ac.at
[2] University of Applied Sciences Campus Vienna, Austria
Competence Center for IT-Security
sigrid.schefer-wenzl@fh-campuswien.ac.at
[3] Vienna University of Economics and Business (WU Vienna), Austria
Institute for Information Systems, New Media Lab
mark.strembeck@wu.ac.at

Abstract. In recent years, business process models are used to define security properties for the corresponding business information systems. In this context, a number of approaches emerged that integrate security properties into standard process modeling languages. Often, these security properties are depicted as text annotations or graphical extensions. However, because the symbols of process-related security properties are not standardized, different issues concerning the comprehensibility and maintenance of the respective models arise. In this paper, we present the initial results of an experimental study on the design and modeling of 11 security concepts in a business process context. In particular, we center on the semantic transparency of the visual symbols that are intended to represent the different concepts (i.e. the one-to-one correspondence between the symbol and its meaning). Our evaluation showed that various symbols exist which are well-perceived. However, further studies are necessary to dissolve a number of remaining issues.

Keywords: BPMN, Business Processes, Empirical Evaluation, Icons, Modeling, Security, Visualization.

1 Introduction

Over the last three decades, organizations moved towards a process-centered view of business activities in order to cope with rising complexity and dynamics of the economic environment (e.g., [1]). Business processes consist of tasks which are executed in an organization to achieve certain corporate goals [2]. Business process models represent these processes of organizations. Typically, the business process models are executed via process-aware information systems

J. Grabis et al. (Eds.): PoEM 2013, LNBIP 165, pp. 236–250, 2013.
© IFIP International Federation for Information Processing 2013

(PAIS) (e.g., [3]). Today, various business process modeling languages exist that support graphical representations of business processes such as the Business Process Model and Notation (BPMN) [4], Unified Modeling Language (UML) Activity Diagrams [5] or Event-driven Process Chains (EPC) [6,7].

To protect sensitive organizational data and services, information systems security is constantly receiving more attention in research and industry (e.g., [8]). In many organizations, process models serve as a primary vehicle to efficiently communicate and engineer related security properties (e.g., [9]). However, contemporary process modeling languages, such as BPMN, EPCs or UML Activity diagrams, do not provide native language support to model process-related security aspects [10,11]. As a consequence, while business processes can be specified via graphical modeling languages, corresponding security properties are usually only defined via (informal) textual comments or via ad hoc extensions to modeling languages (e.g., [12,13]). For example in [13], we outlined current research and practice of security modeling extensions in BPMN. In addition, we conducted a survey to evaluate the comprehensibility of these extensions. The study showed that a mix of visual representations of BPMN security extensions (e.g., use of different shapes, use of text) exists. What is missing is a uniform approach for security modeling in BPMN.

Missing standardized modeling support for security properties in process models may result in significant problems regarding the comprehensibility and maintainability of these ad hoc models. Moreover, it is difficult to translate the respective modeling-level concepts to actual software systems. The demand for an integrated modeling support of business processes and corresponding security properties has been repeatedly identified in research and practice (e.g., [12,14]).

In this paper, we present the preliminary results of an experimental study on the design and modeling of 11 security concepts on different abstraction levels in a business process context. In particular, we investigate the visualization of the following security concepts: Access control, Audit, Availability, Data confidentiality, Data integrity, Digital signature, Encryption, Privacy, Risk, Role and User. This study aims at designing symbols that are semantics-oriented and user-oriented (see Section 2) as outlined in [15]. Based on the suggestions and findings presented in [13,16,17], we designed two studies to obtain graphical symbols for 11 security concepts. Subsequently, we evaluated the symbol set via expert interviews. As most symbols were well-perceived, we plan to use these results and reexamine the symbols that were misleading in further studies. This will yield the basis to convey security-related information in business process models in a comprehensible way.

Our paper is structured as follows. Section 2 introduces background information on the visualization of business processes and security concepts. In Section 3, we outline the methods applied in this paper and corresponding research questions. Next, Sections 4 and 5 describe the design and results of the two experimental studies we conducted to obtain a symbol set for security concepts. The results of the evaluation of the symbols are presented in Section 6. Finally, in Section 7 we discuss results, preliminary options for integrating the symbols into BPMN and UML and impact on future research. Section 8 concludes the paper.

2   Related Work

Visual representations have a strong impact on the usability and effectiveness of software engineering notations [17]. The quality of conceptual models is essential to, e.g., prevent errors and to improve the quality of the corresponding systems [18]. Several frameworks exist that provide guidelines on how to design and evaluate visual notations (e.g., [17,19]). For example, the *Physics of Notations* in [17] consists of nine principles to design visual notations effectively. Further language evaluation frameworks include the cognitive dimensions of notations [19,20] that provide a set of dimensions to assist designers of visual notations to evaluate these designs. A framework for evaluating the quality of conceptual models is presented in [21]. This approach considers various aspects such as learning (of a domain), current knowledge and the modeling activity. It also provides a dynamic view showing that change to a model might cause a direct change of the domain.

Visual Representations of Business Processes. In the context of PAIS, recent publications show increased interest in the visual representation of process modeling languages. For example in [22], an evaluation of the cognitive effectiveness of BPMN using the *Physics of Notations* is performed. Further studies investigate certain characteristics such as routing symbols [23] or the usage of labels and icons [15]. In this paper, we use the terms *symbol* and *icon* synonymously as icons *are symbols that perceptually resemble the concepts they represent* [17, p.765]. In [15], the following guidelines for icon development are outlined based on research in graphical user interface design:

a. Semantics-oriented: Icons should be natural to users, resemble to the concepts they refer to, and be different from each other (so that all icons can be easily differentiated).
b. User-oriented: Icons should be selected based on user preferences and user evaluation.
c. Composition principle: The composition of icons should be easy to understand and learn.
d. Interpretation: The composition rules should be transferable to different models.

Modeling of Security Concepts in Business Processes. Typically, process models are created by process modelers or process managers in an organization. These managers have an expertise in process modeling, but are often not experts in security. A security expert provides know-how and collaborates with the process modeling expert to enforce security concerns in a process. Hence, the integrated modeling of security aspects in a process model is intended to provide a common language and basis between different domain experts. Recent publications try to provide a common language between domain experts (e.g., security experts) and process modelers by proposing process modeling extensions such as to the Unified Modeling Language (UML) (e.g., [24,25,26]) or to BPMN (e.g., [12,13]).

3 Methodology

The main goal of this paper is to assess the design and modeling of security concepts in business processes. Thereby, we expect to obtain an initial set of symbols for security concepts. In contrast to existing security extensions, we do not design these symbols from scratch though. In order to obtain a set of symbols for selected security concepts, we conducted two studies (Experiment 1 and 2) and evaluated the results via expert interviews. In particular, our research was guided by the following questions (RQ):

1. Which symbols can be used to represent 11 different security concepts?
2. How can the drawings from RQ1 be aggregated into stereotype symbols?
   2.1. How do experts evaluate the one-to-one correspondence between the symbols and security concepts?
   2.2. How do experts rate the resemblance between the symbols and concepts?
   2.3. How can the stereotype symbols be improved?
3. How can the security symbols be integrated into business process modeling?
   3.1. Are the stereotype symbols suitable to be integrated into business process models?
   3.2. Which business process modeling languages are suggested for security modeling by experts?
   3.3. In BPMN, which symbols should be related to which process elements?
   3.4. Can color be useful to distinguish security symbols from BPMN standard elements?

Research question RQ1 investigates what kind of symbols people draw for 11 security concepts in Experiment 1. In the first experiment, we retrieved the symbols by setting up an experiment where the participants were asked to draw intuitive symbols for security concepts. Based on these drawings, we aggregate the drawings into stereotype symbols (RQ2) based on frequency, uniqueness and iconic character in Experiment 2. For evaluation, we analyze the stereotype symbols with expert interviews (see Section 6). In particular, we will evaluate the one-to-one correspondence between symbols and concepts, the rating of resemblance between symbols and concepts and if these symbols can be improved. With this expert evaluation, we hope to identify not only strengths and shortcomings of the symbols but also to gain insights on how to enhance the symbols such as with the use of hybrid symbols that combine graphics and text. Moreover, we investigate if security symbols can be integrated into business process modeling (RQ3). For example, we evaluate for each security concept which process elements in BPMN can be associated with it. Thereby, we expect to identify integration options for business process modeling languages.

4 Experiment 1: Production of Drawings

The first experiment addresses research question RQ1 to identify which symbols can be used to represent security concepts (see Section 3). For this purpose, we adapted the experiment design of the first experiment presented in [16].

4.1 Participants and Procedure

In our first experiment, we used a paper-based questionnaire to conduct a survey. In total, 43 Bachelors' and Masters' students in Business Informatics at the University of Vienna and the Vienna University of Economics and Business filled out the questionnaire. Most participants had beginner or intermediate knowledge of business processes and/or security. We expect to find this setting also in research and industry where experts from different domains (e.g., process modelers, security experts and business process managers) interact with each other to discuss and define security in business processes.

The survey contained 13 stapled, one-sided pages and completing the survey took about 30 minutes. It consisted of two parts. The first part, 2 pages long, presented the aim and collected demographic data of the participants, such as knowledge of business processes, knowledge of business process modeling languages and security knowledge. The second part consisted of 11 pages; one for each security concept. At the top of each page, a two-column table was displayed. Its first row contained the name of the security concept in English (see Table 1). Additionally, we displayed the name of the respective concepts in German. In the last row, a definition of the concept was given. All definitions were taken from the internet security glossary [27] except for *Role* and *User* which were taken from the RBAC standard in [28]. Please note that a definition of *Role* is not given in [27] and the *User* definition in [27] and [28] are very similar. *Role* is important as it is an essential concept for access control in PAIS (see [9]). The selection of the security concepts to be included in the survey was based on literature reviews and research projects. The aim was to consider concepts on different abstraction levels, including abstract concepts such as data integrity or confidentiality but also to include its applications (e.g., digital signature (integrity) and encryption (confidentiality)). In the middle of each page, a (3 inch x 3 inch) frame was printed. Participants were asked to draw in the frame what they estimate to be the best symbol to represent the name and the definition of a security concept. At the bottom of each page, we asked the participants to rate the difficulty of drawing this sketch. Additionally, the participants were asked to describe the symbol with one to three keywords in case they want to clarify the sketch.

4.2 Results

In total, we received 473 drawings (blank and null drawings included). We observed that participants often did not only draw a single symbol for a concept but a combination of several symbols e.g., a desk in front of a matchstick man. These drawings often included signs or symbols that resembled the majority drawings.

As can be seen in Figure 1, most participants stated that the task to draw a symbol for *User*, *Encryption*, *Risk* and *Access control* was easy or fairly easy. On the other hand, it was fairly difficult or difficult for many participants to draw *Audit*, *Data confidentiality*, *Digital signature* and *Role*.

Table 1. Names and Definitions of Security Concepts in Experiment 1

Name	Definition
Access control	Protection of system resources against unauthorized access.
Audit	An independent review and examination of a system's records and activities to determine the adequacy of system controls, ensure compliance with established security policy and procedures, detect breaches in security services, and recommend any changes that are indicated for countermeasures.
Availability	The property of a system or a system resource being accessible and usable upon demand by an authorized system entity, according to performance specifications for the system.
Data confidentiality	The property that information is not made available or disclosed to unauthorized individuals, entities, or processes.
Data integrity	The property that data has not been changed, destroyed, or lost in an unauthorized or accidental manner.
Digital signature	A value computed with a cryptographic algorithm and appended to a data object in such a way that any recipient of the data can use the signature to verify the data's origin and integrity.
Encryption	Cryptographic transformation of data (called "plaintext") into a form (called "ciphertext") that conceals the data's original meaning to prevent it from being known or used.
Privacy	The right of an entity (normally a person), acting in its own behalf, to determine the degree to which it will interact with its environment, including the degree to which the entity is willing to share information about itself with others.
Risk	An expectation of loss expressed as the probability that a particular threat will exploit a particular vulnerability with a particular harmful result.
Role	A role is a job function within the context of an organization with some associated semantics regarding the authority and responsibility conferred on the user assigned to the role.
User	A user is defined as a human being. The concept of a user can be extended to include machines, networks, or intelligent autonomous agents.

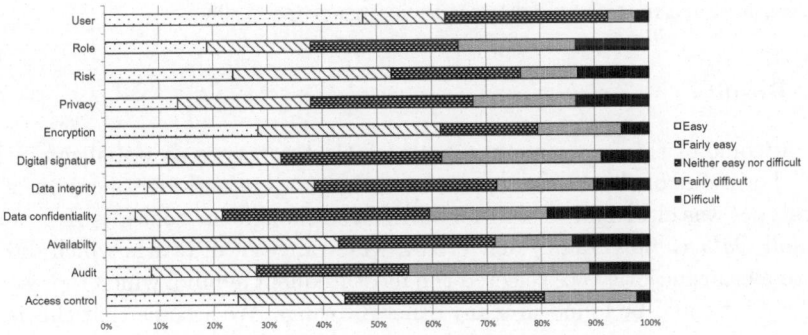

Fig. 1. Participant Rating of Difficulty of Drawing a Sketch

5   Experiment 2: Selection of Stereotypical Drawings

To answer research question RQ2, Experiment 2 is concerned with *producing stereotypical symbols* out of the sketches of Experiment 1 (adapted from [16]).

5.1   Procedure

A stereotype is the best median drawing, i.e. the symbol which is most frequently used by people to depict a concept [16]. The resulting set of stereotypes then constitutes our first proposed set of hand-sketched symbols for visualizing security concepts. However, as mentioned in [16], the drawing that is the most frequently produced to denote a security concept is not necessarily expressing the idea of the respective concept best. Thus, we subsequently evaluated the set of stereotypes via expert interviews (see Section 6).

In accordance with [16], we applied a judges' ranking method in Experiment 2 to identify the stereotypes. We started by categorizing the drawings obtained from Experiment 1. We evaluated (a) the idea it represented, (b) whether it is a drawing or a symbol and (c) the uniqueness and dissimilarity between the drawings. Thereby, each author associated a keyword (i.e. category) that represented the idea with each drawing. Drawings representing the same idea for a particular security concept form a category. Each author performed the categorization independently. Subsequently, we analyzed each categorization and reviewed and agreed on a final categorization in several rounds (see column Experiment 2 in Table 2 for the final number of categories).

To select the stereotypes, we applied the following three criteria to determine the symbol that best expressed the idea of the respective security concept: (1) Frequency of occurrence: For each security concept, we chose a drawing from each category that contained the largest number of drawings. (2) Distinctiveness and uniqueness: To avoid ambiguities and symbol overload [22,17], we tried to select symbols which are not too similar and can be easily distinguished from each other. (3) Iconic character: According to [17], users prefer real objects to abstract shapes, because iconic representations can be easier recognized in a diagram and are more accessible to novice users (see [29]).

5.2   Results

The outcome of this experiment is a set of 11 stereotypes as visualized in Figure 2. For 9 out of the 11 concepts, the categorization and identification of the stereotypes was clear and straightforward. Even though the concepts *Access control* and *Data confidentiality* delivered a wide range of drawings which did not lead to a clear majority, we selected the most frequent symbol which represented an idea that could be found in many other drawings. We assume that this is due to the high level of abstraction of the terms which leads to difficulties in their visual representation. The results also indicate that the participants prefer real objects for representing security concepts (e.g., a house for *Privacy*).

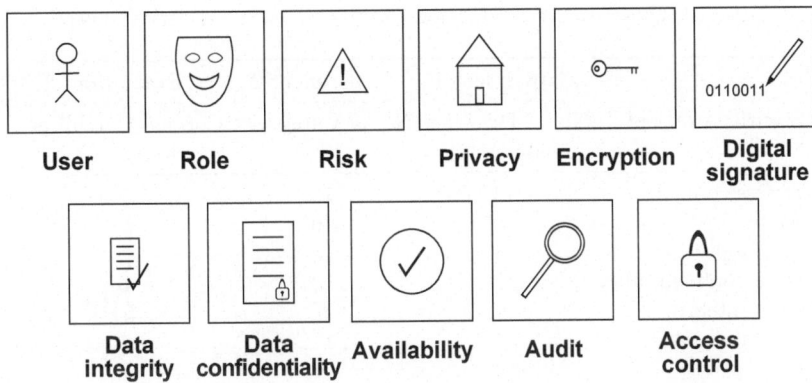

Fig. 2. Stereotype Drawings for Security Concepts

6   Evaluation

This evaluation is concerned with validating the results retrieved form Experiments 1 and 2 via expert interviews and also to initially assess the use of the security symbols for business process models.

6.1   Participants and Procedure

For evaluation, a series of semi-structured interviews were conducted. A paper-based questionnaire served as the basis for these interviews. Moreover, one of the authors observed each expert while filling out the questionnaire. In addition to the questionnaire, a sheet with a list of security concepts and definitions (see Table 1) was provided to the expert. In total, we interviewed 6 experts from the security (2), process modeling (3) and visualization (1) domain. All experts have a high or intermediate expertise in both areas, process modeling and security.

The questionnaire consisted of three different parts. In the first part of the interview, goals and purpose of the interview were presented. Then, demographic data of the experts were collected such as general level of knowledge of process modeling and security. The second part of the interview was concerned with investigating the stereotype symbols (see Figure 2). First, the experts matched the 11 security (stereotype) symbols with corresponding 11 security concepts using thinking aloud techniques (see [30]). With this setting, we expect to gain insight into how the symbols are matched by experts. After the matching, the interviewer pointed out his/her matching. Subsequently, the experts were specifically questioned for the one-to-one correspondence between the symbols and their security concepts to evaluate the semiotic clarity of the symbols (see [17]). Furthermore, the experts were asked to rate the resemblance of the symbols with the concepts they represent. Additionally, we asked if the use of shapes (e.g., triangles or circles), "document" shapes or hybrid symbols (a combination of graphics and text) can be helpful for the stereotype symbols. The third part addressed

Table 2. Quantitative Evaluation Results for each Security Concept

Security Concept	Experiment 1 No. of Drawings (out of 43)	Experiment 2 No. of Categories	Evaluation Correct Matchings (out of 6)
Access control	42	15	3
Audit	38	16	6
Availability	38	15	6
Data confidentiality	39	18	4
Data integrity	41	9	5
Digital signature	37	11	2
Encryption	42	5	5
Privacy	40	20	4
Risk	40	14	6
Role	38	15	4
User	43	5	6

the icons' suitability to be integrated into a business process modeling language. Therefore, we asked if the stereotype symbols are suitable to be integrated into business process models and more specifically into which business process modeling languages. For example, we analyzed to which BPMN elements the symbols could be related to and if color can be helpful to distinguish security symbols from standard BPMN elements.

6.2 Results

In the following, we will summarize the results according to each research question (see Section 3). Table 2 displays the quantitative results of the study: the number of collected drawings by concept in Experiment 1, the number of assigned categories per concept in Experiment 2 (see Section 5) and the number of correct matches of the one-to-one correspondence of the experts for evaluation (RQ2a).

RQ2a: How do experts evaluate the one-to-one correspondence between the symbols and security concepts? In general, all experts could relate most stereotype symbols to the list of security concepts (see Table 2). For example, all (6) experts could identify the stereotype symbols *Audit, Availability, Risk* and *User* (see Figure 2). However, *Digital signature* (2 of 6) and *Access control* (3) were the least recognized symbols.

In case of *Digital signature*, two experts related the pen symbol with the act of writing and signing. However, all other experts could not identify the symbol as pen and binary code. Two security experts could not relate the symbol to any concept or at least to the *Data confidentiality* symbol (see Figure 2). Furthermore, two experts related the padlock symbol for *Access control* to the key symbol for *Encryption* as referring to locking and unlocking something. One expert assigned the concept encryption to the padlock symbol. One could not interpret the symbol at all. In addition, two experts pointed out that the padlock symbol used for *Access control* is also part of the *Data confidentiality* symbol, which might lead to differentiation problems.

RQ2b: How do experts rate the resemblance between the symbols and concepts? All experts agreed on a good resemblance of the symbols *Encryption*, *Risk* and *User*. Four of the experts assessed a good resemblance of the symbols *Availability*, *Data confidentiality* and *Data integrity*. The expert opinions for *Access control*, *Audit*, *Digital signature* and *Role* varied and therefore no clear statement can be made. In the case of *Audit*, at first, experts often associated the magnifier to searching for something. After the interviewer referred to the definition of *Audit*, the expert could link the symbol to review and examine.

RQ2c: How can the stereotype symbols be improved? There were only few suggestions on how to improve the symbols. One important note, however, was the similarity of the *Access control* and *Data confidentiality* symbol (due to the use of the padlock symbol) and of the *Availability* and *Data integrity* symbol (due to the check mark). Also, the relation of the padlock and the key symbol were associated with something that is in a locked or unlocked state. Hence, these symbols need to be reexamined in future studies.

Shapes. The use of additional shapes such as triangles or circles around the symbols can be slightly or moderately helpful. Some experts pointed out that the complexity of most symbols should not be increased by additional shapes. However, the shapes in symbols *Risk* and *Availability* were well-perceived.

Document Shapes. In the first experiment, many participants draw symbols using a "document" shape (e.g., symbol *Data confidentiality* in Figure 2). The experts pointed out that these document shapes should be primarily used to display concepts in relation to data such as data integrity or confidentiality. Additionally, the size of the symbol integrated in the document shape should be large enough to recognize the symbol.

Hybrid Symbols. Most experts found that hybrid symbols combining graphics and text can be very and extremely helpful to display security concepts. However, it is important to use common abbreviations or the full name to display the security concepts.

RQ3a: Are the stereotype symbols suitable to be integrated into business process models? In general, the experts agreed that the symbols are suitable for the integration into business processes. However, they noted that some symbols should be reevaluated or redrawn to avoid symbol redundancy as stated in research question RQ2c. Furthermore, they stated that the use of legends could be helpful to novices.

RQ3b: Which business process modeling languages are suggested for security modeling by experts? The experts proposed mainly BPMN and UML. The choice for BPMN was motivated by the experts as it serves as de facto standard for business process modeling. In addition, UML is suggested because it offers integrated languages for specifying software systems from various perspectives, which includes the process and security perspectives.

RQ3c: In BPMN, which symbols should be related to which process elements? In the following, we will list the experts opinions (of at least 3 or more experts) on the linkage of security symbols and BPMN process elements (events, data objects, lanes, message events, tasks and text annotations).

Tasks can be associated to *Access control, Audit, Privacy, Risk, Role* and *User*. Hence, not only the authorization of end users to tasks is an important factor but also the supervision of these. Furthermore, events can be related to *Audit* and *Risk*. Data objects can be linked to *Availability, Data confidentiality, Data integrity, Digital signature* and *Encryption*. This is not surprising as these security concepts are closely related to data. Moreover, message events are associated to *Data confidentiality, Data integrity, Digital signature* and *Encryption*. As messages represent a piece of data this seems conclusive. Lanes can be linked to *Role*. As lanes can represent job functions or departments it seems feasible that lanes could be also linked to *User*. Lastly, *Audit* was the only symbol associated to text annotations.

These suggestions provide an initial basis to further develop a security extension for BPMN. However, not only the semantic (semiotic) modeling but also the syntactic modeling is important and will be investigated in future work.

RQ3d: Can color be useful to distinguish security symbols from BPMN standard elements? Most experts state that color can be helpful to highlight the security symbols in BPMN. However, the use of color should be moderately handled such as using only one color or coloring the background of the symbol.

In conclusion, our evaluation showed that most symbols could be recognized by the experts. Some symbols such as *Data confidentiality* and *Access control* should be reexamined to dissolve remaining issues (see RQ2b and RQ2c). Furthermore, the integration of security symbols into business processes was in general well-perceived.

7   Discussion

Threats of Validity. In the first experiment, we analyzed the drawings of 43 students. One can argue that this number is not enough to discover stereotype symbols for security concepts. As depicted in Section 5, we evaluated the frequency, uniqueness and iconic character between the drawings to develop the stereotype symbols. Most symbols could be easily identified except for *Access control* and *Data confidentiality*. Our evaluation showed that even though we received a wide range of drawings, the experts rated the resemblance of symbols and their concepts in general positively.

Moreover, the 11 security concepts differ in their level of abstraction. For example, *Privacy* and *Availability* are highly abstract concepts, while *Digital signature* and *Encryption* are more low-level concepts (e.g., applications). In future studies, we need to investigate the need to translate the abstract concepts into further low-level (e.g., implementation relevant) concepts and their use in a business process context.

For evaluation, we interviewed six experts from the security and/or process modeling domain. The purpose of these interviews was to gain qualitative insights on the security symbols and to analyze the one-to-one correspondence matching of the symbols and concepts. Based on these interviews, we will further develop and evaluate the security symbols and continue our research centering on end user preferences.

Integration Scenarios for BPMN and UML. The BPMN [4] metamodel provides a set of extension elements that assign additional attributes and elements to BPMN elements. In particular, the `Extension` element binds an `ExtensionDefinition` and its `ExtensionAttributeDefinition` to a BPMN model definition. This elements could be used to define, e.g., an encryption level or that a digital signature is required. Furthermore, new markers or indicators can be integrated into BPMN elements to depict a new subtype or to emphasize a specific attribute of an element. For example, additional task types could be established by adding indicators similar to the e.g., service task in the BPMN specification (see [4]). The BPMN standard already specifies user tasks; i.e. tasks executed by humans. However, this does not specify how the user is authenticated (*Access control*) nor how the task showed up in his worklist (resolved via *Role* or *User*). We will investigate further if the assignment of *Role* or *User* to tasks is really needed as lanes provide similar functionality in BPMN. For the BPMN symbols for data and message events, we would need to adapt these symbols and determine how to relate security concepts to them.

In case of UML, an integration of the security concepts is possible either by extending the UML metamodel or by defining UML stereotypes (see [5]). In particular, UML2 Activity models offer a process modeling language that allows to model the control and object flows between different actions. The main element of an Activity diagram is an `Activity`. Its behavior is defined by a decomposition into different `Actions`. A UML2 Activity thus models a process while the Actions that are included in the Activity can be used to model tasks.

Several security extensions to the UML already exist, for example SecureUML [24]. However, this extension does not have any particular connection to process diagrams. In addition, several approaches exist to integrate various security aspects, such as role-based access control concepts [31,32,33] or data integrity and data confidentiality [25] into UML Activity diagrams. However, in contrast to the approach presented in this paper, all other security visualizations only represent presentation options. They are suggested by the authors and not evaluated with respect to the cognitive effectiveness of the new symbols. Based on the integration options for BPMN, we derive the following suggestions for integrating the security symbol set into UML. *Access control, Privacy, Risk, Role* and *User* may be linked to a UML Action. *Availablity, Data confidentiality, Data integrity, Digital signature* and *Encryption* can be assigned to UML ObjectNodes. *Audit* may be linked to EventActions or be integrated as a UML Comment.

Future Research. Several opportunities for future research emerge from our paper. As this initial study aimed at a preliminary design and modeling of security concepts, further research is necessary to fully develop security modeling extensions for business processes that can be interpreted by novices and experts, that are based on user preferences and are easy to learn (see Section 2). For example, we plan to use the stereotype drawings as basis to develop icons that can be integrated in process modeling languages. Therefore, we will investigate the icons in business processes, i.e. evaluate icons in a specific context. Furthermore, an extensive survey could assess the end user preferences of security symbols and the interpretation of these symbols (in and out of business process context). This could lead to a general approach to model security in business processes which might be adaptable to various business process modeling languages.

8   Conclusion

This paper presented our preliminary results of an experimental study on the design and modeling of security concepts in business processes. In our first study, we asked students to draw sketches of security concepts. Based on these drawings, we produced stereotype symbols considering the main idea the drawings represented, the frequency of occurrence and the uniqueness and dissimilarity between drawings. For evaluation, we interviewed experts from the area of process modeling and/or security. This evaluation showed that most symbols could be recognized based on the idea they represented. We received an even stronger acceptance for the one-to-one correspondence during the interviews when using a list of symbols and its concepts. In future studies, we aim to further analyze how our symbol set affects the cognitive complexity of corresponding models. In addition, we will evaluate different symbol integration options into process modeling languages.

Acknowledgements. The authors would like to thank the participants of the survey and the experts for their support and contributions.

References

1. Zairi, M.: Business Process Management: A Boundaryless Approach to Modern Competitiveness. Business Process Management Journal 3(1), 64–80 (1997)
2. zur Muehlen, M., Indulska, M.: Modeling Languages for Business Processes and Business Rules: A Representational Analysis. Information Systems 35(4) (2010)

3. Weske, M.: Business Process Management: Concepts, Languages, Architectures. Springer (2007)
4. OMG: Business process model and notation (BPMN) version 2.0. OMG Document formal/2011-01-03, Object Management Group (January 2011)
5. OMG: Unified Modeling Language (OMG UML): Superstructure version 2.4.1. OMG Document formal/2011-08-06, Object Management Group (August 2011)
6. Mendling, J.: Metrics for Process Models: Empirical Foundations of Verification, Error Prediction and Guidelines for Correctness. LNBIP, vol. 6. Springer, Heidelberg (2008)
7. Scheer, A.W.: ARIS - Business Process Modeling, 3rd edn. Springer (2000)
8. Johnson, M.E., Goetz, E.: Embedding Information Security into the Organization. IEEE Security & Privacy 5(3) (2007)
9. Strembeck, M.: Scenario-Driven Role Engineering. IEEE Security & Privacy 8(1) (2010)
10. Leitner, M.: Security policies in adaptive process-aware information systems: Existing approaches and challenges. In: 2011 Sixth International Conference on Availability, Reliability and Security (ARES), pp. 686–691. IEEE (August 2011)
11. Leitner, M., Mangler, J., Rinderle-Ma, S.: SPRINT-Responsibilities: design and development of security policies in process-aware information systems. Journal of Wireless Mobile Networks, Ubiquitous Computing, and Dependable Applications (JoWUA) 2(4), 4–26 (2011)
12. Wolter, C., Menzel, M., Meinel, C.: Modelling security goals in business processes. In: Modellierung, Berlin, Germany. LNI, vol. 127, pp. 197–212. GI (2008)
13. Leitner, M., Miller, M., Rinderle-Ma, S.: An analysis and evaluation of security aspects in the business process model and notation (2013) (in press)
14. Russell, N., van der Aalst, W.M.P., ter Hofstede, A.H.M., Edmond, D.: Workflow Resource Patterns: Identification, Representation and Tool Support. In: Pastor, Ó., Falcão e Cunha, J. (eds.) CAiSE 2005. LNCS, vol. 3520, pp. 216–232. Springer, Heidelberg (2005)
15. Mendling, J., Recker, J., Reijers, H.A.: On the usage of labels and icons in business process modeling. International Journal of Information System Modeling and Design 1(2), 40–58 (2010)
16. Genon, N., Caire, P., Toussaint, H., Heymans, P., Moody, D.: Towards a more semantically transparent i^* visual syntax. In: Regnell, B., Damian, D. (eds.) REFSQ 2011. LNCS, vol. 7195, pp. 140–146. Springer, Heidelberg (2012)
17. Moody, D.: The physics of notations: Toward a scientific basis for constructing visual notations in software engineering. IEEE Transactions on Software Engineering 35(6), 756–779 (2009)
18. Moody, D.L.: Theoretical and practical issues in evaluating the quality of conceptual models: current state and future directions. Data & Knowledge Engineering 55(3), 243–276 (2005)
19. Blackwell, A.F., et al.: Cognitive dimensions of notations: Design tools for cognitive technology. In: Beynon, M., Nehaniv, C.L., Dautenhahn, K. (eds.) CT 2001. LNCS (LNAI), vol. 2117, pp. 325–341. Springer, Heidelberg (2001)
20. Green, T., Blandford, A., Church, L., Roast, C., Clarke, S.: Cognitive dimensions: Achievements, new directions, and open questions. Journal of Visual Languages & Computing 17(4), 328–365 (2006)
21. Krogstie, J., Sindre, G., Jørgensen, H.: Process models representing knowledge for action: a revised quality framework. European Journal of Information Systems 15(1), 91–102 (2006)

22. Genon, N., Heymans, P., Amyot, D.: Analysing the cognitive effectiveness of the BPMN 2.0 visual notation. In: Malloy, B., Staab, S., van den Brand, M. (eds.) SLE 2010. LNCS, vol. 6563, pp. 377–396. Springer, Heidelberg (2011)
23. Figl, K., Mendling, J., Strembeck, M., Recker, J.: On the cognitive effectiveness of routing symbols in process modeling languages. In: Abramowicz, W., Tolksdorf, R. (eds.) BIS 2010. LNBIP, vol. 47, pp. 230–241. Springer, Heidelberg (2010)
24. Lodderstedt, T., Basin, D., Doser, J.: SecureUML: A UML-based modeling language for model-driven security. In: Jézéquel, J.-M., Hussmann, H., Cook, S. (eds.) UML 2002. LNCS, vol. 2460, pp. 426–441. Springer, Heidelberg (2002)
25. Hoisl, B., Strembeck, M.: Modeling support for confidentiality and integrity of object flows in activity models. In: Abramowicz, W. (ed.) BIS 2011. LNBIP, vol. 87, pp. 278–289. Springer, Heidelberg (2011)
26. Sindre, G.: Mal-Activity Diagrams for Capturing Attacks on Business Processes. In: Sawyer, P., Heymans, P. (eds.) REFSQ 2007. LNCS, vol. 4542, pp. 355–366. Springer, Heidelberg (2007)
27. Shirey, R.: Internet Security Glossary. Request for Comments, vol. 2828. IETF (May 2000)
28. Information technology Industry Council: Information technology - role based access control. Technical Report ANSI INCITS 359-2004, American National Standards Institute, Inc (2004)
29. Petre, M.: Why looking isn't always seeing: Readership skills and graphical programming. Communications of the ACM 38(6) (1995)
30. Boren, T., Ramey, J.: Thinking aloud: reconciling theory and practice. IEEE Transactions on Professional Communication 43(3), 261–278 (2000)
31. Strembeck, M., Mendling, J.: Modeling Process-related RBAC Models with Extended UML Activity Models. Information and Software Technology 53(5) (2011)
32. Schefer-Wenzl, S., Strembeck, M.: A UML Extension for Modeling Break-Glass Policies. In: Rinderle-Ma, S., Weske, M. (eds.) EMISA 2012. LNI, vol. 206, pp. 25–38. GI (2012)
33. Schefer, S., Strembeck, M.: Modeling Support for Delegating Roles, Tasks, and Duties in a Process-Related RBAC Context. In: Salinesi, C., Pastor, O. (eds.) CAiSE Workshops 2011. LNBIP, vol. 83, pp. 660–667. Springer, Heidelberg (2011)

"Product-Process-Machine" System Modeling: Approach and Industrial Case Studies

Alexander Smirnov[1], Kurt Sandkuhl[2,3], Nikolay Shilov[1], and Alexey Kashevnik[1]

[1] St. Petersburg Institute for Informatics and Automation of the Russian Academy of Sciences,
39, 14th Line, St. Petersburg, 199178, Russia
{smir,alexey,nick}@iias.spb.su
[2] Institute of Computer Science, Rostock University,
Albert-Einstein-Str. 22, 18059 Rostock, Germany
kurt.sandkuhl@uni-rostock.de
[3] School of Engineering, Jönköping University,
P.O. Box 1026, 55111 Jönköping, Sweden

Abstract. Global trends in the worldwide economy lead to new challenges for manufacturing enterprises and to new requirements regarding modeling industrial organizations, like integration of real-time information from operations and information about neighboring enterprises in the value network. Consequently, there is a need to design new, knowledge-based workflows and supporting software systems to increase efficiency of designing and maintaining new product ranges, production planning and manufacturing. The paper presents an approach to a specific aspect of enterprise modeling, product-process-machine modeling, derived from two real life case studies. It assumes ontology-based integration of various information sources and software systems and distinguishes four levels. The upper two levels (levels of product manager and product engineer) concentrate on customer requirements and product modeling. The lower two levels (levels of production engineer and production manager) focus on production process and production equipment modeling.

Keywords: Product-process-machine modeling, enterprise engineering, knowledge model, product model, production model.

1 Introduction

Enterprise modeling has a long tradition in the area of industrial organization and production logistics, which is manifested in the field of enterprise engineering with its many techniques and developments (see, e.g. [1, 2]). Similar to business modeling or process modeling, the subjects of enterprise models in industrial organization are processes, organization structures, information flows and resources, but for manufacturing and logistics tasks, not for business processes. Global trends in the worldwide economy, like agile manufacturing, value networks or changeable production systems, lead to new challenges for manufacturing enterprises and to new requirements regarding modeling industrial organizations. Traditional enterprise

J. Grabis et al. (Eds.): PoEM 2013, LNBIP 165, pp. 251–265, 2013.

models need to be enhanced with product knowledge, real-time information from operations, and information about neighboring enterprises in the value network. Consequently, there is a need to design new, knowledge-based workflows and supporting software systems to increase efficiency of designing and maintaining new product ranges, production planning and manufacturing.

However, implementation of such changes in large companies faces many difficulties because business process cannot simply be stopped to switch between old and new workflows, old and new software systems have to be supported at the same time, the range of products, which are already in the markets, has to be maintained in parallel with new products, etc. Another problem is that it is difficult to estimate in advance which solutions and workflows would be efficient and convenient for the decision makers and employees. Hence, just following existing implementation guidelines is not advisable (confirmed, e.g., by Bokinge and Malmqvist in [3] for PLM), and the adaptation process to changes has to be and iterative and interactive.

Within enterprise modeling for industrial organizations, this paper focuses on modeling an essential aspect of production systems, the product – process – machine (PPM) system. While a production system includes all elements required to design, produce, distribute, and maintain a physical product, the PPM system only includes design and production of a product, i.e. a PPM system can be considered a subsystem of a production system. The paper presents an approach to "Product-Process-Machine" system modeling, which focuses on integrating product, production and machine knowledge for iterative and interactive product lifecycle management (PLM). The main contributions of this paper are (a) from a conceptual perspective we propose to integrate information at the intersection of product, process and machine models essential for planning changes and assessing their effects, (b) from a technical perspective we propose to use a knowledge structure suitable for extension with domain specific components and (c) from an application perspective we show two industrial cases indicating flexibility and pertinence of the approach.

Based on related work in the field (section 2) and experiences from two industrial cases, the paper introduces the overall PPM system modeling approach (section 3) and shows its use for different roles in PLM (section 4). Section 5 discusses experiences and lessons learned, and summarizes the work.

2   Modeling PPM Systems

Due to the trends and challenges identified in section 1 enterprises need to be quick responsive to changes in their environment, which basically means the ability to identify (a) the potential options how to react to changes and (b) the effects of acting in a certain way, without endangering current operations of customer relations. As a basis for this "agility" an integrated view on knowledge from the product, process and machine perspective and mechanisms tailored to the needs of decision makers in the enterprise are recommendable. In this context, an integrated view to knowledge should encompass:

- Dependencies and relationships within the PPM perspectives:
    - o Product perspective: products consist of components, fulfill customer requirements, are built according to design principles, use certain materials and apply specific design principles and rules.
    - o Process perspective: processes are cross-connected between each other by information, material and control flows
    - o Machine perspectives: machines consist of sub-systems offering capabilities depending on other sub-systems and production logistics components.

    The above are only some examples of information relevant for decision makers in manufacturing enterprises when evaluating options and their effects.
- Dependencies and relationships between the perspectives: products are developed and manufactured in processes; processes are performed using resources, like machines; machines are operated by roles, which in turn are responsible for certain processes and products or product parts. These examples show that there are many relationships between different perspectives that have to be understood when developing and assessing options for reacting on environmental changes.

This integrated view primarily requires information quantifying and qualifying the dependencies between the different perspectives, i.e. not all available information within the different perspective has to be included. Details of product design, operations of productions as provided by CAD or CAX systems usually are not required. Most existing approaches in engineering for manufacturability, PLM and production line engineering strive for an information integration and functional integration covering all life cycle phases. Our focus is on integrating essential information for key roles in a change process (see section 3).

Important roles in an enterprise when it comes to evaluating options and effects are the product manager and the production engineer. They would be among the primary user groups of a PPM system model and knowledge base. The product manager is responsible for the short-term and mid-term development of a product in terms of translating customer requirements to product features (target setting), guidance and supervision of the design process from customer features to the way of implementing them as functions, control of variability indicated by new and existing product functions, interface to sales and marketing, etc. If changes in the environment occur, the product manager has to investigate options on product level how to act or react. In cooperation with the product manager, the production engineer is responsible for making the product "manufacturable", i.e. adjust product design, material or features to what the machines in the production system can manufacture. Furthermore, the production engineer designs the overall production system by developing an appropriate composition of sub-systems and the flow of resources, materials and products.

Modeling in manufacturing and control has a long tradition, which does not only include the above mentioned perspectives, but also business aspects of manufacturing and the design, construction and operations part. This is manifested in reference models and frameworks, such as GERAM [4] and CIMOSA [5], and in a variety of standards for modeling the different perspectives (e.g. STEP [6] and CMII [7]). Furthermore, large European research projects and networks, like ATHENA [8], developed approaches for integrating enterprise system modeling and production system modeling into a joint framework. PLM systems address the complete lifecycle of products including production systems aspects and both, logistics in the supply chain and in production.

Integrated modeling of PPM systems has been investigated before. Many approaches exist which integrate two of the above mentioned perspectives. Examples are [9] that combine product and machine perspective, [10] where Buchmann and Karagiannis partly integrate process and product, and [11] with an approach for integrating product and machine perspective. Sandkuhl and Billig [12] propose the use of an enterprise ontology for product, process, resource and role modeling. However, this approach is limited to the application area of product families in automotive industries. Lillehagen and Krogstie [13] use active knowledge models for capturing dependencies between different knowledge perspectives. They use active knowledge models, which fulfill most of the requirements regarding the knowledge to be included, but their representation as visual models is not appropriate for reasoning and knowledge creation.

3   Approach

The proposed approach to PPM-System modeling originates from experiences in two industrial case studies. These cases served as basis for developing the approach and were used for implementing it and each of the cases implemented a different part. The first case is from a project with a global automation equipment manufacturer with more than 300 000 customers in 176 countries. The detailed description of this project is presented in [14, 15]. The automation equipment manufacturer has a large number of products consisting of various components. The project aimed at product codification, i.e. structuring and coding the products and their components and defining rules for coding and configuration. This coding forms the basis for quickly adapting to new market requirements by facilitating easing configuration of new products and the production system.

The second case is from manufacturing industries and resulted in a tool called DESO (Design of Structured Objects). This tool supports part of our approach and is capable of describing production processes and production facilities [16, 17]. It distinguishes two planning levels: the central planning area and the decentralized planning area of distributed plants. Every production program project or planning activity is initiated by a request asking for manufacturing of a product in a predefined volume and timeframe. Starting from this information, the central planning staff has the task to design a production system capable of fulfilling the given requirements and consisting of different plants. The involved engineers prepare the requests for different plants using the production system design.

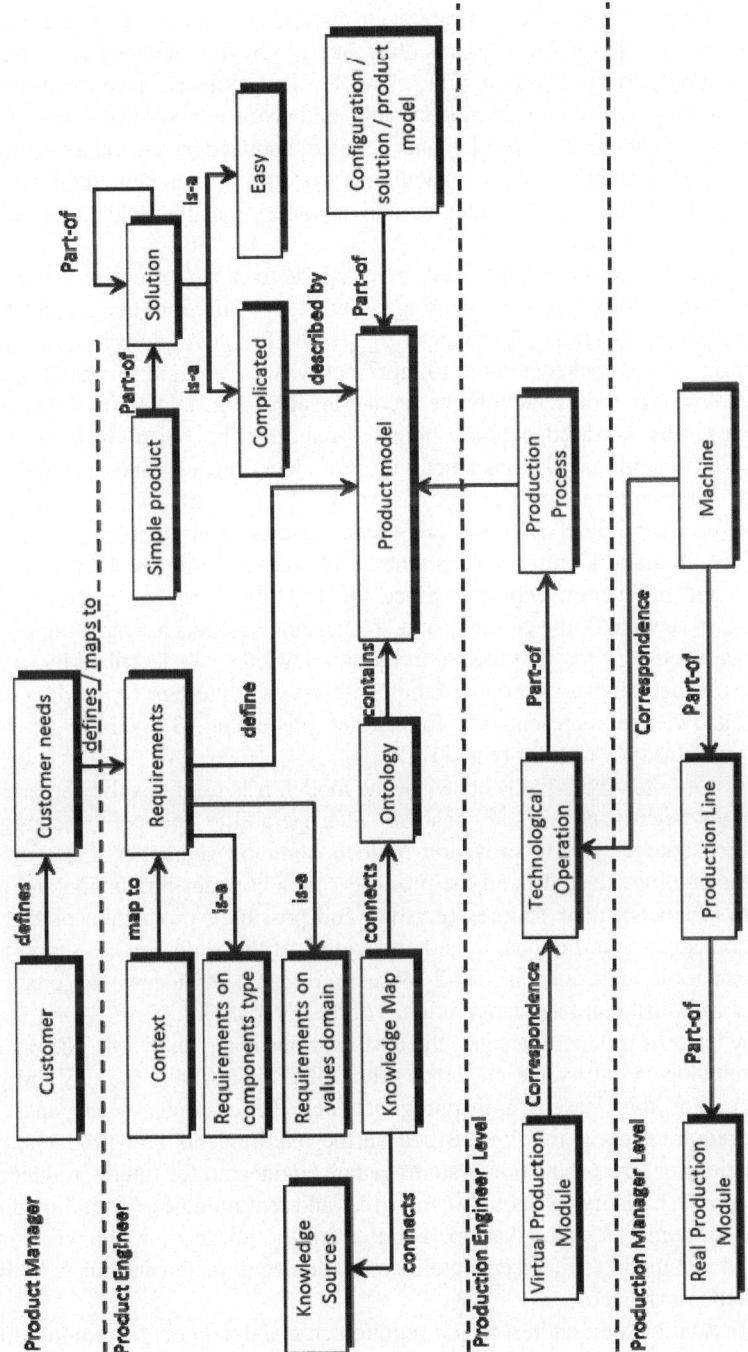

Fig. 1. Multi-level enterprise modelling concept

The engineers harmonize and aggregate parallel incoming requests for different planning periods. The different plants offer their production modules as a contribution to the entire network system. On plant level, engineers have to analyze the manufacturing potentials concerning capacity and process capability of their facilities. Only in the plants is the specific and detailed knowledge and data regarding the selection and adaptation of the machining systems to the new production tasks available. The expertise for developing and engineering of the production modules is available only in the plants.

In the context of these two cases, we propose from a conceptual perspective to distinguish two levels when representing knowledge required for central and decentral planning. The approach is illustrated in fig. 1. The first level describes the structural knowledge, i.e. the "schema" used to represent what is required for the two planning levels. Knowledge represented by the second level is an instantiation of the first level knowledge; this knowledge holds object instances. The object instances have to provide information at the intersection of product, process and machine models essential for planning changes and assessing their effects. What information is essential can be judged from different perspectives. Our approach is to put the demand of the main target groups presented in section 2 into the focus, i.e. product manager and production engineer. Since the PPM perspectives cannot be seen as isolated (see section 2), the common and "interfacing" aspects are most important.

The knowledge of the first level (structural knowledge) is described by a common ontology of the company's product families (classes). Ontologies provide a common way of knowledge representation for further processing. They have shown their usability for this type of tasks (e.g., [18-20]).

The major ontology is in the center of the model. It is used to solve the problem of knowledge heterogeneity and enables interoperability between heterogeneous information sources due to provision of their common semantics and terminology [21]. This ontology describes all the products (already under production and planned or future products), their features (existing and possible), production processes and production equipment. Population and application of this ontology are supported by a number of tools, described in detail in section 4. A knowledge map connects the ontology with different knowledge sources of the company.

At the level of product manager, the customer needs are analyzed. The parameters and terminology used by the customer often differ from those used by the product engineers. For this reason, a mapping between the customer needs and internal product requirements is required. Based on the requirements new products, product modifications or new production systems can be engineered for future production.

The approach distinguishes between virtual and real modules. Virtual modules are used for grouping technological operations from the production engineer's point of view. The real modules represent actual production equipment (machines) at the level of production manager.

The first case study addressed the requirements and support for product manager and product engineers. Production engineers and production managers are supported by the tool developed in the second case study.

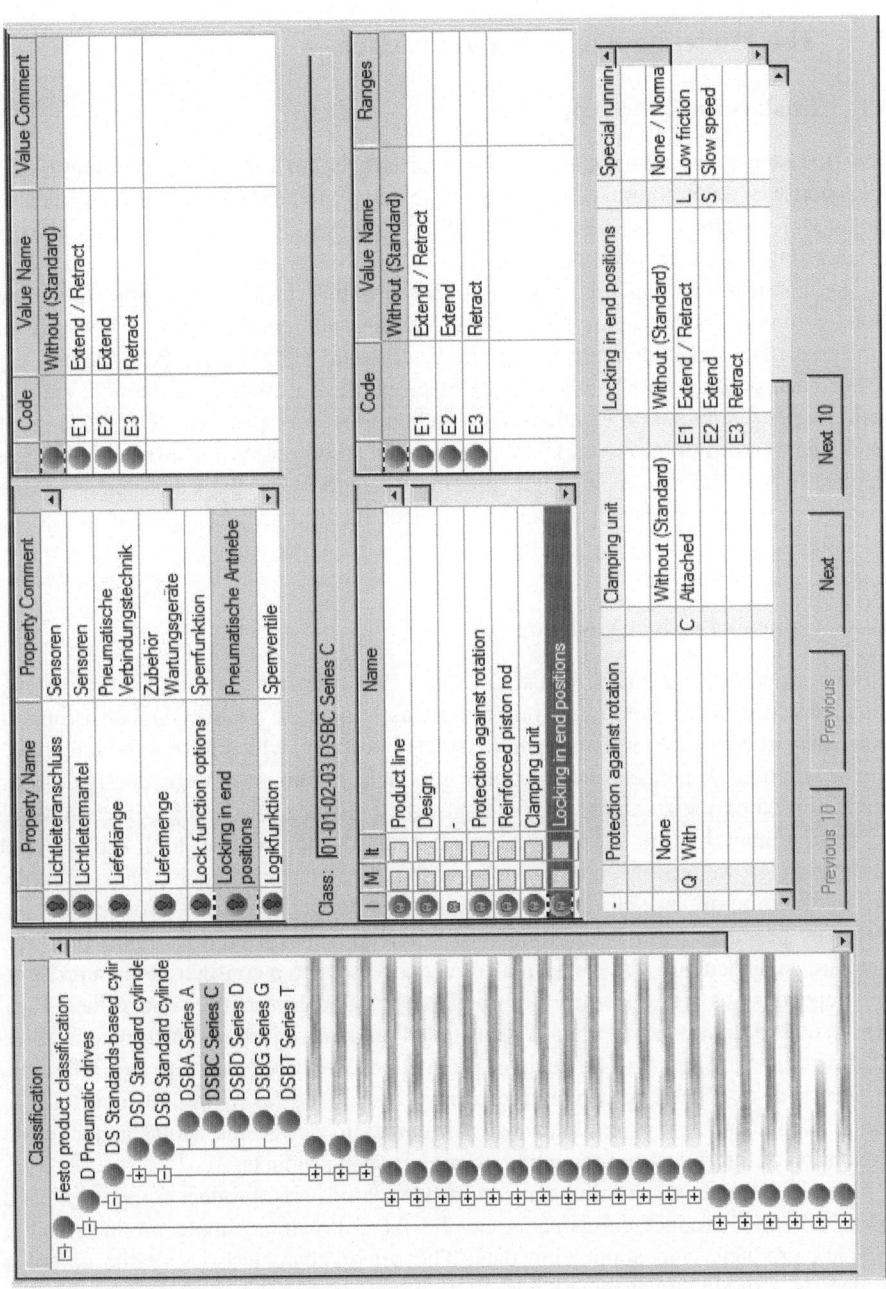

Fig. 2. Main window of the product hierarchy description tool [14]

4   The Modeling Approach in Practice

4.1   Product Engineer Support

The first step to implementation of the approach is creation of the ontology. This operation was done automatically based on existing documents and defined rules of the model building. The resulting ontology consists of more than 1000 classes organized into a 4 level taxonomy (fig. 2).

Taxonomical relationships support inheritance that makes it possible to define more common attributes for higher level classes and inherit them to lower level subclasses. The same taxonomy is used in the company's PDM and ERP systems.

For each product family (class) a set of properties (attributes) is defined, and for each property the possible values and their codes are specified. The lexicon of properties is valid ontology-wide, i.e. the values can be reused for different families. Application of the common single ontology provides for the consistency of the product codes and makes it possible to reflect incorporated changes in the codes instantly.

4.2   Complex Product Modeling

An experience from the first industrial case is that customers nowadays wish to buy complete customized solutions (referred to as "complex products") consisting of numerous products, rather than separate isolated products which have to be integrated into a solution. Whereas such complex products in the past were configured by experts based on the customer requirements, they nowadays to a large extent have to be configurable by the customers, which requires appropriate tool support and automation. However, inter-product relationships are very challenging. For example, the most common use case is the relationship between a main product and an accessory product. While both products are derived from different complex products there are dependencies which assign a correct accessory to a configured main product. The dependencies are related to the products' individual properties and values. E.g., "1x3/2 or 2x3/2-way valve" cannot be installed on a valve terminal if its size is "Size 10, deviating flow rate 1". The depth of product-accessory relationships is not limited, so accessory-of-accessory combinations have also to be taken into account. These relationships can be very complex when it comes to define the actual location and orientation of interfaces and mounting points between products.

Complex product description consists of two major parts: product components and rules. Complex product components can be the following: simple products, other complex products, and application data. The set of characteristics of the complex product is a union of characteristics of its components. The rules of the complex products are union of the rules of its components plus extra rules. Application data is an auxiliary component, which is used for introduction of some additional characteristics and requirements to the product (for example, operating temperatures, certification, electrical connection, etc.). They affect availability and compatibility of certain components and features via defined rules.

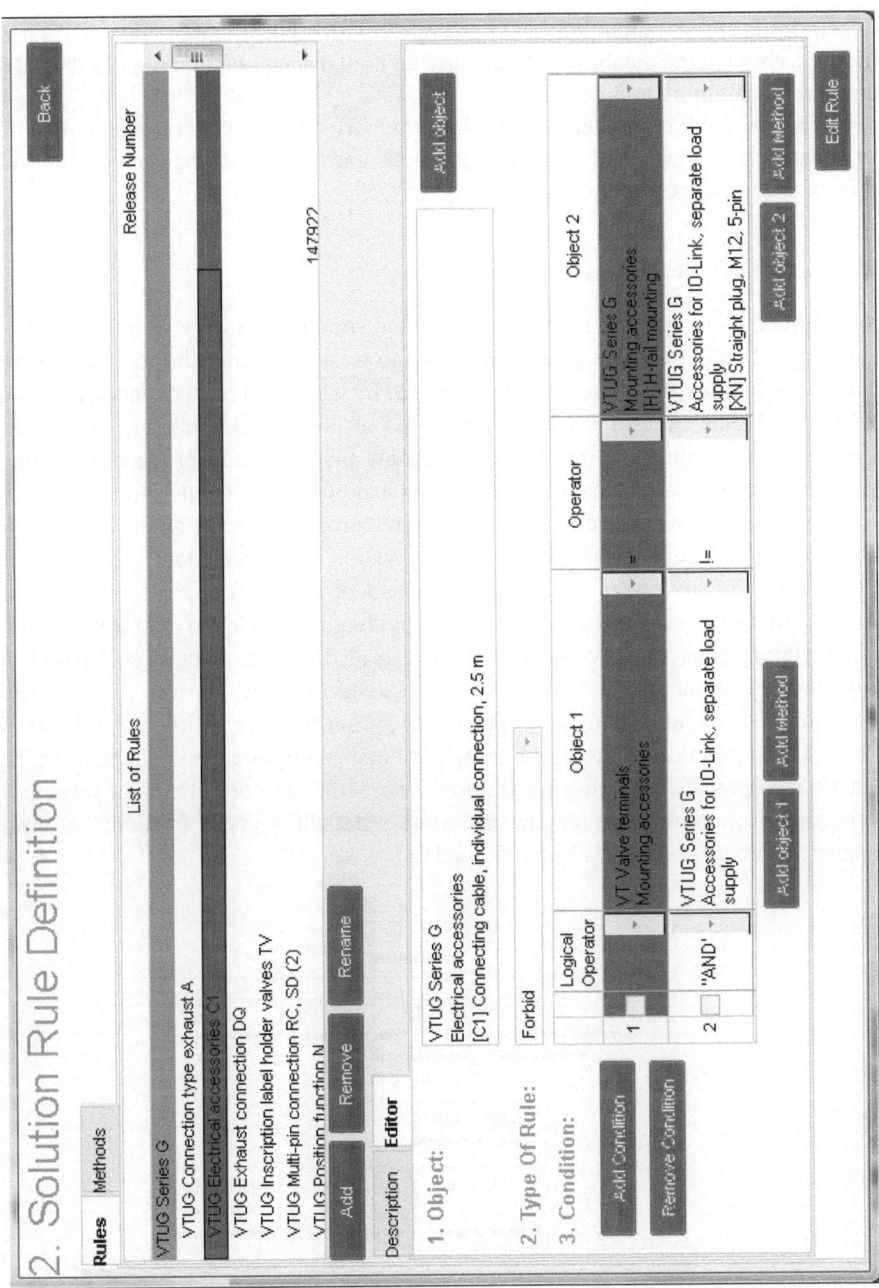

Fig. 3. Solution rules example [15]

Some example rules are shown in Fig. 3. The figure presents a valve terminal (VTUG) and compatibility of electrical accessories option C1 (individual connecting cable) with mounting accessories (compatible only with H-rail mounting) and accessories for input-output link (not compatible with 5 pin straight plug M12). These rules are stored in the database and can later be used during configuration of the valve terminal for certain requirements.

When the product model is finished it is offered to the customers, i.e. the customers could configure required products and solutions themselves or with assistance of product managers.

4.3   Production Facilities Modeling

The DESO system is a tool for management and structured storage of information in knowledge domain, and for processing this information. Depending on the domain under consideration, the system can be extended by additional components for solving specific problems using the information stored in the DESO database. Up to now, components for enterprise production program planning, for production module design, and for industrial resources distribution and planning were developed.

Initially, the DESO system was developed in a project focusing on the early stages of planning investments including (a) derivation of production scenarios, (b) determination of investment cost, (c) assignment of locations and (d) estimation of variable product cost. The system aims at providing a knowledge platform enabling manufacturing enterprises to achieve reduced lead time and reduced cost based on customer requirements through customer satisfaction by means of improved availability, communication and quality of product information. It follows a decentralized method for intelligent knowledge and solutions access. The configuring process incorporates the following features: order-free selection, limits of resources, optimization (minimization or maximization), default values, freedom to make changes in Global Production Network model.

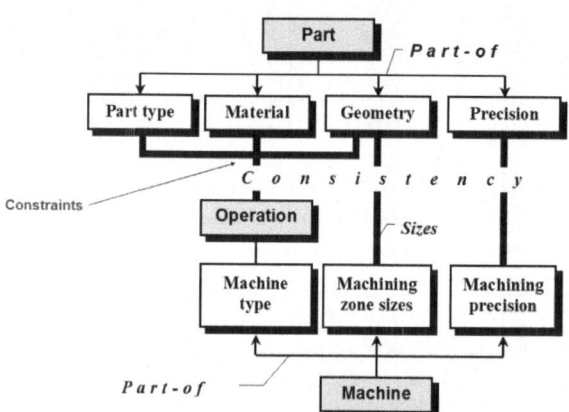

Fig. 4. Product-Process-Machine system modeling

The architecture of the system reflects the structure of "Product-Process-Machine" system. It includes three main IT-Modules or software tools (fig. 4).

The hierarchy editor (fig. 5) is a tool for creating, editing and managing hierarchical relations between objects. These relations may show structures of objects, sequence of operations for a part production, possible alternatives of accommodation etc. The hierarchy editor supports inheriting subordinate objects, what allows creating of complex hierarchical systems of objects by some stages, and using templates automating the user's work.

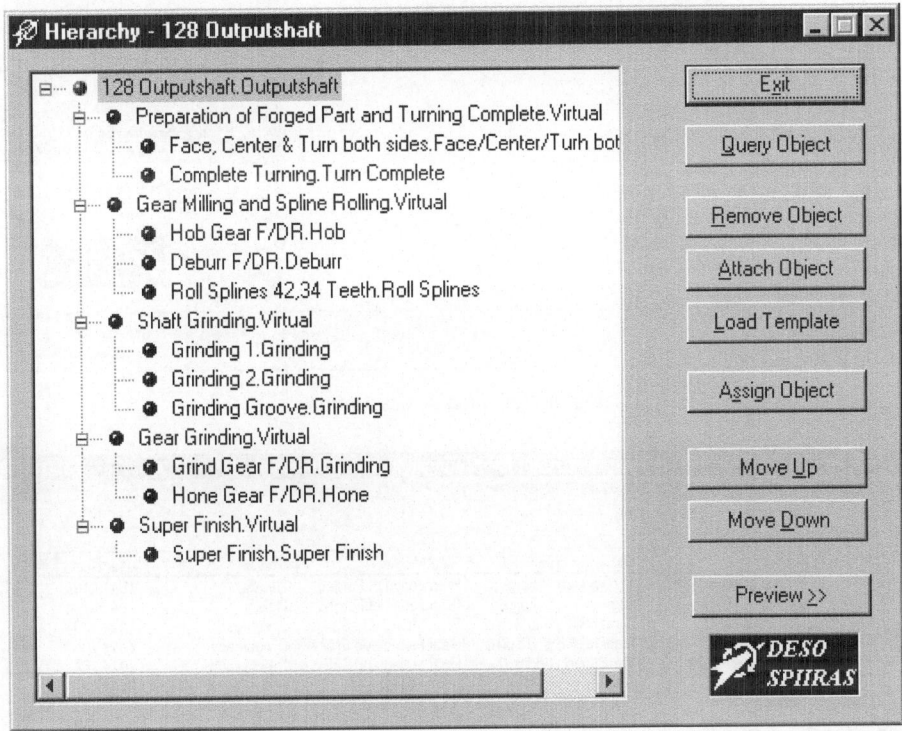

Fig. 5. Hierarchy editor of DESO [16]

DESO distinguishes between virtual and real modules. In accordance with the approach, the virtual modules are used for grouping technological operations from production engineer's point of view (fig. 5). The real modules stand for the real equipment used for the actual production (fig. 6). The production engineer sets correspondences between the technological operations of virtual modules and machines of real modules (fig. 7).

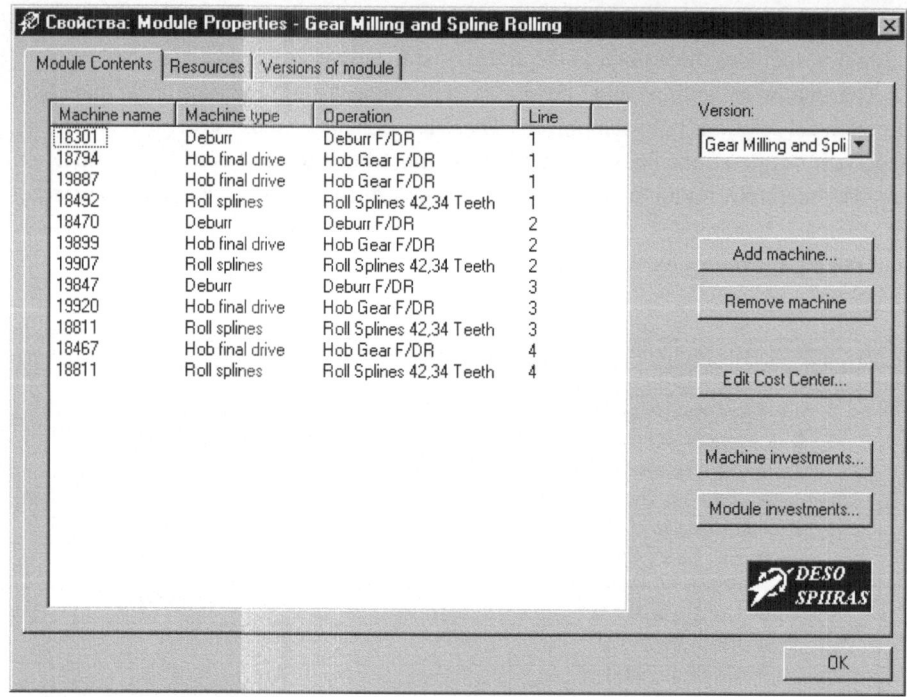

Fig. 6. Real module description

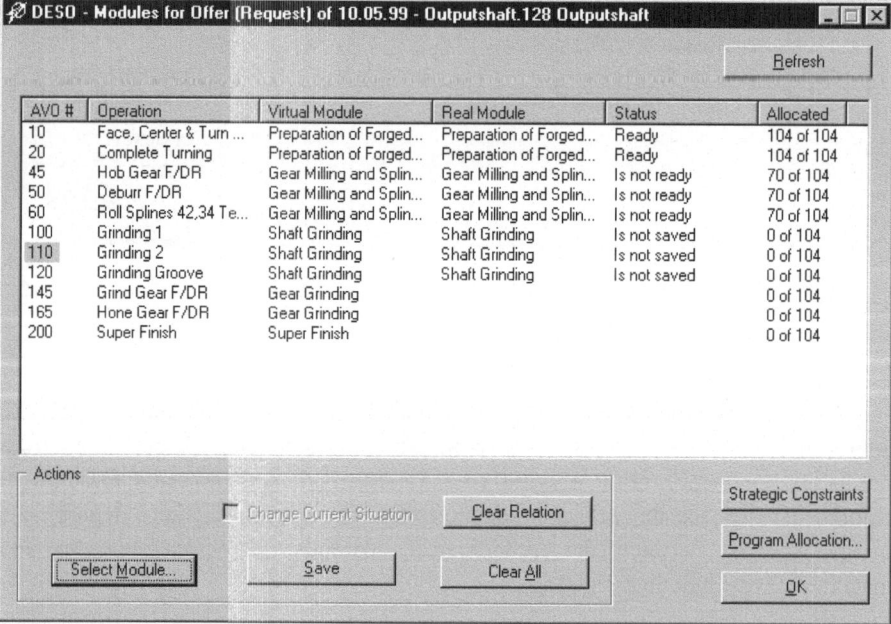

Fig. 7. Setting correspondences between operations of virtual modules and machines of real modules

5   Summary and Discussion

The paper presents an approach to product-process-machine modeling derived from two real life case studies. Compared to existing approaches in the field, which strive for the integration of all available information in the different PPM models, our focus is on integrating essential information for two key roles in an adaptation process to new market requirements, i.e. product manager and production engineer. The approach is based on the idea of integrating various information sources and software systems and distinguishes four levels. The upper two levels (levels of product manager and product engineer) concentrate on customer requirements and product modeling. The lower two levels (levels of production engineer and production manager) focus on production process and production equipment modeling.

As already mentioned, just following existing guidelines for implementing new workflows often is not possible for number of reasons. Engineers and managers do not have sufficient information to decide in advance which solution would be more convenient and efficient for them. As a result, the implementation of new workflows is more a "trial-and-error" process.

This was in a higher degree visible when working with product managers and product engineers in the first case study. In the second case study (aimed at the levels of production engineer and production manager) this issue was less obvious, because the "explorative" production planning could be done in parallel with the actual one. In this context, the modeling of the "product-process-machine" system proved to be an efficient solution.

The model built enabled automation of a number of processes previously done manually. The main advantages of the developed solution are [15]:

- Automatically creating master data in SAP models;
- Automatically creating data for the configuration models and services;
- Automatically generating an ordering sheet for the print documentation (this ordering sheet was generated earlier with much effort manually);
- Automatically generating a product and service list which is needed in the complete process implementing new products.

Based on the experiences from the two cases, our conclusion is that the aim of integrating information from the perspectives product, process and machine was achieved and that it supports identifying potential options in case of changes and the effects of these options. Examples are parallel incoming requests with respect to product features or their effects on re-scheduling and re-configuring the production facilities. Product managers and production engineers are supported in their tasks and responsibilities, both with respect to the central planning level and for the distributed plants.

Experience from the implementation of the mentioned projects shows that deep automation of the Product-Process-Machine system could be achieved if it is considered as one complex system. This requires consideration of all levels of the production system indicated in sec. 3. To facilitate implementation of such projects, first, the structural information has to be collected followed by identification of the relationships. This can be done only through long-term time-consuming communications with experts from the company. As a consequence, we consider using typical structural models or recurring "patterns" for such models as promising and beneficial for such processes.

The limitation of the approach is that it focuses only on the "integrating links" between the different perspectives, i.e. we do not attempt to integrate all existing information regarding construction, design, operation of administrative aspects of products and production systems. Future work will include conceptual extensions and gathering more experiences from practical cases. Conceptual extension will be directed to support more roles in the area of industrial organization by implementing additional features. An example is the extension towards integration of suppliers or partners in the value network.

Acknowledgements. This paper was developed in the context of the project COBIT sponsored by the Swedish Foundation for International Cooperation in Research and Higher Education. Some parts of the work have been sponsored by grants 12-07-00298 of the Russian Foundation for Basic Research, project # 213 of the research program #15 "Intelligent information technologies, mathematical modelling, system analysis and automation" of the Russian Academy of Sciences, and project 2.2 "Methodology development for building group information and recommendation systems" of the basic research program "Intelligent information technologies, system analysis and automation" of the Nanotechnology and Information technology Department of the Russian Academy of Sciences.

References

1. Martin, J.: The great transition: using the seven disciplines of enterprise engineering to align people, technology, and strategy, p. 455. Amacom, New York (1995)
2. Vernadat, F.B.: Enterprise modelling and integration, pp. 25–33. Springer US (2003)
3. Bokinge, M., Malmqvist, J.: PLM implementation guidelines – relevance and application in practice: a discussion of findings from a retrospective case study. International Journal of Product Lifecycle Management 6(1), 79–98 (2012)
4. Williams, T.J., Li, H.: PERA and GERAM - enterprise reference architectures in enterprise integration. In: Information Infrastructure Systems for Manufacturing II, pp. 3–30. Springer US (1999)
5. Kosanke, K., Vernadat, F., Zelm, M.: CIMOSA: enterprise engineering and integration. Computers in Industry 40(2), 83–97 (1999)
6. ISO 10303 Industrial automation systems and integration - Product data representation and exchange (2011), http://www.iso.org/
7. CMII Research Institute: CMII Standard for Product Configuration Management. Document CMII-105C (2010), http://www.cmiiresearch.com
8. Ruggaber, R.: ATHENA-Advanced Technologies for Interoperability of Heterogeneous Enterprise Networks and their Applications. In: Interoperability of Enterprise Software and Applications, pp. 459–460. Springer, London (2006)

9. Osorio, J., Romero, D.: A. Molina: A Modeling Approach towards an Extended Product Data Model for Sustainable Mass-Customized Products. In: PREPRINTS of the International IFAC Conference on Manufacturing Modelling, Management and Control (MIM 2013), Saint Petersburg, Russia, June 19-21, pp. 609–613 (2013)
10. Buchmann, R., Karagiannis, D.: Modelling Collaborative-Driven Supply Chains: The ComVantage Method. In: PREPRINTS of the International IFAC Conference on Manufacturing Modelling, Management and Control (MIM 2013), Saint Petersburg, Russia, June 19-21, pp. 597–602 (2013)
11. Mun, D., Do, N.: W. Choi: Information model of ship product structure supporting operation and maintenance after ship delivery. In: Proceedings of the PLM11 Conference, Eindhoven University of Technology, The Netherlands, July 11-13. IFIP Working Group 5.1 (2013)
12. Sandkuhl, K., Billig, A.: Ontology-based Artefact Management in Automotive Electronics. International Journal for Computer Integrated Manufacturing (IJCIM) 20(7), 627–638 (2007)
13. Lillehagen, F.M., Krogstie, J.: Active knowledge modeling of enterprises. Springer (2008)
14. Oroszi, A., Jung, T., Smirnov, A., Shilov, N., Kashevnik, A.: Ontology-Driven Codification for Discrete and Modular Products. International Journal of Product Development, Inderscience 8(2), 162–177 (2009)
15. Smirnov, A., et al.: Knowledge Management for Complex Product Development: Framework and Implementation. In: Proceedings of the IFIP WG 5.1 10th International Conference on Product Lifecycle Management (PLM 2013), Nantes, France, July 6-10 (2013)
16. Golm, F., Smirnov, A.: ProCon: Decision Support for Resource Management in a Global Production Network. In: The Proceedings of the 13th International Conference on Industrial and Engineering Applications of Artificial Intelligence and Expert Systems (IEA/AIE 2000). New Orleans, Louisiana, USA, Springer Verlag, pp. 345–350 (2000)
17. Golm, F., Smirnov, A.: Virtual Production Network Configuration: ACS-approach and tools. In: Advances in Networked Enterprises: The Proceedings of the 4th IEEE/IFIP International Conference on Information Technology for Balanced Automation Systems in Production and Transportation (BASYS 2000), Bosten/Dordrecht/ London, pp. 103–110. Kluwer Academic Publishers, Berlin (2000)
18. Bradfield, D.J., Gao, J.X., Soltan, H.: A Metaknowledge Approach to Facilitate Knowledge Sharing in the Global Product Development Process. Computer-Aided Design & Applications 4(1-4), 519–528 (2007)
19. Chan, E.C.K., Yu, K.M.: A framework of ontology-enabled product knowledge management. International Journal of Product Development, Inderscience Publishers 4(3/4), 241–254 (2007)
20. Patil, L., Dutta, D., Sriram, R.: Ontology-based exchange of product data semantics. IEEE Transactions on Automation Science and Engineering 2(3), 213–225 (2005) ISSN: 1545-5955
21. Uschold, M., Grüninger, M.: Ontologies: Principles, methods and applications. Knowledge Engineering Review 11(2), 93–155 (1996)

A Business and Solution Building Block Approach to EA Project Planning

Graham McLeod

Inspired, Cape Town, South Africa
University of Cape Town, South Africa
graham@inspired.org

Abstract. Many EA groups battle to establish an overall programme plan in a way that is integrated, achievable and understandable to the stakeholder and sponsor community as well as the downstream implementation groups, including: IT, Process Management, Human Resources and Product Management. This paper presents an approach that achieves these objectives in a simple way. The approach is currently being implemented in a fairly new enterprise architecture function within an aggressively expanding Telco with promising results. The problem is introduced and a solution including meta model and visual representations is discussed. Early findings are made to the effect that the technique is simple to apply as well as being effective in establishing shared understanding between the EA function, project sponsors, project stakeholders and IT personnel. The technique is explicated with an example that should make it easy for others to replicate in their own setting.

Keywords: Enterprise Architecture, Building Blocks, Project Scope, Planning, TOGAF, Inspired EA Frameworks.

1 Introduction to the Problem

The author and colleagues are engaged in a consulting capacity with a rapidly expanding Telco in South Africa. The organization has a newly established enterprise architecture (EA) function. EA is gaining good traction and driving several themes, including: building the EA capability and governance; implementing an ambitious five year growth strategy; providing architectural oversight to active projects and supporting a collection of projects focussed on improvements to the core value chain. A traditional value chain approach, ala Porter, has been employed [1]. A blend of the Inspired [2-3] and TOGAF [4] EA methods and frameworks is being used, with the emphasis on the former. This paper describes a situation and solution relative to the "enhancement of core value chain" projects. The solution will in time be more broadly applied in the strategic theme as well. We believe the approach has general applicability for EA teams in other organizations and settings.

The situation relative to the core value chain involved a number of projects which had already begun, prior to the architecture oversight. Two prominent ones were Quoting and Billing. The core value chain and their position in this can be seen in Figure 1.

J. Grabis et al. (Eds.): PoEM 2013, LNBIP 165, pp. 266–276, 2013.

The Quote and Bill value chain elements were being addressed by active projects at the time of this intervention. Note: The value chain model did not initially include the support capabilities, viz. Product Management and Data and Information Management. The latter was also an active (but early stage) project in the environment. Product Management was a capability supported by a business department. Both the Quote and Billing projects highlighted the need for more capable, flexible, integrated and consistent Product Management, leading to it being identified as a focus area and the creation of a new project to address the related requirements. The evolution of the models and approach is described in the following sections.

2   Problems Identified

Problems in stakeholder expectations, sponsor communication and development project alignment were highlighted by a steering body meeting which reviewed the Quotations project. It emerged that there was little consensus upon the scope of the project, the dependencies between various elements and the release plan. Stakeholders and the sponsor were unclear what would be delivered, in what tranches and when. The EA function was asked to audit the project and make recommendations.

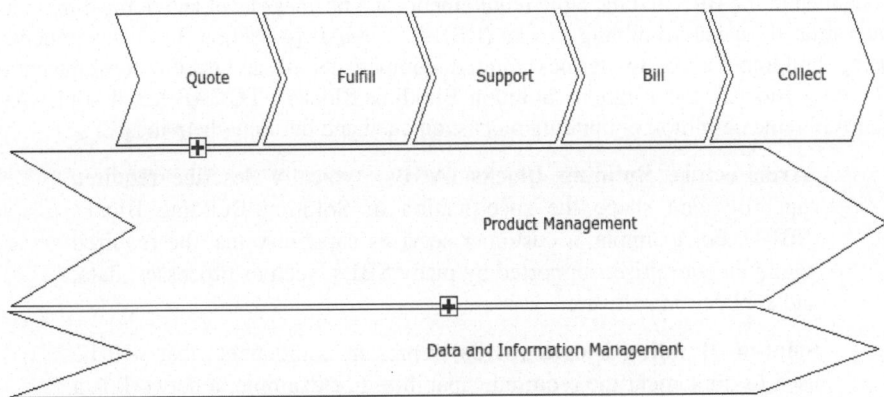

Fig. 1. Core value chain and support capabilities

The audit found that there was a traditional Business Requirements Specification (BRS) which had been done by a business analyst after extensive interviews with personnel in the line functions affected. The BRS effectively sketched an "end state" for the complete quoting automation, including embedded capabilities. The latter included product management, customer information, existing install base information and document generation capabilities. The scope of the BRS was thus large. It was not broken into any releases or delivery packages. The BRS had a tentative solution design, but this was not comprehensive. The major contribution of the BRS was the documentation of the business requirements at a logical level.

The development team in IT, meanwhile, was pursuing an agile project management approach [5-7], with a backlog of requirements managed in a tool. This detailed requirements at a more fine grained level and the team had identified some delivery tranches, which were variously dubbed versions and releases in discussions. The information was not in a form that could be easily packaged for consumption by the sponsor, stakeholders, EA or program management.

Programme management had visibility of the project via the previously mentioned steering body reviews. The discussions were ineffective as the terminology between releases and versions was not standardised, the agile requirements were not visible, and the allocation of capabilities between versions/releases was fluid. The problems could be summarised as follows: scope of requirements not clear; decomposition into releases not clear; definition of release and version terminology not standardised; lack of agreement between stakeholder expectations and project team plan; lack of visibility of capabilities to be delivered, dependencies and timing at program and project management levels; duplication of effort across projects; lack of traceability of requirements from traditional BRS to agile environment; confusion between requirements and solution elements; unclear link between value chain and supporting projects.

3   Towards a Solution

The audit was followed by a facilitated session where we teased out the capabilities contained in the BRS and the agile requirements at a business level and defined these as inter-related business building blocks (BBBs). TOGAF [4 section 37.2] recommends using building blocks to define required components of architecture (Architecture Building Blocks) and solution (Solution Building Blocks). TOGAF has a somewhat schizophrenic definition of building blocks: on one hand defining them thus:

> **"Architecture Building Blocks (ABBs)** typically describe required capability and shape the specification of Solution Building Blocks (SBBs). For example, a customer services capability may be required within an enterprise, supported by many SBBs, such as processes, data, and application software.
>
> **Solution Building Blocks (SBBs)** represent components that will be used to implement the required capability. For example, a network is a building block that can be described through complementary artifacts and then put to use to realize solutions for the enterprise. "

but also at another point [section 33.2] defining them as the elements in the content or meta model:

> "The content metamodel provides a definition of all the types of building blocks that may exist within an architecture, showing how these building blocks can be described and related to one another. For example, when creating an architecture, an architect will identify applications, ''data entities'' held within applications, and technologies that implement those applications. These applications will in turn support particular groups of business user or actor, and will be used to fulfil ''business services''."

This usage is more akin to the "atomic elements" of the Zachman framework [8]. Our usage will be more aligned with the capability based definition. We chose to refer to the higher level capability based building blocks which are independent of technology and implementation choices as Business Building Blocks (BBBs) while we use a similar approach to TOGAF for Solution Building Blocks (SBBs). The former relate to capabilities that the business requires. They can encapsulate services, functionality, data and user access requirements. The latter relate to components chosen to meet the needs of requirements identified in BBBs. They will typically represent commercial off the shelf systems (COTS), data sources or key technologies.

The workshop on BBBs resulted in a whiteboard / Powerpoint model shown as Figure 2. Boxes denote Business Building Blocks i.e. capability; green arrows denote dependencies; dashed arrows denote events; green bubbles are release numbers and yellow text blocks are building block idendities; Generic support capabilities were normalised from the initial diagram and are shown at the base as horizontal lines; User interface modes are shown across the top as horizontal lines. Looking at the figure, we can see that Release 1 would comprise: a web interface; Product Definition (for a limited product set); Price Calculation and an Audit Trail. Release 2 would add: Product Definition for additional products; Workflow and Event handling; Document composition.

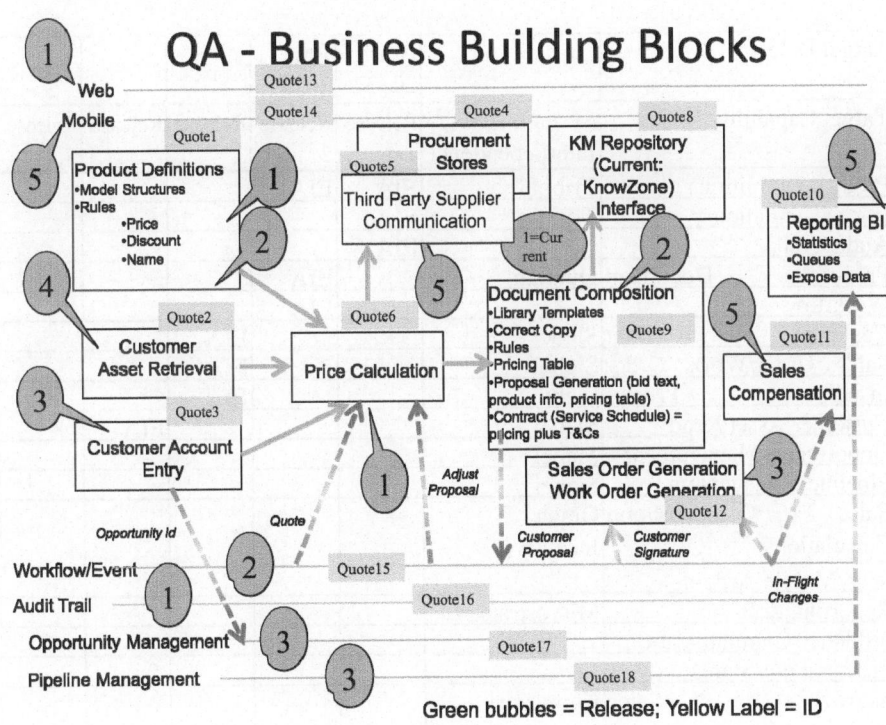

Fig. 2. Business Building Blocks for Quoting

We standardised terminology to describe a release as a package of capability that would be delivered to the business. Versions may be used by the maintenance team within IT to refer to adjustments of a release without major new functionality.

The initial iteration did not have the release annotations (green callout bubbles) or the block ids (yellow text). The initial diagram was validated with the business analyst, the IT project leader and participants from the Billing project who would deal with the results and data downstream. The programme manager, who was also a key player in defining the longer term strategy, participated in identifying dependencies and desirable business capabilities in terms of value. The block ids were subsequently added to provide concise and unambiguous reference as well as support traceability.

A later audit and similar building block definition for the Billing project surfaced common requirements in the Product Management capability. Quoting and Billing projects had been addressing this independently. Other projects in the organization were also finding this a dependency and trying to address shortfalls. Consequently, the EA function initiated a separate Product Management project. Defining the BBBs for Quoting also highlighted the need for a capable document composition solution. This was required in other areas of the business and a project was initiated to investigate this.

Table 1. Release matrix

Target Date =>		April 2013	June 2013			
Target Capability V	Systems Interdependenci	Release 1	Release 2	Release 3	Release 4	Release 5
Product Definitions	Tribold	EIA	EIA			
Price Calculation	Tribold	EIA				
Audit Trail		EIA				
Proposal Document	Qvidian		EIA			
Workflow			EIA			
Customer Account	Siebel			EIA		
Sales Order/Work Order	Siebel			EIA		
Installs Project	Siebel			EIA		
Customer Asset Read	Siebel				EIA	
Opportunity Management	Siebel					
Pipeline Management	Siebel					
Sales Compensation Calculations	Oracle Incentive					
Web/Mobile Access						
Reporting & BI	Microstrategy,					
3rd Party Communication						
Procurement/Stores						
Knowzone Sales Document Creation	Knowzone					
Authority Matrix						

A further scoping issue was related to content of the delivered solution in terms of product/service types to be addressed per release. The initial release of Quoting would only provide support for one major product. Subsequent releases will add additional products, which in some cases involves not only the product modeling and capture into the solution systems, but additional system and interfacing capability, e.g. to handle "bundles" which are products composed from other offerings. We did not want to complicate the BBB diagram with this dimension, so opted to create a matrix which provides a view of capability, release timing and content coverage. The latter is provided in the cells as either (i) a list of product identities or (ii) sub-capabilities of building blocks (also shown in Figure 1 as bullet points within the block text). This is shown as Table 1.

4   Taking It Further

Following the development of the BBB diagram, addition of release tagging, and the release content and timing matrix, a meta model was developed to allow repository and tool support for the building block model techniques. The organization uses the EVA Netmodeler web and repository based EA toolset [9]. Customising the meta model and defining suitable visual notation "model types" allows support for the required techniques in a shared repository. The EA team believed this would enhance rigour, promote sharing and provide visibility across projects. The resultant meta model is shown as Figure 3.

Building Block Categories allow differentiating between business and solution building blocks. Note that multiple own-type relationships exist between building blocks. These are necessary to capture the semantics between building blocks within a layer, as well as between business and solution building blocks. Content elements are related to a building block and a release. They occur in varieties of Feature, Product/Service and Location. These correspond to the cells in the previously presented release matrix (Table 1). The relationship via Model to Value Adding Activity links the building block model to the relevant value chain step.

We were able to define visual model types in the tool to create equivalent business building block diagrams to the Powerpoint model shown earlier. See Figure 4. These do not have the visual cues for release mapping and BBB id but these attributes are captured behind the scenes and can be reported upon or navigated easily.

We also created a visual model type for a solution building block (SBB) diagram. This was completed for the Quoting project, with input from the project team, the business analyst and members of the Billing team who had high knowledge of the existing infrastructure and telecomms processes in general. The resultant SBB model is shown as Figure 5. This shows actual incumbent or anticipated application system components, technologies and data sources. In building this view across the two projects, the need for a messaging infrastructure and consistent data for shared domain objects was apparent. The former was represented in the diagram as an Enterprise Service Bus (ESB) while the latter translates to the Master Data Management (MDM) element. Projects are now underway in the environment to address these requirements.

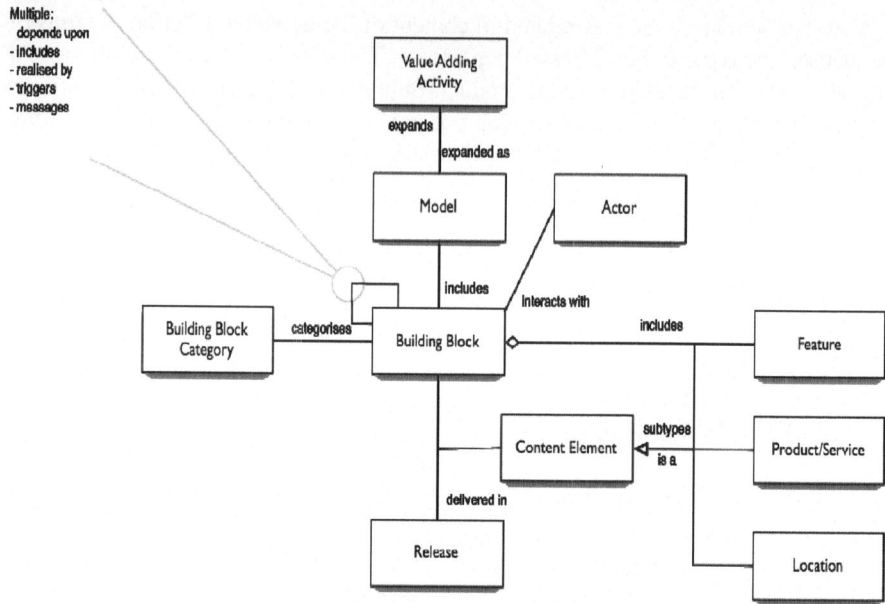

Fig. 3. Meta model for supporting the building block approach

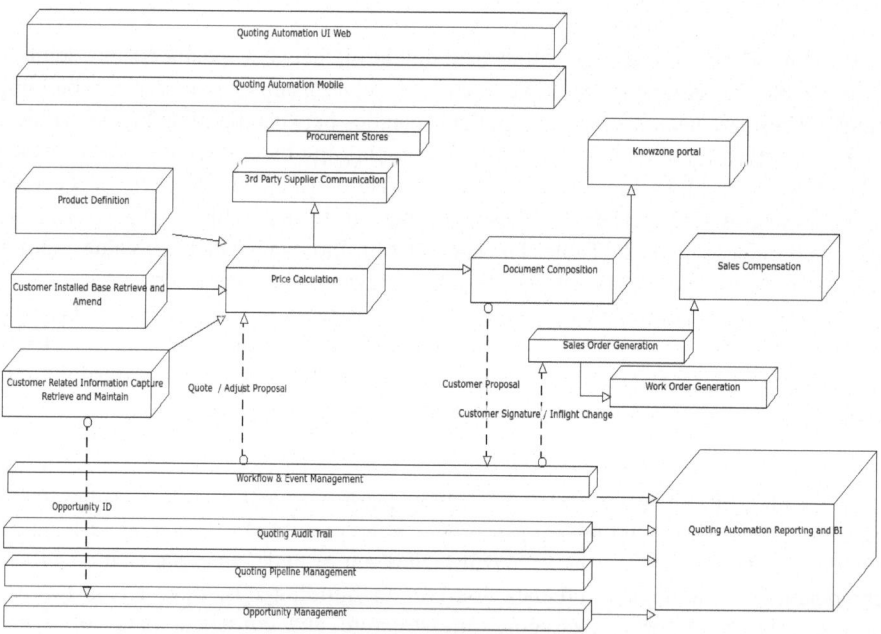

Solid edges: dependency   Dotted edges: Data Flow

Fig. 4. Business building blocks model

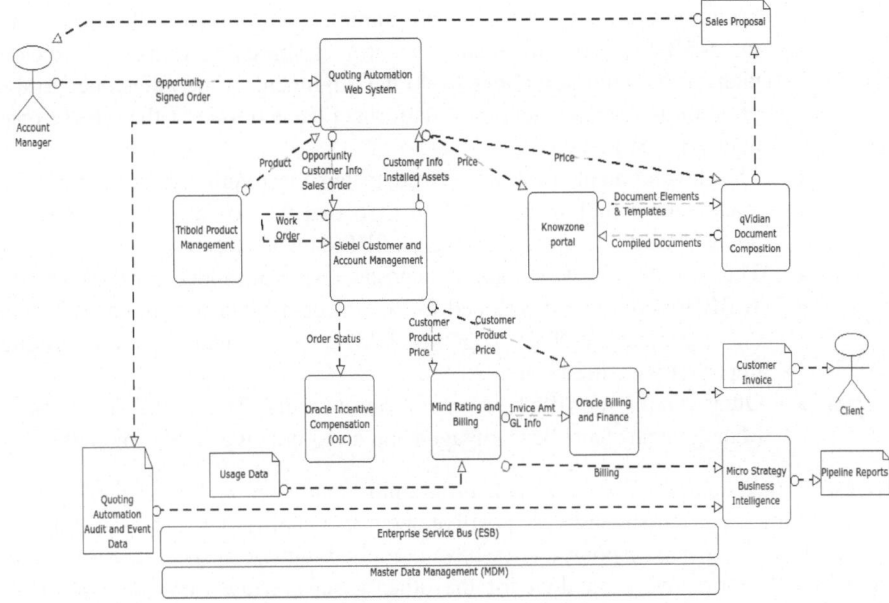

Fig. 5. Solution building blocks model

The revised building block models and the release matrix were presented to stakeholders and the project sponsor in different sessions. Both sessions went extremely well. Stakeholders were easily able to apprehend the business capabilities that were represented and the relationships and dependencies between them. They were also able to grasp the implications of dependencies for release composition. It was clear to them what each release would deliver in terms of functionality and content. With the release matrix, this also relates to delivery time expectations. The three deliverables thus greatly facilitated accurate communication and arriving at a consensus view with stakeholders. Stakeholders expressed their appreciation that they now had a grasp of the scope, capabilities, delivery schedule, release breakdown and dependencies which would enable them to plan properly and engage meaningfully with the development team.

The project sponsor was also delighted with the results, exclaiming that she, for the first time in months, had an accurate and usable picture of what the project was about, what it would deliver, how it was put together and what would be required to deliver it. The programme manager/strategist also expressed her high satisfaction with the clarity which had been achieved.

From an EA perspective we were keen to expand the approach to other projects and to ensure that the clarity prevailed. We thus initiated a number of other activities:

- The business analyst was asked to bring the BBB perspective into the BRS. This was achieved with the BBB ids shown earlier. The BRS was tagged with the relevant ids to show where the requirements mapped onto building blocks. We also encouraged the programme manager and business analyst to align the programme management milestones with the BBB view and to update the project charter to reflect the release plan. In the end they chose to do the alignment in the milestones in the programme management tool, Sciforma [10] and to keep the release map matrix in the BRS.

- The development team was asked to tag the requirements in the agile management tool with the BB ids, so that we could track progress on development, testing and delivery of BB capabilities.
- The Billing team was engaged to produce similar models for their scope.
- A BBB model was developed for the Product Management capability in the organization. This, together with a phase plan, is now driving improvements in this area
- Other teams (Unified Communications and Data and Information Management) have been engaged and are producing similar models.

Sponsors, stakeholders, EA personnel, programme managers and strategist have all embraced the approach and are very positive about its benefits. The jury is still out on the development group response. They have complied, but we suspect that, for them, there is a bit more overhead than for the other groups, while they see less direct benefit to themselves. There may also be an element of resentment that an oversight group has interfered in a work process with which they were happy. Unfortunately other stakeholders were not satisfied. We hope that over time they will be convinced of the benefits in terms of improved stakeholder communication and a happy sponsor.

To summarise, the benefits include:

- Clear scope of projects via BBBs representing business capabilities and their collation into a picture per project
- Clear tie between value chain and project scope via decomposition of value chain activities into models holding the BBBs supporting that business capability
- Clear release content and planning, via the tagging of the BBBs and the collation of these into releases with delivery times
- Improved communications and agreement between strategy, programme management, sponsor, stakeholders and project team via accessible shared and simple pictures and matrix
- Identification of common requirements at both business and technical levels via visibility in respective building block diagrams
- Common basis for prioritisation within and across projects using the shared definitions of building blocks, dependencies identified and stakeholders knowledge of business issues and benefits
- Simple views at business and technical levels which are not arduous to produce and allow rich discussion and a shared understanding
- Traceability of requirements from business to solution to implementation effort via the linkages created between the building blocks views, the BRS and the agile requirements management

5   Limitations

The experience is reported for one organisation only. The techniques have now been applied to several projects and seem to work equally well across these. Some of these projects are core value chain and targeted at operational improvement while some are more strategic, aimed at business change (e.g. introduction of a new product category). Others, such as Product Management and Data and Information Management are broad supporting capabilities across the value chain. However, all projects are still in the same organisational setting and culture. From our experience in many organisations, industries and EA groups we believe that they will have broad applicability and will work in many settings, but this is no guarantee that they will actually work, or work as well there.

Some of the benefits mentioned, particularly those related to commonality across projects and improved traceability are likely to be reduced, or harder to obtain, if the techniques are not supported by a shared and capable repository.

6   Further Work

The EA function is working to integrate the approach with business cases and prioritization in the organization. The models will also be used to underpin estimating for capital budgeting purposes.

More work can be done in the area of integration and feedback with the agile management practices used in the development group.

Integration with programme management is underway, but this could be enhanced, and possibly to some extent automated by feeding project, building block and release information across to the programme management tool.

Integration with portfolio management could be investigated for better reuse of information about the existing solution building blocks and infrastructure elements. Full baselines are still being built in the environment and this would require these and a mapping to reference models (e.g. Telecommunications Application Model (TAM), Shared Information/Data (SID) model, eTOM process model [11] from the TM Forum).

A longitudinal assessment of how the techniques work down the full project lifecycle for requirements traceability should also be undertaken.

References

1. Porter, M., Millar, V.: How information gives you competitive advantage. Harvard Business Review, 149–174 (July-August 1985)
2. Mcleod, G.: The Inspired Enterprise Architecture Frameworks. Inspired/Promis White Papers, 1–28 (2009)
3. Mcleod, G.: An Inspired Approach to Business Architecture (2012),
   http://www.inspired.org/busarch/
   InspiredApproachToBusinessArchitecture.pdf (retrieved)

4. The Open Group, TOGAF ® Version 9.1 (2011)
5. Dingsøyr, T., Dybå, T., Moe, N.B. (eds.): Agile Software Development: Current Research and Future Directions. Springer, Heidelberg (2010)
6. Dybå, T., Dingsøyr, T.: Empirical studies of agile software development: A systematic review. Information and Software Technology (2008), doi:10.1016/j.infsof.2008.01.006
7. Vlaanderen, K., Jansen, S., Brinkkemper, S., Jaspers, E.: The agile requirements refinery: Applying SCRUM principles to software product management. Information and Software Technology 53(1), 58–70 (2011), doi:10.1016/j.infsof.2010.08.004
8. Zachman, J., Sowa, J.: Extending and formalizing the framework for information systems architecture. IBM Systems Journal 31(3) (1992)
9. Inspired (2011), EVA Netmodeler,
   http://www.inspired.org/resources/EVA-Brochure-2-6.pdf
10. Sciforma, Sciforma 5.0 Programme Management (2012),
    http://www.sciforma.com
11. Telemanagement Forum (TMForum), FrameWorkx (2013),
    http://www.tmforum.org

A Demonstration Case on Steps and Rules for the Transition from Process-Level to Software Logical Architectures in Enterprise Models[*]

Nuno Ferreira[1], Nuno Santos[2], Pedro Soares[2], Ricardo J. Machado[3],
and Dragan Gašević[4]

[1] I2S – Informática Sistemas e Serviços, S.A., Porto, Portugal
nuno.ferreira@i2s.pt
[2] CCG – Centro de Computação Gráfica, Campus de Azurém, Guimarães, Portugal
{nuno.santos,psoares}@ccg.pt
[3] Centro ALGORITMI, Escola de Engenharia, Universidade do Minho, Guimarães, Portugal
rmac@dsi.uminho.pt
[4] School of Computing and Information Systems, Athabasca University, Canada
dgasevic@acm.org

Abstract. At the analysis phase of an enterprise information system development, the alignment between the process-level requirements (information systems) with the product-level requirements (software system) may not be properly achieved. Modeling the processes for the enterprise's business is often insufficient for implementation teams, and implementation requirements are often misaligned with business and stakeholder needs. In this paper, we demonstrate, though a real industrial case, how transition steps and rules are used to assure that process- and product-level requirements are aligned, within an approach that supports the creation of the intended requirements. The input for the transition steps is an information system logical architecture, and the output is a product-level (software) use case model.

Keywords: Enterprise Information Systems, Enterprise Modeling, Requirement Elicitation, Model Transformation, Transition to Software Requirements.

1 Introduction

During an enterprise information system development process, assuring that functional requirements fully support the stakeholder's business needs may become a complex and inefficient task. Additionally, the "newfound" paradigm of IT solutions (*e.g.*, Cloud Computing) typically results in more difficulties for defining a business model and for eliciting product-level functional requirements for any given project. If stakeholders

---

[*] This work has been supported by project ISOFIN (QREN 2010/013837), Fundos FEDER through Programa Operacional Fatores de Competitividade – COMPETE and by Fundos Nacionais through FCT – Fundação para a Ciência e Tecnologia within the Project Scope: FCOMP-01-0124-FEDER-022674.

J. Grabis et al. (Eds.): PoEM 2013, LNBIP 165, pp. 277–291, 2013.

experience such difficulties then software developers will have to deal with incomplete or incorrect requirements specifications, resulting in a real problem.

When there are insufficient inputs for a product-level approach to requirements elicitation, using a process-level perspective is a possible approach, in order to create an information system logical architecture which is used for eliciting software (product-level) requirements.

The first effort should be to specify the requirements of the overall system in the physical world; then to determine necessary assumptions about components of that physical world; and only then to derive a specification of the computational part of the control system [1]. There are similar approaches that tackle the problem of aligning domain specific needs with software solutions. For instance, goal-oriented approaches are a way of doing so, but they don't encompass methods for deriving a logical representation of the intended system processes with the purpose of creating context for eliciting product-level requirements.

Our main problem, and the main topic this paper addresses, is assuring that product-level (IT-related) requirements are perfectly aligned with process-level requirements, and hence, are aligned with the organization's business requirements. The process-level requirements express the need for fulfilling the organization's business needs, and we detail how they are characterized within our approach further in section 2. These requirements may be supported by analysis models, that are implementation agnostic [2]. According to [2], the existing approaches for transforming requirements into an analysis model (i) don't require acceptable user effort to document requirements, (ii) are efficient enough (*e.g.*, one or two transformation steps), (iii) are able to (semi-)automatically generate a complete (*i.e.*, static and dynamic aspects) consistent analysis model, which is expected to model both the structure and behavior of the system at a logical level of abstraction.

In this paper we present a demonstration case in which we illustrate the transition between the process-level requirements of the intended system and the technological requirements that the same system must comply with. The transition is part of an approach that expresses the project goals and allows creating context to implement a software system. The entire approach is detailed in [3] as a V + V process, based on the composition of two V-shaped process models (inspired in the "Vee" process model [4]). This way, we formalize the transition steps between perspectives that are required in order to align the requirements the V+V process presented in [3]. The requirements are expressed through logical architectural models and stereotyped sequence diagrams [5] in both a process- and a product-level perspective.

This paper is structured as follows: section 2 briefly presents the macro-process for information system's development based on both process- and product-level V-Model approaches; section 3 describes the transition steps and rules between both perspectives; in section 4 we present a real industrial case on the adoption of the transition steps between both V-Model executions; in section 5 we compare our approach with other related work; and in section 6 we present the conclusions.

2   A Macro-Process Approach to Software Design

The development process of information systems can be regarded (in a simple way) as a cascaded lifecycle (*i.e.*, a development process only initiates when the previous has ended), if we consider typical and simplified phases: analysis, design and implementation. Our approach encompasses two V-shaped process models hereafter referred as the V+V process. The main difference from our proposed approach to other information system development approaches is that it is applicable for eliciting product-level requirements in cases where there is no clearly defined context for eliciting product requirements within a given specific domain, by first eliciting process-level requirements and then evolving to the product-level requirements, using a transition approach that assures an alignment between both perspectives. Other approaches (described further in section 5) typically apply to a single perspective.

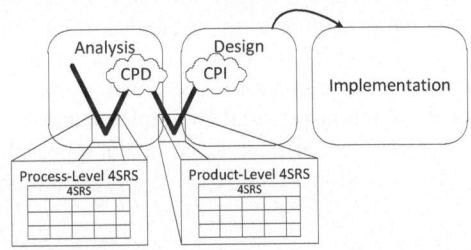

Fig. 1. V+V process framed in the development macro-process

The first V-Model (at process-level) is composed by *Organizational Configurations* (OC) [5], *A-type* and *B-type* sequence diagrams [5] (stereotyped sequence diagrams that use, respectively, use cases and architectural elements from the logical architecture), and (business) *Use Case* models (UCs) that are used to derive (and, in the case of *B-type* sequence diagrams, validate) a process-level logical architecture (*i.e.*, the information system logical architecture). Use cases are mandatory to execute the 4SRS method. Since the term *process* has different meanings depending on the context, in our process-level approach we acknowledge that: (i) real-world activities of a software production process are the context for the problem under analysis; (ii) in relation to a software model context [8], a software process is composed of a set of activities related to software development, maintenance, project management and quality assurance. For the scope definition of our work, and according to the previously exposed acknowledgments, we characterize our process-level perspective by: (i) being related to real-world activities (including business); (ii) when related to software, those activities encompass the typical software development lifecycle. Our process-level approach is characterized by using refinement (as one kind of functional decomposition) and integration of system models. Activities and their interface in a process can be structured or arranged in a process architecture [9]. We frame the process-level V-Model (the first V-Model of Fig. 1) in the analysis phase, creating the context for product design (*CPD*). In its vertex, the process-level 4SRS (Four-Step Rule-Set) method execution (see [6] for details about the process-level 4SRS method) assures the transition from the problem to the solution domain by transforming process-level use cases into process-level logical architectural elements, and results in the creation of a validated architectural model which allows creating context for the product-level requirements elicitation and in the uncovering of hidden requirements for the intended product design.

The second V-Model (at product-level) is composed by *Mashed UCs* model (a use case model composed by use cases derived from the transition steps but not yet being the final product use case model), *A-type* and *B-type* sequence diagrams, and (software) *Use Case* models (UCs) that are used to derive (and, validate) a product-level logical architecture (*i.e.*, the software system logical architecture). By product-level, we refer as the typical software requirements. The second execution of the V-Model is done at a product-level perspective and its vertex is supported by the product-level 4SRS method detailed in [7]. The product-level V-Model gathers information from the *CPD* in order to create a new model referred as *Mashed UCs*. The creation of this model is detailed in the next section of this paper as transition steps and rules. The product-level V-Model (the second V-Model of Fig. 1) enables the transition from analysis to design trough the execution of the product-level 4SRS method (see [7] for details about the product-level 4SRS method). The resulting architecture is then considered a design artifact that contributes for the creation of context for product implementation (*CPI*) as information required by implementation teams. Note that the design itself is not restricted to that artifact, since in our approach it also encompasses behavioral aspects and non-functional requirements representation.

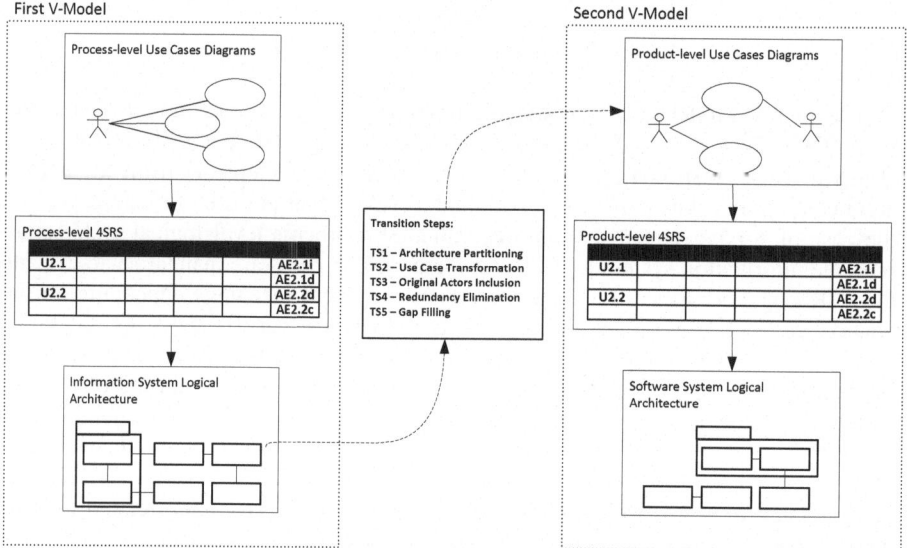

Fig. 2. Derivation of software system logical architectures by transiting from information system logical architectures

The information regarding each of the models and their usage within the V+V process is detailed in [3] and as such is not our purpose to thoroughly describe them, leaving the reader with just a brief explanation on their meaning. The OC model is a high-level representation of the activities (interactions) that exist between the business-level entities of a given domain. *A-type* and *B-type* sequence diagrams are stereotyped sequence diagram representation to describe interactions in early analysis phase of system development. *A-type* sequence diagrams use actors and use cases. *B-type* sequence diagrams use actors and architectural elements depicted in the both the information system or software system logical architectures.

As depicted in Fig. 2, the result of the first V-Model (process-level) execution is the information system logical architecture. The architectural elements that compose this architecture are derived (by performing transition steps) into product-level use cases (*Mashed UCs* model). The result of the second V-Model (product-level) execution is the software system logical architecture.

3   Process- to Product-Level Transition

As stated before, a first V-Model (at process-level) can be executed for business requirements elicitation purposes, followed by a second V-Model (at product-level) for defining the software functional requirements. The V+V process is useful for both stakeholders, organizations and technicians, but it is necessary to assure that they properly reflect the same system.

This section begins by presenting a set of transition steps whose execution is required to create the initial context for product-level requirements elicitation, referred to as *Mashed UC* model. The purpose of the transition steps is to assure an aligned transition between the process- and product-level perspectives in the V+V process, that is, the passage from the first V-Model to the second one. By defining these transition steps, we assure that product-level (software) use cases (UCpt's) are aligned with the architectural elements from the process-level (information system) logical architectural model (AEpc's); *i.e.*, (software) use case diagrams are reflecting the needs of the information system logical architecture. The application of these transition rules to all the partitions of an information system logical architecture gives origin to a set of *Mashed UC* models (preliminary product-level use case models).

To allow the recursive execution of the 4SRS method [10, 11], the transition from the first V-Model to the second V-Model must be performed by a set of steps. The output of the first V-Model must be used as input for the second V-Model; *i.e.*, we need to transform the information system logical architecture into product-level use case models. The transition steps to guide this mapping must be able to support business to technology changing. These transition steps (TS) are structured as follows:

TS1 - *Architecture Partitioning*, where the process-level architectural elements (AEpc's) under analysis are classified by their computation execution context with the purpose of defining software boundaries to be transformed into product-level (software) use cases (UCpt's.);

TS2 - *Use Case Transformation*, where AEpc's are transformed into software use cases and actors that represent the system under analysis through a set of transition patterns that must be applied as rules;

TS3 - *Original Actors Inclusion*, where the original actors that were related to the use cases from which the architectural elements of the process-level perspective are derived (in the first V execution) must be included in the representation;

TS4 - *Redundancy Elimination*, where the model is analyzed for redundancies;

TS5 - *Gap Filling*, where the necessary information of any requirement that is not yet represented, is added, in the form of use cases.

During the execution of these transition steps, transition use cases (UCtr's) bridge the AEpc's and serve as basis to elicit UCpt's. UCtr's also provide traceability between process- and product-level perspectives using tags and annotations associated with each representation.

The identification of each partition is firstly made using the information that results from the packaging and aggregation efforts of the previous 4SRS execution (step 3 of the 4SRS method execution as described in [6]). Nevertheless, this information is not enough to properly identify the partitions. Information gathered in OC's and on the process-level *B-type* sequence diagrams must also be accounted. A partition is created by identifying all the relevant architectural elements that belong to all *B-type* sequence diagrams that correspond to a given organizational configuration scenario. By traversing the architectural elements that comply with the scenario definition (for each *B-type* sequence diagram and aligned with the packages and aggregations presented in the information system logical architecture), it is possible to properly identify the partitions that support the interactions depicted in the OC's.

The rules to support the execution of the transition step 2 are applied in the form of transition rules and must be applied in accordance to the stereotype of the envisaged architectural element. There are three stereotyped architectural elements: *d-type*, which refer to generic decision repositories (data), representing decisions not supported computationally by the system under design; *c-type,* which encompass all the processes focusing on decision making that must be supported computationally by the system; and *i-type*, which refer to process' interfaces with users, software or other processes. The full descriptions of the three stereotypes are available in [6].

The defined transition rules (TR), from the logical architectural diagram to the *Mashed UC* diagram are as follows:

TR1 - an inbound *c-type* or *i-type* AEpc is transformed into an UCtr of the same type (see Fig. 3). By inbound we mean that the element belongs to the partition under analysis;

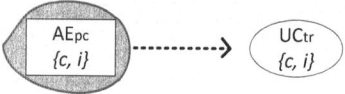

Fig. 3. TR1 - transition rule 1

TR2 - an inbound *d-type* AEpc is transformed into an UCtr and an associated actor (see Fig. 4). This is due to the fact that *d-type* AEpc's corresponds to decisions not computationally supported by the system under design and, as such, it requires an actor to activate the depicted process.

Fig. 4. TR2 - transition rule 2

Rules TR1 and TR2 are the most basic ones and the patterns they express are the most used in the transition step 2.

TR3 - an inbound AEpc, with a given name x, which also belongs to an outbound partition, is transformed into an UCtr of name x, and an associated actor, of name y, being the responsible for representing the outbound actions associated with UCtr$x$ (see Fig. 5).

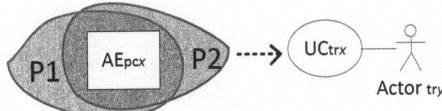

Fig. 5. TR3 - transition rule 3

The connections between the use cases and actors produced by the previous rules must be consistent with the existing associations between the AEpc's. The focus of this analysis is UCtr's and is addressed by the following two transition rules.

TR4 - an inbound d-type UCtr of name x with connections to an (any type) UCtr of name y and to an actor z, gives place to two UCtr's, x and y, maintaining the original types (see Fig. 6). Both are connected to the actor z. This means that all existing connections on the original d-type AEpc that were maintained during execution of TR2 or TR3 are transferred to the created actor.

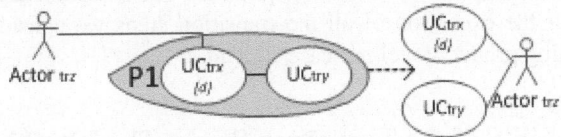

Fig. 6. TR4 - transition rule 4

The previous rule is executed after TR1, TR2 or TR3, so it only needs to set the required association between the UCtr's and the actors, that is to say, after all transformations are executed (TR1, TR2, and TR3), a set of rules are executed to establish the correct associations to the UCtr's.

TR5 - an inbound UCtr of name x with a connection to an outbound AEpc of name y (note that this is still an AEpc, since it was not transformed into any other concept in the previous transition rules) gives place to both an UCtr named x and to an actor named y (see Fig. 7). AEpc's that were not previously transformed are now transformed by the application of this TR5; this means that all AEpc's which exist outside the partition under analysis having connections with inbound UCtr's will be transformed into actors. These actors will support the representation of required external inputs to the inbounds UCtr's created during application of TR1, TR2, or TR3.

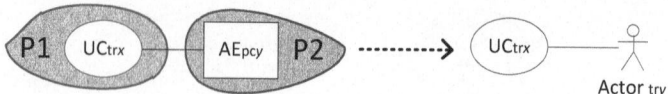

Fig. 7. TR5 - transition rule 5

A special application of TR5 (described as TR5.1) can be found in Fig. 8 where we can see an UCtr with a connection to an outbound AEpc and another connection to an actor. In this case, TR5 is applied and the resulting UCtr is also connected to the original actor. Note that an UCtr belonging to multiple partitions is first and foremost, an inbound UCtr due to being under analysis.

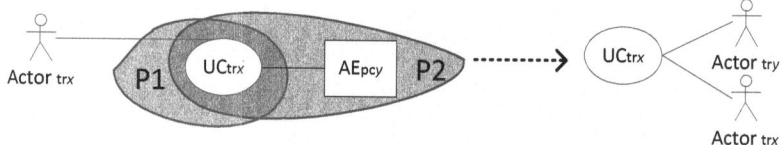

Fig. 8. TR5.1 - transition rule 5.1

The application of these transition steps and rules to all the partitions of an information system logical architecture gives origin to a set of *Mashed UC* models, as we illustrate in the next section using a real industrial case. In the remaining of the transition steps, the purpose is to promote completeness and reliability in the model. The model is complete after adding the associations that initially connected actors (the ones who trigger the AEpc's) and the AEpc's, and then by mapping those associations to the UCtr's. The model is reliable since the enforcement of the rules eliminates redundancy and assures that there are no gaps in the UCtr's associations and related actors. Only after the execution of all the transition steps we consider the resulting model as containing product-level use cases (UCpt's).

4   Applicability of the Transition Steps: The ISOFIN Project

The applicability of the transition steps and rules is demonstrated with a real project: the ISOFIN project (Interoperability in Financial Software) [12]. This project aimed to deliver a set of coordinating services in a centralized infrastructure, enacting the coordination of independent services relying on separate infrastructures. The resulting ISOFIN platform allows for the semantic and application interoperability between enrolled financial institutions (Banks, Insurance Companies and others).

The global ISOFIN architecture relies on two main service types: Interconnected Business Service (IBS) and Supplier Business Service (SBS). IBSs concern a set of functionalities that are exposed from the ISOFIN core platform to ISOFIN Customers. An IBS interconnects one or more SBS's and/or IBS's exposing functionalities that relate directly to business needs. SBS's are a set of functionalities that are exposed from the ISOFIN Suppliers production infrastructure.

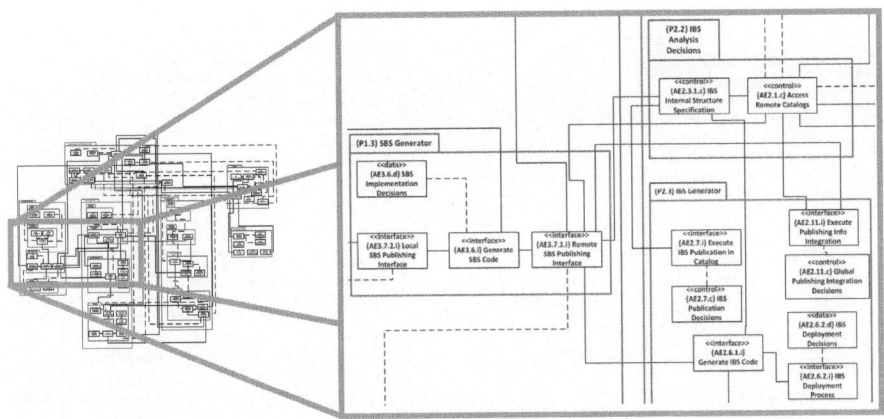

Fig. 9. Subset of the ISOFIN information system logical architecture

From the demonstration case, we first present a subset of the information system logical architecture in Fig. 9, that resulted from the execution of the 4SRS method at a process-level perspective [6]; *i.e.*, the execution of the first (process-level) V-Model. The information system logical architecture is composed by architectural elements that represent processes executed by within the ISOFIN platform.

In Fig. 10, we depict the execution of TS1 to a subset of the entire information system logical architecture (composed by the same architectural elements as Fig. 9), *i.e.*, the partitioning of the information system logical architecture, by marking its architectural elements in partition areas, each concerning the context where services are executed, which resulted in two partitions: (i) the ISOFIN platform execution functionalities (in the area marked as P1); (ii) the ISOFIN supplier execution functionalities (in the area marked as P2). The identification of the partitions will enable the application of the transition steps to allow the application of the second V-Model to advance the macro-process execution into the product implementation. Presenting the information that supported the decisions regarding the partitions in the case of the ISOFIN project is out of the scope of this paper.

Fig. 11 shows the filtered and collapsed diagram that resulted from the P2 partition, which (in the demonstration case) is the partition under analysis. P2 includes the architectural elements that belong to both partitions and that must be considered when applying the transition rules. After being filtered and collapsed, the partitioned information system logical architecture is composed, not only by the architectural elements that belong to the partition under analysis, but also by some additional architectural elements belonging to other partitions that has an association (*i.e.*, the dashed and/or straight lines between architectural elements) with architectural elements belonging to the partition under analysis (*e.g.*, *{AE3.6.i} Generate SBS Code* belongs to P1, but possesses an association with *{AE3.7.1.i} Remote SBS Publishing Interface* that belongs to P1 and P2 partitions). The keeping of these outbound AEpc's assures that outbound interfaces information is preserved.

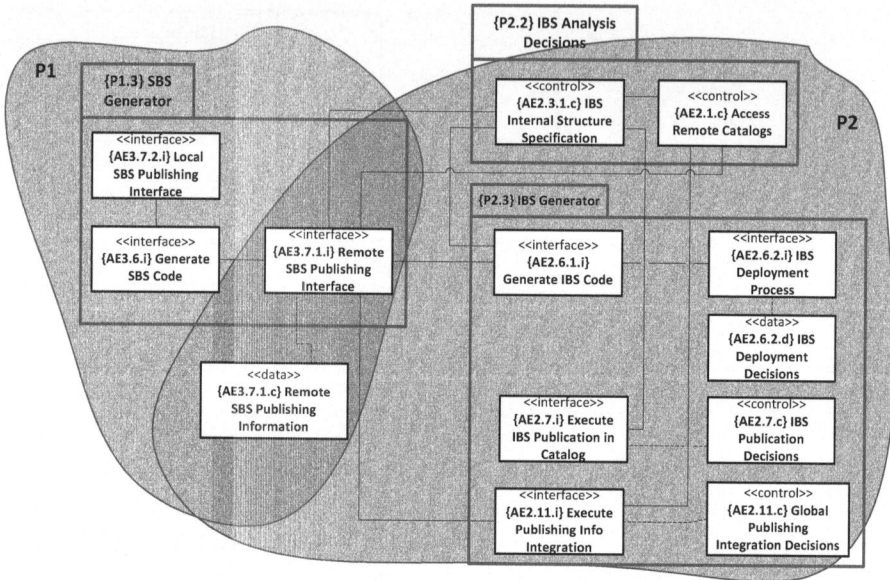

Fig. 10. Partitioning of the information system logical architecture (TS1)

The model is now ready to be transformed. It is during TS2 that the perspective is altered from process- to product-level. We now execute the transition rules presented in the previous section to our demonstration case. We transform from the source model (model from Fig. 11) to the target model (model from Fig. 12), as well as the TR that was applied, are supported in Table 1. Table 1 allows a better understanding of the application of the TR and the result of the transformation executed in TS2.

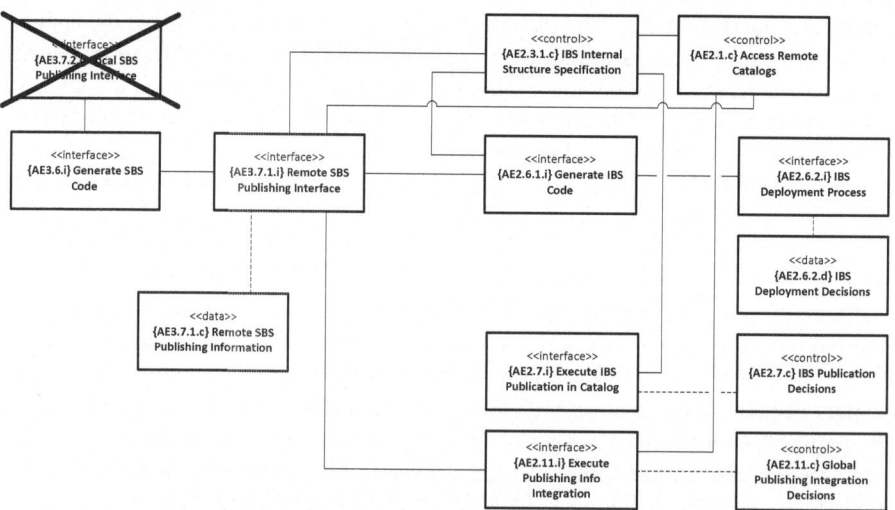

Fig. 11. Filtered and collapsed architectural elements (TS1)

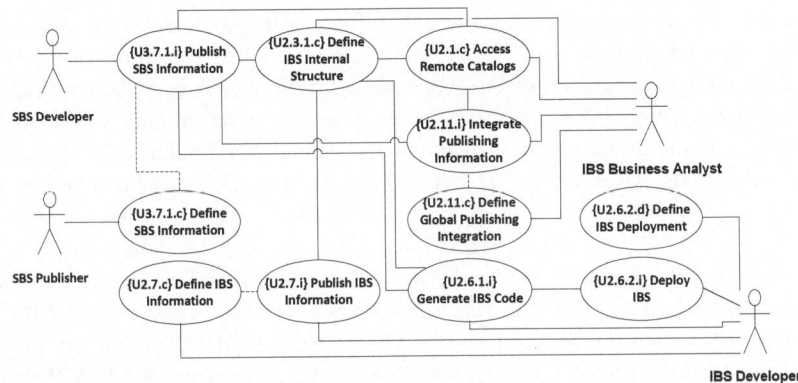

Fig. 12. Mashed *UC* model resulting from the transition from process- to product-level

The resulting model however presents some redundancies and gaps, so it is necessary that the remaining TS are executed. In Fig. 12, we depict the final *Mashed UC* model (the first product-level artifact in the second V-Model), resulting from the execution of TS2-5. Due to space restrictions, we only show the result of the execution of these four transition steps altogether. The resulting mashed use cases are the result of the application of the transition rules in TS2. The resulting model however presents redundancies and gaps, so it is necessary that the remaining TS are executed.

Table 1. Executed transformations to the model

Process-level (transformation source)	TR	Product-level (transformation target)
AEpc *{AE2.1.c}* Access Remote Catalogs	TR1	UCtr *{U2.1.c}* Access Remote Catalogs
AEpc *{AE2.3.1.c}* IBS Internal Structure Specification	TR1	UCtr *{U2.3.1.c}* Define IBS Internal Structure
AEpc *{AE2.6.1.i}* Generate IBS Code	TR1	UCtr *{U2.6.1.i}* Generate IBS Code
AEpc *{AE2.6.2.d}* IBS Deployment Decisions	TR2	UCtr *{U2.6.2.d}* Define IBS Deployment; Actor *IBS Developer*
AEpc *{AE2.6.2.i}* IBS Deployment Process	TR1	UCtr *{U2.6.2.i}* Deploy IBS
AEpc *{AE2.7.i}* Execute IBS Publication in Catalog	TR1	UCtr *{U2.7.i}* Publish IBS Information
AEpc *{AE2.7.c}* IBS Publication Decisions	TR1	UCtr *{U2.7.c}* Define IBS Information
AEpc *{AE2.11.i}* Execute Publishing Info Integration	TR1	UCtr *{U2.11.i}* Integrate Publishing Information
AEpc *{AE2.11.c}* Global Publishing Integration Decisions	TR1	UCtr *{U2.11.c}* Define Global Publishing Information
AEpc *{AE3.6.i}* Generate SBS Code	TR5.1	Actor *SBS Developer*
AEpc *{AE3.7.1.i}* Remote SBS Publishing Interface	TR3	UCtr *{U3.7.1.i}* Publish SBS Information; Actor *SBS Developer*
AEpc *{AE3.7.1.c}* Remote SBS Publishing Information	TR3	UCtr *{U3.7.1.c}* Define SBS Information; Actor *SBS Publisher*

It is possible to objectively recognize the effect of the application of some transition rules previously described. TR1 was the most applied transition rule and one example is the transformation of the AEpc named *{AE2.1.c} Access Remote Catalogs* into one UCtr named *{U2.1.c} Access Remote Catalogs*. One example of the application of TR2 is the transformation of the AEpc named *{AE2.6.2.d} IBS Deployment Decisions* into the UCtr named *{U2.6.2.d} Define IBS Deployment* and the actor named *IBS Developer*. TR3 was applied, for instance, in the transformation of the AEpc named *{AE3.7.1.c} Define SBS Information* into the UCtr named *{U3.7.1.c} Define SBS Information* and the actor named *SBS Publisher*. Finally, we can recognize the application of TR5.1 in the transformation of the AEpc named *{AE3.6.i} Generate SBS Code* into the actor named *SBS Developer*. All the other actors result from the execution of TS3. We must refer, for instance, that the actor *SBS Developer* results from the execution of TS4, since the original actor and the actor resulting from an application of TR2 and TR5.1 and also the inclusion of the original actor in TS3, result in the same actor which brings the need to eliminate the generated redundancy. The resulting model allows to identify potential gaps in use cases or actors (in the execution of TS5), but in this case such wasn't required.

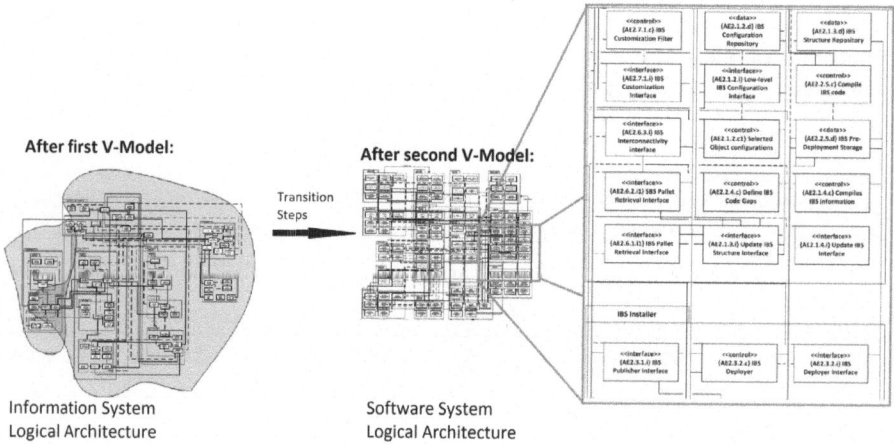

Fig. 13. Subset of the ISOFIN software system logical architecture after V+V process

After the execution of the transition steps, the *Mashed UC* model is used as input for the product-level 4SRS method execution [7] in order to derive the software system logical architecture for the ISOFIN platform. Such architecture is the main output of the second (product-level) V-Model execution. We depict in Fig. 13 the entire software system logical architecture (the second architecture of Fig. 13) obtained after the execution of the V+V process (and, as represented in Fig. 2, derived by transforming product use cases in architectural elements using product-level 4SRS method), having as input the information system logical architecture (the first architecture of Fig. 13) previously presented. The software system logical architecture is composed by architectural elements (depicted in the zoomed area) that represent functionalities that are executed in the platform. The alignment between the architecture elements in both perspectives is supported by the transition steps. It would be impossible to elicit requirements for a software system logical architecture as complex as the ISOFIN platform (the overall information system logical architecture was composed by near 80 architectural elements, and the resulting software system logical architecture by near 100) by adopting an approach that only considers the product-level perspective.

5   Comparison with Related Work

There are many approaches that allow deriving at a given level a view of the intended system to be developed. Our approach clearly starts at a process-level perspective, and by successive models derivation creates the context for transforming the requirements expressed in an information system logical architecture into product-level context for requirements specification. Other approaches provide similar results at a subset of our specification. For instance, KAOS, a goal-oriented requirement specification method, provides a specification that can be used in order to obtain architecture requirements [13]. This approach uses two step-based methods, which output a formalization of the architecture requirements for each method, each of one providing a different view of the system. The organization's processes can be represented by an enterprise architecture [14], and representation extended by including in the architecture modeling concerns as business goals and requirements [15]. However, such proposals don't intend to provide information for implementation teams during the software development process, but instead to provide to stakeholders with business strategic requirements. The relation between what the stakeholders want and what implementation teams need requires an alignment approach to assure that there are no missing specifications on the transition between phases. An alignment approach also based on architectural models is presented in [16].

In [17] it is specified a mapping technique and an algorithm for mapping business process models, using UML activity diagrams and use cases, so functional requirements specifications support the enterprise's business process. In our approach, we use an information system logical architecture diagram instead of an activity diagram, since an information system logical architecture provides a fundamental organization of the development, creation, and distribution of processes in the relevant enterprise context [18]. Model-driven transformation approaches were already used for developing information systems in [19]. In literature, model transformations are often related to the Model-Driven Architecture (MDA) [20] initiative from OMG. MDA-based transformations are widely used but, as far as the authors know, the supported transformations don't regard a perspective transition, i.e., are perspective agnostic since they concern model transformations within a single perspective (typically the product-level one). For instance, [21] describes MDA-based transformations from use cases and scenarios to components, but only in a product-level perspective. Even in cases when MDA transformations are executed using different source and target modeling languages (there is a plethora in literature regarding these cases, like, for instance, [22], where a source model in Business Process Modeling Notation – BPMN, is transformed into target model in Business Process Execution Language – BPEL), the transformation only regards a single perspective. The concerns that must be assured by transiting between perspectives are not dealt by any of the previous works.

The existing approaches for model transformation attempt to provide an automated or automatic execution. [2] provides a systematic review and evaluation of existing work on transforming requirements into an analysis model and, according to the authors, none of the compared approaches provide a practical automated solution. The transition steps and rules presented in this work intent to provide a certain level of automation into our approach and improve the efficiency, validation, and traceability of the overall V+V process.

6   Conclusions

In this paper, we demonstrated through a real industrial case the transition from previously process-level elicited requirements to requirements in a product-level perspective, included in an elicitation approach based in two V-Models (the V+V process). We illustrated a demonstration case that elicits requirements for developing a complex interoperable platform, by adopting a model-based approach to create context for business software implementation teams in situations where requirements cannot be properly elicited. Our approach is supported on a set of transition steps and transition rules that use as basis an information system logical architecture to output a product-level use case model. By adopting the approach, requirements for specifying software system functionalities are properly aligned with organizational information system requirements in a traceable way.

Our approach uses software engineering techniques, such as operational model transformations to assure the execution of a process that begins with business needs and ends with a logical architectural representation. It is a common fact that domain-specific needs, namely business needs, are a fast changing concern that must be tackled. Information system architectures must be modeled in a way that potentially changing domain-specific needs are local in the architecture representation of the intended service. Our proposed V+V process encompasses the derivation of a logical architecture representation that is aligned with domain-specific needs and any change made to those domain-specific needs is reflected in the logical architectural model, and the transformation is properly assured. Since the *Mashed UC* model is derived from a model transformation based on mappings, traceability between AEpc's and UCpt's is guaranteed, thus any necessary change on product-level requirements due to a change on a given business needs is easily identified alongside the models.

References

1. Maibaum, T.: On specifying systems that connect to the physical world. New Trends in Software Methodologies, Tools and Techniques (2006)
2. Yue, T., Briand, L.C., Labiche, Y.: A Systematic Review of Transformation Approaches between User Requirements and Analysis Models. Requirements Engineering (2011)

3. Ferreira, N., Santos, N., Soares, P., Machado, R.J., Gašević, D.: Transition from Process-to Product-level Perspective for Business Software. In: Poels, G., et al. (eds.) CONFENIS 2012. LNBIP, vol. 139, pp. 268–275. Springer, Heidelberg (2013)

4. Haskins, C., Forsberg, K.: Systems Engineering Handbook: A Guide for System Life Cycle Processes and Activities; INCOSE-TP-2003-002-03.2. 1, INCOSE (2011)

5. Ferreira, N., Santos, N., Machado, R.J., Gašević, D.: Aligning Domain-Related Models for Creating Context for Software Product Design. In: Winkler, D., Biffl, S., Bergsmann, J. (eds.) SWQD 2013. LNBIP, vol. 133, pp. 168–190. Springer, Heidelberg (2013)

6. Ferreira, N., Santos, N., Machado, R.J., Gašević, D.: Derivation of Process-Oriented Logical Architectures: An Elicitation Approach for Cloud Design. In: Dieste, O., Jedlitschka, A., Juristo, N. (eds.) PROFES 2012. LNCS, vol. 7343, pp. 44–58. Springer, Heidelberg (2012)

7. Machado, R.J., et al.: Transformation of UML Models for Service-Oriented Software Architectures. In: ECBS 2005, pp. 173–182. IEEE Computer Society (2005)

8. Conradi, R., Jaccheri, M.: Process Modelling Languages. In: Software Process: Principles, Methodology, and Technology, pp. 27–52. Springer US (1999)

9. Browning, T.R., Eppinger, S.D.: Modeling impacts of process architecture on cost and schedule risk in product development. IEEE Trans. on Engineering Management (2002)

10. Machado, R.J., Fernandes, J.M., Monteiro, P., Daskalakis, C.: Refinement of Software Architectures by Recursive Model Transformations. In: Münch, J., Vierimaa, M. (eds.) PROFES 2006. LNCS, vol. 4034, pp. 422–428. Springer, Heidelberg (2006)

11. Azevedo, S., Machado, R.J., Muthig, D., Ribeiro, H.: Refinement of Software Product Line Architectures through Recursive Modeling Techniques. In: Meersman, R., Herrero, P., Dillon, T. (eds.) OTM 2009 Workshops. LNCS, vol. 5872, pp. 411–422. Springer, Heidelberg (2009)

12. ISOFIN Consortium. ISOFIN Research Project; ISOFIN Research Project (2010), http://isofincloud.i2s.pt

13. Jani, D., Vanderveken, D., Perry, D.: Experience Report: Deriving architecture specifications from KAOS specifications (2003)

14. The Open Group. TOGAF - The Open Group Architecture Framework, http://www.opengroup.org/togaf/

15. Engelsman, W., et al.: Extending enterprise architecture modelling with business goals and requirements. Enterprise Information Systems 5(1), 9–36 (2010)

16. Strnadl, C.F.: Aligning Business and It: The Process-Driven Architecture Model. Information Systems Management 23(4), 67–77 (2006)

17. Dijkman, R.M., Joosten, S.M.M.: An algorithm to derive use cases from business processes. In: SEA 2002. Acta Press, Cambridge (2002)

18. Winter, R., Fischer, R.: Essential Layers, Artifacts, and Dependencies of Enterprise Architecture. In: EDOCW 2006, p. 30 (2006)

19. Iribarne, L., et al.: A Model Transformation Approach for Automatic Composition of COTS User Interfaces in Web-Based Information Systems. Information Systems Management 27(3), 207–216 (2010)

20. OMG, MDA Guide Version 1.0.1, OMG Std

21. Kaindl, H., Falb, J.: Can We Transform Requirements into Architecture? In: ICSEA 2008 (2008)

22. Bauer, B., Müller, J.P., Roser, S.: A Model-driven Approach to Designing Cross-Enterprise Business Processes. In: Meersman, R., Tari, Z., Corsaro, A. (eds.) OTM-WS 2004. LNCS, vol. 3292, pp. 544–555. Springer, Heidelberg (2004)

Author Index